Schmid
1/73

SUKARNO AND THE STRUGGLE
FOR INDONESIAN INDEPENDENCE

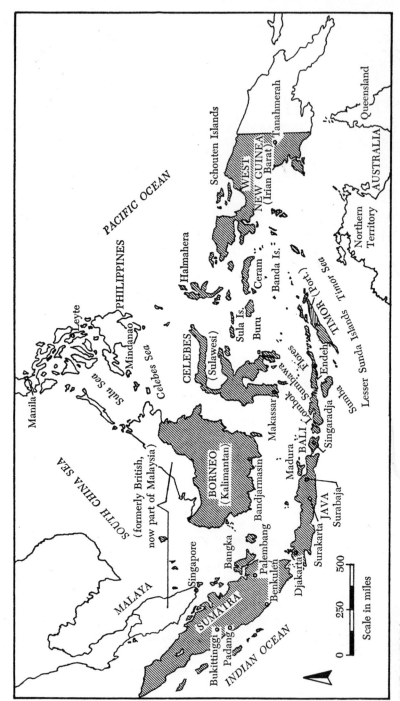

INDONESIA

Scale in miles

0   250   500

Sukarno and the Struggle for Indonesian Independence

Revised and updated edition of *Sukarnos Kampf um Indonesiens Unabhängigkeit*

By BERNHARD DAHM

Translated from the German by
MARY F. SOMERS HEIDHUES

Cornell University Press
Ithaca and London

Title of the original German edition: *Sukarnos Kampf um Indonesiens Unabhängigkeit: Werdegang und Ideen eines asiatischen Nationalisten* (Band XVIII der Schriften des Instituts für Asienkunde in Hamburg)

© Alfred Metzner Verlag, Frankfurt am Main, Berlin, 1966

First published 1969

Standard Book Number 8014–0488–6

Library of Congress Catalog Card Number 69–18356

PRINTED IN THE UNITED STATES OF AMERICA
BY VAIL-BALLOU PRESS, INC.

Foreword

Though there has been an ever-increasing flow of scholarly books on modern Southeast Asia in recent years, it has so far yielded very few biographical studies of importance. Such dearth is more surprising since the region's new nation states have not been lacking in colorful, dominating, and indeed often controversial *dramatis personae.* The writing of biographies is, in any case, difficult enough. But I also suspect that the intellectual curiosity which the "new states," and the problems besetting them, have elicited, notably in the United States, has something to do with this state of affairs. For the greater part, Southeast Asia appears to have attracted social scientists, many of them preoccupied with "patterns," "structures," "models," and "trends"—in other words, with the recurrent, the measurable, the classifiable, if not the predictable, rather than with the idiosyncratic and (dare one say it?) the unique. Dr. Dahm's pioneering effort should do much to remind us once again of the irreducible importance of the individual actor in history. His scrupulously researched and briskly presented intellectual biography of Indonesia's first president, a significant addition to our as yet meager knowledge of that country's modern history, places us in a debt of gratitude to this young scholar. Our thanks also extend to Mrs. Heidhues, who has rendered the text into highly readable English, and to Cornell University Press for its willingness to sponsor the translation, a burden most publishers are unfortunately only too happy to shun these days.

What Dahm has given us here is not, of course, a full portrait of Sukarno the man, but of Sukarno the political leader, ideologue and revolutionary. If it is a remarkably rich portrait, largely drawn from contemporary sources, it will need to be amplified by future biographical efforts to capture other aspects of "Bung Karno's" complex personality—his charm, his wit, his sensuality no less than his phenomenal self-centeredness, his manipulative skills, and all the many other traits that have gone into the making of Indonesia's best-known citizen. It is for this reason that Cindy Adams' *Sukarno: An Autobiography* (1965), for all its obvious shortcomings, is not so much superseded but rather immensely enriched by the present study. It is for this reason, too, that Dahm's book cannot match the quiet intensity of the late Sutan Sjahrir's autobiographical *Out of Exile* (1949) or—to venture beyond Indonesia for a moment— the outrageously fascinating egocentrism of Dr. Ba Maw's *Breakthrough in Burma* (1967). These are comments, not criticisms, for there is more than enough in this book to help us understand the *homo politicus* who was the architect of his country's independence. Dr. Dahm has left no page unturned to extract from the scattered printed records every ounce of useful information, and he has done so in the best tradition of historical scholarship. His accomplishment is the greater since, unlike so many of us, he was not the beneficiary of an academic "area study program" with its vast faculty, library, and financial resources. Rather, he is essentially self-taught, and it was only after his dissertation in the University of Kiel had appeared in print that he was given the chance of paying a short visit to Indonesia.

The careful reader will soon realize the extent of Dr. Dahm's contribution to modern Indonesian historiography. Not the least of its merits are the numerous corrections of several mistaken "facts" (or assumptions) that have bedeviled the field. Often these stem from a single error committed in a secondary source, and repeated, unchecked, by subsequent writers (myself included). But far more important and quite original is the attempt to delineate Sukarno's political thought and to place it in an appropriate framework of the Indonesian, especially the Javanese, political tradition. For Dahm abjures the facile label, whether it be "charismatic leader," "solidarity maker," or "secular nationalist" (the latter being my own questionable coinage), in an effort to come to grips with the intrinsic character of "Bung Karno's" mode of thinking and acting. Of the many elements that Dahm has singled out for emphasis, three seem to me to stand out in graphic detail. Two of them are intimately related to Sukarno's deep-seated "Javanism," the third being a purely personal characteristic. There is, first, what might be called the Djajabaja syndrome: Sukarno's underlying belief in some kind of cyclical movement of history, in which the power of Indonesia's foreign rulers, Dutch no less than Japanese, is viewed as a transitional phenomenon whose "inevitable" ending at the hand of a Just Savior (*Ratu Adil*) was predicted in prophecies widely believed in by millions of Indonesians (especially of course Javanese). Dahm presents, or so I believe, ample and convincing documentation to show how political movements in colonial Indonesia mushroomed if and when a leader invoked these popular Djajabaja myths, and how they waned, and indeed collapsed, as soon as the leadership retreated from them. To study Indonesian nationalism primarily as a result of the implantation of Western values must, in the light of Dahm's compelling findings, henceforth be dismissed as woefully inadequate.

Javanism also lies at the core of the second major factor, Sukarno's inveterate tendency to combine, synthesize, and submerge divergent, even opposite, trends and groups into a spurious unity of his own making. Such disavowal of conflict, such eagerness to reduce opposites to a common denominator are deeply embedded in Javanese thought. Thus Sukarno the oversimplifying "revolutionary" ideologue, no less than Sukarno the crafty politician, hark back to a venerable political tradition—as does, of course, Sukarno the bemedaled oriental potentate, Sukarno the palace and monument builder, and even Sukarno the indefatigable royal lover. Yet there is more to it than that, and, once again, Dr. Dahm deserves full credit for having uncovered a third key factor: "Bung Karno's" uncanny, unbending, and stubborn devotion to a set of notions developed very early in his political career and held, unswervingly, to the bitter end. There is tragic greatness in a man so possessed of his own rightness and self-righteousness, so impervious to the harsh truths of Indonesian political life. From his earliest days as political activist Sukarno insisted that nationalism, Marxism, and Islam were one. And so, in a sense, they—or rather, what he assumed and proclaimed each of them to be—were, by his own Javanese light.

Of course they never were in fact. One only has to read, and reread, the proceedings of the Constituent Assembly of the late 1950's to discover the profound, almost abysmal, and potentially fratricidal ideological cleavages that separate one *aliran* (stream) from the other. Not so to a president obsessed by the notion of unity required by the perennial struggle against Western Imperialism: all could, nay must, be reduced to the *Ekasila,* the intrinsic Javanese oneness, in spite of all the "misunderstandings" (his favorite word) that ostensibly but misleadingly separated Indonesian from Indonesian. And so, Sukarno would time and again endeavor to make reality conform to his *idée fixe*—dissolving the Constituent Assembly, to mention but one symbolically significant example—until catastrophe overtook him in late 1965. True to himself, the "Great Leader of the Revolution" then preferred abdication (if that be the proper term) to presiding, as powerless figurehead, over a reality so obviously and distressingly at odds with the Indonesia of his own imagining.

Having laid bare so much of the essential Sukarno, has his biographer succumbed to his subject's spell? The answer is decidedly in the negative, even though some critics of the German original, enmeshed in an ongoing attempt to pin the blame for Indonesia's manifold ills on the fallen dictator, have taken our author to task for allegedly attempting to whitewash Sukarno. Far from it! Dr. Dahm has not only remained true to his craft, he has also time and again castigated "The Bung" for willfully ignoring reality and for equally willful distortions of the "authorities" that Sukarno has been wont to cite in support of his own conceptions. Above all else, Dahm has clearly shown that Sukarno's political actions have as often as not led not only Sukarno himself, but the nationalist movement in colonial times, and later on independent Indonesia, to the brink of dis-

aster. But Dahm has obviously been more concerned with understanding this complex man than with passing final judgment on
him.

I am not necessarily asserting that he has succeeded in doing
full justice to his chosen task—whoever has? I believe, for instance, that the author has underestimated the purely Machi-
avellian side of Sukarno, the master manipulator, who yet failed
in several decisive moments, not least after the coup of 1965. I
also think that he may have exaggerated Sukarno's bargaining
power vis-à-vis the Japanese during the occupation, in spite of
my admiration for his skillful analysis of that traumatic era as a
whole. Last but not least, as is only natural in a biography,
Dahm's preoccupation with his subject has led him to treat
Sukarno's political opponents, and for that matter too much
of the Indonesian social and political scene, less fully than one
might have wished. But I, for one, having for many years viewed
Sukarno's political actions in terms of an oversimplified "secular
–Islamic" dichotomy, if not in terms, also, of sheer political
cunning, compromising, and manipulation, have been forced to
admit the plausibility of large parts of Dahm's searching
analysis. I believe that many others will join me in saluting
Dr. Dahm for an enviable accomplishment, now that his work
is available to the wider academic public it so amply deserves.

HARRY J. BENDA

Singapore
June 1969

Preface to the American Edition

When the German edition of this book went to press early in 1965, Sukarno still dominated the Indonesian political scene. He was, as his official titles proclaimed, "President for Life," "Great Leader of the Indonesian Revolution," and "Commander in Chief of the Armed Forces." He was the absolute ruler of a nation of more than one hundred million people; his wishes were commands and his words were law. His standing seemed to be unchallengeable among the masses, and even those who did not approve his policies acknowledged his authority.

During the time that has gone by meanwhile, everything appears to have changed. The armed forces have rejected Sukarno's command since October 1965; the Provisional People's Congress restricted his presidency in July 1966, and in March 1967 finally deposed him. His authority has so shrunk that in the streets of Djakarta and elsewhere in the archipelago students can make fun of the "Father of the Nation" without being punished. There have even been rumors that the first President of Indonesia, who lives heavily guarded at Bogor, might be brought to trial on charges of high treason and misconduct.

The reason for this radical change lies in Sukarno's behavior after the attempted takeover by a group of communist-oriented officers on October 1, 1965, which cost the lives of six generals of the Indonesian army. Even though Sukarno was well aware that communists were involved in the "September 30 Movement," he stubbornly refused to accede to demands from all sides for a ban of the Communist Party of Indonesia (PKI). Had he done so in time, he might possibly have prevented the murder of more than one hundred sixty thousand people, killed by an enraged army and by fanatical Islamic youth organizations who then took the settlement of accounts with the communists into their own hands.

"Why didn't you outlaw the PKI?" I asked Sukarno during a visit to Indonesia, a few weeks before he was deposed.

"You cannot punish a whole party for the misbehavior of a few," he answered.

I told him that he had been able to do so in 1960, when he banned the Masjumi and the Partai Sosialis Indonesia for the reason that they had not condemned those of their members who had been involved in the revolutionary government, PRRI, which in 1958 had taken up arms against the republic.

"Masjumi and PSI," he said, "obstructed the completion of our revolution. The PKI, however, was the avant-garde of the revolutionary forces. We needed her for the implementation of social justice and a prosperous society."

I asked whether he was still convinced that his concept of Nasakom, of unifying national, religious, and communist groups, was basically correct.

He said that it was. He spoke of the "historical necessity" of combining all revolutionary (i.e. all anti-imperialist) forces just as in the years before the putsch. The explosive tensions that had developed under his "Guided Democracy" between communists and anticommunists had not shaken his conviction that a strong unity among nationalist, religious, and communist groups was still possible. "These currents," he explained, "are objective factors in our society. And if you want to bring about a change in that society you have to unite them."

This strongly reminded me of the Sukarno of the early 'twenties, who had emerged as a leader of the Indonesian movement with a demand for unity expressed in almost the same words. Obviously his method of dealing with the problems of his own pluralistic society has never changed. And neither has his attitude toward its enemies, colonialism and imperialism. Thus his message had always been the same: to fight imperialism to its very end on the one hand, and on the other, to build up a new order by blending different ideologies into a harmonious whole. This approach was not restricted to the Indonesian scene. He had striven to crown his life work with "Conefo," the Conference of the New Emerging Forces, scheduled for 1966. At this Nasakom Internasional, as he repeatedly called the project, he hoped to rally all anti-imperialist forces of the world under his banner, and after the final victory against imperialism to open the way for everlasting peace in a world without exploitation. Sukarno is now convinced, or so he told me after the Conefo Project had been called off, that he was the victim of imperialist intrigues rather than of his own policy, for all that it has been proved wrong even in his beloved Indonesia.

Much of the hatred to which Sukarno has been subjected in recent years, when he was charged with being a tool in the hands of the Chinese communists, is due to the lack of serious attention to his thinking. In this book an attempt has been made to analyze Sukarno's political ideas, from his early writings down to his nomination as the first Indonesian President in 1945. It is based entirely on sources dating to the Indonesian struggle for independence. Thus, the appearance of *Sukarno: An Autobiography as Told to Cindy Adams* (Bobbs-Merrill, 1965), after my own work was completed, has not necessitated major revisions on my part. Her book contains a number of interesting details and is an important document for the understanding of the man. For his actual role in the Indonesian independence movement, however, contemporary sources provide more reliable information than the not always exact recollections of Sukarno in his sixties.

In the chapters that follow, Sukarno is shown in conflict with political rivals who were often better educated than he, and who occasionally ridiculed his ideas. Again and again, however, those rivals were to see that the masses responded not to rational arguments but to Sukarno's crusading speeches and his promises of a shining future. I have tried to explain his mass appeal by investigating a theme which, since Drewes' classic *Drie Javaansche Goeroes: Hun leven, onderricht en messias prediking* (Leiden, 1925) has been repeatedly discussed in scholarly works [1]

---

[1] As early as 1932, C. C. Berg showed the political implications of the belief in the Ratu Adil ("Indonesia," in H. A. R. Gibbs [ed.], *Whither*

but has not yet been systematically considered in the literature on the Indonesian independence movement, namely, the myths of Java—the belief in the coming of the prophesied Messiah and the impact of the World of Wajang, with all their promises and frustrations.

This book is the result of several years' research in the Netherlands, where Dutch and Indonesian sources could be critically compared. The writer thanks the Koninklijk Instituut voor Taal-, Land- en Volkenkunde, Leiden, and the Indische Afdeeling of the Rijksinstituut voor Oorlogsdocumentatie, Amsterdam, for their kind assistance. In addition, he is indebted to Professors C. C. Berg of Leiden, G. F. Pijper of Amsterdam, E. Sarkisyanz of Heidelberg, and W. F. Wertheim of Amsterdam, for valuable suggestions, as well as to Mary F. Somers Heidhues, Göttingen, for her very conscientious translation of the German original into English. Particular thanks go to Professors Harry J. Benda of Yale University for his guidance in the field of Asian history, and Karl D. Erdmann of Kiel for his unfailing help. And grateful acknowledgment goes to the Southeast Asia Program of Cornell University, which generously assisted in the preparation of the manuscript.

BERNHARD DAHM

New Haven
December 1968

Islam [London 1932], 237–311). In 1955 it was E. Sarkisyanz who drew attention to "Javanischer Chiliasmus als ideologischer Hintergrund der indonesischen Revolution" in his illuminating book *Russland und der Messianismus des Orients* (Tübingen 1955), 297–307. For a perceptive analysis of the belief in the Javanese Messiah, see J. M. van der Kroef "Javanese Messianic Expectations: Their Origin and Cultural Context," *Comparative Studies in Society and History* (1958–59), 299–323. See also S. Kartodirdjo, *Tjatatan tentang segi-segi messianistis dalam sedjarah Indonesia* [Notes on Messianic Aspects of Indonesian History] (Jogjakarta 1959), and a more recent discussion of the subject in his *The Peasant's Revolt of Banten in 1888* (The Hague 1966).

Contents

MAPS

Abbreviations

AR	*Asia Raya*
BPKI	Badan Penjelidikan Kemerdekaan Indonesia
DBR	*Dibawah Bendera Revolusi*
ENI	*Encyklopedie van Nederlandsch-Indië*
GG	Governor General
HBS	Hoogere Burger School
IG	*Indische Gids*
IPO	*Inlandsche Persoverzichten*
Ir.	Ingenieur [Engineer]
ISDV	Indische Sociaal-Democratische Vereeniging
KNIP	Komite Nasional Indonesia Pusat
KT	*Koloniaal Tijdschrift*
Masjumi	Madjelis Sjuro Muslimin Indonesia
NICA	Netherlands-Indies Civil Administration
NIP	Nationaal-Indische Partij
Partindo	Partai Indonesia (1931–36)
Peta	Pembela Tanah-Air
PI	Perhimpunan Indonesia
PKI	Partai Kommunis Indonesia
PNI	Perserikatan (after 1928, Partai) Nasional Indonesia
PNI–Baru	New PNI = Pendidikan Nasional Indonesia
PPPKI	Permufakatan Perhimpunan Politik Indonesia
Putera	Pusat Tenaga Rakjat
RVO–IC	Rijksinstituut voor Oorlogsdocumentatie, Indische Collectie
SI	Sarekat Islam
SIM	*Suluh Indonesia Muda*
SRI	*Suluh Rakjat Indonesia*
VR	Volksraad

SUKARNO AND THE STRUGGLE
FOR INDONESIAN INDEPENDENCE

I

Introduction: The Appeal of Ratu Adil—the Javanese Messiah and the Indonesian Independence Movement

The Ratu Adil of Tangerang

On Sunday, February 10, 1924, late in the afternoon, a strange procession made its way along the road from Tangerang to Batavia in Western Java. In it were some forty white-clad Javanese, surrounded by police, soldiers, and civilian employees of the Dutch colonial administration. At Tanah Tinggi, near a newly constructed prison, it finally came to a stop.

The leader of the Javanese, Bapak (Father) Kajah, was completely covered with Djimats, charms designed to confer invulnerability upon the wearer. As the procession came to a halt, Bapak Kajah answered a summons from the automobile of a high-ranking colonial official; in a moment he had been seized and overpowered by two policemen. As he fell to the ground, his followers, armed only with knives and bamboo spears, rushed blindly at the soldiers and police, who responded with swords and bullets. After a few minutes, the place was littered with dead and wounded, among them Bapak Kajah, who had managed to free himself in the mêlée but had then been shot dead in attempting to fight his way through to his followers.

Thus occurred the very sort of bloodbath that the Dutch colonial official, by isolating its leader, had hoped to avoid. Because the event acquired such catastrophic proportions, there were detailed reports on it, and it is easy enough to reconstruct today.[1]

It was the intention of Bapak Kajah and his followers to set up a new kingdom, about which he hoped to receive further instructions from his "royal father," whose spirit was supposed to have called him repeatedly from its "residence" on the volcano Gunung Gédé. After that he planned to ask the colonial government to approve his rule. Only if recognition were denied did Bapak Kajah threaten Perang Sabil, or holy war. Against that eventuality he had also supplied Djimats to his followers, who believed that by day-long fasting they had acquired magical powers. Bapak Kajah had recruited these followers mainly in his capacity as a Dalang.[2] As such he inhabited a world of fantasy and miraculous happenings, whose heroes regularly overcame a vastly superior force with effortless ease, deflecting arrows, for example, with a mere wave of the hand.

Such magical superiority was not limited to the dim mythical past. The *Babad Tanah Djawi* (Chronicle of Java) relates similar occurrences no longer ago than the arrival of the Dutch, as for instance in describing the Battle of Djakarta in the early seventeenth century:

The Dutch saw Prince Purbaja approaching; they had heard that he commanded unusual magical powers and was able to fly. So they showered him with gunfire, but the Prince was untouched. . . . Approaching the fort, he called, "Why do you shoot at me, you Dutchmen? Do you still believe in the strength of your fort?" He pointed to the fort, and as he did so a hole the size of a man opened in it. Having thus given proof of his magical power, the Prince returned to his ship.[3]

[1] See *De Locomotief, Overseeseditie,* beginning with the issue for February 11, 1924, as well as the reports on Tangerang in the unpublished collection of R. Kern (Advizeur voor Inlandsche Zaken) at the Koninklijk Instituut voor Taal-, Land- en Volkenkunde, Leiden.

[2] The Dalang is the performer of the Wajang, the Javanese shadow play, which takes its themes chiefly from the great Indian epics but offers its own interpretations.

[3] *Babad Tanah Djawi,* translated into Dutch by W. L. Olthof (1941), pp. 142ff.

The thirty who died at Tangerang were a horrible demonstration that the belief in Djimats and supernatural powers could only miscarry as soon as an attempt was made to transpose this belief from its magical world of imagination into reality. But they were also evidence that in the twentieth century this belief was still very much alive.

In 1924 alone, three more attempts to establish "kingdoms" are known to have occurred in other parts of Java, where it was possible to separate the "king" from his "palace" without bloodshed, although not without resort to force and a defiant attitude on the part of his followers.[4] All these instances involved the belief of the Javanese in the promised advent of the Ratu Adil, a "just prince" who would set up a flourishing kingdom, bestowing upon its inhabitants such benefits as prosperity, freedom from taxes, and houses built of stone. In view of the number of Ratu Adil movements appearing in a single year, it seems appropriate to give brief attention to the character of these messianic expectations before going on to investigate their connection with the Indonesian independence movement.

Djajabaja's Prophecies of the End of Alien Domination

Wiselius notes that in 1872, when riots broke out in central Java, it was whispered everywhere that Djajabaja was behind the agitation. To the question of who Djajabaja was, the usual answer went, "Djajabaja was a king and a prophet who made prophecies to the Javanese people of the disasters and humiliations they must suffer before they could have power and esteem."[5]

In the passage that follows Wiselius gives one version of the prophecy. Djajabaja, who forecasts the future by means of food set before him, sees intermittently happy and unhappy times for Java, until the arrival of the seafarers (i.e., the Dutch):

[4] See *Inlandsche Persoverzichten* (IPO), 1924, No. 8, pp. 327ff., and No. 11, p. 454.

[5] J. A. B. Wiselius, "Djajabaja. Zijn leven en profetieën," *Bijdragen tot de Taal-, Land- en Volkenkunde van Nederlandsch-Indië*, Third Series, VII (1872), 172.

In this time seafarers will come to Java to engage in trade. They will become involved in the struggle [a family quarrel of the princes of Mataram] and will encompass the land from every side; finally they will lay siege to the kingdom and divide it. . . . When, over a period of a hundred years, four kings will have reigned over the land, a time of disorder will begin. The wrath of God will descend upon Java, the wealth of the land will disappear, and great disasters follow one upon another. God's anger will increase from year to year, the nobility will be accursed and the people will suffer want. . . . Truth will have vanished. . . . The judgments of the princes will be uncertain, wavering and without strength. Their commands will bring the people to ruin.[6]

But then the end of the kingdom would likewise be near. Natural disasters would announce the arrival of Si Tandjung Putih; [7] he would come from Mecca, a descendant of the Walis (Holy Ones). He would be poor and unknown at first, but God himself would do battle for him and destroy all his enemies. Then justice would reign. The blessings of the reign of this priest-prince are depicted in the same detail as the preceding depravity, expressing sympathy with the people, who would then be richly compensated for all the hardships they had suffered.

Nevertheless, the "last" kingdom was not yet. This kingdom too would decline, and be replaced by a new age of self-seeking. Thereafter a kingdom of happiness would once again arise under the priest-prince Erutjakra,[8] with favorable prospects for the population as under Si Tandjung Putih. But this kingdom too would not last. Once again an unjust age would be followed by a just, until in the year 2000 the history of Java would have come to an end.

At first glance this distorted mixture of Islamic and Hindu-Buddhist ideas is bewildering. Although on the one hand Si

[6] Wiselius, *op. cit.*, pp. 183ff.

[7] Si Tandjung Putih (King of Champa?) and Erutjakra (or Eruçakra; derived from Vairoçana, the highest Buddha), are both names for the Ratu Adil. Because various princes claimed to be Erutjakra, "predecessors" later had to be invented. On the meaning of the name, see Th. Pigeaud, "Eruçakra Vairoçana," in *India Antiqua* (1947), pp. 270–73.

[8] See note 7, above.

Tandjung Putih is recognizable as the Mahdi figure that had evolved in Islamic tradition up to the end of the nineteenth century [9]—as the priest-prince whose enemies God himself destroys—on the other hand, the prophesied end of the reign of peace and its replacement by a reign of selfishness, a prophecy that certainly has no parallel in Islam, points to Hindu Yuga images. Can, perhaps, a vestigial succession of Kertayuga and Kaliyuga periods be seen in the alternation of ages of happiness and misery? [10]

The expectations that are linked with Si Tandjung Putih and Erutjakra, however, bring to mind the Buddhist Maitreya, who as Buddha-designate and bearer of the Tree of Wishes brings wealth to his followers. As such he was already important in medieval Javanese literature; [11] and that he remained a familiar figure throughout the period of the Islamization of Java may be inferred from the preservation of the name Vairoçana, that is, Erutjakra. But these Hindu-Buddhist traits are overshadowed in turn by the abrupt prediction that the end of Java's history will have come by the year 2000.

This peculiar juxtaposition of Hindu, Buddhist, and Islamic images is an outstanding trait of Javanese culture. Without disassociating itself from the influences of Hinduism and Buddhism, which operated for centuries, and which very early became one in the popular consciousness,[12] that culture was also able to assimilate Islamic traits and to gather them all into a synthesis. By around 1870 the Islamic character of the prophecies was already dominant, as the predicted end of the history of Java clearly suggests. In the earliest known reference to the Javanese Messiah (at the beginning of the eighteenth century), the proportions are reversed: the names of the months, and such

---

[9] C. Snouck Hurgronje, "Der Mahdi" (1885), in *Verspreide Geschriften,* Vol. I (1924), pp. 145–81.

[10] Cf. H. W. Schomerus, *Indische und Christliche Enderwartung und Erlösungshoffnung* (1941), pp. 12–53.

[11] W. Aichele, "Oudjavaansche bijdragen tot de geschiedenis van den wenschboom," *Djawa,* VIII (1928), 28–40.

[12] So taught Vairoçana in the *Kunjakarna:* "All are one, we are Çiva, we are Buddha." (See H. Kern, *Verspreide Geschriften,* Vol. X, p. 36.)

a statement as that Java was still "heathen" (kafir) when the Brahmans arrived, indicate no more than the beginning of a gradual Islamization. The prophecy ends with the words: "This prince . . . will reign one hundred years. Then it will be as in the Tretayuga." [13]

This oldest preserved text appears still to be a formulation from the court. Brandes, who reproduces it, regards it as a "prototype of the Djajabaja prophecies." That the name of Djajabaja is not mentioned is, he thinks, a mere accident.[14] The Javanese princes, however, hardly needed to invoke the authority of a prophet to guarantee further a reign whose future had already been magically certified. The prediction that the Tretayuga would begin after the golden age chiefly reflects the conviction of the royal theologians about what was to occur after Dvaparayuga and Kaliyuga.

By the beginning of the eighteenth century the Dutch East India Company had been active in Java for some time. Similarly, in the official Javanese annals of this time it was regarded not as an opponent but as a power allied to the court. The statement was made, after the first unsuccessful attempts to "drive the Dutch out of Djakarta," that by "Allah's foreordained will, the princes who are my successors should be aided by the Dutch." [15] At first it was inconceivable to the royal theologians that foreign traders could overthrow the power of their kingdom; accordingly, they revised the facts rather than the courtly tradition, in which opponents could be easily transformed into allies.

But eventually the reality of their subjection could no longer be concealed. The division of the kingdom of Mataram, imposed by the Dutch about the middle of the eighteenth century, branded the fiction of an alliance for what it was, and the introduction of a prophet became necessary. This could have been the birth hour of Djajabaja, the harbinger of release from foreign domination. The name Djajabaja had been familiar to the

[13] J. Brandes, "Iets over den ouderen Dipanegara in verband met een prototype van de voorspellingen van Jayabaya," *Tijdschrift voor Indische Taal-, Land- en Volkenkunde*, XXXII (1889), 387.

[14] Brandes, *op. cit.*, p. 373.   [15] *Babad Tanah Djawi*, pp. 140, 143.

Javanese since the reign of the historical Jaya Bhaya of Kediri (c. A.D. 1150), at whose order parts of the Indian *Mahabhrata* had been newly set down in Javanese, under the title *Bharata Judha*. Because his name had been handed down in connection with this popular depiction of the struggle between Pendawas and Kaurawas, Djajabaja is generally regarded by the Javanese as a king from the remote past. Thus the scholars of the court, casting about for a name with sufficient popular authority to become their mouthpiece in prophesying a new age under the rule of native princes, turned quite naturally to Djajabaja.[16]

The earliest known prophecy invoking the authority of Djajabaja was discovered in 1816, in the library of the Sultan of Jogjakarta, by Sir Thomas Stamford Raffles. It contains the following reference to foreign rule and eventual liberation:

In 1950, the seat of government will be removed to Kediri, where it was of old. The Pringi people (Europeans) will then come, and having conquered Java, will establish a government in the year 1955. The Prince of Kling [i.e., India, or foreign countries in general], however, hearing of the conquest and ruin of Java by the Pringis, will send a force which will defeat and drive them out of Java; and having given up the island once more to its Javan government, will, in the year 1960, return to his own country.[17]

It is possible that this prophecy originated only after Raffles had arrived in Java at the head of a British expedition from India, which occupied Java in return for the participation of the Netherlands in Napoleon's continental blockade of England. Perhaps Raffles himself was seen as the liberator or the envoy of the Prince of Kling, who must now (after a rule of exactly five years) be called upon to return the island to Java-

[16] It should be pointed out here that the matter of whether the prophecy was xenophobic from the beginning—as we are led to assume—has yet to be established. Likewise, that Dutch colonial power was the target cannot be taken as proved unless an examination of the prophetic manuscripts circulated among the people of Java in the nineteenth century, and now collected in the Leiden University Library, should bear out such an interpretation.

[17] T. S. Raffles, *The History of Java* (1817), Vol. II, p. 70. The dates are arbitrary, in keeping with the nature of the prophecy.

nese authority. The essential thing, however, is the mention of the conquest and destruction of Java by the Europeans, who could then only be expelled again by means of help from abroad.

In the nineteenth century this prophecy, with its open confession that Java itself was powerless to expel the foreigners, receded into the background. Not until a century later, after Japan's rise to the status of a great power, did the hope of outside aid reappear, and this time it was to have great political significance.[18]

In the meantime—especially during the second half of the nineteenth century—hope was concentrated on the coming of the Javanese Messiah in the manner described by Wiselius. After Diponegoro, the hero of the Java War of 1825–30, adopted the name Erutjakra, the prophecy connected with it became widely known. Moreover, after the end of the war the Javanese rural population became conscious for the first time of the heavy hand of the foreign masters, when in response to demands from the European market the enforced cultivation of certain products (Cultuursteelsel) was introduced, and the peasants were made to abandon their customary rhythm of life.

As a result of this oppressive system, indebtedness and expropriation, especially after crop failures, laid the groundwork for wild speculation and anticipations of the Messiah who was to come. Itinerant teachers proclaimed the imminent arrival of the Ratu Adil and instructed the people on how he was to be received.[19] Great importance was attached to earthquakes, volcanic eruptions, and other natural disasters; anything out of the ordinary became a sign. In addition, the appearance of the "Sudanese Mahdi" at the beginning of the 1880's and the growing animosity of the Moslem world toward "unbelievers" nourished the general expectations.

Thus even trivial causes gave rise to Ratu Adil movements such as the one at Tangerang. As early as 1888, when serious clashes occurred near Tjilegon in connection with somebody's

[18] See Chapters III and VII, below.

[19] For details, see G. W. J. Drewes, *Drie javaansche goeroes. Hun leven, onderricht en messias prediking* (1925).

claim to be the Ratu Adil, the editor of the *Locomotief* had information on nineteen such incidents, and wrote that "all these attacks and revolts bear a resemblance to the events in Tjilegon: the same ambiguous character, because of which no one can say with certainty which way the wind is blowing; and yet each time the same elements of popular discontent, alleged descent from a Sultan, and religious fanaticism are manifested." [20]

For the Dutch, any notion that underlying these unpredictable events was an anti-foreign sentiment, inseparable from the idea of Ratu Adil, still appeared too unlikely for serious consideration. After all, the decisive steps they had taken toward establishing a colonial government throughout the Indies were meeting with some success. But a wish to be free of foreign domination was the only way to explain those signs of discontent—alleged descent from a Sultan and religious fanaticism—which were expressed in the Ratu Adil movements everywhere; for the alien rulers were the main hindrance to achieving the benefits to which the people looked forward.

Another development which the Javanese nobility had certainly not intended took place when, after 1750, they set out to popularize the old Maitreya image of the court—namely a decline of their own authority. By degrees, the hope for the just prince promised by Djajabaja ceased to be focussed exclusively upon the court. The prophecy of 1870 announced that the Messiah would be poor and at first quite unknown.[21] With this the door to speculation was opened so wide that eventually it would be possible for any Javanese at all to be proclaimed or chosen Ratu Adil.

This "socializing" of the court's ideas of Maitreya had three important preconditions:

1. The increasing dissemination of Islamic teachings, in the consciousness that all men are equal before Allah.
2. The rising expectations of a Mahdi throughout the Moslem world in the second half of the nineteenth century.

[20] *De Locomotief* (J. P. M. Brooshooft, editor), July 26, 1888. For an analysis of one such revolt, see the recently published doctoral dissertation of S. Kartodirdjo, *The Peasants' Revolt of Banten in 1888* (1966).
[21] See note 6, above.

3. A growing dissatisfaction with the role of the Javanese nobility, who had permitted themselves to be used by foreign rulers in implementing a system of indirect control.

These three developments only reinforced the anti-foreign sentiment whose connection with the prophecies of Djajabaja perhaps dated to their inception after 1750, transforming the age-old Maitreya image into a political instrument and paving the way for nationalist ideas even among the rural population.

Introduction of the Ratu Adil Idea into the
Nationalist Movement

The "Ethical Policy" [22] proclaimed by the Dutch from the beginning of the twentieth century was first put into practice in the field of education.[23] After 1903, when the principle was established that the children of all native-born Javanese could attend European schools—a privilege hitherto enjoyed only by the nobility—the slogan "Freedom from Holland," in diametric opposition to the hoped-for "Association with Holland" gained currency in the Indonesian movement and largely determined its further course.

The founding on May 20, 1908, of Budi Utomo ("Pure Endeavor"), the first Javanese association, is generally accepted as the birth date of the Indonesian nationalist movement.[24] This association planned to work for better educational opportunities for the Javanese people, for improvement in the fields of agriculture and trade, and for the general dissemination of humanistic ideas, with the ultimate aim of securing the Javanese people an existence consonant with human dignity.

But because Budi Utomo was founded by students of a medi-

---

[22] The discussion was launched in an article by C. Th. v. Deventer, "Een eereschuld," *De Indische Gids* (IG), March and June 1899. The phrase originated with J. P. M. Brooshooft, author of *De ethische Koers in de koloniale politik* (1901).

[23] I. J. Brugmans, *Geschiedenis van het onderwijs in Nederlandsch-Indië* (1938), pp. 289ff. ("De ethische koers").

[24] The history of the birth of Budi Utomo is given in Akira Nagazumi, *The Origin and the Earlier Years of the Budi Utomo, 1908–1918* (1967).

cal school [25] that had previously been open only to the Javanese nobility, it had from the beginning an aristocratic stamp from which it was never willing or able to free itself. Thus it gained no popular support whatever; people believed they must regard it as an interest group representing the nobility rather than the poor rice farmers, craftsmen, and petty traders who largely made up the population.

That respect for the nobility, because of the key positions they occupied under the rule of the Dutch, had sunk, was already discernible in the phrasing of the prophecy of 1870: "The nobility will be accursed and the people will suffer want. . . . The judgments of the princes will be uncertain. . . . Their commands will bring the people to ruin." And so objections were soon raised to the vague program of Budi Utomo: "What good is the art of writing and thinking to the native who at every turn is exposed to the arbitrary actions of the police; what good to us are the finest irrigation schemes if we may lose our rice fields at any moment? . . . Men seek justice above all else. From their official superiors they have always sought it in vain." [26]

Budi Utomo thus could not possibly become the vehicle of the gathering popular discontent, or the bearer of the idea of Ratu Adil. Of this the general indifference, if not the criticism, among the populace were sufficient proof. But neither was the Indische Partij, founded in 1912, able to win the masses, even though its founder, E. F. E. Douwes Dekker, declared in provocative language that independence was the only alternative to colonial domination.[27] The lack of support from the ranks of the people is possibly attributable to the prompt expulsion from the country of the most important leaders of the new party.[28] But more important was the dominant role played in it

---

[25] The so-called STOVIA (School ter opleiding van inlandsche artsen).

[26] Cited in B. Alkema, *De Sarikat Islam* (1919), p. 26.

[27] E. F. E. Douwes Dekker, *De Indische partij. Haar wezen en haar doel* (1913).

[28] Douwes Dekker, Tjipto Mangunkusumo, and Suardi Surjaningrat, *Onze Verbanning* (1913).

by Eurasians, who were only too ready to pass along the humiliations to which they had been subjected by the white race. The distrust of the masses toward them was certainly even greater than toward the Javanese nobility, who could at least base their claim to authority on a long-standing tradition.

The lack of support for both parties from the ranks of the people may also be attributed to a total lack of academic training. A system of basic education involving a broader spectrum of the population was then being introduced only by degrees.[29] It would be easy to argue that a certain amount of education is a prerequisite for the acceptance of new ideals. But it has already been observed that in the Ratu Adil movements the urge to be free of foreign domination gave expression to a lively proto-nationalist sentiment among the people.

And even in this period of national awakening the Ratu Adil movements had not died out. Shortly before the foundation of the Indische Partij, Ratu Adil proclamations and attempts to establish "kingdoms" had sprung up in seven different places.[30] In addition, a utopian communist movement, which could not be traced to the Ratu Adil tradition but which used equally unpromising methods, likewise manifested an anti-foreign character, and found a remarkable number of adherents.[31]

Thus was revealed among the masses, in spite of their political indifference and their lack of education, a latent urge toward organization which seemed only to await its cue. And once that cue had been given, there arose in Java, beginning about the middle of 1912, a development without parallel in the history of modern independence movements.

Suddenly, tens of thousands of new members flocked to the Sarekat Dagang Islam, an Islamic trading association originally set up to resist the power of Chinese middlemen in Java. And after its name had been changed to Sarekat Islam, or "Islamic

[29] Brugmans, *Geschiedenis*, pp. 305ff.

[30] IG, 1914, p. 69; *Koloniaal Tijdschrift* (KT), 1913, pp. 21ff.

[31] This was the Samin movement. Analyses of the movement are given in *Het Saminisme* (1918), by Tjipto Mangunkusumo, and in "The Samin Movement," a paper presented to the Congress of Asian Studies in Kuala Lumpur (1968) by Harry J. Benda and Lance Castles.

Association," the number of new members reached hundreds of thousands in the course of a single year.

The phenomenal growth of the Sarekat Islam (SI) is made clear in the following table:

Table 1. Sarekat Islam Membership
in Java, 1912–14 [32]

April 1912	4,500
December 1912	93,000
April 1913	150,000
April 1914	366,913

In April 1914 a peak was reached. From then until 1917, a decline was noticeable; in 1918, however, there was again a great increase in membership:

Table 2. Sarekat Islam Membership
in Java, 1915–18 [33]

April 1915	319,251
June 1916	273,377
October 1917	268,355
October 1918	389,410

Thus far there has been no critical study of the membership statistics of the SI. Its increasing propaganda in other islands of the archipelago had recruited many members, giving rise to a supposition that the SI had continued to grow at the original pace and had soon passed the million mark. Thus A. K. Pringgodigdo believes that the SI had 800,000 members in 1916 and over 2,000,000 by 1919.[34] These figures, taken from propaganda statements of the time and accepted in more recent schol-

[32] Sources for the number of members: (April 1912) KT, 1912, p. 724; (December 1912) KT, 1913, p. 482; (April 1913) KT, 1913, p. 1032; (April 1914) IG, 1914, p. 1004f.

[33] (April 1915) KT, 1915, p. 1243; (June 1916) *Sarekat Islam Congres. 1-e nationaal congres* (1916) p. 69f.; (October 1917) *2-e nationaal congres* (1919), p. 60ff.; (October 1918) *3-e nationaal congres* (1919), p. 61. All figures pertain only to the island of Java.

[34] A. K. Pringgodigdo, *Sedjarah pergerakan rakjat Indonesia* [History of the Indonesian People's Movement] (1950), pp. 16ff.

arly works,[35] do not stand up under critical examination. At the Sarekat Islam Congresses of 1916–18, for which fairly exact statistics are available, the representation was as follows:

Table 3. Representation at SI Congresses, 1916–18 [36]

1916: 354,800 members, including 81,423 from outside Java
1917: 350,954 members, including 92,599 from outside Java
1918: 450,099 members, including 60,689 from outside Java

Although it is possible that thousands or even tens of thousands were not represented at these congresses, it can still hardly be assumed that the membership in the SI movement at any given time exceeded half a million. Therefore, the explosive growth of the movement from 1912 to 1914 takes on even greater importance.

In April 1912, as can be seen from Table 1, the Islamic Trading Association, founded in 1909, had 4,500 members. Figures for the rest of that year are as follows:

Table 4. Membership in Sarekat
Dagang Islam, 1912 [37]

April	4,500
June	40,000
August	66,000
December	93,000

The reason for this sudden influx into the Trading Association was its successful boycott of Chinese batik dealers in Solo.

---

[35] H. J. Benda, *The Crescent and the Rising Sun* (1958), p. 42; R. Van Niel, *The Emergence of the Modern Indonesian Elite* (1960), p. 120. Though Van Niel is well aware of the Ratu Adil aspect of Sarekat Islam (pp. 106, 114, 119) and has some doubts concerning actual participation of the masses in SI policies (p. 157), he does not compare the statistics presented at the several SI congresses and can thus speak of a "continued adherence of members" and minimize the influence of the belief in the Ratu Adil (p. 114).

[36] Sources for the numbers of members from Table 3: *Sarekat Islam Congres, 1-e nationaal congres* (1916), pp. 69f.; *2-e nationaal congres* (1919), pp. 60ff.: *3-e congres* (1919), pp. 61f.

[37] KT, 1912, pp. 724, 1122.

All over Java—first in the cities, then gradually in the rural areas as well—people suddenly became aware of their own power against the monopoly of trade by Chinese middlemen. They joined together in associations of Moslems to resist the dictation of prices by the Chinese. Encouraged by this unexpected response—which came first from the ranks of the Indonesian middle class—the leadership of the Sarekat Dagang Islam, who in the meantime had announced an attractive program to recruit new members,[38] called a congress to be held at Surabaja in January 1913. Here a new program was agreed upon, and the name of the association was changed to Sarekat Islam. Raden Umar Said Tjokroaminoto was elected chairman.[39]

Most of the approximately one hundred thousand members of the SI up to this time had been Javanese who were ready to throw themselves behind the aspirations of the indigenous people in a strong organization. These members lived mainly in the cities, where since 1905 they had seen the Japanese, and after 1911 the Chinese, grow more and more overbearing, and it was a source of pride to counter them with an organization of their own. A large number may have joined the Islamic Association on account of the religious label, although at that time general knowledge about Islam was still inadequate, and the word for "Moslem" was frequently used as a synonym for "Javanese." [40]

Islam, into which the veneration of tombs and the animism of rural Java had gradually been incorporated, had remained for the Javanese population in the period of foreign domination very much their own. With the advent of the Sarekat Islam it took on a new importance. This movement had in fact, as stated by one of its followers,[41] become a vehicle of the Ratu Adil idea, the largest such vehicle ever to appear in Java.

[38] De Locomotief, July 25, 1912. Among other things, help was promised to members who got into difficulties through no fault of their own.

[39] KT, 1913, pp. 755f. The four points of the program of the SI were: promotion of trade without conducting trade itself; support of all who innocently got into difficulties; development of the natives; promotion of the Mohammedan religion.

[40] See, for instance, Alkema, Sarekat Islam, p. 26.

[41] See R. M. S. Suriokusumo in Wederopbouw, III (1920), 104.

From the beginning of its stormy history, the SI was linked with the name Djajabaja. According to an article appearing in the Chinese-managed newspaper *Bintang Surabaja* in the fall of 1912, Djajabaja had declared that Java would receive its independence only after 250 years, and attempts to shorten this span of time could not but have ruinous consequences.[42]

But little attention was given to this comment by worried Chinese who hoped to avoid ruinous consequences for themselves. Soon the rumors took a more concrete form. In the spring of 1913 it was being said all over Java that a child of Mohammed had fallen from heaven and was destined to free the Javanese from their subjection.[43] Pamphlets were circulated, telling of the imminent arrival of the Mahdi.[44] Religious zeal increased, and in June 1913 *Pewarta Surabaja* called the widespread disturbances a sign to the masses that the prophecy of Djajabaja was now to be fulfilled.[45]

Interest began to center on the leaders of the Sarekat Islam. It was above all Tjokroaminoto, as he came more and more into prominence, who caught the imagination of the masses. "Could he not be the long awaited Prabu Heru Tjokro, the traditional Ratu Adil? He came, and was accepted in the name of the Tjokro. In a world permeated with mystical relationships and beliefs, this was no mere coincidence of names." [46] It had been prophesied that the coming of the Messiah would be heralded by natural calamities. Was it not a sign that 1882, the year of Tjokroaminoto's birth, had witnessed the volcanic eruption of Krakatau, the greatest such event within memory of Java? [47] Wherever Tjokroaminoto appeared, crowds gathered about him, reaching out to touch his clothes; they were enthralled by the way he spoke out against the status quo.[48]

---

[42] KT, 1913, p. 484.   [43] *Ibid.,* p. 1042.   [44] *Ibid.,* p. 1347.
[45] *Ibid.,* p. 1339.   [46] R. Van Niel, *Emergence,* p. 106.
[47] See, for example, V. Singh, "The Rise of Indonesian Political Parties," *Journal of South East Asian History,* II (1961), 52. From this it follows that in the biography of Tjokroaminoto (Amelz, ed., *H. O. S. Tjokroaminoto: Hidup dan perdjuangannja* [H. O. S. Tjokroaminoto: His Life and Struggle] [1952]) the coincidence of these events is plainly emphasized.
[48] The authority for this statement is Professor Hazeu, who was then Adviizeur voor Inlandsche Zaken, as cited by his pupils C. C. Berg and Th. Pigeaud in conversations with the author, 1962–63.

Capitalizing on the widespread speculations, the propagandists of the SI promised the people, as their reward for joining the movement, houses built of stone, prosperity, and freedom from taxes and forced labor, among other things. All this is proof, not—as Alkema has it—of a "childish wishful thinking," [49] but rather of an exact acquaintance with the promises of the Ratu Adil tradition. Even the reception of new members into the various branches was conducted according to the traditional formulas for welcoming the Ratu Adil.[50] Secret practices were followed, such as the taking of oaths, the drinking of holy water, and the distribution of variously colored membership cards, so as to remove any shadow of doubt that a new era had begun. And the masses rushed forward to buy these membership cards so as to make certain that they had a place in it.

In July 1913, Governor General Idenburg denied Sarekat Islam the right of legal incorporation, on the ground that the many thousands who had joined it that year were of the "least developed class of the people." [51] Only local SI groups might be formed. But by 1916—when the influx into the SI dwindled as suddenly as it had begun—it was possible to bring these together into a central organization.

Never again did the Indonesian movement, which the Javanese belief in the Ratu Adil had played a decisive part in calling forth, reach a total membership even approaching that of the Sarekat Islam while this belief in the coming of the righteous prince was alive.

For Europeans, the time was one of fear,[52] aroused by the hostile character of this movement which had come so suddenly and so menacingly to life, and which—despite all its leaders'

[49] Alkema, *Sarekat Islam,* pp. 16, 21.

[50] See, for example, Drewes, *Goeroes,* p. 181.

[51] The wording of the excuse appears in J. Th. Petrus Blumberger, *De nationalistische beweging in Nederlandsch-Indië* (1931), p. 61. For the preceding history, see KT, 1913, pp. 1041f. There are indications that Idenburg wanted to protect the SI against itself, by denying legal status to the central organization, because of the radicalism of some of its branches. See Van Niel, *Emergence,* pp. 95ff.

[52] "Vrees," *De Locomotief,* April 26, 1913; "Vrees voor den Sarekat Islam," IG, 1913, pp. 949ff.; and numerous other articles of the time in IG and KT, as well as the daily press.

protestations to the contrary—had as its true impetus the desire to be rid of foreign domination.

From the speeches at the congresses, it might appear that the Sarekat Islam had originally been "loyal" and had developed only gradually, under the influence of radical ideas, into a political movement calling for independence.[53] Officially, its leaders could not speak otherwise; ever since the middle of the nineteenth century, Article 111RR of the Netherlands-Indian law, dating to 1854, had strictly forbidden all political associations. Yet from the beginning, once it had assimilated the heritage of Djajabaja, the Sarekat Islam had been radical; it was obliged to be so in order to attract the masses. For the bearer of the Ratu Adil idea there could be no alternative. Members were sought and won under the slogan "freedom from foreign rule." [54] In July 1913, the journal of the SI, *Utusan Hindia,* declared quite openly, "It is God's will that the SI should come and that you should become free men, unhampered in praising God." [55]

It was only after the "great draft of fishes" that the leaders of the association pledged themselves to loyal cooperation, since their earliest experiences had shown that in this way alone could gradual recognition be achieved. Each year thereafter, tens of thousands withdrew in disappointment (see Table 2, above). But among the masses the hope for a new era lived on, and even during the years of submission—as a Dutch writer observed in 1916—it was clear that the SI envisioned nothing short of the complete overthrow of the Dutch rule throughout the archipelago.[56]

In 1918, when the revolutionary events in Europe threatened to spread to the Netherlands, the anti-foreign character of the SI once again came swiftly to light. On November 15, 1918, van der Jaagt told the Volksraad that had been inaugurated in May 1918 of the many indications that the Ratu Adil was being preached in the villages, and with him the end of the constituted authority. Such things as freedom from taxation and the

[53] See, for example, W. Weise, *Entstehung,* p. 45, and finally Van Niel, *Emergence,* p. 137. The latter believes he can identify an open call by the SI for eventual freedom only in 1917.

[54] KT, 1913, pp. 1044, 1047, 1343, *et passim.*   [55] *Ibid.,* p. 1416.

[56] W. K. S. van Haastert, *De Sarekat Islam* (1916), pp. 11f., 39ff.

division of forest reserves were being promised, he said; and with each new demonstration by the SI, there had been threatening letters, unmistakably directed against the government.[57]

These observations are borne out by the soaring membership figures of the SI (see Table 2: from a low point of 268,355 members in October 1917, the total had leaped by October 1918 to 389,410—the highest membership ever reached in Java). Thus even after the beginning of a "modern" movement, Djajabaja and his prophecies of the end of white domination lived on in the popular consciousness and were capable of asserting themselves, especially in times of crisis.

The leaders of the SI, who owed their success to this belief among the people, could not always keep it under control. Thus, for example, it was accidentally discovered in 1919 that a conspiracy within the association, formed under the name "Section B," was cultivating the anti-foreign aspects of the belief in the Ratu Adil,[58] no doubt in order to keep the SI attractive to the masses, who were still awaiting the benefits as prophesied by Djajabaja.

But gradually, as the influence of socialist ideas became powerful, the concept of national independence faded into the background among the leaders of the SI, who sought to introduce socialism as the new vehicle of the idea of Ratu Adil. Thus, although in 1918 Tjokroaminoto still saw in self-government the fulfillment of the idea of Ratu Adil,[59] at a meeting some three years later he declared: "We await a new messenger of God, the successor of Moses, Jesus, and Mohammed, who will drive all evil desires from the hearts of men. This is the messenger called Ratu Adil. All of us, whatever our religion, await him. But this Ratu Adil will not appear in human form; rather, he will appear in the form of socialism. It is to this that the SI looks forward." [60]

[57] *Handelingen Volksraad,* Second Session (1918/19), p. 201. On the Volksraad itself, see Chapter III, below.

[58] See the reports of the trial in *De Locomotief,* beginning February 5, 1920.

[59] *Sarekat Islam Congres, 3. nationaal congres* (1919), pp. 33f.

[60] Padjadjaran, April 29, 1921, in *Inlandsche Persoverzichten (IPO)* (1921), No. 21, pp. 400f. In the article by Padjadjaran, Moses (radja Piraun) is wrongly translated as Pharao (fir-aun).

Thus the Sarekat Islam broke away from the spell of Djaja-baja and largely lost its mythical significance in the eyes of the masses. Djajabaja would come to life again only when national independence, and with it the fulfillment of all material wishes, was again preached by a popular party and a Messiah-like leader. But then it would be no longer the work of the Sarekat Islam or its leader Tjokroaminoto, but of the Partai Nasional Indonesia and its leader Sukarno.

PART ONE
APPRENTICESHIP

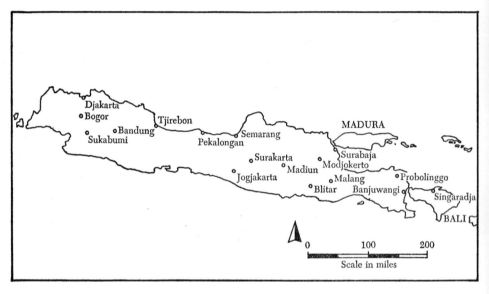

JAVA

II

Sukarno and the Indonesian Movement to 1926

Childhood—the School of the Wajang

Sukarno's father, Raden Sukemi (b. 1869) [1] belonged to the lesser Javanese nobility, as the title "Raden" signifies, and was thus able to attend a teacher training institute ("Kweekschool") that had been established about 1870 in Probolinggo (East Java). His first teaching position, near the end of the century, was at a school in Bali for the training of native administrators. There he married a Balinese girl of about his own age who, after the Islamic marriage ceremony, was expelled from her Brahman caste. At the turn of the century, he was transferred to Java, where Sukarno, his second child, was born on June 6, 1901. [2]

Kusno—this was Sukarno's childhood name—spent most of his childhood in Tulung Agung (Kediri) with his grandfather, who, although he raised the boy "always to be truthful and just," [3] appears also to have been very indulgent, allowing him to follow his own inclinations. For example, little Kusno was quite early permitted to watch the Wajang shows, which ran from nightfall until the early hours of the morning.

[1] His later name was R. Sosrodihardjo; he died on May 8, 1945, at the age of seventy-six (*Asia Raya*, May 8, 2605 [1945]).

[2] Sukarno had an older sister who was born on the island of Bali. See M. Y. Nasution, *Riwajat ringkas penghidupan dan perdjuangan Ir. Sukarno* [Sketch of the Life and Struggle of Engineer Sukarno] (1951), p. 11. The stubbornly persistent rumor in Holland casting suspicion on his origin ("Ir. Soekarno is feitelijk een Indo-European"—*Haagse Post*, November 3, 1956) is thus without foundation.

[3] As later recalled by Sukarno in *Djawa Baroe*, I (1943), 6.

The Wajang,[4] a shadow play projected by a Dalang using leather puppets before a lighted screen to portray events of a mythical Javanese history, meant far more to the Javanese than simple amusement. A little of its original cultic function (the exorcism of ancestral spirits) still remained attached to it; in addition, it had become for the Javanese a dream world in which their secret hopes and wishes were fulfilled, and in which they looked for models and guiding precepts for their own lives.

In 1914, for example, Tjipto Mangunkusumo, who later became Sukarno's teacher, wrote during his Dutch-imposed exile: "The rising of the sun will be accompanied by the final victory of the Ksatrija, by the bearer of the idea of the good, who—in order to reach his ideal—does not hesitate to risk his life, knowing that the victory belongs to him if he is strong enough to follow the ideal without questioning." [5] This was more than an objective description of the Wajang, which just then, was Tjipto's task. It represented a feeling for, if not a total identification with, the heroes of the Wajang, from whose victory he appeared also to conclude that his own ideals would be fulfilled. The identification was complete in the words of Suardi Surjaningrat, who, when along with Tjipto he was expelled from Java in 1913, called out in farewell to his comrades in the struggle: "Consider the outcome of our Wajang myths. Let the eve-

---

[4] On the Wajang, see G. A. J. Hazeu, *Bijdrage tot de kennis van het Javaansche tooneel* (1897); W. H. Rassers, "Over den zin van het Javaanse drama," *Bijdragen tot de Taal-, Land- en Volkenkunde van Nederlandsch-Indië*, LXXXI (1925), 311–81; and "Over den oorsprong van het Javaansche tooneel," *ibid.*, LXXXVIII (1931), 317–450; L. Serruier, *De Wajang poerwa* (1896); Tjan Tjoe Siem, *Hoe Koerapati zich zijn vrouw verwerft. Jav. Lakon in het Nederl. vertaald* (1938), Introduction; "Wajang purwaka," in *Encyklopedie van Nederlandsch-Indië*, Vol. IV, under "Toneel"; also the essays by R. M. S. Suriokusumo, "De Wajang of het schaduwenspel," *Wederopbouw*, IV (1921), 121ff.; "De Wajang als leidraad tot karaktervorming," *ibid.*, 174ff.; "Het Heilige Schrift in beeld, de wayang," VI (1923), 30ff.; and finally Tjipto Mangunkusumo, "De Wajang," IG, 1914, pp. 530ff.

[5] Tjipto Mangunkusumo, *ibid.*, p. 533.

ning go to our Kaurawas, and be content with the early morning of the Pendawas. The sacred heritage will come to us." [6]

This was a reference to the *Bharata Judha* that tells of the struggle of the Pendawas with the Kaurawas for the kingdom of Ngastina, which rightly belonged to the Pendawas but of which the Kaurawas had taken possession. Such themes from the *Mahabhrata,* and likewise those of the *Ramayana,* offered to the Dalang and to the nationalists abundant possibilities of expressing their own aspirations in a language that could be understood by every Javanese.

Even before the movement began, while little Kusno crouched night after night in front of the screen, the desire for independence was being fed by the Wajang, as it was by the Ratu Adil idea.

In Java at the middle of the nineteenth century, the Dalangs sometimes even refused to perform the *Bharata Judha,* arguing as follows: "Later a time will come when the *Bharata Judha* can be performed again—when Java will again be free, when the shame of defeat in the struggle of the *Bharata Judha* will have been avenged, and Java will return flourishing and prosperous to its former state." [7]

Written half a century before the expulsion of Tjipto and Suardi Surjaningrat, this suggests that the Wajang had already been identified with the reality of events in Java. The rule of the Europeans was regarded as a shame that had to be avenged in the *Bharata Judha* of reality. Only then could the *Bharata Judha* of the Wajang again be performed.

Since clearly we are concerned here with two different *Bharata Judhas,* a brief account of their development, so characteristic of the Javanese mentality, must be attempted.

After the Indian epic of the *Mahabhrata* came to Java, the depiction of the struggle of the Pendawas and Kaurawas as having a final outcome was gradually but intentionally pushed into the background. The concept of "either-or" was basically alien

---

[6] Douwes Dekker, Tjipto Mangunkusumo, Suardi Surjaningrat, *Onze verbanning* (1913), p. 77.

[7] L. Serruier, *Wajang poerwa* (1896), pp. 4f.

to a culture that saw itself as a reflection of the cosmos, as a microcosm within the macrocosm in which both good and evil had a right to exist. The two were conceived to be interdependent; for, in the words of a Javanese text on the reawakening of the Kaurawas after their defeat in the *Bharata Judha*, "How could order [in the world] be maintained, if no Kaurawas and Pendawas existed? They are the very substance of the world." [8]

The culture that was so preoccupied with the maintenance of order had, indeed, not yet experienced the jarring disturbance of that order by influences from the outside, and still less the experience of being completely ignored. Both Hinduism and Buddhism, and Islam in its turn, had adapted themselves to the conditions of Java, and had given way to the philosophy that at bottom "all things are one." [9] Only after the arrival of the Europeans, who brought with them an order of their own, were the Javanese faced with the question of an "either-or." The development of the Ratu Adil idea has made it clear that this intervention was not accepted passively. The same development appears to have occurred in the Wajang: a polarization of the once harmonious Pendawa-Kaurawa relationship, to remove from the sphere of the native order the intruder who would not fit into it. Only then could the traditional *Bharata Judha,* as representing an order made up of contending Pendawas and Kaurawas, again be performed.

For the Javanese, this development found a parallel in the role of Bima, the second of the Pendawas, as this swaggering, outspoken warrior of the Indian epic [10] was for a while made practically into a saint, who strove incessantly to grasp the

[8] J. L. Swellengrebel, *"Korawaçrama,"* een oudjavaansch prozageschrift, uitgegeven, vertaald en toegelicht (1936), p. 14.

[9] See Chapter I, note 12, above; also H. Kraemer, *Een javaansche primbon uit de zestiende eeuw* (1921). An example of the numerous maxims to be found in other Javanese writings is the advice of Vairoçana to Bima in Prijohoetomo, *Nawaruci . . . vergeleken met de Bhimasoetji* (1934), notably the twelfth verse (pp. 197ff.).

[10] See, for example, J. Dowson, *Hindu Classical Dictionary* (1913, popular reissue 1914), pp. 99ff.

meaning of all existence.[11] But with the polarization of the Pendawa-Kaurawa relationship, his old significance came back into play, and in the struggle for the reestablishment of order he once more took the part he had had in the Indian epic, that of an uncompromising, relentless crusader,[12] a terror to his enemies until victory had been achieved and the Kaurawas defeated; whereas toward friends he was always helpful and unselfish. In this aspect of Bima, a fragment of the saintly hero of Javanese tradition lived on: relentless though he was in battling the disturbers of order from outside, he was nevertheless ready to work out a compromise with those in his own ranks who were prepared to submit to that same order.

It is quite possible that this beloved Wajang figure impressed the young Kusno more than any other,[13] and certainly there is no better clue to the Sukarno of later years than this Bima with his uncompromising attitude toward outsiders and his readiness for compromise within his own ranks. But other elements may also have excited the boy's imagination: for example, the fate of the reawakened Kaurawas, who certainly took on symbolic importance after the "reawakening of the Javanese" with the founding of the Budi Utomo (1908), the more so because their victory in the coming battles had been prophesied.

At any rate, it was their leader and hero, Karno, who became the sponsor of the young Sukarno when his father brought him to his new official post at Modjokerto (East Java). Sukarno recalled several decades later: "My father intended me . . . to become a Ksatrija who would serve the fatherland. His desire

[11] Prijohoetomo, *Nawaruci*, pp. 148ff.; also W. F. Stutterheim, "Een oudjavaansch Bhima-Kult," *Djawa*, XV (1935), 37–64.

[12] R. Goris, "Stormkind en geestes zoon," *Djawa*, VII (1927), 110–13; M. v. Moens-Zorab, "De intocht der Pendawas in Ngastina," *Djawa*, IV (1924), 146.

[13] Nasution, *Riwajat*, p. 12. Nasution's statement that Sukarno was so strongly influenced by Bima that he later wrote articles using that name as a pseudonym has not been confirmed by my research; however, his defiant appearance in "Jong Java" later caused him to be known among his comrades as Bima (*Asia Raya*, December 12, 2602 [1942], p. 2). See also "Sukarno's Early Political Views," below.

was so strong that he changed my name, which at first was Kusno, to Sukarno. Sukarno comes from Karno; that is the name of a Ksatrija from the Mahabhrata who was honest and fearless." [14]

With the transformation of little Kusno into the "Ksatrija Sukarno," the time of the Wajang, which in Tulung Agung had actually interfered with his performance at school,[15] was for a while at an end. It was his father's ambition to give him a good education and make it possible for him to enter the European elementary school (in Dutch, the "lagere school"). A prerequisite for this was the knowledge of Dutch, which a Dutch lady was hired by his father to teach him. At the age of twelve, Sukarno was admitted to a European elementary school, and in 1915 he passed the "klein ambtenaars-examen" which was equivalent to graduation.[16]

At that time it was still unusual for a native to enter a European school. Those who succeeded in taking a place among the sons of the white masters and the children of the Indo-Europeans (who were no less arrogant toward those below them) were often, therefore, still victims of race prejudice. As Sukarno later recalled, in every dispute that flared up he continually "defended the honor of his nation." [17] Here the meaning of the portrayal in the Wajang of the relations between rulers and ruled, or of justice and injustice, must have been made painfully clear to Sukarno. Like Tjipto Mangunkusumo and Suardi Surjaningrat, he must have begun to believe in the promise of the Wajang, "knowing that the victory belongs to him, if he is strong enough to follow the ideal without questioning."

First European Influences

After completing elementary school, Sukarno found the opportunity for further study in nearby Surabaja, in the home of Umar Said Tjokroaminoto, the charismatic leader of the Sarekat Islam. It would appear that Tjokroaminoto used funds from the SI to conduct an "open house" for needy countrymen, since Sukarno was not his only guest. In 1921, about thirty persons

---

[14] *Djawa Baroe,* I (1943), 6. See also *Sukarno: An Autobiography as Told to Cindy Adams* (1965), p. 26.

[15] Nasution, *op. cit.,* pp. 13f.   [16] *Ibid.,* p. 14.   [17] *Ibid.*

were living in his household and paying a modest fee for room and board; in addition, many guests stayed there temporarily while visiting Surabaja.[18]

In Surabaja, Sukarno came into contact with a world completely new to him. Surabaja was the most important commercial city in the Indonesian archipelago, with a population at that time of about 145,000.[19] Here Sukarno encountered not only harbor facilities for ships from all over the world, but also an extensive railroad network to all parts of the country, paved thoroughfares, streetcars, business districts, and much else—a great contrast to the conditions under which he had lived up until then. Although wealth and luxury also existed in the country, they were limited to European circles and Javanese families of the upper nobility. In Surabaja, however, the colonial caste system had already been overcome, and businessmen, no matter what their nationality, had been able to acquire considerable wealth since the opening of free trade in 1870. In short, there was a well-to-do bourgeoisie.[20]

In the Hogere Burger School (HBS) in Surabaja, which Sukarno attended for five years, the racial dividing line did not appear so clear-cut as in the country. But the percentages of secondary-school students throughout the entire colony of the Netherlands Indies, separated according to population group, still reflected a shocking disproportion between Europeans, foreign Asiatics, and the native-born:

Table 5.[21] Secondary-school Students by Population Group, 1920

Total Population		Students	Ratio
European	169,708	1,344	1: 126
Chinese, etc.	854,568	145	1: 5,894
Indonesian	48,304,620	78	1: 619,290

[18] IPO 1921, No. 13, p. 21.

[19] Cf. *Encyklopedie van Nederlandsch-Indië* (ENI) (1921), Vol. IV, pp. 31ff. ("Soerabaja").

[20] On the development of the Indonesian city in general, see Wertheim, *Indonesian Society in Transition,* pp. 170ff.

[21] The figures are from ENI: number of inhabitants, Vol. 5 (Supplement), "Bevolking," pp. 114f.; number of pupils, Vol. 3, "Onderwijs," p. 98.

Or, if the proportion of graduates of these schools out of the Indonesian population is calculated: in eleven years (1917–27), seventy-eight Indonesians passed the final examination, giving a yearly average of seven native graduates, or one graduate each year for every seven million Indonesians.[22] The concentration of these few Indonesian students in the four existing secondary schools did, however, make possible an alliance based on their common interests, such as occurred for the first time in 1915.[23]

Little is known of Sukarno's experiences in the HBS. That the instruction was "entirely directed to the needs of the Europeans, especially of those who would not always remain in the Netherlands Indies," was openly stated in an article on the system of education in secondary schools that appeared around this time.[24] But for the Indonesians this was only right. They were eager to discover the secret of European progress, and their interest soon went beyond the subject matter of the classroom.

Thus, Sukarno later recalled, "as a mere youngster" he made his "first acquaintance with Marxist theory" from the mouth of C. Hartogh, a teacher in the HBS.[25] From 1915 to 1921—that is, approximately from the beginning to the end of Sukarno's school days—C. Hartogh was instructor in German at the HBS in Surabaja. In addition, he belonged to the Indische Sociaal Democratische Vereeniging (ISDV), established in 1914. In 1917, after it had become increasingly radical, with others of similar convictions he founded the more moderate Indische Sociaal-Democratische Partij (ISDP).[26] In contrast to the left wing, which was soon to become active in the Indonesian movement and finally to split it apart, most of the adherents of the ISDP, along with Hartogh, favored a gradual native develop-

[22] *Publicaties Hollandsch-Inlandsch Onderwijs-commissie No. 2* (1929), Table 45, "Overzicht van het verloop der Inlandsche mannelijke leerlingen op de HBS 5 jc. (absolute cijfers) berekend over 11 generaties."

[23] See note 61, below.   [24] ENI, Vol. 3, p. 97.

[25] "Mendjadi pembantu Pemandangan [Becoming an Assistant of Pemandangan]," in *Dibawah bendera revolusi* (DBR) [Under the Banner of the Revolution], 510—an essay from about the middle of 1941.

[26] For data on C. Hartogh, see *Regeeringsalmanach voor Nederlandsch-Indië*, 1915ff.

ment before making an all-out fight against capitalism. Their spokesman, D. M. G. Koch, argued that the native population would not be served for the time being by a struggle against European capital, which had the task of bringing them to a higher level of development.

> For this reason, our Marxist views require of us first of all not the struggle against Western capitalism, but rather the campaign for a rapid and continued development of native society. . . . Its interest demands, along with effective social legislation, the rapid development of an indigenous capitalism, the only means of putting an end to Western domination.[27]

During the next few years, European social democrats in the Dutch East Indian colonies adhered consistently to this position. They were just as critical of the demands of a revolutionary nationalist movement for immediate independence as they were of a too-rigid stand on the part of the colonial government. Thus, for example, Sukarno's teacher Hartogh declared in 1920, after the "Section B" affair in the Sarekat Islam had come to light, that he must reject all such activity "at this stage of economic and political development." [28] On the other hand, he also took a public stand against the government's intention to build a theater in Surabaja at a cost of 400,000 guilders. That Sukarno himself held up this stand to his countrymen as an exemplary one [29] suggests that the contact between students and teacher outside of school was not limited to theoretical explanations of Marxism, and that perhaps Hartogh exercised a moderating influence on Sukarno. In this first political stand, at any rate, there is little to be seen of the radical spirit of the left wing of the Sarekat Islam, with which Sukarno became acquainted during the same period. Before Sukarno's early political views can be discussed, however, there must be some attention to the development of the Sarekat Islam.

[27] "Marxisme in Europe en hier," in D. M. G. Koch, *Koloniale vraagstukken* (1919), pp. 48f.

[28] *De Taak,* III, 316f. (criticism of Tjokroaminoto).

[29] Sukarno in *Utusan Hindia,* January 22, 1921; IPO 1921, No. 4, p. 24.

The School of Sarekat Islam [30]

Sukarno was received by Tjokroaminoto at a time when the latter had not yet lost any of the universal respect in which he was held all over Java. At the First National Congress of the Sarekat Islam in June 1916, he could still say of himself, with no little justice, "I alone am the one who determines the direction of our movement." [31] This self-assurance was shown also at the Congress, where his domination of the proceedings and the hypnotic effect of his speeches were especially noted by neutral observers.[32]

The universal trust that had been reposed in the person of his foster-father, and the hopes which were centered upon him, must from the beginning have impressed Sukarno deeply. He came to Surabaja after he had first been made aware of the colonial caste system in the European elementary school. Now, after slights and humiliations, at Surabaja he suddenly experienced a completely changed atmosphere: he absorbed the pride and self-confidence of a man who knew that his voice would not go unheeded even in the highest circles of the colonial regime. On the eve of the First Congress, in March 1916, the legal incorporation that had originally been denied the mass organization had been granted. From quasi-illegality, the association had entered into what amounted to a partnership with the colonial power. In view of such progress, it is no wonder that Tjokroaminoto could declare:

Self-help—this is the key that will open the door to the realization of one's own wishes, no less for your private interests than for the interests of an entire people whose aim is to achieve equal status with other nations: it is on our own strength that we must learn to rely. Above all we must have self-confidence, otherwise we cannot

[30] On the development of Sarekat Islam in general, see the article by C. C. Berg, "Sarekat Islam" in *Enzyklopaedie des Islam*, Vol. 4 (1934), pp. 174–81; also J. Th. Petrus Blumberger, *De nationalistische Beweging in Nederlandsch-Indië* (1931), 55–89.

[31] *Sarekat Islam Congres, 1. nationaal congres*, p. 15.

[32] See "Algemeene indruk," *ibid.*, p. 50.

gain the confidence of others. To be in possession of self-confidence and love of truth is already to be halfway to the goal.[33]

Tjokroaminoto made no attack on the colonial regime. Very early he must have realized how much importance there could be in a single paragraph in the legal code of a national power, and how little in the hundred thousand members of a movement that had no such power. Although he left no doubt that his followers wanted self-government and wanted it quickly, he showed himself otherwise loyal and grateful to a government that was prepared to set up councils to grant the natives a right to be heard. His people must pass through that school before they could take the government into their own hands. And so he declared: "We must be patient, for it is the people who can show patience who are certain of reaching their goal. Patience is the guarantor of victory; impatience, on the other hand, is a sign of weakness. The leaders of our movement recognize this point, and I hope they really understand it." [34]

But even in 1916 there were some leaders who did not want to understand it, although at the time they were not capable of any great effect on Tjokroaminoto's position. Thus the youthful Semaun called down a strict schoolmaster's rebuke when he rejected the proposed "colonial council" [35] because it lacked "any sort of independence." Tjokroaminoto's answer was that no one wanted to repeat what had happened in the Negro republic of Haiti, which quickly came to ruin because its citizens had no notion of government.[36]

This brief dialogue between Tjokroaminoto and Semaun was the omen of an approaching storm, the fierce argument that was to take place in the Sarekat Islam before another year was out. Semaun, who was strongly influenced by the left wing of the ISDV and later headed the Indonesian Communist Party, and Tjokroaminoto, who tried in every way possible to avoid splitting the movement, became the representatives of two tenden-

[33] *Ibid.,* p. 9.   [34] *Ibid.,* p. 6.

[35] On the later Volksraad, see "The Permissible Field of Activity," below.

[36] *Sarekat Islam Congres, 1. nationaal congres,* p. 18.

cies. Their opposition grew more and more rigid, until the rift was made final by the founding of the Communist Party of Indonesia (1920) and the introduction of party discipline into the Sarekat Islam (1921).

Thus Sukarno was a witness from the beginning of this power struggle within the movement and of the discords that accompanied it. In 1917, he himself came temporarily under the influence of communist slogans as the socialist A. Baars, who had also won over Semaun to the left, exhorted him to renounce nationalism and to commit himself to the socialist brand of international humanism.[37]

Sukarno later recalled that he recovered from this cosmopolitanism in 1918 through becoming acquainted with Sun Yat-sen's "San Min Chu-I." Although at that time Sukarno had perhaps already heard of Sun's "Three Democratic Principles" from accounts in the press,[38] it is likely that Abdul Muis, who was close to Tjokroaminoto and a very influential leader of the Sarekat Islam, had the decisive role in supplanting his internationalism. At the Second National Congress of the Sarekat Islam (October 1917), Muis had unmistakably declared: "Because our own conditions are now so miserable, they demand all our strength. They demand the effort of nationalists, whose force must not be dissipated. For the betterment of the whole world, we need not begin by turning into internationalists."[39] However, Abdul Muis did more than turn against the internationalists when he exclaimed: "One who calls himself a leader of the people must revive national feeling in the hearts of his countrymen. Only if we have that national feeling can we expect that our wish for independence . . . may soon be fulfilled."[40] Abdul Muis's plea for nationalism set forth the nature of the Sarekat Islam for those outside as well as those within it. To those colonial masters who hoped gradually to deprive the movement of all the radical character it had originally possessed, and to remold it into a loyally constituted organization,

[37] Sukarno, *Lahirnja Pantjasila* [The Birth of Pantjasila] (1952), p. 23. This was a speech given June 1, 1945.

[38] Sukarno later used the edition of *San Min Chu I* printed in Shanghai in 1928. See his speech of defense, *Indonesia menggugat* [Indonesia Accuses] (1930). p. 201.

[39] *Sarekat Islam Congres, 2. nationaal congres,* p. 5.   [40] *Ibid.,* p. 4.

remarks made in passing—such as that the one burning goal in the hearts of all Indonesians was "to free themselves from their chains" [41]—came as an unmistakable warning. Within the movement, the emphasis on nationalism was a first attempt to curb the rise of socialist ideas and to safeguard its members against those "who become tools for the suppression of national feeling" or "who would sow discord among us." [42]

Thus began the struggle of the Sarekat Islam to preserve unity within the movement. To meet the leftward tendency halfway, a compromise formula was agreed upon, calling for a fight against "sinful [that is, foreign] capitalism." [43] In this formulation the significant idea was that of gathering heterogeneous forces into a united front. Wertheim's opinion that the Sarekat Islam "was really mainly concerned about the interests of the rising middle class," is questionable.[44] The main concern of Sarekat Islam was to unite all classes of the people in the movement and so to constitute a kind of "state within a

[41] *Ibid.*   [42] *Ibid.,* p. 5.   [43] *Ibid.,* p. 83.

[44] See Wertheim, *Transition,* p. 215: "Though in the Sarekat Islam propaganda much was made of the 'interests of the people,' there are many signs that the union was really mainly concerned about the interests of the rising middle class, the 'third estate.' " The source to which Wertheim refers here is an official government publication written in 1919 by D. M. G. Koch. When Koch learned of the plan to print his sociological analysis of the movement as "official opinion," he warned the authorities that what he had set down was his own opinion, "the scientific basis of which is criticized by many" (Koch, *Verantwoording,* p. 112). Even so, it was published (*Mededeelingen der regeering omtrent enkele onderwerpen van algemeen belang,* 1920, Part 1). The reasons given by Koch for a "rising capitalism" are, however, not convincing. The demands by the Sarekat Islam for better training of craftsmen, traders, etc., are put forward as the strongest argument. Why should the Sarekat Islam not demand this, provided they were really interested in all the people? This arbitrary interpretation of the aims of the Sarekat Islam brings to mind a report by the communist Baars in *Het vrije woord,* after the first Sarekat Islam Congress (1916). Baars, who had himself participated in the Congress, wrote that the leaders "really felt that they spoke for the whole people and saw a concession achieved as in fact their victory. But this in no way alters what we are taught by our theory, that we are to look for the driving social forces hidden behind the thought, so that then it becomes clear" (*Sarekat Islam Congres, 1. nationaal congres,* p. 67). It is here that the "scientific basis" becomes questionable.

state." [45] That it also attempted to find support among the nobility therefore appears only natural.[46]

That the Sarekat Islam really worked for general improvement on behalf of the people (and not merely for the purposes of propaganda) can be concluded from its support of a reform movement up to now has received little consideration in scholarly studies. This was the Djawa Dipa ("Noble Java") movement, founded in March 1917, which took as its task the removing of a serious obstacle from the path to development of a new self-confidence among the Javanese people. The obstacle was the "caste system" in the Javanese language, through which the medieval Kawula-Gusti (master-servant) relationship had been handed down into the twentieth century. It required the mass of the Javanese to use Kromo, a language of studied politeness, in every relation with a superior, whereas a superior speaking to an inferior used Ngoko, a language devoid of submissiveness. After the Djawa Dipa had been founded, the Sarekat Islam, by systematically promoting Ngoko as the language of all Javanese attempted to remove the most obvious symbol of oppression.[47]

If the Djawa Dipa movement enjoyed only a brief existence, this was first of all because in the 1920's the concept of Java was more and more supplanted by that of Indonesia. Thereupon another language, Malay, automatically came into prominence. Formerly the language of traders among the islands, taken up by Islam and later by the colonial government as a medium of communication in a polyglot region, Malay finally became the weapon of the nationalists. Too proud to speak the language of the rulers,[48] from the beginning of the Sarekat Islam move-

[45] Cf. Van Haastert (*op. cit.*, pp. 24f.) on the position of Hazeu in 1916.

[46] Wertheim displays surprise when he writes, "In some parts of Sumatra this popular movement was even [*sic*] combined with feudal resistance against Western rule" (*Transition*, p. 69).

[47] On Djawa Dipa, see *Sarekat Islam Congres, 3. nationaal congres* (1918), pp. 40ff.; IPO 1919, No. 6, p. 23; No. 21, p. 15; No. 22, p. 14, among many others; also the criticism in *De Locomotief*, June 14, 1921.

[48] Thus, for example, Tjokroaminoto in the spring of 1913, when he was first received by Governor General Idenburg, refused to speak Dutch, although he knew the language (KT 1913, pp. 1041f.). On the develop-

ment they found in Malay an infallible means of distinguishing themselves from foreigners and of spreading their ideas from Java (which remained from beginning to end the head and center of the Indonesian movement) to the surrounding islands.

But the growing left wing of the movement was still not satisfied with proclaiming the fight against "sinful capitalism" and preaching the idea of equality (Djawa Dipa). Spurred by revolutionary events in Europe, those concerned with "class struggle" progressively strengthened their own position and put the "race strugglers" on the defensive. At the end of 1918 Tjokroaminoto's newspaper was still insisting, "The existence of both groups need not endanger the unity of the Sarekat Islam nor weaken our work, for our principles are so broadly defined that they can embrace all possible tendencies. . . ." [49] But in 1920 it became clear which tendency was dominant. On July 12, *Utusan Hindia* contained the statement: "We are pursuing not independence but freedom. We call for the freedom of mankind, for wiping out the difference between rich and poor." [50] The transformation of the Ratu Adil idea had already made it evident that the Sarekat Islam was moving in the direction of socialism. In order to prevent a break in the movement, step by step the national aspect was dropped, and one concession after another was made to the pressure of the communists. Thus far, Tjokroaminoto's striving for unity had been respected by the communists, he had been exempt from abuse,[51] and his "breadth of principle" had been to their advantage. However, after their own Communist Party (Partai Komunis Indonesia,

---

ment of "Bahasa Indonesia," see T. Alisjahbana, "The Indonesian Language—By-product of Nationalism," *Pacific Affairs*, XXII (1949), 388–92; C. C. Berg, *Indiës Talenweelde en Indiës taalproblemen* (1939); A. A. Bodenstedt, *Sprache und Politik in Indonesien. Entwicklung und Funktionen einer neuen Nationalsprache.* (Heidelberg: Südostasien Institut, 1967); *Indonesia*, anniversary number of Perhimpunan Indonesia (1938), pp. 249ff.

[49] *Sarekat Islam Congres, 3. nationaal congres* (1918), p. 78.

[50] IPO 1920, No. 29, p. 30.

[51] Cf. Semaun's remark before the Third Congress: "About brother Tjokroaminoto I do not wish to say anything, because I value his effort to unite our people in the Sarekat Islam" (*3. nationaal congres,* p. 79).

or PKI) had been founded in the summer of 1920,[52] and the Second Congress of the Third International had recommended support for "bourgeois democratic liberation movements" but a fight against "Pan-Islamism and similar tendencies,"[53] the Indonesian communists regarded Tjokroaminoto as no longer under a taboo. Up until then the infidel revolutionaries had tried in vain to undermine Islam and the place of Allah. This aspect of Sarekat Islam, which in its earlier years was often overlooked, had now in fact come more and more into prominence. In the autumn of 1920 a communist, Darsono, published a series of articles which through personal attack and slanderous insinuations did serious harm to the prestige of Tjokroaminoto.[54] He never regained the status or the respect he had enjoyed for nearly a decade in the Indonesian movement.

The decline of Tjokroaminoto's reputation signaled the breakup of the first indigenous Indonesian movement. It had attempted through compromise to bring together all the forces of liberation and therefore had accepted the "confederate from the West," who soon converted it into his own tool and split it apart. With the introduction of party discipline into the Sarekat Islam in the fall of 1921, the break in the movement became final. It was symptomatic that this break occurred while Tjokroaminoto was in prison.[55] For another leader of Sarekat Islam, Hadji Agus Salim (a native of Sumatra), the "weapon of unity"[56] acclaimed by the Javanese Tjokroaminoto was of no account so long as real harmony was absent, and from the previous behavior of the communists he arrived at the only possible conclusion.

Be it noted that Tjokroaminoto, even after his return to the

[52] For further information on the origins of the PKI, see Ruth McVey, *The Rise of Indonesian Communism* (1965), and J. Th. Petrus Blumberger, *De communistische beweging in Nederlandsch-Indië* (1928).

[53] A. Stern, ed., *Lenins 21 Punkte: der 2. Kongress der 3. Internationale* (1920), p. 24 (Point 11).

[54] In *Sinar Hindia,* October 1920; IPO 1920, No. 41, pp. 9ff.; also commentaries in succeeding numbers.

[55] More details below.

[56] Tjokroaminoto's phrase; see IPO 1919, No. 11, p. 22.

movement, held fast unflinchingly to the ideal of unity,[57] even though in the past this readiness to compromise had brought only failure. Elsewhere an attempt will be made to establish the motivations behind this striving for unity. When, a dozen years later, a similar incident occurred in the Indonesian movement, the champion of unity was to be Tjokroaminoto's eager disciple Sukarno.[58]

Sukarno's Early Political Views

In the Sarekat Islam, Sukarno had known a succession of political currents: first the new self-respect, then nationalism, and finally the rise of socialist thought, which were brought together by the movement in a remarkable blending with belief in Allah and vestiges of Hinduism. The following, for example, appeared in *Utusan Hindia* in the spring of 1921: "Socialism, communism, incarnations of Vishnu Murti, awaken everywhere! Abolish capitalism, propped up by the imperialism that is its slave! God grant Islam the strength that it may succeed. . . ."[59] This Hinduized Communist Manifesto and Islamic oath could certainly not have appeared in any place on earth but Java. Everything runs together, for "all things are one" . . . Sukarno was at the time a contributor to the journal which gave the new synthesis so picturesque an expression. He was by now no longer an unknown; in May 1921 it was reported that at a large May Day demonstration Tjokroaminoto had made his way through the masses to the speaker's platform accompanied by the "popular young leader Sukarno." [60]

Renown had first come to Sukarno in the Surabaja section of "Jong Java" (Young Java), an association founded in 1915 under the name "Tri Kara Darma" (Three Noble Objectives), and in fact intended to be the youth organization of Budi Utomo.[61] The three guiding principles were: (1) to forge a

[57] See, for example, Blumberger, *Nationalistische beweging*, pp. 68, 71, 72, 76, 79, 81.

[58] See Chapter IV, below.   [59] IPO 1921, No. 26, p. 572.

[60] *Ibid.*, No. 20, p. 315.

[61] See, for example, "Jong Java als deel van de inlandsche Volksbeweging," *Djawa*, 1924, pp. 69f.

bond linking native students in intermediate and secondary schools; (2) to awaken and cultivate a feeling for indigenous culture; and (3) to spread knowledge (through lectures etc.). The association was renamed "Jong Java" at the First Congress (1918) in Solo, and sections were then established in all parts of Java. The Surabaja section was founded on February 1, 1920.[62]

As is already obvious from the program of "Jong Java," it was anything but a "national revolutionary association." [63] For Sukarno—who for years had been exposed to the problems of the larger nationalist movement—its Java-centered and purely cultural character must have presented something of a challenge. He conducted his work within it accordingly.

The earliest contemporary sources contain the following report: At the annual plenary gathering of the Surabaja section of "Jong Java" in February 1921, Sukarno was to give a lecture on the educational system. He began by speaking to an association that had set as its goal the preservation and encouragement of traditional Javanese culture—in Djawa Dipa, the language of the "innovators"! The chairman promptly deprived Sukarno of the floor, demanding, after a brief debate, that he continue in Dutch, since he would not speak Kromo. This Sukarno likewise refused to do, and after fierce discussion the meeting finally broke up in disorder, amid shouting, cheers, and the music of the gamelan.[64]

Matters were no less uproarious a month later, when in the same organization it was again Sukarno who caused tempers to flare. This time he proposed to admit to its membership not only secondary and intermediate school students, but also those in elementary schools, and also to publish the journal of "Jong Java" in Malay rather than in Dutch alone. During the debate that ensued on the value of the Malay language, Sukarno once again became so impassioned that the chairman threatened to

[62] IPO 1920, No. 6, pp. 15f.

[63] "Jong Java" is so described in "Indonesien: Politik und Weltanschauung des Präsidenten Dr. Achmed Sukarno," *Aus Politik und Zeitgeschichte;* Supplement to *Das Parlament,* No. 18 (1958), p. 209.

[64] IPO 1921, No. 7, p. 20.

expel him. And this time a speech Sukarno had planned, on the theme of "Poverty and Want," was never given.[65]

After these turbulent events, it is no wonder that in the association Sukarno acquired the name of Bima, the warrior from the Wajang who had been the hero of his childhood. That he still tended to identify himself with that same hero at this time —as he was about to take his final examinations—may be inferred from a veiled hint, in *Utusan Hindia,* that even to God Sukarno spoke Djawa Dipa [66]—an enormity not permitted to anyone but the valiant Bima, in whom it was looked upon as a mark of distinction.[67]

Sukarno's participation in "Jong Java" was merely an episode. His conscious superiority toward it is clear from an article he wrote for *Utusan Hindia,* published on April 7, 1921, under the title "Intellectuals?", in which he inveighed against the plan for a federation to unite "Jong Java" with the newly formed association, "Jong Sumatra." What did these associations, one striving for a greater Java and the other for a greater Sumatra, hope to gain from a federation? If, instead of pursuing vague and foggy notions, they were to devote themselves to the people, and to helping them out of their misery, the "intellectuals" would then have reached a correct decision.[68]

This frankly anti-nationalist and apparently anti-Indonesian article shows the degree to which Sukarno, at the time he was about to graduate, had come under the influence of socialist ideas: both the desire for independence and the "Indonesian" concept implicit in the Sarekat Islam had been completely subordinated to the slogan of "freeing the people from their distress." But Sukarno did not enter the communist camp. Even though—as he brought out in the article just quoted—Sarekat Islam and the Communist Party had "the same goal, namely the welfare of the people of the Netherlands Indies," their paths and methods were different. And where those paths diverged, Sukarno opted for the "Indonesian" party, the Sarekat Islam. He rebuked those others who "would undermine the organiza-

---

[65] *Ibid.,* No. 13, pp. 14f.   [66] *Ibid.,* No. 25, pp. 524f.
[67] *Sarekat Islam Congres. 3. nationaal congres* (1918), p. 41.
[68] IPO 1921, No. 15, pp. 90 ff.

tion," those "who have become untrue to the principles of the Sarekat Islam," and he favored the introduction into the Sarekat Islam of party discipline, which the communists had so vehemently opposed.[69]

In another article from this same period, Sukarno also dealt with relations to the colonial power. He wrote that the need of the people had called the Sarekat Islam to life, and that "one of its goals" was self-government. The critical problems could be solved only when the people had a government of their own, and when a solid community of interest between it and them had come into existence. That, however, could not happen all at once: "First the Indonesian people must learn." For this, the planned decentralization of the government offered an excellent opportunity: councils must be set up which would really represent the people, as the councils of the time—including the Volksraad [70]—did not. The people's own government would then bring about political and economic justice.[71]

Sukarno thus conceded that at this time the Dutch still had a place in the colony. He did not demand their immediate departure because he saw that the Indonesian people still had much to learn before they could take the control of their destiny into their own hands. Never in later years did such words come from Sukarno; but in them the moderating influence of his teacher C. Hartogh—and perhaps also of Tjokroaminoto, whose criticism of the colonial government was always held within limits—becomes especially evident.

To conclude, Sukarno also took a stand on the question of what was to be done after independence had been achieved:

Once the proper conditions emerge, and a parliament of our own, truly representative of the people, has come into being, the Sarekat Islam must not then end its activity; rather, it must continue to work for the strengthening of democracy and of Islam in Indonesia, and for the abolition of capitalism. What use is a government of

[69] *Utusan Hindia* (UH), May 6, 1921; (IPO 1921, No. 19, pp. 262f.: "Kiesrecht").

[70] On the Volksraad, see "The Permissible Field of Activity," below.

[71] UH, April 22, 1921 (IPO 1921, No. 17, p. 182: "Zelfbestuur").

our own if it is still controlled by adherents of capitalism and imperialism [72]

From these statements it is evident that by 1921 Sukarno had already brought into synthesis the political currents that made up the Sarekat Islam. There was nationalism, which in the years 1917–18 had been riding high, but which since then had suffered a decline; Sukarno nevertheless adhered to it, under the somewhat labored phrase "the proper conditions." Then there was socialism, which at this time dominated everything and thus for Sukarno likewise occupied an important place. Indeed, he went beyond the Sarekat Islam when he asserted the necessity of abolishing capitalism in his own country. But this leaning toward the communists was at the same time modified by a call for the strengthening of Islam in Indonesia, the third component in the young Sukarno's political thinking. He was not yet concerned primarily with charting a common course for all the political tendencies then operating in Indonesia, but rather with fixing a standpoint for himself in the welter of diverse ideologies. And this he did by way of synthesis, after the time-honored Javanese maxim that "all things are one."

This synthesis of nationalism, socialism, and Islam, here first recognizable in an embryonic form but doubtless already in existence for some time, was later brought to perfection by Sukarno and is the real key to understanding him.

Student Days in Bandung (1921–1926)

The Technical College

Sukarno passed the final examination at the HBS in Surabaja in June 1921—not, as Nasution and all the brief biographies since would have it, in the spring of 1920.[73] The boast of the Technical College in Bandung, which opened in the spring of 1920, "that one of the first students to sit on its benches was later to become the great leader of Indonesia" [74] thus turns out

[72] UH, May 6, 1921 (IPO 1921, No. 19, p. 263). At this time Indonesia was still spoken of as "East India."

[73] Nasution, *Riwajat*, p. 17; *Ensiklop. Indonesia*, p. 1265. See, however, IPO 1921, No. 24, p. 490.

[74] Nasution, *op. cit.*, p. 17.

to be incorrect. Sukarno was first enrolled there (under the title "Raden") for the second school year (1921–22), and received his engineering diploma (with the design for a harbor installation) only in the summer of 1926.[75] He took a year longer to complete his studies than the period officially fixed at four years. This was largely because shortly after his matriculation he was obliged to leave Bandung for some time, since in the fall of 1921 Tjokroaminoto—who meanwhile had become his father-in-law—was arrested, and Sukarno had to take over the management of his household.[76] At the beginning of 1922, however, Sukarno returned with his young wife [77] to Bandung, where he could now devote himself to his studies without interruption.

Whereas at the HBS the ratio of European to Indonesian students was still about twenty to one (see Table 5), at the Technical College this ratio dropped to four to one. During the years while Sukarno was studying in Bandung, the number of newly enrolled students, grouped according to nationality, amounted to:

Table 6.[78] Enrollment in the Technical College

Year	Europeans	Indonesians	Chinese, etc.
1920/21	22	2	4
1921/22	29	6	2
1922/23	30	8	4
1923/24 *	10	5	3
1924/25	20	8	2
1925/26	10	3	1
Total	121	32	16

* The drop in numbers for the academic year 1923/24 is explained by the plan to open an additional college, for the study of law, at Batavia in 1924; until then the Technical College in Bandung had offered the only opportunity for higher study.

[75] *Jaarboek der Technische Hoogeschool te Bandoeng, 17. Cursusjaar* (1937), pp. 40f., 51; IPO 1926, No. 24, p. 517; Nasution (who believes it was 1925), *op. cit.,* p. 25.

[76] IPO 1921, No. 49, p. 445; Nasution, p. 18.

[77] IPO 1922, No. 2, p. 50.

[78] *Mededeelingen der regeering omtrent enkele onderwerpen van algemeen belang* (May 1929), pp. 88ff.: "Het hooger onderwijs in Nederlandsch-Indië."

The reason for the establishment of the Technical College had been "the scarcity of specialists in technical fields" and the increased difficulty, after the war, of recruiting specialists in Europe for the Netherlands Indies.[79] The catalogues of the first years further indicate that the Technical College was purely a trade school, offering no opportunity for a broader education.[80] The studies were so strictly regulated, moreover, that there could be little leisure or freedom of activity. According to Article 5, "No choice of studies is allowed those enrolled; they are required to adhere to the plan of study and to hand in assignments as scheduled. They must take part in receptions and excursions as well as in each of the examinations conducted at the end of the school year." [81] From all this it is clear that Sukarno could hardly have had time for political agitation, even if the directors of the College had permitted it. So much for the legend, one of many from his student days, concerning essays in *Sama Tengah* that "attracted great attention from the public and the Dutch colonial government." [82] *Sama Tengah*—which was, moreover, a neutral journal—was obliged to cease publication in May 1922,[83] so that at most Sukarno could have contributed to only a few issues. The only article traceable to him was a Marxist analysis of prostitution which Sukarno had already published in *Utusan Hindia* in spring 1921.[84]

Politics for Sukarno, at least in the earlier period of his studies, was limited to attendance at evening lectures and discussions in small groups. Thus he was present, for example, at an evening lecture in the house of a Dutch engineer where the need to improve Indonesian culture was discussed. During the debate, he took the floor to argue that the improvement of economic conditions should have precedence. People forced to live in misery were, he said, like a sick man whose handicap was

[79] *Mededeelingen* . . . (January 1, 1920), p. 53 ("Hooger onderwijs").
[80] See *Programma der Technische Hoogeschool te Bandoeng,* 1921 and later years.
[81] *Ibid.,* year 1921/22, p. 24.
[82] *Soekarno—President of Indonesia* (1956), p. 7.
[83] IPO 1922, No. 20, pp. 239f.; No. 39, pp. 470f.
[84] IPO 1921, No. 17, pp. 180f.; IPO 1922, No. 13, p. 472.

mental as well as physical.[85] From this statement it may be concluded that Sukarno had not meant, when he said earlier, "First the Indonesian people must learn," the long path of cultural reeducation; but there was still nothing to indicate a rejection of the colonial power. On the contrary, implicit in the demand for an improvement of economic conditions was a recognition that the colonial government still had a task to carry out. The moderating influence of Hartogh and Tjokroaminoto was still present, although it was soon to be lost in a Bandung alive with radical ideas.

The School of the Ksatrijas

Up until then, Sukarno had never seen his father-in-law Tjokroaminoto deal at all effectively with obstacles to the movement. At protest meetings he did speak boldly, and when the atmosphere of the gathering called for it, he would perhaps give voice to a threat. At the Sarekat Islam Congress in the fall of 1918, for example, Tjokroaminoto declared, to the tumultuous applause of the delegates, that if the government did not comply with the demand to have their views represented within five years, they would set up their own councils, and they would do it alone.[86]

Such bold words remained the exception; the modern Ratu Adil was just as likely to have recourse to magical spells. Thus in an especially critical period in the fall of 1920, Tjokroaminoto provided two organizations with powerful incantations —the "Tjondobirowo" and the "Pantjasana"—which in the Wajang enabled heroes, in spite of all disappointments, always to reach their goal.[87]

Tjokroaminoto was not a crusader. He went to prison not because he had defied the colonial authorities, but because he had been accused of perjury.[88] Far from being the Ksatrija of the Wajang, "who . . . does not hesitate to risk his life, knowing that the victory belongs to him," he placed himself, even

[85] IPO 1921, No. 32, p. 261.

[86] *Sarekat Islam Congres. 3. nationaal congres* (1918), p. 5.

[87] IPO 1920, No. 50, p. 27.

[88] On Tjokroaminoto's arrest, see IPO 1921, Nos. 36, 37, 38.

though the masses saw in him the bearer of the Ratu Adil idea, with the rest who looked for the coming of the Messiah. The Ratu Adil, he had said, would appear in the form of socialism, and, he went on, "It is to this that the Sarekat Islam looks forward." [89]

At Bandung another spirit prevailed. Sukarno could have observed this difference, for example, at a lecture one evening in March 1923, at which he must have been present, and to which a student organization, the TAO,[90] had invited J. E. Stokvis, a Social Democrat and party colleague of C. Hartogh, as well as a tireless defender of Indonesian interests in the Volksraad. Stokvis spoke on colonial relations, particularly their psychological aspect. He gave an objective description of the existing differences—arrogance on the one side, servility on the other—from which nobody was exempt. Europeans were thrust into the position of master from the moment they arrived, and it was up to them to do away with this obstacle through every possible form of assistance. In addition, every European had "to work so as to make himself superfluous as rapidly as possible," for the colonial relationship was an injustice both in theory and in practice.[91]

For Sukarno, the same note had already been struck by Hartogh, and in a sense also by Tjokroaminoto, both of whom had made pleas for European guidance. After such an address, it was customary in the Sarekat Islam to thank the speaker for his "distinguished speech." And it was of course expected of young people that they should take part in the development of their country according to their abilities, attempting, by means of university training in a suitable subject, to become equal partners with the Europeans.

But that night in Bandung, Stokvis's lecture was followed by criticisms. One of those present was not at all in favor of Euro-

---

[89] See the end of Chapter I, above.

[90] TAO—"Ter Algemeene Ontwikkeling"—was an association formed by native-born and other Asian students, was in striking contrast to the Bandung "Studentencorps," to which only Europeans could belong (*Jaarboek T. H. Bandoeng* [Lustrum I, ed., 1935], p. 95).

[91] See the speech in *De Locomotief,* March 12, 1923, pp. 2–4.

pean guidance because Europe was the prisoner of capitalism, and capitalism was incapable of providing any culture at all. Turning finally to the students who were present, the same speaker exhorted them to concern themselves less with their studies and more with the liberation of their country. The speaker was Douwes Dekker,[92] founder of the revolutionary Indische Partij, who for the first time, more than ten years before, had made a party program of the slogan "Freedom from Holland." Shortly afterward he had been exiled, along with Tjipto Mangunkusumo and Suardi Surjaningrat, for the public proclamation of this goal.[93]

The three leaders had meanwhile been pardoned and had returned to Java. They had taken over the leadership of the National-Indische Partij (NIP), the successor to the Indische Partij, whose headquarters were at Bandung. Not only Douwes Dekker, but also Tjipto Mangunkusumo, the crusading Ksatrija, had taken up residence there. In 1920 he had been assigned to the west Javan city as his "permanent abode" because, in the opinion of the colonial government, he had too much political influence in his home territory of central Java. Suardi Surjaningrat, finally, lived in Jogjakarta, where he published the journal of the NIP, *Panggugah,* and where in 1922, bypassing the colonial power, he had launched a national school system, later known as the Taman Siswa, in which Indonesian students became the teachers of their countrymen.[94]

As is already clear from this brief account of the three leading personalities of the NIP—Douwes Dekker's challenge to the Bandung students, Tjipto Mangunkusumo's house arrest in Bandung, and Suardi Surjaningrat's competition with the schools of the colonial government—they had lost hardly any of their early radicalism. Although their influence failed to reach the masses, it was increasingly effective among smaller groups, in which Sukarno now became more and more active.

In 1922 the Bandung section of the NIP was especially eager

[92] "Bandoengsche Brieven," *De Locomotief,* March 13, 1923, p. 15.

[93] See above, Chapter I.

[94] On the Taman Siswa schools, see R. McVey, "Taman Siswa and the Indonesian National Awakening," *Indonesia* (Cornell) No. 4, Oct. 1967, pp. 128–149.

to revive the "Radical Concentration," a coalition of all parties (even European ones) that had first been formed in 1918 to work toward autonomy or independence for the colony.[95]

At the beginning of 1923 a manifesto signed by seventeen different organizations, including all the Indonesian parties, was published.[96] It proclaimed the need for renewed coopera-tion without regard to principles and points of view, and for protection from oppressive measures by the government, which were becoming more and more frequent. The newly announced economy measures that affected the national schools, were, for example, rejected; the lack of legal protection, which made pos-sible all sorts of arbitrary interference by the police, and a plan for government reform that had fallen far short of expectations, were criticized. The manifesto concluded by saying:

For years we believed that Holland really wanted to change existing conditions, to blot out the memory of past wretchedness. But again and again these expectations were disappointed, and so mistrust arose among us. Now we must trust in our own strength alone. And it is in our unity, brothers, that this strength is to be found.

A week after the drafting of this manifesto, mass demonstra-tions were organized in all the larger towns of Java, at which the representatives of the most important parties expressed their views on particular points within it.

Nasution reports that on this occasion Sukarno took the floor in Bandung and so inflamed the passions of his hearers that the police stepped in and dragged him from the podium.[97] There is no record of this episode in contemporary sources. Even less likely is the purported "dialogue" at the Technical College.[98]

95 On the development of the "Radical Concentration," see the article under this heading by P. Blumberger in ENI, Part 5 (1927), pp. 370ff.

96 Cited in *De Locomotief,* February 14, 1923, pp. 30f. (But see *Utusan Hindia* as early as January 9, 1923 [IPO 1923, No. 2, pp. 74f.])

97 *Riwajat,* p. 24.

98 Nasution asserts (*ibid.*) that the incident was reported to the Rector of the Technical College, Professor Klopper. One morning, when Sukarno came to school, the Rector said to him, "My son, you must promise me not to mix in politics from now on." "Sir," answered Sukarno, "I promise not to miss your lectures." "I did not ask you that," retorted the profes-sor. "But that is the only promise I can give," Sukarno told him.

It is possible that a few weeks later a rather more moderate discussion took place between the Rector and Sukarno, when the latter publicly defended his father-in-law Tjokroaminoto at the Congress of the Communist Party in Bandung against the attacks of the "Red Hadji" Misbach, and forced the Hadji to apologize to the assembly.[99] Only party representatives spoke at the organization of the "Radical Concentration," however, and at the time, although he still nominally belonged to the Sarekat Islam, Sukarno held no post in any party.

The widely promoted "Radical Concentration" was by no means an empty threat, as can be seen from a plan that was frequently discussed in February 1923, of employing the tactic of noncooperation against the colonial government. The proposal to refuse to work with the Volksraad, new elections to which were to take place in 1923, came from the Ksatrijas, the leaders of the NIP, and in particular from Suardi Surjaningrat, who in mid-February 1923 wrote a lengthy article giving reasons for the tactic. In noncooperation he saw the beginning of a struggle between the Sini- and the Sana-parties,[100] the friends and foes of independence. The NIP was convinced, he continued, that the entire Indonesian people stood behind this movement, that it was the best means of forcing a government that had neglected its responsibilities back onto the right path. The cooperation then in effect was simply useless, for the will of the people was not respected. Should the government cooperate with the Sana-party, it would lose the last shred of the people's confidence. Finally, noncooperation would serve to unmask all those who had joined the movement only for the sake of appearances and who basically were on the side of the Sanas.[101]

Such was the language of the warriors, of the Ksatrijas, who favored a sharp drawing of the lines, so that the struggle could

[99] Nasution, pp. 24f. The one piece of contemporary evidence for this appearance by Sukarno is in *Neratja*, March 17, 1923 (IPO 1923, No. 13, p. 660).

[100] Sini and Sana—literally, "those standing here" and "those standing there." The Pendawa-Kaurawa concept had gradually been reduced to this easy formula. Its meaning was that those standing "here" wanted independence, whereas those standing "there" wished to obstruct it.

[101] *Panggugah*, February 21, 1923 (IPO 1923, No. 9, pp. 440ff.).

begin. There was no attempt to achieve unity at any price, an attempt that would necessarily have throttled every kind of activity. The emphasis was on the decision to fight.

A few days later, a sensational "unmasking" took place. In the midst of preparations for establishing the principle of non-cooperation, news came from a Sarekat Islam Congress that Tjokroaminoto was to be a delegate to the Volksraad.[102]

Sukarno, who for a year had been under the influence of NIP slogans, may have felt that criticism of Tjokroaminoto, which now became outspoken, was justified. That criticism came not only, as might have been expected, from the communists; the Ksatrijas were even more vehement. Suardi Surjaningrat publicly called on Tjokroaminoto "to withdraw from the movement, in view of all the suspicions of outward and inward corruption." [103]

Sukarno's break with Tjokroaminoto dates from this time, and was underscored by the divorce from his young wife, Tjokroaminoto's daughter, after a marriage that had lasted barely two years.[104] At the same time, he moved closer to the circle of the NIP; and in September 1923 he was first mentioned as a teacher in the national school system organized by Douwes Dekker.[105]

At this point the NIP itself had very nearly fallen apart. In summer 1923, it was split by internal tensions between Indo-Europeans and Indonesians, which had placed a heavy strain upon the movement from the beginning.[106] But as a party, its importance had never been great. What counted was the radicalism alive within its ranks, which continued to be effective after the organization had been dissolved. In a kind of testament, *Panggugah* stated, "The spirit of the NIP will be found where the parliamentary path is abandoned" [107]—that is, in the realm of self-help.

This idea had not been alien to the Sarekat Islam. But now, in 1923, Tjokroaminoto himself had prevented his own threat

---

[102] IPO 1923, No. 12, p. 592. For criticism, see Nos. 12–15 *passim*.
[103] *Ibid.*, No. 19, p. 274; also No. 26, p. 456.   [104] Nasution, pp. 19ff.
[105] IPO 1923, No. 38, p. 503.   [106] *Ibid.*, No. 46, p. 298.
[107] *Ibid.*, No. 31, pp. 226f.

of 1918—"In five years . . . we will do it alone"—from being carried out. Tjokroaminoto's conduct in 1923 once more pointed to the vacillating character of the Sarekat Islam, which had first sacrificed the goal of independence to socialist ideas and then devoted itself to yet another ideal, Pan-Islam.[108]

But the NIP had remained true to the spirit and program of 1912. Its slogans—"Indonesia for the Indonesians"; "Religious Tolerance"; "Equality of the Races"; "Struggle against Capitalism"; "Noncooperation to Bring the Fulfillment of Promises" [109] —were hardly new to Sukarno. But they were stated in clear and militant language and were concentrated on the one goal of national independence.

During a time of political change throughout Asia, Sukarno found this goal more and more worth working for. In Bandung it was Tjipto Mangunkusumo with whom he formed close ties, and who made him into a convinced nationalist.

The Appeal of the Indonesian Students in Holland

Officially, however, after the NIP was dissolved in July 1923, the nationalist idea in the Indonesian movement was dead. Near the end of 1923, when there were rumors of a resurrected NIP, the communist journal *Sinar Hindia* asserted that the nationalist idea was outmoded, and that it would be better for the association to remain in its grave.[110]

On the political scene, the "Pan"-movements set the stage: Mecca and Moscow were the points of orientation; in the Sarekat Islam, as in the Communist Party, the idea of "Indonesia" had receded completely into the background, and the family quarrel between the two was carried on without restraint.

This development caused concern among a small community of Indonesian students in Holland, the "Perhimpunan Indo-

---

[108] H. O. S. Tjokroaminoto in *Islam dan Socialisme* [Islam and Socialism] (1924; reissued 1950) explained (p. 111) the transition from socialism to Pan-Islam: "In order to achieve true socialism, efforts must be directed first of all to the realization of the ideal of Pan-Islam."

[109] Cf. the slogans of 1923 with those of 1913, as recorded in E. F. E. Douwes Dekker, *De Indische Partij. Haar wezen en haar doel* (1913).

[110] On December 11, 1923 (IPO 1923, No. 51, p. 572).

nesia" (Indonesian Association) or PI. Begun in 1908 as a loose federation "for strengthening the sense of community," it had become over the years a genuine reflection of the indigenous movement. Toward the end of 1922, the PI had promptly put into effect the change of tactic expressed in the call for a new Radical Concentration.[111] It isolated itself from the supporters of closer cooperation with the colonial government, and by choosing for itself, after many changes, the name "Indonesian Association," it introduced for the first time the hitherto purely geographical term Indonesia, which was to become the political designation for the islands within it.

The PI was to give more precise reasons for this choice at the beginning of 1924, when its journal, previously entitled *Hindia Putera* (Son of India), appeared for the first time under a title that expressed its program, *Indonesia Merdeka* (Independent Indonesia).

The more the fatherland was involved in international relations, it was explained, the more clearly the lack of a specific name began to be felt. "Indonesia" had been chosen to distinguish the archipelago from its great neighbor India and to avoid confusion. That their nation should be called the "Netherlands Indies" was now for the Indonesians as unbearable as, in its time, the designation "Spanish Netherlands" had been for the Dutch. "Merdeka" (independence)[112] denoted the goal and endeavor of the people; and "Indonesia Merdeka," the editors of the journal concluded, was from now on to be the battle cry of young Indonesia in its struggle for independence.[113]

In the years that followed, the Perhimpunan Indonesia con-

[111] For an account of the origin and development of the Indonesian Association, see the "terugblik" in *Gedenkboek Indonesische Vereeniging 1908–1923* (1924). The name "Perhimpunan Indonesia" was first used on February 8, 1925, and regularly thereafter.

[112] "Merdeka" comes from the Sanskrit word "mahardikkha," and originally meant "rich." The change in meaning to "independent, free" can be explained by the grants of land by the princes to the monasteries, which thereby became "rich," but also—in relation to the princes—"independent." The author is indebted to Professor C. C. Berg for this information.

[113] *Indonesia Merdeka*, II, No. 1 (March 1924), Foreword.

tinued to speak out for nationalism—which in the Indonesian movement was being supplanted by communist and Islamic slogans—in thoroughly revolutionary terms. That it was able to do so shows clearly the liberal climate and the firm legal security that prevailed in the Netherlands. In the colony, by contrast, arrests, prison sentences, and exile for spoken or written offenses were an everyday occurrence.[114] Indeed, mail from the Netherlands was examined, and very often the magazine *Indonesia Merdeka* was confiscated by the postal service and not delivered to the addressee.[115]

The March 1924 issue of *Indonesia Merdeka* had directed an appeal to the movement in the homeland, challenging it to bring about "self-reliant mass action, based on its own strength" —action which, in view of the twofold foreign domination (economic and political), also had a twofold task, "preparation for political independence and a stand against parasitic foreign capital." For this the prerequisite was an Indonesia at one with itself, in which all divisiveness was thrust aside; only thus could the power of the overlord be broken.[116]

Indonesians returning from Holland undertook the first steps toward this unity when they set up what were called Study Clubs, in which the problems of unity were to be discussed. Thus in the fall of 1924, the physician Dr. Sutomo founded the Indonesian Study Club in Surabaja. In January 1925 he resigned from the executive committee of Budi Utomo, the Javanese organization to which he had belonged since its founding (1908), as a proof of his "Indonesian" stand.[117] Another step that attracted attention occurred in March 1925, when Dr. Sutomo left the municipal council in Surabaja as a protest against the impotence of the representatives of the Indonesian population.[118] At a meeting he called in July 1925 to discuss a co-

---

[114] Thus by 1925, among the better-known communists alone, Sneevliet, Baars, Tan Malaka, Bergsma, Semaun, Misbach, Zainuddin, Datuk, Darsono, and Mardjohan were exiled one after the other. Documentation in detail is given in IPO 1925, No. 49, pp. 466ff.

[115] IPO 1926, No. 24, p. 517.   [116] *Indonesia Merdeka,* II, No. 1, p. 3.

[117] IPO 1925, No. 5, p. 239. On the founding of the Study Club, see IPO 1924, pp. 592ff.

[118] IPO 1925, No. 14, pp. 22f.

ordination of activities, no less than six Indonesian associations were represented. At this high point of his career, Dr. Sutomo boasted that July 11 would become as important a date for Indonesians as May 1 was for the Internationals.[119]

After this notable beginning, however, Sutomo's fame rapidly dwindled.[120] New Study Clubs were founded not as subsections of his Indonesian Study Club, but rather as competitors with it. This was true of the Study Club of Indonesia at Batavia and the General Study Club ("Algemeene Studieclub") founded at Bandung early in 1926, as well as the Study Clubs founded later that year at Solo and Jogjakarta.[121]

In the Algemeene Studieclub of Bandung, which held its founding meeting on January 17,[122] we meet again with Sukarno. Although he was still a student faced with final examinations, he was elected "first secretary"—not chairman, as is now officially stated.[123] The chairman was Mr. Iskaq Tjokrohadisurjo, who had just finished his law studies in Leiden and who hoped to carry on in Indonesia the spirit of the PI.

An example of the difference between the Bandung Study Club and the Surabaja Study Club appears from the position they took toward noncooperation. Sutomo's Study Club regarded it as a tactical weapon for use now and then in forcing the Dutch finally to yield to the demands of the Indonesians for a share of responsibility, and thus to further the principle of a genuine cooperation. On a speaking tour through Java in the summer of 1926, the secretary of the Surabaja Study Club, Mr. Singgih, gave expression to this view.[124] But the radicals from Bandung had a very different attitude. In a speech to an audience of young Indonesians at the beginning of April 1926, Mr. Iskaq declared that it was no longer the time to beg and entreat

[119] *Ibid.,* No. 30, pp. 167ff.   [120] See next chapter.

[121] See, in the following order, IPO 1926, No. 5; pp. 219, 222; No. 23, p. 453; No. 35, p. 421.

[122] IPO 1926, No. 5, p. 222.

[123] *Ensiklopedia Indonesia,* p. 1265. The notion that Sukarno had already completed his studies in 1925, and had then founded the Study Club in Bandung at the beginning of 1926, is widespread. See also Nasution, pp. 25f.

[124] *De Locomotief,* August 9, 1926, p. 9; also IPO 1926, No. 34, p. 384, and No. 36, p. 462.

the government; that had gone on long enough. The one remaining weapon for the Indonesians was noncooperation, with a trust in their own strength and abilities.[125]

Tactical noncooperation in Surabaja, absolute noncooperation in Bandung: they wanted to "do it alone" with no heed to the power of the Dutch. What Tjokroaminoto had threatened to do in 1918, what the radicals in Bandung in 1923 had wanted to do, was now about to begin. And such was now the political creed of Sukarno.

In his student days he had become acquainted with two fundamentally different views of action toward the colonial regime: a passive one in Tjokroaminoto, who was looking forward to the victory of socialism and who in 1919 had said, "If everything we ask is refused, then it is better for us to spend two days and two nights, in a mosque, commending our souls to Almighty God and asking him to fulfill our desires." [126]

On the other hand, he encountered a militant attitude in his teacher of the Bandung period. Tjipto Mangunkusumo, although he had spent long years of his earlier life in exile, nevertheless called on his followers again and again to have the courage of their convictions and to fight for the fatherland of the Pendawas.[127] In Tjipto, Sukarno had found again the language of the Ksatrijas from the Wajang, which had left so deep an impression upon his childhood, and which had been more persuasive than the expectation that the questionable promise of the Ratu Adil community around Tjokroaminoto would be fulfilled. At the beginning of the month of June 1926, having completed his studies and received his engineering diploma, he announced that he did not intend to enter the service of the colonial regime.[128] Thus, for him, the struggle for Indonesian independence under the banner of noncooperation had begun.

[125] IPO 1926, No. 19, p. 263.   [126] IPO 1919, No. 36, p. 28.
[127] IPO 1923, No. 7, pp. 309f.   [128] IPO 1926, No. 24, p. 517.

PART TWO
UNDER THE BANNER OF NONCOOPERATION:
SUKARNO'S STRUGGLE FOR
INDONESIAN INDEPENDENCE AGAINST
THE DUTCH COLONIAL POWER

III

The Nationalist Phase
(1926–1931)

For the Unity of the Pendawas

"The Single Goal"

Whatever differences Sukarno's teachers Tjokroaminoto and Tjipto Mangunkusumo may have had, they were one in demanding a united front of the Pendawas, for the settlement of internal disputes. In this they were strongly supported by Indonesian students in Holland who had followed with concern the unwelcome development of the movement in the homeland after the break between Sarekat Islam and the Communist Party (PKI) in 1921. So as a matter of course Sukarno turned, after completing his studies, to the work of unifying the movement.

In the summer of 1926, chaos dominated the political stage in Indonesia. First there were the large parties who represented the all-Indonesian idea: the PKI, which at this time was the most active party; the Sarekat Islam, still living off the fame of its first great years; the NIP, which, although it had been officially dissolved, was still widely influential; and finally the Study Clubs that had recently been founded by students returned from Europe.

In addition, there were many smaller associations that had nationalistic tendencies but at the same time exhibited dangerous leanings toward separatism. Budi Utomo did not remain unique; competitors had arisen even in Java, such as the West Javan Pasundan and a group with still more special interests, the Batavian Kaum Betawi. Even the Outer Islands had begun to organize: there were, for example, the Minahasa Union, the Ambonese Union, the Young Sumatrans, and, in North Sumatra, the Young Bataks. Although all had their headquarters on the island of Java, it was no secret that many federations kept alive a pronounced anti-Javanese accent, and that they were working more for the autonomy of their own regions than for anything that might possibly mean a new dependence on Java.

The religious organizations also exercised great influence, for example the Muhammadijah, an association founded in 1912 with the aim of reforming and deepening Islamic life, and later the orthodox membership of the Nahdatul Ulama, who opposed reform. There were some Christian associations, soon to be gathered into a Protestant and a Catholic party. And there were, finally, a number of labor unions under communist influence or direction, composed of railway workers, sailors, teachers, postal employees, pawnshop personnel, sugar-mill laborers, etc. All these associations, organizations, and parties wherever possible set up their own youth groups, organized their own congresses, and published their own newspapers or journals.[1] In short, there could not be said to be any unity or even an accommodation of the various tendencies to one another; instead, many were involved in private feuds. Within the camp of the potential forces for independence, greater divisions prevailed than at the front, as compared with the Kaurawas.

Up until then, hardly any attempt at unification had been undertaken. After the failure of the Radical Concentration in 1923, there had been increasing apathy; only Dr. Sutomo, in the spring of 1925, achieved any success.[2] But soon afterward he had committed the unpardonable error of providing the communists with material for a devastating campaign against him. He was said to have declared in a speech, "Every powerful state must devour a weaker one. This is what is meant by the Marxist theory of historical materialism. The strong devour the weak." [3]

[1] The weekly issues of IPO (*Inlandsche persoverzichten*) offer a vivid impression of the many associations and their problems.

[2] See the end of Chapter II, above.

[3] IPO 1925, No. 31, p. 193; also the articles on "Dr. Sutomo and Historical Materialism" in *Api,* July 18–25, 1925 (*ibid.,* pp. 193ff.), and other statements in IPO, Nos. 31 and 32.

The derisive clamor that ensued in the communist press greatly undermined Sutomo's standing as a nonpartisan intellectual, and his subsequent vacillation concerning the government—especially on the question of becoming a candidate for the Volksraad in the spring of 1927—laid him open to criticism.[4] Also, nearly every year he had a new falling out with the Moslems.[5] Thus Sutomo, throughout all his efforts on behalf of the Indonesian movement, was notably unsuited for one task, that of mediating among the various political tendencies—a role attributed to him, for example, by Benda.[6]

But Sutomo was not alone in his failure to produce unity. Others, likewise former members of the Perhimpunan Indonesia in Holland, fell short of the success they had hoped for. For one thing, after their stay in Europe they could readjust only with difficulty to colonial conditions, under which even their academic titles did not shield them from deliberate harassment. In Europe, they had become accustomed to a certain status and above all to legal guarantees. There they had been exposed to an aspect of the Kaurawas quite different from what they had previously known in the colony, so that many privately questioned the necessity of a Bharata Judha. Furthermore, upon returning they were frequently assigned to government posts, which amounted to the total relinquishment of political activity.[7] And they had almost entirely lost contact with their own people, who now seemed to them stupid, backward, and

[4] See, for example, the sharp criticism in "Politieke Streberei," *Indonesia Merdeka*, Vol. V, No. 3 (May 1927), pp. 70ff.; also IPO 1927, No. 2, pp. 44ff.; No. 3, pp. 76, 78f., 88f.; No. 14, pp. 10f.; No. 17, pp. 108f., 122ff.; etc.

[5] At the end of 1926 he differed with the Sarekat Islam (IPO 1927, No. 2, pp. 44ff.; No. 21, pp. 226ff.); in mid-1928 with the Ahmadijah (*Suluh Rakjat Indonesia* [SRI, "Torch of the Indonesian People," Sutomo's own paper], 1928, Nos. 36, 37; in 1930 with Moslems generally because of his articles on "Digul and Mecca," which assigned greater value to the journey into exile than to the pilgrimage to Mecca required of all Moslems (IPO 1937, p. 849, note).

[6] H. J. Benda, *Crescent*, pp. 59, 215 (note 55). Benda here incorrectly (on the basis of wrong information in H. Bouman, *Beschouwingen*, p. 47) ascribes the articles on "Digul and Mecca" to Sukarno.

[7] See "The Curbs: Penal Regulations," below.

superstitious. On the other hand, they themselves were no longer understood because their views had become too modern or too "Western." [8]

None of this was true of Sukarno. He had never left the country, and during his student days the guidance of the Ksatrijas had only added to his conviction of the inevitability of a Bharata Judha. He was acquainted with the Kaurawas only under their colonial aspect; European conditions were totally unfamiliar. What he knew had a strong ideological coloring: like a true Marxist, he accepted the thesis of the suffering, exploited masses, the tyranny of the capitalists, the irreconcilable antagonism between classes, and the imminent triumph of the proletariat. But Sukarno was also aware of a strong bond with Islam; one need only recall his statement in 1921 that the position of Islam must be further strengthened. His once-vague nationalism ("the proper condition") had since then become a conviction within the NIP.

Sukarno was thus well acquainted with all the political currents in the Indonesian movement, and he brought ideal qualifications to the task of unification, without having to reckon at once with embittered opposition from any quarter. For each of the bewildering profusion of parties and associations, almost without exception, could be traced to one of the three underlying political currents—nationalism, Islam, or Marxism. Sukarno was at home with all these ideologies, and had lately added to his theoretical knowledge of Marxism and the revival of Islam.[9]

In the fall of 1926—about three months after completing his studies—Sukarno published in *Indonesia Muda* ("Young Indo-

[8] Cf. Sjahrir's recollections in Sjahrazad, *Indonesische overpeinzingen* (1945), pp. 34f.

[9] On his preoccupation with Marxist literature during this period, see D. M. G. Koch, *Verantwoording*, pp. 191f. Sukarno had borrowed the books from Koch himself. However, Koch's chronology is in error; thus he supposes that Sukarno had already completed his studies in 1923. For his knowledge of the Islamic revival, Sukarno is greatly indebted to Lothrop Stoddard, *The New World of Islam* (1921), a book he acquired for himself and later sent on to Tjipto Mangunkusumo in exile (SRI 1930, No. 36, p. 541: Sukarno's testimony at the 1930 trial).

nesia"), the journal of the Bandung Study Club, the first of a series of articles on "Nationalism, Islam, Marxism," in which he called for closer cooperation among the three groups.[10]

But first he hailed the journal itself as a "true child of Bima," born in the midst of struggle, the struggle of an awakened Asia. The time was past when the peoples of Asia could passively leave their political and economic fate in the hands of foreign powers. Their faith that the peoples ruling them would one day voluntarily withdraw and, like an older brother, give young nations that had grown up or become mature their independence, was all but dead.

The loss of confidence stems from the *knowledge,* the *conviction* that colonization arose not out of the quest for fame, or the desire to visit foreign lands, or the love of freedom, or even overpopulation in the colonizing region—but rather from the very start out of the passion for riches.[11]

An absence of prosperity at home drove Europeans to seek it abroad, and to establish colonies wherever they found it. And for this reason they would never again give up those colonies voluntarily, since "no one simply hands over his rice basket, if that means his own undoing." [12]

And so the Kaurawas were unmasked. With a single gesture every possible motive for colonization other than the economic had been swept away, and at the same time the facile delimitation of fronts could not but be obliterated. Decade after decade —he continued—the people of Europe ("but above all Western Europe") had sent the riches of Asia flowing into their own lands. There was no mention now, as there had been in 1921, of "worthy instruction" or of a "need for economic improve-

[10] In *Dibawah Bendera Revolusi* (DBR), where the article is reprinted (pages 1–23), the source is mistakenly given as Sukarno's later newspaper *Suluh Indonesia Muda* [Torch of Young Indonesia]—which, however, first appeared only in December 1927. For a contemporary source on the article "Nationalism, Islam, Marxism," see IPO 1926, No. 48, p. 347.

[11] DBR, p. 1 (italics in original).

[12] *Ibid.,* pp. 1f.: "Orang tak akan gampang-gampang melepaskan bakul nasinja, djika pelepasan bakul itu mendatangkan matinja. . . ."

ment." Teachers and guides had become outside interference, which must now be expelled.

Awareness of the colonialist tragedy, Sukarno continued, had led to protests all over Asia, for the "Spirit of Asia" would not give way to oppression. Even in Indonesia, a popular movement had arisen; it had found expression in three political currents, "albeit with the same goal" [13]—one nationalist, one Islamic, and one Marxist. It was now the duty of all to strive for the unity of these three currents and to prove that in a colony they need not be mutually hostile. Were they but united, they would become an irresistible flood. With unflagging zeal, never despairing, they must take up this great and difficult task: "For we are convinced that unity alone can lead us one day to the fulfillment of our dream, to Indonesia Merdeka!" [14] Thus for the first time Sukarno gave clear and unmistakable formulation to the idea that was to dominate all his actions, that was the key to the fulfillment of his hopes: unity within the movement alone could give its actions sufficient force to reach the goal.

That Sukarno was not pessimistic about the task of unification appears from his casual remark that for all the currents the goal was the same. Thus there must first of all be a turning away from internal dissensions. With the unmasking of the colonial power, the setting forth of the true motive of colonization, and the conscious identification with the protests throughout Asia, a common adversary had been found: the people of Europe, "above all Western Europe." They were the adversary of the nationalists because of their territorial claims in Asia; of the Moslems because of their Christian missionary activities; and of the Marxists, finally, as upholders of the capitalist system, who hindered the spread of socialism. For Sukarno it was self-evident that nationalists, Moslems, and Marxists must unite in the struggle against the foreign masters.

However, he had spoken not only of the common opponent, but also of a single goal. He had spoken once before of that "single goal," when the Sarekat Islam and the Communist Party

[13] *Ibid.,* p. 2: "Pergerakan rakjat . . . jang walaupun dalam maksudnja sama ada mempunja tiga sifat. . . ."
[14] *Ibid.*

had parted company—and when the nationalist thinking had been overwhelmed and largely replaced by socialist concepts. In 1921 he had said that the "single goal" of the Sarekat Islam and the Communist Party was "to bring about the well-being of the people of the Netherlands Indies" (sic).[15]

But Sukarno had been schooled meanwhile by the nationalists, and soon the goals of the major parties had shifted for him as well. Now he saw them all as working for Indonesia Merdeka, for an independent Indonesia: the Sarekat Islam, which for some years had regarded the realization of Pan-Islam as its most important task; [16] the PKI, which in its early years likewise appeared definitely internationalist; [17] and finally the nationalists, striving, as Budi Utomo did on the one hand, for a "greater Java," or as the Minahasa Union did on the other, for a "greater Celebes," etc., but not at all for an independent Indonesia— such was the real background of the so-called "common goal." Showing the same skill and assurance as he had done in ascribing profit the sole motive of the colonial powers, Sukarno now suddenly presented the divergent groups of the Indonesian movement with a new "common goal." And showing the same lack of concern as he had for all possible arguments in favor of colonization, he proceeded to gloss over whatever differences of aim in fact existed; he now spoke of a "single goal," and of Indonesia Merdeka as the "fulfillment of all our dreams."

From these preliminary statements, Sukarno already strikes an objective observer as one given to shocking oversimplifications, who regards his own opinion as absolute, who avoids inconvenient details as though they did not exist, and whose own standpoint determines what is true or false, good or evil. None of this was ever to change. Throughout the entire period under consideration here, Sukarno never once lost his proneness to consider himself infallible. It was his weakness, but it was also

[15] See Chapter II, note 69, above. That is, Sukarno spoke neither of "the people of Indonesia" nor—as was then usual—of those of "East India" (Hindia Timur).

[16] See Chapter II, note 108, above; also J. Th. Petrus Blumberger, De nationalistische Beweging, p. 82.

[17] See Chapter II, note 110, above.

his strength. His rigidly one-sided certitude worked like a charm upon the Indonesian movement. After suffering for years from internal dissensions, in an atmosphere charged with accusation and exculpation, in which actions were begun without plan and abandoned without having any effect, it had now suddenly been told that the quarrels were needless and out of place, that at bottom all it members had a "single goal," which could be achieved only if they came together in a united front.

Sukarno could thus not be content with showing them a common enemy; he had also to find a common basis on which this united front could be built.

Nationalism as a Common Denominator

The reaction of the communists to Dr. Sutomo's Darwinist interpretation of historical materialism had demonstrated that the effort toward unification could succeed only if its initiator had a clear conception of the fundamental ideas of nationalism, Islam, and Marxism. Sukarno had meanwhile added to his own knowledge, and accordingly came well armed to the task of unification.

In his appeal to the nationalists, the first group on whom he called to prepare for cooperation, he began by showing that theirs was the prevalent terminology. He cited Ernest Renan's "désir d'être ensemble" and Otto Bauer's definition of the nation as "aus Schicksalsgemeinschaft erwachsene Charaktergemeinschaft"; but it is unnecessary to establish whether these scholars really influenced him, since Sukarno himself lost no time in fleeing the world of abstract ideas: "Whatever explanation these scholars may offer, it is certain that the nationalist sense evokes a sense of self-confidence, a sense that is very necessary if we are to defend ourselves in the struggle against conditions which would keep us in an inferior status." [18] In his emphasis on subjective feeling, however, Sukarno identified himself with another school, namely the Sarekat Islam. At the Sarekat Islam Congress in 1917, Abdul Muis had used almost

[18] DBR, pp. 3f.

the same words in summoning the leaders of the movement to rekindle their nationalist feeling: "Only when there is nationalist feeling can we expect our wish for independence . . . soon to be fulfilled." [19] Even Tjokroaminoto had expressed himself this way when he declared, for example, that belief in oneself created self-confidence, and that with self-confidence half the goal had been achieved.[20]

Such words from indigenous leaders held out more promise than the objective pronouncements of European thinkers. A goal to be reached "soon," or one already half achieved, had greater meaning than, say, the consciousness of forming a "Charaktergemeinschaft"—even though that definition was especially appropriate for making clear to the nationalists that they, with Moslems and Marxists, had "for centuries formed a community of fate, for centuries endured together the fate of the oppressed." [21] But difficulties immediately arose over Renan's "désir d'être ensemble," for such a condition could not be seriously attributed to either Moslems and communists or, for example, to Budi Utomo and the Ambonese Union.

With his emphasis on feeling, Sukarno took refuge in a realm of contemplation such as flourishes in the Orient, in which the sharply defined concepts of European thinkers have no part, and boundaries become fluid. Thus Gandhi could be taken as a model. Sukarno quoted his declaration, "My love of the homeland is a part of my love for all mankind. I am a patriot because I am a man and a human being. No one is excluded [from my love]." [22] This, Sukarno said, was the secret that had given Gandhi the power to unite Moslems, Hindus, Parsees, Jains, and Sikhs.[23] He too sought such a secret to bring about his union of Moslems, nationalists, and Marxists, and it was doubtless to be found in the traditions of the Orient rather than in the terminology of European scholars. Nevertheless, Sukarno had undergone a long search before arriving at a formula that could satisfy

[19] See "The School of Sarekat Islam," above.   [20] *Ibid.*

[21] DBR, p. 4.

[22] Sukarno having given no source, this has been translated from the Indonesian.

[23] DBR, p. 5.

not only the nationalists but the Marxists and Moslems as well. The result of that search, given here in its entirety, is an excellent example of Sukarno's didactic style.

True nationalists, whose love of the fatherland is grounded in a knowledge of the structure of the international economy and of history, and not merely in national arrogance—nationalists who are no chauvinists not only should but must reject all narrow-minded exclusivist ideas. True nationalists, whose nationalism is not merely a copy or imitation of Western nationalism but is based on a feeling of love of man and humanity—nationalists who receive their nationalist feeling as a divine inspiration [Wahju] and express it as an act of devotion [Bakti] are free of all pettiness and narrowness of thought. For them, the love of country is great and wide, giving space to other views, just as the air is vast and spacious and offers all living things a place and all they need for life.[24]

It is necessary to pause briefly over this, the only definition Sukarno gave of his nationalism, and one he regarded as so significant that two years later he still quoted extensively from it.[25]

If a comparison is made with Gandhi's "love for all mankind," it becomes clear that Sukarno, although using the same words, nevertheless observes a distinction here. Whereas for Gandhi "no one is excluded" from his love, Sukarno apparently stops short of the West. Although only Western nationalism is specifically excluded, nevertheless the unmistakable implication is that such a nationalism could exist only in the West. What Sukarno understood by "Western nationalism" is explained more precisely in what follows: "European nationalism has an aggressive character, is a nationalism which is concerned only with its own needs, a commercial nationalism that can lead to profit or loss, but that in the end must perish or be destroyed." [26]

In this opinion Sukarno agreed so completely with the Indian Chita Ranjam Das that he quite forgot to mention him here as

[24] DBR, p. 6.

[25] In his article "Indonesianisme dan Panasiatisme [Indonesianism and Pan-Asianism]," July 1928 (DBR, p. 76), as well as in the article "Kearah persatuan [Toward Unity]," August 1928 (DBR, pp. 112f.).

[26] DBR, p. 6.

his authority, despite having drawn this description from him word for word.[27]

With the sharp distinction from the West ("Eastern nationalism is much purer"), Sukarno made it clear that he refused to see nationalism as "love for all mankind"; rather, he saw it as a common denominator for all participants in the Bharata Judha, the decisive conflict. He offered a possible basis to Marxists as well as Moslems, for a "knowledge of the structure of the international economy" was no less a prerequisite for "true nationalists" than the view of nationalism as "divine inspiration" or, as it was even more clearly expressed at another point, the awareness of becoming, through nationalism, an "instrument of the Lord." [28] Should there be still other allies, there was still space enough in nationalism, which was "great and wide as the air."

Thus nationalism was for Sukarno at first the common denominator of all anti-imperialist, anti-Western elements, not only in Indonesia itself, but, as he later added, in all of Asia. All Asian peoples could easily, in the definition of "true nationalism" as being "like the air," be united "in the greater and more important problem, Asia against Europe." [29] But from the moment this occurred, nationalism had exceeded its usual bounds and had become, through the circumlocution of "Eastern nationalism," a form of internationalism. For Sukarno these terms were always interchangeable, as is still evident from his Pantjasila address of June 1945.[30]

The extent of the common denominator, which could be broadened at will, had not been the discovery of Sukarno. Along with his high regard for national feeling, it was firmly grounded in the Sarekat Islam. In 1918 Tjokroaminoto's newspaper had declared, "Our principles are so broadly defined that all possible tendencies can be contained in them." [31]

[27] Sukarno made use of the same passage as a quotation two years later (DBR, p. 76).

[28] "Nasionalisme kita adalah nasionalisme jang membuat kita mendjadi perkakasnja Tuhan" (DBR, p. 76).

[29] See the article, "Indonesianisme dan Panasiatisme," July 1928 (DBR, pp. 73–77, especially p. 74).

[30] See Chapter XI, below.　　　　[31] See Chapter II, note 49, above.

Earlier, Islam had played a role similar to that attributed by Sukarno to nationalism. It is significant that in the heyday of the Sarekat Islam, the propagation of the teachings of Mohammed had occupied fourth and last place in its program.[32] The important thing was that Islam should be seen as the symbol of self-reliance, of anti-Westernism, and finally of anti-imperialism. This breadth of principle for a long time served as a guarantee that all political currents motivated by such forces could be united in the Sarekat Islam. Sukarno drew upon the strength of Tjokroaminoto when he made the same breadth the basis of his nationalism. His statement at that time that "I learned politics from Tjokroaminoto" [33] received its best confirmation in the way he began his work of unification.

The "Misconceptions"

Once nationalism was considered "broad as the air," Sukarno no longer found it a problem to summon the nationalists into closer cooperation with the Moslems and Marxists. He referred to the example of India—to the "indissoluble union" between the nationalist Gandhi and the Pan-Islamites Maulana Mohammed Ali and Sjaukat Ali—or of China, where the Kuomintang had readily acceded to Marxist ideas in its rejection of militarism, imperialism, and capitalism.[34]

Nationalists who were not satisfied with these examples might have recalled that Islam had become the bearer of the spirit of freedom in the East, thereby pledging its adherents in the entire "Dar ul Islam" (world of Islam) to the welfare of the region and the people, wherever they lived. Marxism, on account of its "basic principle," was already the natural ally of the movements for freedom in Indonesia and in all of Asia.

Accordingly, in Sukarno's opinion, there was no further obstacle to closer cooperation by the nationalists with Moslems and Marxists. If they were nevertheless to refuse, then they would have to answer before the "tribunal of history." [35]

In the appeal he now made to the Moslems, Sukarno gave a

---

[32] See Chapter I, note 39, above.
[33] IPO 1932, Vol. I, pp. 101f. (The statement is from the year 1928.)
[34] DBR, p. 5.   [35] Ibid., p. 7f.

remarkable demonstration of his skill. He made a historical survey of the rise and decline of the Islamic world and the great importance of the recent reform movements for the revival of the spirit of freedom in the Asian world. Nevertheless, he pointed out, the charge was often leveled at Moslems, by nationalists as well as Marxists, that Islam was responsible for the subjection to the West of most peoples who professed belief in Allah. "They have confused the terms! Not Islam, but those who adhere to it are at fault. From a national as well as a social point of view, Islam originally set so high a standard that virtually nothing could be compared with it." [36] Its decline had begun only with the debasement of the real Islam, after the Caliphate had been usurped by secular dynasties. Thus it was an error and a misconception for nationalists or Marxists to be hostile toward Islam as such. It was also an error for Moslems to be suspicious of nationalism and Marxism as a matter of principle.

In addition to the nationalist mission of the Dar ul Islam to bring about the well-being of the homeland, Islam had still another nationalist aspect: Moslems were to bear in mind "that their agitation against the infidels will certainly awaken nationalist feeling, for the groups who are called infidels are for the most part of another nationality, not Indonesians!" [37] For cooperation with the Marxists there was likewise a common basis. In particular Sukarno mentioned that surplus value in the Marxist sense stood for "nothing other" than what the concept of usury was for Moslems. That both movements had a socialist character was already enough to permit their working together, even though the socialism of Islam had a spiritualistic and not a materialistic foundation. If the Moslems nevertheless refused to cooperate with the other groups, they would one day have to answer for that before God.[38]

Sukarno now turned to the Marxists. Here, too, he gave a notable display of knowledge, showing, in addition to wide reading, his familiarity with Marxist terminology. He explained the theories of surplus value, accumulation, and pauperization, noting casually that Marx had not discovered most of the theories but had simply translated them into a language easily

[36] *Ibid.*, p. 10.   [37] *Ibid.*, p. 11.   [38] *Ibid.*, pp. 12–14.

understood by the people. He even issued a testimonial when, for example, he noted that Vandervelde's opinion was completely correct, that revisionism had begun not with Bernstein but with Marx and Engels themselves.[39]

After thus vindicating his right to speak, Sukarno reminded the Marxists that they had a new tactic. The old tactic, calling for the demise of nationalism and for opposition to religious associations, had been superseded; the new tactic now plainly recommended the cooperation of Marxists with both nationalists and Moslems. He praised as exemplary the friendship between Marxists and nationalists in China (where the split had not yet occurred) and between Marxists and Moslems in Afghanistan.[40]

Sukarno was referring to resolutions by the Fifth Comintern Congress at Canton in June 1924, and by the meeting of the Enlarged Executive of the Communist International at Moscow in March and April 1925, in which the communist parties of Asia and the PKI in particular were exhorted to cooperate "with all political movements of a revolutionary nature." [41] He probably was acquainted with the Perhimpunan Indonesia's declaration of sympathy with the Comintern, to which the latter's resolutions had led in 1925.[42] It is doubtful, on the other hand, whether he knew that the Comintern had demanded in its letter to the PKI that in any cooperative effort the communists must assume the intellectual leadership.[43]

Nowhere, however, had any lifting of the edict of the Third International against "Pan-Islamism and similar tendencies" been mentioned. Thus Sukarno's assertion that the new tactic called for cooperation between Moslems and communists could well have been truly "new" for one group, namely the Indonesian communists themselves, since at this time, quite justly, they

[39] *Ibid.,* pp. 14ff.

[40] *Ibid.,* pp. 17, 19. On the instructions to the PKI from the Enlarged Executive of the Communist International in Moscow, March 21–April 6, 1925, see *Westkust-Rapport,* Vol. I, pp. 47–52.

[41] On the Canton Congress see Blumberger, *Commun. beweging,* pp. 56 f.

[42] *De Locomotief,* November 9, 1930 (on the trial of Sukarno).

[43] *Indisch Tijdschrift van het Recht,* CXXXIII (1931), 628.

did not consider the Sarekat Islam one of the "revolutionary" associations.[44]

But Sukarno had still other surprises in store for the communists (whom he alone, in continually referring to them as "Marxists," seems to have linked anew with the Second International). He made it plain to them that Otto Bauer had made national autonomy a prerequisite for realizing the goals of the proletariat, and thus he concluded: "This is why it is the very first duty of the working class in Asia to work for national autonomy. This is why it is their duty to work together with and to support movements in Asia which also strive for national autonomy, without exploring the principles of the other movements." [45] With this bold leap from the opinion of the Austrian Marxist Bauer on the duty of the Social Democrats in Europe [46] to the communist-led camp of the working class in Asia, Sukarno masterfully arrived at the "single goal" mentioned at the beginning of this chapter. Like the other movements, "which also [!] have national autonomy as their goal," they were brought by Sukarno to a common denominator through which cooperation appeared quite possible, once their prejudices were abandoned. No one, Sukarno repeatedly declared, was to give up his own standpoint; no nationalist was to become a Moslem, or vice versa.

With the exposure of the "misconceptions" and the elucidation of the goal common to all, it might have appeared that enough had been done for the sake of tactical cooperation. But Sukarno, it seemed, was not yet satisfied. He still wanted to clear up the "chief misconception," because of which in his day the break in the Indonesian movement between the Sarekat Islam and the communists had been inevitable. This had to do with the answer to the crucial question: what of religion?

[44] In an open letter to the PKI, Semaun, elaborating on the decisions of the Comintern, called for infiltration into the Sarekat Islam "in order to draw the revolutionary masses to the side of our party" (McVey, *The Rise of Indonesian Communism*, p. 280).

[45] DBR, pp. 19f.

[46] Otto Bauer, *Die Nationalitätenfrage und die Sozialdemokratie* (1909, 1924). Bauer was primarily concerned here with the attitude of the Social Democrats on questions related to the Austrian multinational state.

At the time of the last attempt at unification, Semaun, representing the communists, had answered with the words, "We are neutral toward religion." This had not satisfied the leadership of the Sarekat Islam, and the attempt at unification had failed.[47] What had not been enough for the Sarekat Islam was for Sukarno, however, an important advance. Not only the tactics but also the theory of Marxism had changed. Marx and Engels were not prophets who had laid down guiding principles valid for all time; even their teachings had been outdated with the passage of years. Thus, for example, present-day Marxism no longer demanded, as the Communist Manifesto had done in 1847, that religion be "abolished." [48]

Such was the introduction to Sukarno's remarkable disclosure that the entire conflict between Marxism and religion was at bottom likewise an error. He then proceeded to explain that a distinction must be made between historical and philosophical materialism. "We must recall that the intent of historical materialism is different from that of philosophical materialism." [49] Philosophical materialism inquired into the nature of thought, historical materialism inquired into the reason for changes in thought; philosophical materialism was philosophical, historical materialism was historical. Having made this artificial distinction, as though dealing with two completely different or at any rate mutually exclusive concepts, Sukarno declared:

Both these concepts have long been confounded and misrepresented by the enemies of Marxism in Europe, especially those in the Church. In their anti-Marxist propaganda they have constantly misused these concepts, they have never tired of charging the Marxists with proclaiming that thought was only a secretion by the brain, as saliva was by the mouth or gall by the liver; they never ceased to call the Marxists worshipers of earthly goods and idolaters of matter.

[47] IPO 1923, No. 10, pp. 482ff.; also Blumberger, *Commun. beweging,* 32.

[48] DBR, pp. 19ff.

[49] "Kita harus memperingatkan bahwa maksudnja Historis-Materialisme itu berlainan dari pada maksudnja wijsgerig-Materialisme tahadi" (*ibid.,* p. 21).

This was the reason for the hate of the European Marxists for the Church, and for the hostility of the European Marxists to religion. And this hostility grew fiercer and more hateful wherever the Church used religion to protect capitalism, to defend the interests of the ruling class, to carry out an exceedingly reactionary policy.[50]

Sukarno was not content simply to describe the Church in general as the handmaid of capitalism. For this thesis he would easily have found examples in Marxist literature—which of course likewise reckoned Islam among the supporters of the "ruling classes." [51] But this was just what Sukarno wanted to avoid; therefore, he took refuge here in the proved formula of misconceptions. What underlay the conflict between theists and Marxists was not the irreconcilable antagonism of two systems of belief supported by dogma—one of which promised paradise on earth, the other only in the hereafter—but rather a confusion of terms.

Here, it would appear, Sukarno had stepped outside the frame of tactics and gone in search of a standpoint of his own. As grounds for cooperation, the "common enemy" and the "common denominator," along with the "single goal," would have sufficed. But even as early as 1921, his unusual combining of the Marxist belief in progress with belief in God could already have been observed. His problem was to unite these two beliefs—which, according to the old Javanese philosophy that "all things are one," was not an impossibility.[52] Sukarno believed he had found the key to solving the problem in the difference between philosophical and historical materialism. Philosophical materialism was "philosophical"; it was, like so many other theories, speculation that one could either believe or not believe. Historical materialism, on the other hand, was "historical"; it was a

[50] *Ibid.*

[51] See, for example, K. Kautsky, *Ethik und materialistische Geschichtsauffassung* (1906), p. 132: "The kind of morality that must be held up before the people in the interest of the ruling class, of course urgently needs the support of religion and the entire ecclesiastical superstructure." Kautsky refers to the "new" (monotheistic) religions, in which Islam is included.

[52] See Chapter I, note 12, and Chapter II, note 9, above.

science that made use of exact reasoning, in which one had to believe and in which, as will presently be demonstrated, Sukarno himself believed slavishly, for the reason that from it could be deduced the victory of the oppressed.

For Sukarno, philosophical materialism was thus not the self-evident foundation of historical materialism that it was, for example, for Lenin, who declared, "Only the philosophical materialism of Marx showed the proletariat the way out of the intellectual servitude in which all oppressed classes had until then been imprisoned." [53] For Sukarno, the separation of philosophical and historial materialism meant rather that it left room for a Creator-God whom he had to "accommodate." It was then quite easy to speak of "misconceptions," "deceptions," and "distortions," and to dispose of the entire dispute between believers in God and Marxists as an error.

Sukarno—whose relations with Marxism and with Islam will be examined later in more detail—had given to his synthesis of nationalism, Islam, and Marxism which was recognizable in embryo by 1921 a "philosophical foundation." [54] It was no more difficult for him, finally, to assure the Marxists that, in contrast to Christianity in Europe, where it protected the upper class, Islam in Indonesia was the religion of the oppressed—and that once this difference had been understood they would undoubtedly stretch forth their hands once again and say, "Come, brothers, let us unite." [55]

At the end of his series of articles Sukarno once again issued this advice to the three movements, nationalism, Islam, and Marxism: "We must know how to receive, but we must also know how to give. That is the secret of unity. Unity cannot be achieved unless each is also willing to give a little." [56] That advice was also the secret of Sukarno himself. He took away philosophical materialism from Marxism and gave it Allah; he took from Islam its "encumbering past" and gave to it the Marxist idea of progress; he took from the nationalists their "narrow-

[53] Lenin, *Karl Marx* (Dutch edition of the biography originally published in 1913; 1933), p. 55.
[54] See "Sukarno's Early Political Views," above.   [55] DBR, p. 22.
[56] DBR, p. 23.

mindedness" and gave them his own "broad nationalism," as well as allies. Where serious difficulties stood in the way, they turned out on closer examination to be "misconceptions," which could easily be swept aside. With this accomplished, all ideologies could be conveniently adapted to the "common denominator," so as to fight side by side toward the "single goal" of all. After his own fashion, by passing tolerantly over inconvenient details, Sukarno had theoretically opened the way for at least an attempt at a united front.

The Indonesian Federation PPPKI

The crucial question was over what position the communists would take toward the plan for closer cooperation. They had demonstrated often enough that they did not shrink from indulging in accusation and personal attack if objective discussion afforded them no advantage.

By one of the greatest strokes of luck in Sukarno's political career, this question never had to be raised except in theory; for while his articles were appearing in *Indonesia Muda*, communist revolts broke out in Java (November 1926) and in Sumatra (January 1927),[57] leading to the suppression of the Communist Party in Indonesia. Thus from the beginning of Sukarno's public career until the end of the war in the Pacific (the PKI was also illegal under the Japanese), this unpredictable ally was unable to restrict Sukarno's actions and influence. Despite the sympathy for the Communist Party that originally existed in the Study Club at Bandung, which Sukarno led after completing his studies—a sympathy whose effect in 1930 was to make the verdict against Sukarno more severe [58]—it was more than doubtful that the communists would have submitted in the long run to a nationalist leadership. Lenin's Twenty-one Points contained the directive, confirmed in the new tactic of

---

[57] On the Communist revolts, see details in the reports gathered by the colonial government, known as the "Bantam-Rapport" and the "Westkust-Rapport" (complete titles in the bibliography). These have recently been made available in English: see H. J. Benda and R. T. McVey, *The Communist Uprisings of 1926-27 in Indonesia* (1960).

[58] *Indisch Tijdschrift van het Recht*, CXXXIII (1931), 629.

the communists, that in cooperative efforts they were to attempt "to give the noncommunist organizations a communist tinge, on no account to merge with them, and to preserve the independence of the proletarian movement down to the smallest detail." [59] There would have been no question of "giving" in Sukarno's sense.

Thus the self-imposed elimination of the Communist Party by its attempted putsch in 1926 and 1927 was in any case a gain for Sukarno in the work of unification. Instead of the three movements—nationalism, Islam, and Marxism—there was now only a question of gathering the many groups of nationalists and Moslems into a united front.

In December 1926, Tjokroaminoto's new journal *Bandera Islam* ("Flag of Islam") [60] contained the interesting announcement of a change of character. On February 7, 1927, *Bandera Islam* appeared for the first time in its new form: in addition to the Islamic section under the direction of Tjokroaminoto, there was a nationalist section under the editorship of Mr. Sartono and Ir. [Ingenieur] Sukarno.[61] On the front page of the paper the new Islamic-nationalist cooperation was graphically shown in the emblems of both ideologies: the crescent moon and star of the Moslems, together with the wild-buffalo head that symbolized the nationalists.[62]

Thus Sukarno once again joined forces with his old teacher

[59] Point 11, Paragraph 5. See A. H. Stern (ed.), *Lenins 21 Punkte*, p. 24; also a similar letter from Moscow to the PKI, dated May 1925 (*Indisch Tijdschrift v. h. Recht*, p. 628).

[60] *Utusan Hindia* had been replaced in the Spring of 1923 by *Dunia Islam*. Thus "Messenger of Ind[ones]ia" had become "World of Islam"— a sign of the changed interest in the Sarekat Islam (IPO 1923, No. 12, p. 580).

[61] IPO 1927, No. 7, p. 211. Mr. Sartono, a former member of the Perhimpunan Indonesia in Holland, subsequently came to be more and more a confidant of Sukarno.

[62] The buffalo's head derived its meaning for the Indonesian nationalists from a Dutch apocalyptic poem by Roorda van Eysinga, "The Last Day of the Dutch on Java," from the mid-nineteenth century, found in Multatuli, *Max Havelaar* (Appendix), under the title "Song of Sentot." In this poem, the buffalo—"exasperated with his driver"—tosses him into

Tjokroaminoto—a rapprochement that became advantageous when, after the events in the Near East in the years 1924–26, the Pan-Islamic idea once more receded into the background. That Tjokroaminoto had no longer blamed Sukarno for the rupture of 1923 is best shown by the continued public appearances of both men at the same events during the years that followed, and by their continuing to speak on the same themes.[63]

In other ways, Sukarno worked enthusiastically to spread the Indonesian idea. Surmising that among the older generation the idea of a greater Java or an independent Sumatra would give way only by degrees to that of "Indonesia," he concentrated his efforts on the youth. Thus at Bandung he was influential in founding an association called "Jong Indonesia." The various Boy Scout organizations were introduced to the new ideal of an independent Indonesia, and the duty was laid upon them of considering themselves above all to be Indonesian patriots.[64] The "Indonesian idea" gained ground rapidly; by July 1927, according to one newspaper, a real "Indonesian period" had already begun.[65]

This development came to its natural expression with the establishment on July 4, 1927, of what was to become Sukarno's Partai Nasional Indonesia. Originally called "Perserikatan Nasional Indonesia" (Indonesian National Association), it was better known by the initials PNI. The repeated misreading of PNI as "Persatuan Nasional Indonesia" (Indonesian National

---

the air and then tramples him. The Perhimpunan Indonesia had taken this as a symbol; see Mohammed Hatta, *Indonesia vrij* (1928), pp. 30f. The buffalo's head, as well as the traditional colors, also appears on the title page of the *Gedenkboek Indonesische Vereeniging* (1908–23). The statement by H. J. de Graaf (*Geschiedenis van Indonesië*, p. 473) that the nationalists had adopted the buffalo's head as a symbol from the Scouts, should properly be reversed: the Scouts adopted the symbol of the "Kepala banteng" from the nationalists.

[63] See, for instance, IPO 1927, No. 12, p. 381.

[64] *Mededeelingen der regeering* (1928), p. 31; also IPO 1927, No. 4, p. 111; No. 12, pp. 379ff.

[65] See the article "Indonesianism" in *Bintang Timur*, mid-July 1927 (IPO 1927, No. 30, pp. 179f.).

Unity) [66] makes it clear that Sukarno's wish for a united front had not diminished, but that even as chairman of a new party he continued to devote himself zealously to it.

The renewed contact with the Sarekat Islam promptly led to Sukarno's receiving an official invitation to a Sarekat Islam Congress in Pekalongan, at the end of September 1927. Here he presented the Moslems with his ideas on a united front— namely that although a single party was the ideal, the course taken by the development of society meant that different interest groups were still in existence. The PNI therefore aimed first at a federation, whose member groups would cooperate on certain questions and would give the necessary force to their demands upon the colonial power.[67]

Thereupon Hadji Agus Salim, the very SI leader who had brought about the break with the communists in 1921, got up to praise Sukarno's initiative. The Sarekat Islam was ready to cooperate, and wanted to help in bringing the federation into existence. Finally, Sukarno was officially entrusted with working out the plans. His optimism was contagious: upon appearing once again before the Congress, he had already been greeted with joy.[68]

Sukarno worked quickly. Within a few weeks, the most diverse political groups had received invitations to take part in the establishment of a federation. And on December 17, 1927, the representatives of the seven major parties [69] met for the founding session of the PPPKI or, as it was called in full, the "Permufakatan Perhimpunan Politik Kebangsaan Indonesia" (Consensus of Political Associations of Indonesia).

In his keynote speech, Sukarno explained the structure and working methods of the federation [70]—in which the most di-

[66] IPO 1927, No. 39, p. 605; No. 41, pp. 77f.; etc.

[67] *De Locomotief*, October 1, 1927, p. 38.

[68] *Ibid.*, October 3, 1927, p. 4.

[69] They were Sukarno's new party, the Perserikatan Nasional Indonesia; Partij Sarekat Islam; Budi Utomo; Pasundan; Sumatranenbund; Kaum Betawi; and Dr. Sutomo's Indonesian Study Club.

[70] For details, see *Suluh Rakjat Indonesia* (SRI), December 28, 1927, pp. 11ff.; also *Suluh Indonesia Muda* (SIM), No. 2 (January 1928), pp. 37ff., 48ff.

verse interest groups were represented—and particularly urged that themes which could give rise to dissension ought, as much as possible, to be kept out of the discussions:

Let us refer to no matters that could endanger our consensus. Let us, for example, not discuss cooperation and noncooperation—the question of whether we are to work with the government or not. But let us seek that which brings us closer to one another. Let us put into the foreground all that unites us.[71]

The question of cooperation with the colonial government at this time nevertheless dominated the Indonesian movement. Sukarno, as will presently be shown, became the spokesman of the camp of the noncooperators, who ignored the Dutch colonial regime in their attempt to create a mass movement, and who relied exclusively on their own strength and ability—or so, at least, it was said officially. They were the warriors, the Ksatrijas. On the other hand, there was just as strong a group of "cooperators" who foresaw no advantage in a willful severing of ties with the government, or who even still believed in promises of a gradual share in responsibility. They sat in the councils which the Ksatrijas boycotted.

If there was now to be a really effective coordination of the different associations, the first requirement was that they be of one mind on the decisive question of their relation to the Kaurawas. But at this juncture, there was no such unanimity. Sukarno's tested formula was once again simply to avoid these questions. For him the important thing was that all associations first be brought closer together, and that they begin with the common discussion which had so long been shunned by the movement. Their decisions, finally, ought to represent to the world at large the wish of the entire Indonesian people.

Consequently these decisions were to be reached unanimously. The federation had been named the "Consensus of Political Associations." The Indonesian word "Mufakat"—to be in agreement, to agree unanimously—had always played an important role in Indonesian tradition. From the village communities on up to the highest advisory bodies, decisions were taken

[71] SIM, p. 51.

not according to majority rule, which was too alien to syncretistic thinking ("all things are one"), but rather according to the Mufakat system. In general discussions ("Permusjawaratan"), wherever opposition developed, compromises were made by the opposing sides until Mufakat had been reached. And it was this system that Sukarno now wanted to adopt in a modern organization, proudly calling it a "return to our own selves." [72] In concluding his appeal, he had already spoken of the secret of unity, that each must "give [in] a little." [73] That was exactly in the style of the traditional "Permusjawaratan," which had Mufakat as its culmination. In Sukarno's opinion, the Western system of voting on the basis of majority rule was unjust. It led too easily, he explained, to a "tyranny over the minority," and the world's history had shown that great and decisive impulses frequently originated with just such minorities. The PPPKI would not reject the opinion of the minorities; therefore, the decisions must be reached unanimously.[74]

Here, once again, Sukarno was seeking a common ground for all Pendawas. No one was to be excluded or to find himself disadvantaged from the outset. In the permanent advisory council (Madjelis Penimbangan), each of the member organizations was represented with a vote.[75] Whether this "Indonesian solution" actually worked can be judged only at a later juncture.[76] For the moment, at least, it appeared to be a great success for Sukarno: he had accomplished the feat not only of theoretically overcoming all "insurmountable contradictions," but also of uniting in one organization such diverse groups as the noncooperators and the cooperators, the fervent Javanese and the fervent Sumatrans, and even the brother organizations that had quarreled all through the year 1927—the Sarekat Islam and Dr. Sutomo's Study Club [77]—all this by the end of that same year.

In no more than a year and a half, Sukarno had accomplished the work of unification, first in theory and then in practice, and had created a "state within a state." The Sarekat Islam had attempted the same thing, but had been decisively prevented

[72] *Ibid.*, p. 58.   [73] See "The 'Misconceptions,' " above.
[74] SIM, No. 2, p. 52.   [75] SRI, December 28, 1927, pp. 12f.
[76] See Chapter IV, below.   [77] See note 5, above.

from succeeding by "allies from the West" who showed no understanding of "Indonesian solutions." Now that the Communist Party had been outlawed, the united front succeeded without any notable difficulty.

The "Brown Front"

At the congress in Pekalongan, however, Sukarno had already indicated that he would not be satisfied with the "state within a state," as at that time the federation was repeatedly called.[78] With the PPPKI, he intended to call a "brown front" into being. His speech at the congress in Pekalongan, under the title, "Toward a Brown Front," later appeared in the first issue of his new journal, *Suluh Indonesia Muda* (Torch of Young Indonesia), on the eve of the founding of the federation.[79] In it, Sukarno declared that the idea of a "white united front" had been suggested in the white press as a means of defense against the "murderousness" and "bloodthirstiness" of the "natives." That the idea had not taken hold could have two explanations: either the white man really wanted to work toward brotherhood, toward mutual understanding and respect, or he felt "that the formation of a white front will irrevocably call forth a brown front, in which the browns can throw into the scale the weight of their superior numbers, which could no longer be neutralized by better organization on the side of the whites alone." [80]

Against the first supposition—or so went Sukarno's startling contention—was the way the whites had up to then consciously separated themselves from the browns; *for* the second hypothesis was the way they began to "overflow with brotherly love" at a time when the Indonesians had been able to gain strength by consolidating power in a number of organizations, and when from a mass of unorganized illiterates they had become a mass of organized illiterates, whose members were aware that the

[78] IPO 1927, No. 42, p. 132; No. 46, p. 317; etc.

[79] See the article "Naar het bruine front," SIM, No. 1 (December 1927), pp. 2–5 (also DBR, pp. 37ff.), and the report in *De Locomotief* (October 1, 1927, p. 38) of Sukarno's speech at Pekalongan.

[80] DBR, p. 37.

academic education they lacked was more than made up for by their great numbers.[81]

Sukarno did not trouble at first to weigh the pros and cons of his two hypotheses against each other. The notion that a fraternal impulse could exist was so unwelcome to him that he wished only to look for arguments against it. On the other hand, the notion that those on the "side of the whites" had already begun to be afraid was so attractive that it was accepted *a priori*. It gave his side reason to speak triumphantly of their own strength, and by dialectic means (the white front would irrevocably call forth the brown front) to work themselves into a position of power that was without any foundation in reality.

For had not the Dutch colonial government, by its supression of the badly organized communist uprising only a few months before, easily demonstrated that it was master of the situation? Was not the lack of any response whatever to the proposal of a "white front" the best proof that it was regarded as totally unnecessary?—an argument that Sukarno appeared to have omitted entirely from his pros and cons.

However, Sukarno deliberately evaded any idea that the Indonesian movement was not just then being taken very seriously. In the same way that the "fraternal impulse" merely served as a pretext for sarcastic remarks ("Why, suddenly, these loving glances?"), he ignored every other possibility that might have diverted him from his predetermined conclusion. "A white front would weaken the European position in our land. From this it follows that a brown front will strengthen our position." [82] Had these words been spoken at the Pekalongan congress alone, it might be argued that Sukarno had been speaking there simply as a demagogue who wished to intoxicate the people momentarily with a sense of their own power—something he was later to do successfully at his rallies, over and over again.

But Sukarno also published this speech in the first number of his new periodical, where it appeared, surprisingly enough, in Dutch.[83] It thus became obvious that Sukarno intended not

[81] *Ibid.*, p. 38.   [82] DBR, p. 38.

[83] It is, so far as can be learned, the only article written by Sukarno in Dutch.

only to give his own countrymen "courage and self-confidence" because, as Tjokroaminoto's old slogan had it, therewith "victory was already halfway won," but also, in the manner of the Ksatrijas, to let the Kaurawas know that his countrymen were aware of their own strength. For him, the position arrived at dialectically had become one of real power:

Unquestionably, we the Indonesians understand that as we become more and more conscious of the strength in our numerical superiority, accompanied by the constantly declining prestige of the rulers, the situation will become more and more acute. We understand that to draw a mathematically exact line of division between the browns who desire power and the whites who are holding fast to it will mean opening the way for a crisis in the deteriorating relations between brown and white. But we also understand that the sooner and the more sharply the antithesis is posed, the more clear-cut the struggle will be. And to the degree that the antagonism is recognized, the direction of the struggle will be all the more precise.[84]

This was nothing other than a call to the Bharata Judha, to the decisive struggle of the Pendawas against the Kaurawas, which Sukarno, once he had completed the task of unification, meant to see enacted on the Indonesian stage. Before going on to an account of that struggle under the banner of noncooperation, however, it is necessary to give brief attention to the opposing camp.

The Power of the Kaurawas

The Permissible Field of Activity: The Volksraad

Was it sheer arrogance that led the noncooperators to reject the means granted by the Dutch colonial power for working toward their aims as loyal subjects, or did they have a real justification? This question may be briefly examined by using the example of the Volksraad, considered as a political training ground for the exercise of an awakened national ambition.[85]

[84] DBR, p. 38.

[85] On the Volksraad, see S. L. van der Wal, *De Volksraad en de Staatkundige ontwikkeling van Nederlandsch-Indië* (2 vols., 1964, 1965), an important source on the origins and development of the VR; also the stenographic record of the Volksraad meetings, *Handelingen Volksraad*

In July 1913, when with the awakening of the Indonesian movement the rush of the masses to the Sarekat Islam was at its height, the "long-planned" formation of a colonial council was decided upon. Its function, as an advisory board of independent subjects, was to assist the Governor General (GG), whose decisions were law in the colony. Once the movement had declined, however, much time was allowed to elapse before, in December 1916, the functions of what was now called the Volksraad (VR) became law; and those functions were strictly adhered to once the VR had opened in May 1918.

According to the law, the VR was to consist of a chairman nominated by the King of the Netherlands, and thirty-eight members (forty-eight after 1921), of whom half might be elected, but the other half had to be nominated by the GG. The election process, however, not only was indirect and extremely complicated,[86] but also was so unmistakably controlled by representatives of Dutch interests that the power of nomination, which had actually been intended as a safeguard, was used now and then by the GG to invite a few "extremists" into the council. Thus it happened that Sukarno's teachers, Tjokroaminoto and Tjipto Mangukusumo, were both nominated for the first session (1918–20).

Nor were these the only safeguards to the position of the Kaurawas. During the three first sessions an absolute majority of foreigners dominated the VR, so that even had all Indonesians become infected by the extremists, the colonial masters would have had no reason for apprehension.

But there had been no such danger. The delegates who pleaded either secretly or openly for autonomy, even in the

---

(1918ff.), and the rather sketchy surveys (which are, however, useful for their nearly exhaustive bibliography on the VR) in *Tien jaar Volksraadarbeid (1918–1928)* and *Tien jaar Volksraadarbeid (1928–38)*; and from 1928 on, the irregularly published survey of the annual sessions, issued by the Volksraad. As secondary sources, see the very detailed account by Nederburgh in *Encyklopaedie van Nederlandsch-Indië* (ENI), Part 4 (1921), pp. 612ff. ("Volksraad"), and the continuation in ENI, Part 6 (Supplement 1932), pp. 438ff.; also the dissertation of I. Samkalden, *Het college van gedelegeerden uit den Volksraad* (1938).

[86] Explained in detail in ENI, Part 4, p. 614.

moderate fashion of the representatives of Budi Utomo or the Social Democrats (e.g., Stokvis), were a hopeless minority. In the three sessions of the VR up to 1926, the council was composed as follows:

Table 7. Volksraad Membership, 1918–26 [87]

	Indonesians	Non-Indonesians	Total	Favoring Independence
1918–20	15	23	38	8
1921–23	20	28	48	5
1924–26	20	28	48	5

One could hardly expect the nationalists to flock to this training ground, in which there were ten Kaurawas for every Pendawa. But even had any of the Pendawas dared raise the Indonesian question, he would have influenced no decisions whatsoever, for the reason that the VR had no decisions to make. It had been set up as an advisory board authorized to take a position on matters submitted by the GG; but it could not bring about changes in proposed laws or regulations. On such matters, the GG was required to obtain the advice of the VR only when they concerned the budget. The sole right of the VR was the "right of petition," either to the King of the Netherlands or to the GG.

When in 1927 the status of the Volksraad was raised in principle to that of co-legislator, its essentially minor function was scarcely altered. Indeed, a few new rights were granted, and its composition was revised in the Indonesians' favor; but independence of decision and the exercise of any measurable influence on policy were denied the VR even after a new government regulation had been established for the Netherlands Indies.

This new regulation was the final disillusioning outcome of promises made by the GG in the fall of 1918, six months after the VR had been installed. When political upheavals brought about by the revolutionary events in Europe temporarily threatened the Netherlands, and the link between Asia and Europe could be maintained only with difficulty, Governor General van

[87] From data in Tien jaar Volksraadarbeid (1928–38), pp. 31ff.

Limburg Stirum on November 18, in a message to the VR, had spoken of a "shifting of powers." [88] Then, a few weeks later, the government representative, Mr. Talma, spoke before the VR of a "fundamental change in the character of this body"; it was gradually to become a true component of the government, with an actual right to be heard and to exercise control over the administration.[89]

Although a commission was soon appointed by the GG to work out a reform in the government of the Netherlands Indies, the results [90] did not begin to satisfy the wishes of the nationalists. So in 1925 the final "new order," with its meager concessions to the VR,[91] came as proof to those Indonesians who had still hoped for genuine progress that the colonial government had no thought at all of granting the population an "actual right to be heard." For the extremists, this was the signal for seizing the initiative to act on their own, as Tjokroaminoto had proclaimed them ready to do in 1918 and as there had been repeated talk of doing, but without any serious moves.

Although the VR gave the nationalists no opportunity for independent negotiation or accountability to themselves, it did have another sort of value, in that it brought together representatives of the entire archipelago. Thus the delegate from the Celebes necessarily developed an interest in events in West Sumatra, and the representative of the Moluccas in the prob-

[88] "Verschuivingen van bevoegdheden." See *Handelingen Volksraad,* second session, 1918–19, pp. 251f.

[89] *Ibid.,* p. 430 (address by Mr. Talma on December 12, 1918).

[90] *Verslag van de commissie tot herziening van de staatsinrichting van Nederlandsch-Indië* (1920).

[91] The VR was granted the "right of initiative"—i.e., it could work out proposals for governmental measures—as well as the "right of amendment" (proposals for changes), and finally the "right of interpellation," i.e., it could ask the Governor General to explain measures. But in no case was the GG required to submit to the proposals of the VR; if he chose to make an independent decision, there were a number of possible excuses (lack of time, the need for secrecy, the right to settle matters in dispute as the "representative of the crown," etc.). The College of Delegates (one-third of the membership of the VR, which had been raised to sixty), who met in continual session, likewise had no further powers (I. Samkalden, *Het college van gedelegeerden uit den Volksraad,* 1938).

lems of Borneo, with the result that in this much-abused "parliament" there was actually a symbol of the Indonesian idea. And as a further advantage to the nationalists, the Volksraad offered the opportunity—of which ample use was made—for critical statements immune to criminal prosecution.

These hazardous side effects of the "innocent Volksraad" were also recognized by the supporters of permanent Dutch colonial rule in Indonesia. H. Colijn, the spokesman for this group—which had a powerful influence in Holland and an even greater one in the colony—in a book published in 1928, significantly titled *Colonial Problems of Today and Tomorrow*, called the Volksraad a "tree that is rotten at the root, and must be grubbed out." [92] It was unfruitful for the Indonesians because it could grant them no authority of their own "in the humanly foreseeable future"; [93] it was intolerable for the colonial power because it was a haven for agitators and unbridled critics, whom it protected from "getting their knuckles rapped." [94]

As a way out satisfactory to both sides, Colijn suggested what he called "island councils," parliamentary bodies in which the residents of the several islands would gradually work their way up into responsible positions, with the final goal of a locally restricted autonomy. In thus propounding, quite without scruple, a policy of divide-and-rule, he let it be known that the most serious threat from the Volksraad had not been lost on him, namely the increased feeling of unity throughout the archipelago—although even in 1928 he still found it possible to say: "The term Indonesia, which it pleases them to use as an expression of unity, is lacking in content. The islands that make up the East Indian archipelago are a unity for the reason that they compose the Netherlands Indies, and for that reason alone." [95] For those who did not regard Indonesia as a term "lacking in content," but rather as the sacred heritage of the Pendawas that had been unlawfully usurped by the Kaurawas— those who preferred not to enter the councils of the rulers but

[92] H. Colijn, *Koloniale vraagstukken van heden en morgen* (1928), p. 71. Colijn had criticized the VR from the very beginning; see S. L. van der Wal, *Volksraad*, Vol. I, p. 250.

[93] *Ibid.*, pp. 49, 59.   [94] *Ibid.*, p. 56.   [95] *Ibid.*, pp. 59f.

rather to oppose them publicly—the colonial regime had an abundance of regulations designed, as Colijn put it, for "rapping their knuckles."

The Curbs: Penal Regulations

Some attention must be given to these penal regulations, as an indication of the curbs Sukarno encountered in his struggle under the banner of noncooperation.

When in 1919 the hated Article 111RR, dating to 1854 and forbidding all forms of political activity, was finally withdrawn, Tjokroaminoto had prematurely rejoiced that he could now express his political views "straight from the heart." [96] In the same year a much more significant motion, to abolish what were known as "exorbitant rights," was rejected in the Dutch parliament by a large majority.[97]

These rights permitted the GG, without a court decision, to exile from the Netherlands Indies persons "regarded as dangerous to the public peace and security" or, where Dutch subjects born in the Netherlands Indies were concerned, to assign them for an unlimited time to a permanent residence somewhere in the archipelago.[98]

In addition to this radical measure—which was often used after 1920, particularly against the communists [99]— a series of regulations authorized prison sentences or fines for offenses that gradually came to be regarded as dangerous and which, through legal devices, were transformed into penal offenses. A leading master of this was GG Fock, originally a lawyer, who governed in the Netherlands Indies at the beginning of the 1920's. He was aware of the disillusionment among the nationalists after the promised reforms of 1918 failed to be carried out, but he believed the movement could be restrained by taking harsh measures. Among the laws designed to hold it in check were the following: [100]

[96] IPO 1919, No. 36, pp. 28f.

[97] Blumberger, *Commun. beweging*, p. 144.

[98] Dealt with in articles 35–38 of the criminal code; see the text in Blumberger, *Commun. beweging*, pp. 142ff.

[99] See Chapter II, note 114, above.

[100] See Blumberger, *Commun. beweging*, pp. 142ff., for a compilation of all laws against revolutionary activity up to 1928.

* 1919: The so-called Muzzle Law, which prevented civil servants and employees of the government, under pain of dismissal, from taking part in, or merely giving support to, any movement to undermine the authority of the government.

*1923: The notorious Article "161 bis," which penalized every move to strike, and even propaganda in favor of strikes, with prison sentences of up to five years.

*1924: The regulation of travel within the archipelago, including a passport requirement that made it practically impossible for the spokesman of a political party to promote its goals outside Java.

*(May) 1926: Articles "153 bis" and "153 ter," issued against communist subversion, but in fact leading to just such subversion by forcing the communists underground,[101] whence they contributed to the autumn 1926 uprising.

Article "153 bis," which went into effect a few weeks after Sukarno completed his studies, enabled the police to lay hands on nearly everyone who spoke publicly of freedom for Indonesia, even as no more than an ultimate goal. It read:

Whoever deliberately by speaking, writing, or pictures—even if only indirectly, by implication or veiled suggestion—praises or spreads propaganda for a disturbance of public order, for the overthrow of or insurgency against the existing government in Holland or the Netherlands Indies, will be punished by imprisonment up to six years or a fine of up to 300 guilders.[102]

From without, Dutch rule in the colony thus appeared indeed "as firmly anchored as Mont Blanc in the Alps" (Colijn), since whatever might have been "forgotten" by the penal regulations could easily be put together whenever there was a threatening development—as, for example, the "wild" (nationalist) schools in the early 1930's.

But internally, what had been sanctioned by the legal machinery of the 1920's, instead of fulfilling the promise of "genuine participation," was the final failure of the idea of associa-

---

[101] The reaction in the Malay-language press was collected and published by the communist paper *Api* in its final number before being compelled to cease publication at the beginning of May 1926 (IPO 1926, No. 17, pp. 157ff.).

[102] Blumberger, *Commun. beweging* p. 150.

tion. Trust in the "older brothers"—as Sukarno himself demonstrated—had vanished; the schoolmasters had become adversaries.[103]

It was disastrous that at this time the School of Leiden—Snouck Hurgronje, van Vollenhoven, Hazeu, and others—could exert no influence on policy in the colony. The warnings by these leading authorities on Indonesia against underestimating the movement, and their proposals of greater concessions to the Indonesians,[104] accomplished only one thing: the establishment of a Faculty of Indology at Utrecht, in obvious competition with Leiden.[105] In this way, business circles sought to prevent the influence of the School of Leiden from becoming too great in the colony. For, as Mr. Treub, chairman of the Dutch businessmen's association, said in an exchange with Hazeu—the man who over a decade as Advizeur for native affairs closely followed the awakening of the Indonesian movement—"The gentlemen of the Leiden Faculty of Indology see apparitions. And if those are something more than apparitions, then they are the children of their own imagination." [106] This was the voice of those who made policy. And if they met the "apparitions," as Treub did in February 1923, when during a visit to Bandung he was challenged to a debate by Sukarno's new group, the NIP, they remained consistent; thus Treub rejected the invitation by saying, "One doesn't talk with such people." [107] Such was the exalted language of the Kaurawas, who thus provided the Pendawas with a catchword for their deliberate noncooperation in the years that followed.

[103] See "Sukarno's Early Political Views," above.

[104] Van Vollenhoven in NRC (*Niewe Rotterdamsche Courant*), April 3–6, 1922; also Hazeu, in a series on W. F. M. Treub, *Nederland in de Oost* (1923), under the title "Het inlandsche vraagstuk en Mr. Treub" (*ibid.*, February 1924); and Snouck Hurgronje in *Colijn over Indië* (1928), written in reply to Colijn's much-quoted *Koloniale vraagstukken*.

[105] See, for example, "Leiden of Utrecht," *De Locomotief*, February 7, 1925.

[106] Treub, replying to Hazeu's attack in NRC, February 1924.

[107] *De Locomotief*, February 21, 1923.

Bharata Judha (Part One)—
Challenge and Conflict, Wajang Style

The Struggle for the Antithesis

Once Sukarno had drawn his "mathematically exact dividing line" between the Sinis and Sanas, the friends and enemies of the independence movement, he welcomed men like Colijn and Treub, advocates of another century of colonization and thus of severe measures against the "extremists," as demonstrating the effectiveness of the Indonesian movement. Thus at the beginning of 1928, in an article called "Cry of Alarm," [108] he quoted with satisfaction a few sentences from Treub, who had demanded in a new pamphlet that every activity of the Indonesians that had independence as its goal be suppressed, by force if necessary.[109]

To this Sukarno's reaction was reminiscent of Prince Purbaja's, mentioned in the introduction, as he brushed aside the Dutch bullets with a cry of "Why do you shoot at me?" [110] His response to the threat by the influential Dutch politician was literally, "Kita bersenjum—We smile." True to the Bima of the Wajang, he mockingly continued:

> Is Treub's alarm, and that of his party, already so great that they no longer heed the lessons of history, the experience of the colonialists, on the suppression of a people's movement with force? . . .
>
> We Indonesian nationalists regard the cry of alarm of Professor Treub, chairman of the association of Dutch capitalists, as a symptom. It shows that our opponent indeed already feels the earth tremble under his feet. It shows that the course we, the Indonesian nationalists, have taken, and the course taken by our brothers the Pan-Islamists, are both correct and must be continued.[111]

Like Prince Purbaja, Sukarno had a sense of magical superiority. It was true that he could not fly like the prince, but he had now conjured himself into a position whose power was in reality

---

[108] "Djerit kegemparan," DBR, pp. 51ff.; also SIM, No. 3–4, pp. 61ff.
[109] W. F. M. Treub, *Het gist in Indië* (1927).
[110] See Chapter I, note 3, above.   [111] DBR, p. 53.

nonexistent. His magic consisted of dialectics; thus, for example, he asserted in the same article, "The colonial problem is essentially not a problem of rights but rather a problem of power." [112] But it became clear a few sentences later that for him, as for the Ksatrijas of the Wajang, rights actually were the central idea and the key to victory:

On the grounds of self-preservation, the party of the rulers has the right to obstruct, oppose, and pursue our movement; but on the same grounds of self-preservation *we too have the right* to be active, the *right* to seek for ourselves a way out of the present circumstances, the *right* to seek our freedom. Their right in this matter is opposed to ours; the right of reaction is opposed to the right of action. —And the problem of the opposition of right against right at once becomes a problem of the opposition of power against power: power opposes power.[113]

Sukarno here treated the relation between "rights" and "power" as loosely as he did the "misconceptions" within the movement. For him, there was obviously no difference. The manner in which a question of right could become a question of power, and finally even an actual confrontation of one power by another, shows clearly how everything flows together. The conviction that every action produces a reaction allowed him to see "reactions" everywhere, thus in dialectic fashion assuring himself of an imaginary position of power, from which he soon detected a wavering in the genuine power of his opponents.

So long as the antithesis from which he derived this conviction was firmly anchored in reality, there was likewise no reason to doubt his own power. "The sooner and the more sharply the antithesis is posed, the more clear-cut the struggle will be," [114] he had said, and for this reason Treub and Colijn, since they helped to strengthen the antithesis, were for him more partners than opponents.

There was more danger from those who attempted to undermine the antithesis, who were in fact friends of the movement.

[112] *Ibid.*, p. 51: "Soal djadjahan itu dalam hakekatnja bukanlah soal hak ia soal kekuasaan."

[113] *Ibid.*, p. 54. Sukarno's emphasis.

[114] See "the 'Brown Front,' " above.

"All efforts to narrow or to eliminate the line between Sinis and Sanas [115] are bad for our movement; every attempt to unite Sinis and Sanas is bad for our movement. But everything that perfects the division between us and them is good for our struggle," Sukarno declared in August 1928, before the first Congress of PPPKI, the federation he had created.[116] And he behaved according to this maxim; he accused the movement's friends of hypocrisy the instant they violated the antithesis. That was what happened, for example, to Sukarno's old acquaintance, the engineer A. Baars, who in 1921 had been expelled from the Netherlands Indies as an ardent communist, whereupon he went to Russia, worked six years at Soviet posts, and during this time was converted away from communism. At the beginning of 1928 he warned his friends in Indonesia not to press their demands, arguing that Indonesia was not yet ripe for its own government and that he did not wish to see the chaos he had witnessed in Russia repeated in Indonesia. Sukarno then took the field.[117] He did not believe, he declared, that the article had been written out of "pure motives," or out of "compassion" or "sympathy" for the "still immature" Indonesian people. This opinion was reinforced by noting that Baars had aired his views not in an Indonesian journal but in that of the Sana party. Baars had only criticism for conditions in Russia; he expressed no admiration for the progress in the field of education, the improved lot of the Jews, and still other gains that could have been cited.

"Nearly all reports of conditions in Russia are unjust," [118] declared Sukarno, who up until then had never been outside Java. By way of proof he quoted lengthy passages from his own article, "Nationalism, Islam, and Marxism," in which he had blamed the intervention of the Western powers for the cata-

[115] On Sinis and Sanas see Chapter II, note 100, above.

[116] "Menjambut Kongres PPPKI [On the Occasion of the PPPKI Congress]," DBR, p. 84.

[117] "Berhubung dengan tulisannja Ir. A. Baars [On the essay of Ir. A. Baars]," SIM, No. 3–4, pp. 86ff.; also DBR, pp. 57ff. (Sukarno first gives a summary of the article by Baars.)

[118] "Terhadap pada keadaan di Ruslan ini memang hampir semua chabar kurang adil" (DBR, p. 58).

strophic situation in Russia.[119] Baars, the communist who had accepted exile from Java for the sake of his ideals, returning from a land where for six years he had experienced the greatest disappointments, now had to learn from Sukarno that in Russia everything was quite different. What could more clearly document the unreality of Sukarno's position, his one-sidedness, and at the same time his self-assurance, than this judgment against his former teacher, who for a while in 1917 had been able to win over Sukarno himself to communism?

Baars erred, by Sukarno's reckoning, in that "his article does not once mention the word independence, but says only that we must 'ascend to a much higher stage than the one we have now reached.' " [120] This, for Sukarno, was proof that Baars no longer belonged in the Camp of the Sinis; he belonged with the opponents who were to be suspected of no longer writing from "pure motives." [121]

The Second International, at its congress in Brussels in August 1928, committed the same sacrilege of finding Indonesia not yet ripe for independence. Mohammed Hatta, who at the time was chairman of the Perhimpunan Indonesia in Holland, then proceeded to write for the Indonesian press an article strongly attacking the decisions of the Congress on colonial matters.[122] Hatta found it especially suspicious that the socialists had proposed a division of colonies into four groups, consisting of those (a) on which freedom must be conferred; (b) to which the right of self-determination would be granted; (c) whose right to self-government was acknowledged; and (d) which must still remain under the domination of the whites. Hatta was surprised that, for example, Iraq and Syria were to obtain freedom; India, the Philippines, Annam, and Korea the right of self-determination; and Indonesia (along with the peoples of North Africa), only the right to self-government. In Marxist fashion,

[119] Cf. DBR, pp. 18, 59.   [120] DBR, p. 58.

[121] There was a similar "reckoning of accounts" with the *Indische Courant,* which was sympathetic to the Indonesian movement, in Sukarno's article "Dubbele Les," early in 1928 (DBR, pp. 45ff.).

[122] "Socialist Internasional dan kemerdekaan Indonesia [The Socialist International and Indonesian Freedom]," reprinted in SIM, No. 10–11 (October 1928), pp. 254ff.

Hatta examined the economic grounds for this classification, and concluded

that all colonies except for Iraq and Syria, which consist mainly of desert, are regarded by the Socialist International as not ready for independence. It becomes clear [also] that each year the lands not yet considered ready present the ruling peoples with hundreds of millions of guilders. It is for this reason that they are not yet ready, that they are not yet permitted to be independent—even in the opinion of the socialists, who call themselves the defenders of the oppressed.[123]

This the Marxists took as a real challenge, and J. E. S. Stokvis produced a rejoinder. The congress in Brussels, he said, had tried to achieve only what could actually be achieved at present. The freedom of Syria and Iraq was demanded not *because* these lands were economically unimportant, but rather *despite* the rich oil deposits of Iraq, and Syria's profitable trade. Thus Iraq and Syria actually offered proof that the resolutions were no mere "hypocrisy." The socialists wished to confine themselves to what was possible, and not simply cause an uproar in the manner of the League against Imperialism and Colonial Oppression,[124] whose protests and resolutions up to now had met with no success.[125]

After this defense by Stokvis, in which the arguments of Hatta were refuted, Sukarno in his turn declared that although it was understandable for Stokvis to resist the attacks on his party, his protest contained a "great error":

We ask, is it true, is it really true, that economic motives are not at all involved in this matter? Can it be that this attitude of the Euro-

[123] *Ibid.*, pp. 259f.

[124] The League was set up on February 10, 1926, by Willi Münzenberg in Berlin; at its first congress, held February 7–14, 1927, in Brussels, Hatta and Semaun (who lived in Russia) participated as representatives of "Indonesia." Further meetings were held in September 1927, at Cologne, and in December 1927, once again at Brussels. Each time the colonial policy of the Netherlands was vehemently denounced (Blumberger, *Commun. beweging*, pp. 130ff.).

[125] Sukarno summarizes Stokvis's arguments (as set forth in *Het Indische Volk*, 1928, No. 29) in "Mohammed Hatta—Stokvis," SIM, No. 10–11, pp. 239ff. See also DBR, pp. 87ff.

pean working class has no economic basis whatever? Does not the
basic concept of the socialists themselves teach, does not historical
materialism itself teach that all conditions, all events in this world,
whether they have to do with thought or politics or religion, are essentially grounded in economic factors? Does not historical materialism itself teach, "It is not the consciousness of men that shapes
their existence, but rather their social existence that shapes their
consciousness"? [126]

So this was the "great error" of the Marxist Stokvis, that he did
not think in Marxist terms. Sukarno, thereby providing an example of his theoretical attachment to Marxism, demonstrated
that "error" by piling up economic arguments to the effect that
for England and France respectively, Iraq and Syria were losing
concerns, which actually placed a burden on the workers of Europe. "Ergo," he concluded "the independence of Syria is
profitable to the French just as the independence of Iraq is
profitable to the British. So is it still surprising that the Congress in Brussels should demand the freedom of these lands?" [127]

Whereupon, in Sukarno's opinion, Hatta's thesis that the resolutions in Brussels amounted to hypocrisy was proved anew. In
his eagerness to banish the Social Democrats to the camp of the
Sanas, however, Sukarno was quite unaware that according to
this scheme, everything in the world, and in particular the demands of immediate independence for Indonesia, could be
given an economic explanation and unmasked as hypocrisy.
Their not having demanded independence could have been
offered with equal logic as proof of hypocrisy, as the same thing
could have been proved by their demand for freedom.

Sukarno was, in short, not so much interested in exact analysis as he was above all in finding evidence to support a precon-
ceived idea. The same article contained further proof of this.
The chief fault of which he accused Stokvis and his party asso-
ciates was that they did not condemn colonization in principle.
Sukarno reminded the Social Democrats of the Stuttgart congress of the Second International (1907), at which every "capitalist-imperialist colonization" had been condemned. He recalled the words of Karl Kautsky, who, he asserted, had said that

[126] DBR, pp. 89f.   [127] DBR, p. 92.

the socialists must not only demand political freedom for the colonies, but also "wage a relentless struggle against *'every possible colonial policy,'* if not, indeed, *'every conceivable colonial policy.'* " [128]

And this, Sukarno went on, pleased at being able to cite so eminent an authority by way of proof, was the understanding of Mr. Stokvis's party colleague, Karl Kautsky. But in fact this had not been Kautsky's opinion. He had called on the Social Democrats in 1907 to be "opponents of every possible, although not of every conceivable, colonial policy." [129]

With a single word, which Sukarno had dropped in making his translation, the "radical Kautsky" had shown himself unwilling to reject in principle every form of colonization, as Sukarno was attempting to prove. For the socialists, there was indeed a "conceivable colonial policy." [130] The distortion of his patron's opinion was, to borrow the expression Sukarno had used against Treub, a "symptom"; it shows that at heart Sukarno was not at all interested in the opinions of others, but invoked them in support of his own without ever seriously coming to terms with them. In later "proofs," the same thing was to recur in a more pronounced fashion.[131]

In this instance Sukarno was satisfied to have demonstrated to the socialists that they had strayed from the right path. But having done so, they no longer belonged to the Sinis:

When they declare that Indonesia should not yet "be given" independence, but only later; when they say that Indonesian independence is still no more than problematical, that self-government is the most we can obtain— . . . then the socialists—however unwit-

---

[128] "Kaum sociaal-democraten haruslah djuga menentang keras kapada 'tiap-tiap koloniaalpolitiek-apa-sadja jang dapat diadakan,' kalau tidak kepada 'tiap-tiap koloniaalpolitiek-apa-sadja jang dapat difikirkan.' . . ." (DBR, p. 95; Sukarno's emphasis.)

[129] Karl Kautsky, *Sozialismus und Kolonialpolitik* (1927), p. 78, wrote that the Social Democrats should be "Gegner jeder möglichen wenn auch nicht jeder denkbaren Kolonialpolitik." Sukarno dropped the "auch."

[130] *Ibid.*

[131] See his quotations from Liebknecht (Chapter IV) and Ameer Ali (Chapter V), below.

tingly—are at one with the imperialists, at one with their enemies, who say that we are "not yet ripe" for independence.[132]

The ejection of the socialists, the only friends of the Indonesian movement from whom real help could be expected, into the camp of its opponents had been achieved.

Nor was the matter simply one of objective analysis. In his effort to make the antithesis between white and brown as rigid as possible, Sukarno did not shrink from further reproaches: the Social Democrats were too faint-hearted, too opportunistic, too often bogged down in details, completely losing sight of the whole picture. This was also the reason for their continual fighting with the radical left.[133]

The socialists had been put in their place. With his aggressive language, his didactic arguments and pontifications, Sukarno had long since abandoned all reasonable discussion. The struggle had begun against the "temporizers" who stood between the two sides, against those "most dangerous adversaries" who sought to bridge the gap between the hostile parties and thereby to destroy the antithesis. Tjipto Mangunkusumo, who had trained Sukarno to be such a Djago, such a "wild fighter," wrote with alarm from Bandaneira, a thousand miles away (having been exiled for the third time), warning Sukarno above all not to break with the Social Democrats, not to declare war on them unless it became unavoidable.[134]

The Weapons of the Partai Nasional Indonesia

Trust in Their Own Strength

Sukarno was soon widely known as, on the one hand, the unrelenting warrior, already recognizable in his theoretical discussions, who banished to the opposite side of his antithesis everything that in his opinion might hurt the movement or delay its course—and on the other hand as the pivot of unity, the hero who had succeeded in the first attempt at bringing the diver-

[132] DBR, pp. 93f.   [133] DBR, pp. 95ff.

[134] Presented at Sukarno's trial. See *De Locomotief,* November 5, 1930, p. 36.

gent political movements in the camp of the Pendawas together under one organizational roof. His fame grew rapidly.

This attacker and conciliator combined in one person, this Bima of the Javanese myth, had never before appeared in the Indonesian movement. Sukarno brought together in ideal fashion Tjokroaminoto's tireless efforts for unity within his own ranks and Tjipto Mangunkusumo's bold stand against foreign rule. Nor was this all. For Tjipto, who at no time shrank from speaking openly against the Sanas, still had a secret weakness. He regarded the Kaurawas not as totally opposed but rather (in the manner of Javanese tradition) as the "necessary evil"; he still expected concessions from them, and was at bottom in favor of a harmonious solution.[135]

This became apparent in the spring of 1927, when Tjipto, after the storm of the communist uprising had cleared the air, pleaded openly for cooperation based on trust in the new government.[136] And Tjipto, as a protest, refused to take part in the founding of Sukarno's Perserikatan Nasional Indonesia (PNI) on July 4, 1927, after a resolution calling for "fundamental noncooperation" had been adopted.[137]

Although before the end of 1927 Sukarno might have regarded Tjipto's position as a possible alternative, after that all doubt was removed by the colonial regime itself. Tjipto Mangunkusumo, the advocate of cooperation and trust in the government, was arrested, and in December 1927, for reasons that are obscure, he was exiled.[138]

[135] This becomes clear in the work of Tjipto Mangunkusumo, *Het communisme in Indonesië,* particularly the chapter "Attempt to reestablish equilibrium [*sic*]," pp. 22ff.

[136] *Ibid.;* see also IPO 1927, No. 36, pp. 471ff.; 1929, No. 25, p. 333. De Graeff, the new GG, in September 1926, at the beginning of his term, had called on the nationalists for cooperation; even after the communist revolt, he had once more emphasized his positive attitude toward the nationalist movement (*De Locomotief,* March 12, 1927).

[137] See *De Locomotief,* August 21, 1930, p. 6; also SRI 1930, p. 554.

[138] The official reason was that Tjipto had (financially) "supported" communists who later participated in the uprisings. As revealed in the trial of Sukarno in 1930, the communists were indeed keenly interested in

For Sukarno, the exiling of his "chief"—the title had been given to Tjipto, in an explicit reference to the name given Gandhi by his followers [139]—was simply proof of the correctness of his antithesis. Governors General such as Mr. Fock might counter the "extremists" with open hostility, or they might, like Jonkheer de Graeff, speak of a "positive attitude" toward the nationalist movement; [140] but one way alone could lead to the cherished goal of independence, and that was through the struggle of the brown masses against the aliens—the way of Bharata Judha.

At first, Sukarno was noncommittal about Tjipto's arrest: "We are Orientals. And as Orientals, we are *believers*. If we believe in the necessity of everything that happens, then we must believe that whatever happens is good and necessary for the future." [141]

After Tjipto's exile became a certainty, Sukarno sought through it to give new momentum to the movement. He assured Tjipto, in a farewell article,[142] that his cheerful sacrifice had provided Indonesian nationalists with an object lesson such as Krishna had given to Ardjuna in the *Bhagavad Gita*, namely that one had to fulfill one's duty without thinking of the consequences. He quoted the assertion of Sir Oliver Lodge that "no sacrifice is wasted"; he referred to the task handed down by the communists, who had now been sent into exile in

winning over Tjipto, and made every effort to do so. Their circle had, for example, a code name for Tjipto, which must have been known to the colonial officials (*De Locomotief*, September 3, 1930, p. 22, September 5, 1930, p. 8). The government may also have believed that Tjipto Mangunkusumo must be considered responsible for the new radicalization of the nationalists under Sukarno. Also, since Tjipto already had a full measure of convictions the de Graeff government probably believed it must make an example of him. See the bitter comment on this unfortunate measure by D. M. G. Koch in *Batig Slot* (1960), pp. 146f.

[139] "Saudara Dr. Tjipto—my chief, sebagai Gandhi disebutkan oleh pengikut-pengikutnja . . ." (SIM, No. 1, p. 30).

[140] *De Locomotief*, March 12, 1927.

[141] SIM, No. 1 (December 1927), p. 30.

[142] "Sampai ketemu lagi [Till We Meet Again]," SIM, No. 2, pp. 34ff. See also DBR, pp. 41ff.

vast numbers,[143] and also—since the federation was just then being established—to the opening of a "new front." So there was no reason to become faint-hearted; the slogan of the movement could only be "Forward, forward, ever forward, never a step backward, never yielding by a finger's breadth; forward, ever forward in the drive toward happiness." [144] For the next two years, Sukarno himself adhered to this motto above all. Once his work of unification had been completed for the time being, he traveled tirelessly back and forth through Java to make the Nationalist Party known and to proclaim its message.

The European peoples—Sukarno usually began by saying [145]—were not in any way forced to come to Asia, there to fulfill a task, but had come "only to fill their rumbling bellies." [146] If they were asked, however, why they had come to Asia, then they would answer that they had come to seek fame, to spread knowledge and civilization, etc. But why, then, it must be asked, had they come to lands that had possessed a high civilization for longer than the Europeans themselves? Why did they go to Egypt, to India, to Indonesia, and not to the Zulus, the Hottentots, or the Eskimos? No, greed alone was the reason for colonization.

But this greed still existed today, and it was therefore only too understandable that the rulers should speak of three centuries more of colonization; no concession could be expected of them—that was impossible. Only through their own efforts, through self-help, could anything be achieved. The councils— the local bodies as well as the Volksraad—were hopeless, even supposing that the natives would one day be represented by a larger percentage. Therefore the Partai Nasional Indonesia (PNI)—as the nationalist association was officially called after the first party congress in May 1928—had decided on nonco-

[143] More than 2,000 were sent to Boven Digul, the notorious prison camp in the jungle of West New Guinea; see *Mededeelingen der regeering* (1929), p. 3.

[144] DBR, p. 44.

[145] He would first make a few remarks on local particulars. What follows is from a speech of Sukarno before Sutomo's Indonesian Study Club at Surabaja (SRI, Vol. 2, No. 7 [February 15, 1928], pp. 25ff.).

[146] "Untuk mengisi perutnja jang kerontjong belaka."

operation, knowing that self-help was the only path to freedom. Noncooperation was thus based not on hate but on a "return to one's own self," [147] or to a form of what Gandhi called "self-realization."

Along with thus proclaiming the principles of the PNI, Sukarno set forth its relation to other parties. It was the friend of all associations that had set for themselves the goal of independence; it had not included Islam in its party program so as to leave the way open for those professing other beliefs as well. Since class struggle would disrupt the united front, the PNI likewise did not profess communism, although class struggle "might" come later, once Indonesia had become independent. But first of all the task was to strive together for freedom. "All Indonesian groups must be united, must become one, so that freedom may come."

This appeal was followed by those images from the myths that Sukarno, like his teacher Tjokroaminoto, knew how to command, certain of their effects: from the *Mahabhrata,* the example of the Pendawas, who fought for their fatherland; from the *Ramayana,* the example of the monkeys' army whose power overcame the demon Rahwana, into whose clutches the abducted goddess Sita had fallen. In Sukarno's account, the beauty of the goddess and of Indonesia gradually became one and the same, so that it was not hard to guess who the Dewi Sita was, who the demon Rahwana, and who the monkeys' army—but above all there was no question of the outcome, either in the struggle of the Pendawas or in the battle against Rahwana. In conclusion, Sukarno urged each of those present to join some party, the one where he felt "at home"; the important thing was for them all to be organized.

With such speeches, all through 1928, Sukarno raced from one triumph to another; through his mastery of rhetoric he transported his listeners into enthusiasm and himself into ecstasy. Thus a reporter for *Pembrita Kemadjuan* wrote in May 1928 that he had been so carried away by Sukarno's imagery that he suddenly believed he was already "merdeka." [148] A high-level civil servant, instead of taking notes, applauded so

147 "Sifat-kembali kepada diri kita pribadi."
148 IPO 1928, No. 24, pp. 507f.

wildly at the end of a speech of Sukarno's that shortly afterward he was dismissed from his post.[149] At a meeting in Djakarta—as what the Dutch knew as Batavia had been called by the nationalists from the start, in memory of Jacatra, which had stood on the same site and had been destroyed by the Dutch [150]—when Sukarno had to break off his speech for some time, 1,600 persons remained in their places despite the unbearable heat, because they were afraid of losing them if they moved.[151]

Not only were the people intoxicated with Sukarno; he was likewise intoxicated by them and their adulation. Thus it was reported that at one meeting where Sukarno had been called upon to speak, as he stood before the microphone, absorbing the waves of applause, he was heard whispering to himself, "Don't speak yet—look at the audience a little longer." [152]

But even then the criticism had begun. In *Bintang Timur* on July 19, 1928, an article under the caption of "Sukarnoism" asserted that Sukarno's constantly repeated "trilogy"—that a "national consciousness" must be awakened, so that a "national will" could arise, from which finally "national deeds" would result—was in fact very old, and that the consciousness and the will had already been brought into being by Tjokroaminoto and Tjipto Mangunkusumo. It was now time for Sukarno to produce the deeds. The paper wound up by inquiring, "It may perhaps be rude to say so, but haven't we talked enough by now?" [153]

Even after that, however, the PNI did not devote much attention to "national deeds." Although at its first congress in May 1928 in Surabaja it had resolved to undertake a vast "program of action," [154] it did not in fact attempt a single one of the many projects that might have been accomplished without

[149] *Bintang Timur*, December 27, 1928; IPO 1929, No. 1, p. 17.
[150] The name Djakarta was officially reintroduced by the Japanese in December 1942 (*Djawa Baroe*, No. 1, Year 1, Chronik). On the earlier Jacatra (destroyed at the beginning of the seventeenth century), see Chapter I, above.
[151] IPO 1928, No. 29, pp. 133f.
[152] "Tak berbitjara—memandang publiek sedjurus," SRI 1929, p. 479.
[153] IPO 1928, No. 30, p. 182.
[154] "Daftar usaha," SIM, No. 5 (April 1928), pp. 119ff.; SRI 1928, pp. 108, 180f.

opposition from the colonial regime—for example, the fight against usury; promoting an intra-Indonesian migration to relieve the overpopulation of Java; giving work to the unemployed; setting up a health service; or combating child marriage, drug addiction, and alcoholism, among many others. These programs would all have required a great deal of time, and above all they would not have advanced, but rather would have hindered, the drive against foreign rule. Also, not much could have been accomplished without coming to an agreement with the government. Sukarno's aversion to details and unspectacular effort coincided with his fear that the "main outline" would be lost sight of; and that "main outline" was the struggle for independence. In October 1928 he declared:

> It must be understood that we are to think above all of the great question, we are to think continually of the first goal of our movement—that is, of Indonesia's independence. Yes, no more and no less than that: an independent Indonesia, by the quickest way possible. Therefore we must strive for independence not merely by reforming the disordered living conditions in our land; rather, we must strive first for Indonesian independence, so that our living conditions may then be improved. Independence is the first, it is the primary goal.[155]

Thus for the Partai Nasional Indonesia the all-important thing was struggle. The positive program of self-help had been adopted largely for its propaganda value, and as a legitimation in the eyes of the colonial government, whose attitude for the time being was to wait and see. The real drive was toward stirring up resentment, preaching the irreconcilable antithesis, and calling for the Bharata Judha, and at the same time toward strengthening internal unity and gradually forging it into a united front.

Thus in the autumn of 1928, on the occasion of the first congress of the PPPKI, Sukarno declared that a "consensus of spirit" was not enough, that the PPPKI must also arrive at a consolidation of power. "The PPPKI must understand that what we ordinarily call 'Indonesian unity' is only the path and

155 SIM, No. 10–11, p. 248; DBR, p. 96.

the drive toward power, power to achieve all that we desire." [156]

That this power could be achieved was, for Sukarno, beyond question. There was for him no reason to doubt, and here again his certitude came from the antithesis:

The consolidation of power is certain; power will be achieved! For essentially the consolidation of power is nothing other than the consequence arising from the arbitrary rule of imperialism itself. It is a historical necessity . . . a reaction imperialism itself has produced. For imperialism and capitalism are both "their own grave-diggers." [157]

Playing dangerously at applying Marxist promises to a situation completely lacking in the economic conditions and motivating forces on which those promises were based, Sukarno had raised himself, by the end of the year 1928, into a position of "power" that permitted him to be more and more defiant. He now believed that he had found the key to absolute success—namely, "trust in our own strength and our own ability." This doctrine, based on a belief in the operation of Marxist prophecies, which appeared up until then to have been fulfilled in Indonesia, was proclaimed by the PNI everywhere. Gradually his party began to take root and to branch out further and further.

That Sukarno himself believed implicitly in the Marxist slogans and in "historical necessity" is especially clear from a criticism of the Indian movement of which he delivered himself in December 1928. Sukarno declared:

Too often, the leaders who wish to guide the Indian people on the way to the light have set off on paths which do not appear to be the best and shortest. Too little attention is given by the spiritually gifted Indian to the material side of the fight against materialistic imperialism; all too often he forgets that politics, if it is to bear sound fruit, must rise on the basis of actual, concrete, substantial conditions, and not lose itself in the vague clouds of philosophy and abstraction; still less can it oppose the iron laws of social evolution. Above all Mahatma Gandhi—no matter how gifted he may be—has

[156] SIM, No. 10–11, pp. 270f.   [157] Ibid., p. 271.

to a great degree sinned in this; and society has thus, as a logical consequence, turned cruelly against him.[158]

Proud and all-knowing: this was Sukarno toward the end of 1928. He knew the way not only for the Indonesian movement but for the Indian movement as well. Exactly a year was to pass before it became clear who stood "on the basis of actual, concrete, substantial conditions"—Sukarno or Gandhi. Gandhi, in his "offense" against social evolution, had at any rate not forgotten one thing: colonial power. Sukarno, on the contrary, believed that with the espousal of noncooperation he could completely ignore that power.

From the day of his first public appearance, he might have been punished simply for saying the words "Indonesia Merdeka: Freedom for Indonesia." For six months he had already been speaking in such a way that in the summer of 1928 a leader just released from prison exclaimed with astonishment, "He speaks a hundred times more strongly and fiercely than I did, and still the police say nothing . . . !"[159]

And in fact the police did say nothing; they had their orders. Governor General de Graeff, having settled accounts with the communists and exiled Tjipto Mangunkusumo, was serious about his "positive attitude" toward the nationalist movement. He wanted the trust of the people, and he knew that it could not be won with new punitive measures. Thus he allowed Sukarno scope for activity, of which the latter made radical use. Once, in October 1928, while Sukarno proclaimed the "irreconcilable antithesis," a policeman did actually intervene and forbid Sukarno to speak.[160] This move raised such a storm that in December 1928 de Graeff drafted a letter to the Residents ordering them to take no ill-considered measures against the PNI. Otherwise, he feared there might be excesses as there had been from the side of the PKI in 1926; and in his opinion, a

[158] Sukarno's foreword, Tjipto Mangunkusumo, *De beweging in India* (1928).

[159] Sudadi, in August 1928; "Dia berkata seratus kali keras dan pedes dari apa jang saja dulu katakan, tetapi polisi tinggal diam sadja" (SRI 1929, p. 241).

[160] This was in Semarang; see IPO 1928, No. 43, pp. 108f.

radical wing of the people's movement was perfectly natural.[161]

Thus it becomes clear how effective the slogan calling for trust in one's own strength still was toward the end of 1928. The power of suggestion in Sukarno's antithesis, to the effect that this movement was a "historical necessity," had penetrated even the palace of the Governor General.

Trust in Foreign Assistance

In 1929 the incidents at PNI meetings multiplied. Despite the appeals of Governor General de Graeff, gradually a campaign against the "extremists," in which the police and the "lying white press" took an equal part, was begun in all parts of Java. Even the normally restrained *Locomotief* gave voice to an angry statement:

From now on, these reports [on the boldness of the PNI] will appear regularly in our paper, so as to make known what the authorities are now permitting, and how they have lapsed into the old errors of the previous government—too late to intervene, too late to step forward, too late to put an end to this provoking demagoguery.[162]

The "white front" that Sukarno for so long had tried in vain to provoke was suddenly there—not, however, with the result foretold by Sukarno, that the brown front would also "irrevocably" come into being. On the contrary, in the PPPKI it began to be rumored that the cooperators and noncooperators could not reach Mufakat unless such drastic concessions were made on both sides that there could be no further basis for action, and the sum total of their activity would be a few declarations.[163]

[161] See the secret letter of GG de Graeff dated December 28, 1928 (Gobee Collection, Koninklijk Inst. v. Taal-, Land- en Volkenkunde, Leiden).

[162] Issue for May 23, 1929; subsequent issues regularly carried reports in which the government was vehemently criticized for its attitude of restraint.

[163] See the report on the effectiveness of the PPPKI up to the end of 1929 in IPO 1929, No. 49, pp. 305f.

But for Sukarno there could be no retreat. Again and again he proclaimed the necessary antithesis, he spoke of the conflict of interest between the colonial peoples and the white masters, he demanded—such was the irony of all noncooperation—that the government send intelligent spies, since the informers and simple-minded police could not follow his "scientific disputation." [164] But his reputation as Djago, as the wild fighter, became greater and greater, and the masses flocked to hear him as they had once done to hear Tjokroaminoto. "When Ir. Sukarno gives a speech, then they come by the thousands and all shout at the tops of their voices," reported *Bintang Mataram* on August 24, 1929. "But," it went on, "that is all. For when they are urged to become members, they explain that they want to think it over first, or they are afraid." [165]

It was no secret that the membership of the PNI was not growing at the rate its leaders would have liked. Despite two years' intensive propaganda, in the Priangan (Bandung and its environs) up to September 16, 1929, there were no more than 2,740 members; [166] and this remained by far the largest section of the PNI, accounting for over 50 per cent of the entire membership. Compared with the gigantic numbers of the Sarekat Islam in its first two years,[167] the successes of the PNI in the same amount of time were "nothing." And although Sukarno's newspapers again and again published the assertion that the PNI was born of pressure from the people themselves, this was dialectical self-hypnosis rather than a description of reality.

The reasons why a party that won favor everywhere gained members only gradually were plain: on the face of it, the style assumed by the PNI in its struggle all too closely recalled the disbanded PKI, of whose heritage it "had gratefully taken pos-

[164] Statement by Ir. Kieviet de Jonge, the government official responsible for interior affairs in the Volksraad. At the trial of Sukarno, it transpired that Sukarno had spoken with him three times—in December 1928, April 1929, and December 1929 (*De Locomotief,* October 22, 1930, p. 36).

[165] IPO 1929, No. 36, p. 292.

[166] *De Locomotief,* September 6, 1930, p. 32 (material on Sukarno's trial).

[167] See Table 1, above. Between 1912 and 1914, the SI reached a total of 366,913 members.

session." [168] Thus those who had been appalled by the harsh punishment of the communists involved in the uprising of 1926–27 [169] could not summon the courage to step out of the role of interested bystanders and once again take part in the "struggle." Also, it was more difficult to become a member than in the great days of the Sarekat Islam. At that time, to acquire a membership card and to take an oath to abide by the rules of the association had been enough. But Sukarno attached importance to the formation of cadres: there were courses for candidates, who had to pass a final examination in order to become full-fledged members.[170] After spies appeared at these courses, the fear of summary prosecution by the government was added. Nevertheless, the number of members grew by leaps and bounds from September to December 1929, just when pressure against the PNI was strongest, and when it was regarded as virtually an illegal organization. In the Priangan there were a total of 2,740 members from July 4, 1927 to September 16, 1929; for the period from September 16, 1929, to December 28, 1929, the figure rose to 5,746.[171] An average of one thousand new members joined each month.

What was it that sent thousands who up to then had consciously stayed aloof suddenly flocking to the outlaw party?

To this question, the answer is Djajabaja. The Nationalist Party had taken up in its propaganda a theme in which the respective superstitions of the people and of Sukarno himself coincided: this was the much-discussed possibility of a war in the Pacific.

It will be recalled that in the prophecy unearthed by Raffles, it had been predicted that Java would be freed from foreign domination by troops of the "Prince of Kling." [172] After the rise of Japan as a world power at the beginning of this century,

[168] This was Sukarno's explanation during a course attended by prospective members of the PNI; see, in the Gobee Collection, the "spy's report" on a course given by the PNI toward the end of 1928.

[169] See note 143, above.

[170] For details see the transcript of the proceedings in SRI, 4th Year (1930), pp. 538ff.

[171] *De Locomotief,* September 6, 1930, p. 32.

[172] See "Djajabaja's Prophecies of the End of Alien Domination," above.

there had been a slight change in the prophecy: Japan had taken the place of India. As long ago as 1920, in the proceedings against Section B of the Sarekat Islam, a defendant had declared that Japan would help in expelling the Dutch from Indonesia.[173] But in the versions of the prophecy then current, the benevolent foreign power was not referred to directly as Japan or Nippon but was wrapped in circumlocutions so secretive that Tan Malaka, a communist who was exiled in 1923, and who related the prophecy in a pamphlet issued in 1926, interpreted it incorrectly. According to him the text went, "In Java a revolution will break out, which will be led by a man with a yellow skin; he will reign for the period of a year of corn." [174]

Tan Malaka believed in 1926 that this prophecy concerned an event from the past, an uprising led by a Java-born Chinese that had already taken place.[175] But Sukarno knew better. As later appeared, not only did he know the prophecy in the form that had meanwhile become current in Java—that a government of yellow men would replace the whites in Java, and would thereafter relinquish the government to the natives themselves —but he had also used this prophecy in his courses.[176]

Nor was Sukarno alone in using it. The great theme of the Partai Nasional Indonesia near the end of 1929 was that they were to "be prepared," that the coming war in the Pacific would bring an end to white rule in Indonesia.[177] From the leaders' lips the word traveled down through the villages, and soon the air was thick with rumors that in 1930 the "national revolution" was to break out. At the beginning of December 1929, *Suara Publiek* actually interviewed a number of popular leaders about their views on the approaching national revolution,[178] and *Suluh Rakjat Indonesia* for December 4, 1929, contained

---

[173] *De Locomotief,* February 6, 1920.

[174] Tan Malaka, *Massa-actie* (new ed., 1947,) pp. 9f.: "Suatu revolusi dipulau Djawa akan timbul, jang dipimpin oleh seorang jang berkulit kuning dan . . . akan memerintah setahun djagung."

[175] *Ibid.*   [176] SRI, 4th Year (1930), pp. 574f.

[177] This was openly stated, in the autumn of 1929, in *Banteng Priangan* (a PNI newspaper at Bandung); IPO 1929, No. 38, p. 340; No. 44, p. 141. See also Blumberger, *National. beweging,* pp. 241f., 244; also *De Locomotief,* November 4, 1930, p. 23.

[178] IPO 1929, No. 51, p. 380.

the statement: "It is evident at this time that many men believe in the coming of the Ratu Adil, and it is clear that they await him with great hope, so that they are already working to prepare a joyous reception for him." [179] Dr. Sutomo's newspaper went on to say that this belief that the Ratu Adil would come in 1930 had no contemporary political background but could be traced to religious sources; it had been said decades before that the Ratu Adil would appear in 1930. But this only drew attention to the rumors that something was generally expected to happen. The closer the year came to its end, the more fantastic the expectations became, and all hopes were centered on the PNI.[180] Even Sukarno felt something brewing here that had not been foreseen in his antithesis, and he let the government know that he was ready to take steps to counteract the popular superstition, insofar as he could bring it into harmony with his propaganda.[181]

The government, on the other hand, thought it more advisable to put an end to the scare, since its patience was exhausted. For several years the de Graeff regime had been ridiculed from the right as a weak and incompetent regime,[182] and mocked from the left as though its behavior had been the result of pressure, not benevolence. Uncertain how to behave toward the phenomenon of noncooperation without doing violence to its often-emphasized positive attitude toward the "good" nationalists, for two years it had maintained an attitude of restraint, and had already once voiced mild warnings in the

---

[179] "Ratu Adil–Heru Tjokro," SRI, 3rd Year (1929), December 4, 1929, pp. 738ff. See also the article "Tahun 1930 [The Year 1930]," ibid., November 4, 1929, pp. 679ff.

[180] See the government declaration in the Volksraad in De Locomotief, January 10, 1930, p. 15.

[181] Testimony of Kieviet de Jonge, to whom Sukarno himself had made the proposal (De Locomotief, October 22, 1930, p. 36).

[182] These charges had dogged the regime of de Graeff from beginning to end—as, for example, in the provocative words of Karel Wijbrand (Het Nieuws van den Dag, June 25, 1927): "Go on, get out—you are a good fellow and mean well, but the Netherlands Indies right now needs a stronger hand than yours." The end of 1929 saw constantly increasing agitation against the government as well as the PNI in the entire "white press."

Volksraad; but now, as disturbances began to occur openly, it struck. On December 29, 1929, with unnerving ease, the Pendawas' entire dialectically based power structure was shown to be an illusion. Within an hour, all the leaders of the PNI, wherever they were, had been arrested. Their houses were searched for evidence, and all the documents thus turned up went finally to a Landraad in Bandung for judicial investigation.[183]

Did Sukarno make use of propaganda concerning "foreign assistance," which in the autumn of 1929 had taken the leadership of the movement out of his hands, only as a tactical means of strengthening the movement by references to the "approaching outbreak of war in the Pacific"? This question, to which Sukarno at his trial would indignantly answer in the negative,[184] will be considered briefly here after the events themselves have been described.

In May 1929, at the second congress of the PNI, Ali Sastroamidjojo, a prominent member of the Perhimpunan Indonesia (PI) who had just returned from Holland, had spoken on the theme, "Our Propaganda Abroad." He had explained, basing his reasoning on the statutes of the PNI and on the belief in one's own strength and one's own ability, that this propaganda was not meant to "seek help abroad from anyone at all," but was intended simply to make the Indonesian movement known abroad.[185]

For the PI, which had followed with great interest the sudden flaring of the movement in Indonesia under Sukarno's leadership, this was perhaps appropriate. As will be shown, the PI took as the complement of "trust in one's own strength" a trust in the master, as the one who would give them scope for developing that strength. Noncooperation, for the PI, was not primarily aimed at arousing resentment, but rather, as had been set forth in its program, at preparing the people for independence.[186]

But Sukarno rejected such preparation as unnecessarily pro-

---

[183] Details in SRI, 4th Year (1930), Nos. 1ff.; also *De Locomotief*, January 2, 1930ff.

[184] See Chapter IV, below.   [185] SRI, 3rd Year (1929), pp. 302f.

[186] See "The Appeal of the Indonesian Students in Holland," in Chapter II, above.

longing the way to the "primary goal." [187] For him, there could likewise be no confidence that the master would give them scope to develop their own strength. For him, therefore, as opposed to the PI, hope for outside help did play an important role; it became the complement to a "trust in one's own strength." At the end of the congress at which Sastroamidjojo so firmly rejected the thought of "outside help," Sukarno declared that all those who in the future obstructed the movement should beware, that trouble was in store for them as soon as the Pacific War broke out.[188]

Very early, Sukarno had extended his propaganda to the outside world. During the days of the Study Club at Bandung he had established contact with foreign organizations. He had, for example, received an invitation from the Pan-Pacific Labor Congress in Canton (1926), which only a lack of time prevented him from accepting. He did, however, send to Canton a detailed response from the Study Club, which, he said, regarded itself as an "outpost in the Pacific" and was convinced "that it is necessary to solve national problems in common." [189]

Sukarno was an ardent adherent of Pan-Asianism, or "Interasianism," as he himself called it. In his definition of nationalism, he had left room for all other Asian peoples.[190] For him "the great problem of the time" was "how Asia could shake off the yoke of England and America." [191] He called for unlimited cooperation among all Asian peoples,[192] no doubt under the

[187] See note 155, above.

[188] Blumberger, *Nationalistische beweging,* pp. 241f.

[189] *Mededeelingen der regeering* (1928), p. 27.

[190] See section on Nationalism as a Common Denominator, above.

[191] Thus Sukarno declared, for example, at a meeting on December 4, 1927, in "Djakarta"; see *De Locomotief,* December 6, 1927, p. 24.

[192] Later Sukarno was fond of using his "Asian circus" to explain the cooperation. Innumerable times he used the parable: if the Indonesian Banteng (the wild buffalo) worked together with the Nandi (sacred cow) of India, the Liong Barongsai (dragon) of China, the Sphinx of Egypt, the white elephant of Thailand, etc., then the days of imperialism would be numbered. In the period of the Japanese occupation, the Asian circus at once became the "Greater East Asian circus," and the teamwork of the animals he named was of course "bathed in the rays of the rising sun" (of Dai Nippon). See, for example, *Asia Raya,* December 7, 2602 (1942), p. 2.

influence of Sun Yat-sen, who in a speech at Kobe in 1924 had declared that the nationalist movements in Asia could expect success only "if all Asian peoples unite and stand as one." [193]

Sun Yat-sen had then spoken a few flattering words to the host country, Japan—saying, for example, that the leading role in the liberation of Asia belonged to it. Sukarno had likewise included the Japanese in his "Interasianism," and had ascribed to them a critical importance. In July 1928, in the article calling on Indonesians to cooperate with other Asian peoples, he had written:

The time will shortly call upon us to become the witnesses of a great struggle in the Pacific, among the imperialist giants, America, Japan, and England, who will engage in a struggle for plunder and domination; time may soon hurl us into the midst of the typhoon that will overwhelm the Pacific. The first rumblings of the thunder can already be heard. Like a lion that has unsheathed its claws, ready to destroy Japan at whatever moment it may choose, like the [ten-headed] demon Dasamuka, who has opened wide his many mouths, ready to devour his enemy, so America has encircled Japan with heavy and powerful naval bases, in Dutch Harbor, Hawaii, Tutuila, Guam, and Manila. And likewise Japan is adding to its arsenal, while England builds a naval fortress at Singapore.[194]

This passage, which gives an impression of Sukarno's eloquence, with its abundantly metaphorical style, shows unmistakably how Sukarno had assigned precise individual roles to each of the "imperialist giants": the West—which here meant America— would attack, and Japan would defend herself; thus, one imperialist was not the same as another. Thus a statement (not by himself) in an earlier issue of *Suluh Indonesia Muda*—"In fact, Japan for us is an imperialist country and nothing more. . . . For its neighbors, it is just as dangerously imperialistic as those of white imperialism are" [195]—was at least modified by Sukarno.

[193] For further details, see W. H. Elsbree, *Japan's Role in Southeast Asian Nationalist Movements, 1940–45* (1953), p. 7.

[194] "Indonesianisme dan Panasiatisme," SIM, No. 8 (July 1928), pp. 176ff.; also DBR, p. 77.

[195] SIM, No. 6–7, p. 150.

The attitude of the PNI toward Japan was expressed still more clearly in 1929, when the thunder had grown even louder. A Japanese believed he had detected a certain anti-Japanese character in the PNI.[196] On the same subject, a writer for a Chinese newspaper observed that, although nothing in the statutes of the PNI expressly said so, it was known from discussions with the leaders that Japan was numbered among the capitalist-imperialist nations.[197] Sukarno's newspaper *Persatuan Indonesia* (Indonesian Unity) now entered the discussion, and declared on July 11, 1929, that the PNI did not exclude Japan from the "Asian lands." Although it had to be admitted that Japan was imperialistic, the article went on, Japan itself would have to decide between a rising East and a West that was rushing to its downfall.[198]

This change of attitude toward Japan is possibly explained by a statement appearing in *Banteng Priangan,* Sukarno's newspaper in Bandung, on July 7, 1929, which asked what could be expected from communists of the type of Stalin, who shut themselves up in their own country, or from nationalists like Chiang Kai-shek, who flirted with foreign capitalists.[199]

For the time being, neither Russia nor China could be expected to give aid against Western imperialism. And so all hopes once again centered more and more on Japan, to which, despite its imperialism, the opportunity was now open of deciding between East and West. In all these approaches to world politics there was an element of frank speculation about foreign assistance, a tacit admission by the Indonesian nationalists that their own strength would not suffice to defeat the opponent. The Pacific War would not produce freedom, Sukarno now explained, but it would hasten the coming of freedom.[200]

That one day the Pacific War would break out, there was for him no question. At his trial in 1930, he told the judges of what lay behind the Pacific War propaganda: "We do not affirm that the Pacific War will break out this year. Nor do we affirm that it will occur within a short time. We only insist that, given the

[196] IPO 1929, No. 25, p. 339.   [197] *Ibid.,* No. 27, pp. 21f.
[198] *Ibid.,* No. 29, p. 77.   [199] *Ibid.,* No. 30, p. 99.
[200] SIM, No. 8, p. 479.

present competition between America, England, and Japan, this war is bound to take place." [201]

Here again Sukarno derived his certainty from Karl Marx. Like the irreconcilable antithesis between brown and white, with final victory going to the oppressed, the outbreak of the Pacific War, with its prospects for Indonesia, was for him a foregone conclusion. This was what constituted the meeting point between popular superstition and the "superstition" of Sukarno, which in the autumn of 1929 permitted Djajabaja to hold sway.

No less intensely than the Javanese people believed in the prophecies of Djajabaja, Sukarno, himself a Javanese, believed in the promise of that other "Djajabaja," Karl Marx, the prophet of the downfall of capitalism. He no longer believed in Djimats that conferred invulnerability, but he trusted in other "Djimats"—in the irreconcilable antithesis, in dialectics. But these gave him no more real power than the amulets carried by the followers of the Ratu Adil movements that have already been described. Once noncooperation was espoused, the existing power relationships were denied but not abolished. Sukarno's assertion in the summer of 1928, that "if an authority is confronted by 'nonrecognition' of its rule . . . then it must of necessity begin to waver," [202] was valid only as long as noncooperation inhabited the magic realm of imagination. On the evening of December 29, 1929, Sukarno's position of power was shown to be pure illusion, just as five years earlier, for example, the power of Bapak Kajah had likewise been proved an illusion.[203] And similarly the reaction of his followers was one of helplessness, as it had been for the adherents of the Ratu Adil after their leader, who had won them by the sheer force of his eloquence to a belief in the "new kingdom," was taken from them.

[201] *Indonesia Menggugat* (Indonesia Accuses), Sukarno's speech in his own defense before the Landraad at Bandung in December 1930 (1961), p. 171.

[202] "Djikalau sesuatu gezag disambut dengan 'ontkenning' daripada gezagnja . . . maka ta' boleh tidak, ia tentu mendjadi gojang" (SIM, No. 9, p. 216).

[203] See "The Ratu Adil of Tangerang," in Chapter I, above.

In such moments, trust in Djimats and in magical incantations vanished, and people turned with their distresses to that greater power which in Javanese culture was also the refuge of the disappointed: to Allah. In August 1930, just as Sukarno and three co-defendants were about to be tried, Sukarno's newspaper *Persatuan Indonesia* contained this call to the Indonesian people: "But God will be the greatest witness at this trial; therefore we have faith that God will protect our four brothers. And we have faith also in the truth and justice of our principles and our aims." [204] To the Partai Nasional, which had so boldly put its power to the test, faith was the only thing left.

The Trial of Sukarno (1930)

The proceedings [205] against Sukarno and three co-defendants before the Landraad in Bandung began on August 18, 1930, and went on until the end of that year. In all the material brought to light in the search of their houses, nothing was found to indicate that the Partai Nasional Indonesia had actually planned an uprising.

For weeks the chief witness for the prosecution, Police Commissioner Albreghs of Bandung, sought in vain to establish that there had been "communist subversion" of Sukarno's party. The nationalists' intimate association with the communists at the time of the Study Clubs appeared to him just as suspicious as the joining of the PNI by various former PKI members after the Communist Party had been abolished. But that out of the abundance of confiscated material not one incriminating document could be produced was clear proof instead that the Indonesian communists, who at that time were based in Singapore, could not possibly have exerted an influence over the PNI.

In addition, the prosecution attempted to uncover a direct

---

[204] *Persatuan Indonesia,* August 8, 1930 (reprinted in SRI, August 23, 1930, p. 515).

[205] The section that follows is based on the detailed reports of the trial in *Suluh Rakjat Indonesia* and *De Locomotief.* The author's request to the Dutch government for a study of the records of the trial made in February 1962 had, at the time the present work was completed, received no reply, either positive or negative.

link between the PNI and the Perhimpunan Indonesia in Holland. Since up until the autumn of 1929 the latter had been affiliated with the League against Colonial Oppression, it might in this way have been possible to infer an indirect communist influence. But Sukarno insisted—quite justly—on the independence of the Partai Nasional. Despite such common principles as noncooperation and self-help, no closer contact had existed. Even though most members of the PI who returned to Indonesia had assumed leading positions in the PNI, and even though all the co-founders of the PNI, except for Tjipto Mangunkusumo and Sukarno, had once been in the Perhimpunan Indonesia, the fact remained that the development of the party under Sukarno's leadership had not been at all in accord with the ideas of the PI, since it had thus far placed little value on "preparing the people." [206]

This was what emerged from the testimony of the 113 witnesses who had been called. Their statements, sometimes of appalling naïveté, revived in the courtroom the rumor-filled days of autumn 1929. Thus one witness, Aspai, declared that he had heard that freedom was to come in a certain January, although he didn't know in exactly which year; [207] another, Nailun, testified to having heard that in 1930 an uprising was to take place, but did not know against whom it was to be directed.[208] More than thirty witnesses linked the PNI in one way or another with the prophecies of Djajabaja,[209] and fourteen witnesses independently declared that it had been proclaimed at PNI meetings that freedom would come in 1930 if the Pacific War were used to force the government then in power to abdicate.[210]

It was obvious that the references to the Pacific War had evoked a more powerful response in the popular consciousness than all the rest of the party's propaganda. Neither the neglected self-help nor the demons of capitalism and imperialism, which were constantly proclaimed the arch-enemy, could be de-

[206] See Chapter IV, below.   [207] SRI (1930), p. 772.
[208] *Ibid.*, p. 773.
[209] *Indisch Tijdschrift v. h. Recht*, CXXXIII (1931), 664.
[210] *Ibid.*, p. 666.

fined with even a remote approach to accuracy by the great majority of witnesses in the courtroom. "Saja sudah lupa—I don't remember"—was the most frequent answer to questions about such things.[211]

Even though the prosecution did not bother to introduce Sukarno's well-trained disciples into the courtroom, for him and the other party propagandists the outcome must have been disappointing. It had been clearly shown how two years of intensive propaganda had failed to bear fruit among the people.

The judge now also believed that the inclusion of the Pacific War in the propaganda of the PNI constituted proof of Sukarno's hostile intent toward the government of the Netherlands Indies. As early as the second day of the proceedings, Sukarno was asked no less than four times how the PNI would behave in the event that the Pacific War actually broke out. Four times, Sukarno gave an evasive answer: the matter had not yet been considered, the PNI had nothing to do with it, etc.[212]

In another context, however, it was to become clear what the PNI would have done once it came to consider that eventuality. To a question by the chairman on what he expected of his "Interasianism," Sukarno answered, "Suppose there should be hostility between one Asian people and, for example, the English imperialists. Then I would hope that that Asian people would receive help from other Asian peoples." [213] The judge, immediately on the alert, then asked whether Japan was to be included in this "Interasianism," and Sukarno again gave an evasive reply; he was not referring to states but rather to peoples striving for freedom.

Although later, speaking in his own defense, he unequivocally placed Japan among the imperialist powers, declaring that to see in it a "Savior of Asia" that would call a vigorous halt to Western imperialism had been an "empty dream"—instead, Japan had itself become a threat to the Pacific area [214]—such statements must always be considered against the background of the trial. There was a question of obliterating the impression

---

[211] See the collected testimony in SRI (1930), pp. 710ff., 738, 751ff., 772ff.
[212] SRI (1930), p. 524.   [213] *Ibid.,* p. 554.
[214] *Indonesia Menggugat,* pp. 31f.

that had arisen from PNI propaganda and the testimony of the witnesses. But from these statements it is impossible to conclude anything about Sukarno's later behavior toward the Japanese—as, for example, that he must therefore have cooperated with them subsequently only under pressure.[215] Sukarno never again spoke directly of Japan as a threat to other Asian peoples; rather, as will be shown, he constantly placed his hope in it, just as did all the Javanese who accepted the word of Djajabaja about where to look for liberation.

During the trial, the chairman brought up the connection between PNI propaganda and the prophecy of Djajabaja, and asked Sukarno whether he had ever represented the Pacific War as a fulfillment of that prophecy concerning the disappearance of the white peoples. Sukarno replied angrily that he had used the Pacific War as no more than a point of departure, "only because I wanted to educate my people positively and not delude them with false hopes." [216] Faced with the threat of war and its dangers, the people ought simply to draw closer to one another, so as better to withstand economic need and other difficulties.[217]

Sukarno had in fact never deliberately attempted to profit from the superstition of the people, as had the communists in the period before the uprising (1926), when they declared that a Ratu Adil was coming and that he would recognize nobody as his subject who did not possess a membership card.[218] Rather, Sukarno took the attitude of Tjokroaminoto, who made a constant effort to give new meaning to the prophecy, and who thus interpreted the Ratu Adil first as independence, then as participation in the government, and finally as the coming of socialism.[219]

Indeed, Sukarno frequently became annoyed with the "back-

---

[215] As was done, for example, in the essay, "Indonesien—Politik und Weltanschauung des Präsidenten Dr. Ahmed Sukarno," *loc. cit.*, p. 215.

[216] *De Locomotief,* November 6, 1930, p. 6.

[217] *Indonesia Menggugat,* pp. 165f., 176.

[218] IPO 1926, No. 31, p. 225. Cf. also IPO 1925, No. 47, p. 382.

[219] See "The Introduction of the Ratu Adil Idea into the Nationalist Movement," above.

wardness" of the peasants, "who still believe in the Ratu Adil or Heru Tjokro, who will come from heaven and bring to earth the blessings of Paradise." [220] When the prophecies of Djaja-baja nevertheless revived around him in the autumn of 1929, it was because of the charisma that he had for the masses, and that was lacking in those who liked to style themselves emissaries of the Ratu Adil. In them it was lacking because they did not be-lieve as the people did, but only exploited that belief.

Sukarno, on the other hand, was very close to the thinking of the people. This he made clear to the judges during the trial, with the very example of the Ratu Adil. In his defense he de-clared:

If you could only understand, honored Sirs, why the people con-tinue to believe in the coming of the Ratu Adil and to await him, why the prophecies of Djajabaja up to the present still inflame the hopes of the people; why we so often hear that in this or that village an Imam Mahdi, or Heru Tjokro, or a descendant of Wali Sanga has appeared. For this there is only one explanation—that a suffer-ing people unceasingly, endlessly wait and hope for aid, like a man in darkness; every hour, every minute, every second, they wait and hope; when, when will the sun rise at last? [221]

But groping in darkness and waiting for sunrise were also Su-karno's constant image for the Indonesian movement, repeat-edly telling itself that somewhere in the distance the light of the rising sun was already to be seen. Just where its gaze was di-rected was not hard to guess, thanks to the predictions of a Pacific War; and in a sketch dated 1932, he himself gave the an-swer still more clearly; it was toward Japan, the Land of the Rising Sun.[222] On the waiting and the direction of hope, Su-karno and the people of Java were thus completely in agree-

[220] As, for example, in the article "Marhaen dan proletar" in the sum-mer of 1933 (DBR, pp. 254f.).

[221] *Indonesia Menggugat*, p. 75.

[222] The sketch appeared in the first number of *Fikiran Rakjat* [Thought of the People], on July 1, 1932. The otherwise strictly objective editor-ship of the IPO put aside a little of its reserve to note that the reference to the Japanese sun was certainly "rather daring" (IPO 1932, No. 27, pp. 27f.).

ment, even though they had different prophets. It was this consonance that led, in the fall of 1929, to the wild rumors and finally to Sukarno's arrest.

During the trial it became evident that the government had fallen victim to a psychosis. If the main point of the prosecution, that the PNI planned a violent revolution, had already been seriously undermined by a total lack of conclusive evidence and by the confused testimony of the witnesses, that point was made all but meaningless by the testimony in October 1930 of a representative of the government [223] who declared from the witness stand that Sukarno had asked permission to denounce the rumors of an uprising.

Nevertheless, a verdict of guilty was handed down, and in December 1930 Sukarno was sentenced to four years in prison. In the eyes of the Indonesian public, who had followed the trial with increasing interest, Sukarno consequently became a martyr of the drive toward freedom, made to suffer innocently for an ideal. Even in circles where he had been little known up to then, a lively discussion of his fate began. Within the Indonesian movement, his fame reached unexpected heights.[224] This was the reward of Djajabaja, who in the autumn of 1929 had taken the control of the movement out of Sukarno's hands: he had assured Sukarno of a lasting place in the hearts of the masses.

The Landraad, which in Bandung handed down the judgment and pronounced the sentence, acted in the sincere belief that it must assess and punish the struggle for independence as a dangerous rebellion. In the opinion of its members, the realization of independence could occur only through a violent revolution. But this Sukarno had expressly denied. Asked several times about the "final step" toward realizing the goal of the PNI, Sukarno had explained that it had not yet been considered, that more exact plans could not be made at the time be-

[223] The representative was Kieviet de Jonge. See *De Locomotief,* October 22, 1930, p. 36.

[224] See the voluminous comments in IPO after the verdict on December 21, 1930 and its confirmation by the Raad van Justitie on April 17, 1931; also S. Djojopuspito, *Buiten het gareel* (1940, 1946), an informative novel about this period which also discusses the trial (p. 56) and provides a useful impression of Sukarno's growing fame (pp. 54ff.).

cause conditions were bound to change continually. Since the people's movement had not come into being by itself, but had been called to life as the antithesis of imperialism, it must likewise continue to be linked with the development of imperialism.[225]

With this interpretation of the movement as "historical necessity," however, the court did not agree. It believed rather that the entirely earnest arguments offered by Sukarno (who had invariably used the same dialectical style to assure himself of the correctness of his actions) must be seen as "excuses" and "hiding behind speculative hypotheses." In a sixty-two-page decision, the court manufactured an ingenious linkage of the PNI to the PKI and PI—both of which were said to approve the use of force and to have plotted violent revolution—for which there was not one piece of valid substantiation.[226] Sukarno and his three co-defendants, who received milder sentences, were convicted on the basis of Article 169 (taking part in an association which plans to commit crimes) and Article "153 bis" (advocating the overthrow of Dutch rule in Indonesia).[227]

Whereas Article 169 was invoked on grounds of sheer conjecture,[228] Sukarno could already have been thrown into prison on the basis of Article "153 bis" from the time he first mentioned the goal of independence, without any miscarriage of existing justice. For the nature of that justice was still determined by the existing power, and that power, as before, remained firmly in the hands of the Kaurawas.

Sukarno had raised the question of power, and the answer he

[225] SRI (1930), pp. 517, 603; also *Indonesia Menggugat*, pp. 69ff., 190ff.

[226] On the final day of the proceedings, what the prosecution had offered as its trump card, a letter purportedly written by Sukarno and advocating a resort to force, was investigated by a handwriting expert, who concluded that the letter was *not* Sukarno's (*De Locomotief*, November 7, 1930, p. 22).

[227] The verdict was published in *Indisch Tijdschrift van het Recht*, CXXXIII (1931), 608–70.

[228] After the confirmation of the verdict by the Raad van Indië, there appeared a brochure—*Het vonnis in de PNI-zaak* (1931)—in which the author, Professor J. M. J. Schepper, dissociated himself from such manipulations, in the name of the Dutch legal tradition.

had received had exposed his dialectic maneuvers ("out of right comes power") as mere illusion. That the fiction of Indonesian "power" could have been maintained for more than two years was entirely due to the forbearance of the then Governor General, de Graeff, who as a last concession, before his return to Holland in the fall of 1931, cut Sukarno's prison sentence from four to two years.[229] Thus—having been credited with time served during the investigation—Sukarno regained his freedom on December 31, 1931.

[229] It was said, by way of explanation: "The verdict of guilt handed down by the Landraad and the Raad van Justitië is acknowledged, but the government is of the opinion that the idealistic motives of Ir. Sukarno must be taken into consideration." See IPO 1931, No. 39, p. 559.

IV

The Marhaenist (Marxist) Phase (1932–1933)

The Split between the Indonesian Nationalists

The Two Nationalist Parties

The degree to which Sukarno for several years had dominated the Indonesian movement first became really clear after December 29, 1929, when he was removed from the political scene for two years. With his arrest, the soul appeared to have gone out of the people's movement; a "pensive stillness" [1] took command after years of feverish agitation. Neither of the organizations Sukarno had founded—the PPPKI and the PNI—was to survive the trying period during which their founder and driving force had been taken from them.

The federation of Indonesian parties, which had sprung to life with such élan but which up to then had scarcely gone beyond a "consensus of spirit," might have taken the opportunity, after the police action against the PNI, to give an impressive demonstration of solidarity with its founder Sukarno. However, as the journal of the Perhimpunan Indonesia in Holland observed in a critical comment,[2] "apart from a few half-hearted protest meetings, the PPPKI was able to do nothing more than make a public display of its impotence." Following the verdict, the PPPKI seemed incapable even of that much; it no longer reacted at all, although the doubtfulness of the verdict, which

[1] Cf. J. M. Pluvier, *Overzicht van de ontwikkeling der nationalistische beweging in Indonesië in de jaren 1930 tot 1942* (1953), p. 46.

[2] "De Crisis der PPPKI," *Indonesia Merdeka,* VIII (1930), No. 5, pp. 75ff.

even aroused the protest of a Dutch legal scholar,[3] would seem
to have provided one of the very rare occasions for arriving at a
Mufakat. But by then the PPPKI was already falling apart;
early in 1931 the Partai Sarekat Islam Indonesia—as the old SI
had meanwhile been named—announced its withdrawal from
the federation.[4]

A critical examination of the PPPKI makes it clear that this
very system of Mufakat, celebrated as a "return to ourselves,"
had blocked every action from the start. The need for unanimity crippled the federation, and if its impotence was openly exposed only after Sukarno's arrest, that merely proved the skill
with which, again and again, he had mollified the individual
parties to private quarrels. But the unresolved points of friction, above all between the Sarekat Islam and Dr. Sutomo's
Study Club, had not been eliminated. Following the arrest of
the magician of unity, they broke out with renewed force.

As a "state within a state," the PPPKI might have found a
raison d'être in representing, for example, the still unfulfilled
ideal of an entire Indonesian people, by avoiding needless internal quarrels, and so on. On the other hand, it was totally unable to function as a weapon, as Sukarno had intended it to do.
Mufakat was the enemy of clear-cut decisions, since every view
had to be taken into account; but the struggle against the party
of the Sanas required clear-cut decisions, such as could never be
reached between cooperators and noncooperators.

Thus in founding the PPPKI Sukarno had achieved, for his
purposes, only a dubious success. And what of the PNI? In a
short time it had succeeded in broadcasting the ideal of independence across the land on a tide of nationalism. With contagious optimism, it had called forth the illusion of being
powerful and near to the goal, so that by degrees a dangerous
state of euphoria had been produced—until the Kaurawas put a
stop to the goings-on and shut up the Dalang of this Bharata
Judha in jail. That the battle had been a mere shadow play became evident almost immediately. No new leaders stepped into
the breach left by Sukarno; the reaction of the Brown Front was
one of resigned helplessness.

[3] See Chapter III, note 228, above.
[4] *Indonesia Merdeka,* IX (1931), No. 1–2, p. 21.

This came especially to the notice of the Perhimpunan Indonesia in Holland, where from the first the revival of the Indonesian movement under Sukarno's leadership had been followed with intense interest.[5] Its members had believed that Sukarno was working to realize what had been the program of the PI in 1924, namely to call to life a self-sufficient mass movement, one that would rely on its own strength. Now, with great disappointment, they saw how with the arrest of Sukarno the movement had come to a standstill. After the confirmation of the sentence, when the acting leadership of the PNI under Sartono ordered the dissolution of the party, because under Article 169 the PNI had been branded virtually illegal,[6] Mohammed Hatta, for years chairman of the PI in Holland, concluded that he must actively intervene in the events at home.

In July 1931 he addressed a letter [7] to various Indonesian newspapers, outlining in detail the following views: The dissolution of the Partai Nasional Indonesia had been a great mistake; even though the verdict had made it suspect as well, there was reason to suppose that the government had shied away from outlawing the PNI in order to avoid a reaction by the movement such as had happened after 1926.

In this Hatta may have been wrong. He had lived in the Netherlands since 1921 and certainly no longer had a clear idea of the legal practices then prevailing in the colony. But more important was the charge he now made, that the dissolution of the PNI had taken place in a "dictatorial manner" without consulting the thousands of members. Obviously a democratic attitude did not exist in the party, even if the leaders always insisted that it did. Hatta waxed caustic: "The people are treated as a doormat for the leaders to wipe their feet on; they are regarded as the necessary audience, so there will be applause when a leader makes a brave speech. But they are not taught to take on responsibility or duties themselves." [8]

This was undisguised criticism not of the acting leaders of the

[5] *Indonesia Merdeka,* VI, beginning with M. Hatta's article, "De nieuwe opmarsch" (May 1928).

[6] Pluvier, *Overzicht,* p. 48.

[7] The complete text is reprinted in IPO 1931, No. 32, pp. 262ff.

[8] IPO 1931, No. 32, p. 266.

PNI, who were nominally being attacked by Hatta, but of the style of leadership Sukarno had developed. For anyone who had not yet read it into this letter, the charge was made more directly, a few months later, in *Daulat Rakjat* ("People's Sovereignty"), the organ of Hatta's adherents: "Mohammed Hatta has said that Ir. Sukarno had too little contact with the people, merely gathering applause at meetings. But the people must become totally infused with the spirit of Ir. Sukarno. This cannot be achieved by agitation alone." [9]

Presently Hatta advanced his idea of what must be done with the movement in the future. It was necessary to educate the people on economic, political, and social matters, so that they could acquire a grasp of their own worth and their own rights. At first the education of leaders who would in themselves embody the spirit of the people must begin. Therefore, according to this outline of the task, "noncooperation is a social-pedagogic system." [10]

That was the core of Hatta's criticism, that Sukarno used noncooperation only to provoke and not to educate, or, as it had been put in 1924, to "prepare" the people. Where agitation alone would lead had been shown in 1929 and 1930: a daring charismatic leader stood high above the people, knew what to do in every situation, promised help to them all, thought for them all, acted for them all. Then, after his arrest, hope, thought, and action vanished. If the movement ever became a genuine force against the colonial power, a Bandjir (flood) as Sukarno had constantly urged, it would do so only through the education of the masses and the training of an elite that did not intoxicate the people but rather gave them enlightenment.

Hatta, a large number of whose close friends among the members of the PI had returned to Indonesia, was thus well acquainted with the weaknesses of the movement. He was given leave to make such criticism by the fame he had acquired among Indonesians as their representative at European congresses of colonial peoples and of the League. But even more than to his speeches in these congresses,[11] his fame was due to

---

[9] IPO 1931, No. 44, p. 195.   [10] IPO 1931, No. 32, pp. 266f.

[11] Most of Hatta's speeches are included in Mohammed Hatta, *Verspreide Geschriften* (1952).

another incident. In the summer of 1927, the homes of PI members were searched, and Hatta was taken prisoner along with other members of the executive committee. Although the outcome of his trial in the spring of 1928 was a verdict of not guilty, in the meantime, thanks to the use the PNI made of the event as propaganda, Hatta had come to be considered a martyr in the cause of freedom.[12]

Hatta's letter gave the signal for a split among Indonesian nationalists. All those who shared his interpretation of the people's movement stayed aloof from the Partai Indonesia (Partindo), which was named the successor to the PNI after the dissolution of the latter. They now established what were known as Independent Groups (Golongan Merdeka). Toward the end of 1931, a few days before Sukarno's release from prison, these Independent Groups were merged into a "new PNI" (PNI-Baru),[13] in which the old initials did, to be sure, herald a new program: the Partai Nasional Indonesia had become the Pendidikan Nasional Indonesia (Indonesian National Education).

On the other hand, those who had thus far been content with the style of leadership joined the Partindo. Among them, Hatta's criticism was seen as rude meddling in the movement, and some reacted with great vehemence.[14] Essentially there was no difference between the Partindo and the old PNI. It was obvious that only the name had been changed, so as to avoid harassment based on the judgment against the old PNI. For the

[12] In the summer of 1927, the PNI accompanied its appearance in the Indonesian movement with vehement protest demonstrations against the "despotic persecution of our brothers in Holland." See *De Locomotief*, August 15 and 16, 1927 (IPO 1927, No. 30, p. 169); Blumberger, *Nation. beweging*, p. 207. On the trial, see M. Hatta, *Indonesia vrij* (1928), an expanded version of his speech of defense before the judges, which in its clear organization and sober, unprejudiced account of the origin and goal of the movement clearly contrasts with Sukarno's *Indonesia Menggugat*. On his release, Sukarno wrote for SIM, No. 5, an article, "Pemandangan dan Pengadjaran (Observation and Lesson)," in which he attempted to reduce the rising sympathy for the Dutch judges (see also DBR, pp. 63ff.). To this Sukarno received an interesting reply from a former PI member ("There are still judges in The Hague"; SIM, No. 6–7, 172, and Sukarno's "Last Word," *ibid.*, p. 173).

[13] Pluvier, *Overzicht*, pp. 48f.

[14] People began to tear up pictures of Hatta (IPO 1931, No. 27, p. 14).

same reasons as before, its members espoused noncooperation; the Partindo's basic platform announced that in a colony the interests of the government and of the people must be in continual conflict, and thus only a movement that relied on its own strength and ability could win freedom.[15]

Exactly the same view was adopted by Hatta's party.[16] The differences between the two groups were over the manner of the struggle, the question of how the popular consciousness could be developed—through mass agitation, the method thus far pursued by Sukarno, or by the less spectacular educational means which Hatta had come to advocate, because in his opinion success was possible only in this way.

Viewed superficially, it was only a difference over tactics that had led to a split in the nationalist camp. And thus Sukarno, when he came back into the movement, made a solemn pledge to reunite the two "hostile brothers."

Sukarno's Vain Attempt at Unification

Nanggala, the Miraculous Weapon

Sukarno's optimism was understandable. Never before had a leader in the Indonesian movement been honored with such enthusiasm as welcomed Sukarno after his release from prison. The split that took place among the Indonesian nationalists during his imprisonment, and the internal disintegration of the PPPKI, only added to his fame. Under Sukarno, people told each other, this would not have happened. His continual efforts at compromise had caused him to be regarded everywhere as the symbol of Indonesian unity.

For this reason, the talk about him that had gone on even during his imprisonment had still not died down by the autumn of 1931, when news of his pardon and approaching release nourished anew the hopes that had meanwhile gathered about his name.[17] Even in the eyes of those who did not embrace noncooperation, he was the Great Sukarno, who could drive the

[15] *Persatuan Indonesia,* June 24, 1931 (IPO 1931, No. 27, p. 14).

[16] *Siang Po,* August 26, 1931 (IPO 1931, No. 37, p. 485).

[17] Cf. the statements appearing in Indonesian papers for the autumn of 1931 (IPO 1931, No. 37, pp. 493ff.; No. 38, pp. 553ff.).

dark clouds from the political firmament, restore unity, and move the leaders to regard one another not as enemies but as brothers.[18] Devotion to Sukarno even took on the aspect of a cult: at their meetings, various associations would honor him by standing for two minutes of silence,[19] bringing an energetic protest from *Suara Islam:* the Prophet himself had declared that people were not to rise to their feet for him, but only for Allah.[20]

The adulation of Sukarno reached its peak at the Indonesia Raya (Greater Indonesia) Congress in Surabaja, at the beginning of 1932, the first event in which Sukarno took part after his release, and one that had been postponed until then on his account. Newspapers put out special Sukarno numbers, and the journey by train from Bandung to Surabaja became a triumphal procession without precedent. The masses jammed the railroad stations to see him ride past.[21] At Surabaja, finally, 6,000 enthusiastic followers were on hand to meet him,[22] in a reception that could only confirm him in the belief that the path he had chosen was the correct one, and one that he must continue to walk. On the following evening he told the Congress:

The joy and the honor which you, brothers, have accorded me by this reception is, I know, not meant for myself, not for my own person, but for Sukarno the leader, whose highest ideal and burning inspiration it is to serve the people and the fatherland of Indonesia; it is meant for your leader who has taken up the torch that he may bring light to the people still living in darkness, who so long as life remains in the body of Sukarno will continue on this road to Indonesia Merdeka, to an independent Indonesia [stormy applause].[23]

[18] So went the statement of the cooperation-minded Budi Utomo (*ibid.*).

[19] See, for example, IPO 1931, No. 43, p. 176.

[20] IPO 1931, No. 52, p. 369.

[21] Cf. the exuberant comments on Sukarno's release in IPO 1932, No. 1 and 2.

[22] Sukarno's arrival in Surabaja is described in I. Supardi, *Bung Karno sebagai Kokrosono* [Bung Karno as Kokrosono] (1950), pp. 5f. (The brochure deals only with Sukarno's appearance at the Indonesia Raya Congress.)

[23] *Ibid.*, p. 10.

Sukarno was entirely in his element. Thus he might have pictured his return to the movement in the cramped cell where his suffering had been so intense. There, he had not succeeded in divesting himself of his own ego, for Sukarno as a person experienced acutely the injustice that had been inflicted on Sukarno the leader.[24] Now he had been rewarded, and Sukarno as a person enjoyed to the full the homage given to Sukarno the leader; for the two aspects, the leader and the man, could not be separated. Sukarno the man needed the response to Sukarno the leader in order to regain his confidence and persuasive power. As soon as the echo failed to sound, the confidence likewise failed him; this was to become evident all too soon after the euphoric reception at Surabaja.

In the very next sentences that Sukarno spoke, he sounded the theme to which he was to devote himself without stint in the weeks that followed.

He compared himself to Kokrosono,[25] a figure from the Wajang who, when he reappears out of the life of a hermit, is at once happy and sorrowful—happy because he has won the miraculous weapon Nanggala, sorrowful because he has had to stand by watching from afar while two of his children were in great danger. For him it was the same. He was happy once again to be able to devote himself entirely to the movement, but distressed at having to see his followers split into two separate parties. This split, he said, could only mean a weakening of the movement. And now he gave his word, which was received with

[24] During his imprisonment, Sukarno had attempted to take Nietzsche's "Superman" as an example. But he soon gave up, and concluded, "The way I live, evenings in my little cell, is in his view a very trifling evil." If Nietzsche had tried to have anyone in prison live as a Superman [he went on], he would certainly have had no success. See the letter of May 17, 1931, "Keadaan dipendjara Sukamiskin [Conditions in Sukamiskin prison]" (DBR, pp. 115–17).

[25] In the Lakon, "Kongso adu djago," Kokrosono is the legitimate heir to the land of Mandura, ruled by the demon Kongso. The father of Kokrosono cannot defend himself against the usurper. Kokrosono withdraws to live as a hermit, and after his purification receives from a god the magic weapon Nanggala, with which after various adventures he succeeds in overcoming the demon Kongso. Cf. I Supardi, *Bung Karno,* pp. 22ff.

enthusiasm: "Brothers, be sure that for as long as Bung Karno [26] has life within him, for as long as he feels power in himself, he will stake all his energy on reuniting the two wings with their body." [27]

Sukarno, who had achieved in theory the unification of Moslems, Marxists, and nationalists, and who believed he should have no difficulty in uniting nationalist with nationalist, now brought out the tested formula:

In my opinion, the split among the brothers is nothing more than a misunderstanding. Truly, misunderstandings often lead to divisions and schisms. And so I shall take up the [miraculous] weapon Nanggala to bring back together those who misunderstand one another, so that they will again be united with the whole people, and so that our movement can at last bring independence to Indonesia.[28]

For Sukarno the miraculous weapon Nanggala, by which he thought he could once more reconcile the hostile brothers, was thus the denial of any real difference and the disclosure of "misunderstandings." Up until then this had worked in most of his attempts at unification because people believed in it, believed that unity was necessary and must be achieved at any price. As a newspaper commented at the time on Sukarno's new attempt at unification, "One on whom God's blessing falls will surely bring about a miracle." [29]

But the miraculous weapon Nanggala could no longer work when people had ceased to believe in it, when they could make no sense of unity and when, rather than strive for Mufakat, the general consensus, they shunned it, seeing it as the cause of evil —as they did, for example, in the party of Hatta's supporters, the PNI-Baru, which was responsible for the split. Its young chairman, Sutan Sjahrir, upon his return from Holland to Indonesia in the summer of 1931, to become Hatta's confidant,

---

[26] Bung Karno was the popular way of addressing Sukarno; it means about the same as "Comrade Karno." Sukarno had dropped the "Su" (perhaps so as to be named exactly for the Karno of the *Mahabhrata*); see, "Childhood—the School of the Wajang," in Chapter II, above.

[27] I. Supardi, *Bung Karno*, p. 13.   [28] *Ibid.*

[29] *Darmokondo*, January 28, 1932 (IPO 1932, I, p. 66).

talked not of "misunderstandings" but of the "difference in underlying character and goal" between the two associations.[30]

Differences in the Thinking of Sukarno and Sjahrir

Sjahrir had no sooner appeared in Indonesia than he made this exceedingly stern demand: that everyone taking part in the political movement and the struggle for independence must first carefully analyze the previous history of the independence movement, must examine carefully the false steps and all tendencies that had endangered the movement, and learn from them. Only then could the movement make progress.[31]

Under Sukarno's leadership there had been no progress, nor was there to be any in the future. Thus, according to Sukarno, the failure of the PNI to bring about any mass action was neither his fault nor that of the PNI itself, but solely the fault of the rulers: "Before the party could begin to be organized, it was hastily put behind bars." [32] For Sjahrir the explanation was altogether different. His analysis of the movement led him to this conclusion: "In our movement the atmosphere of the Holy War, of allowing passions to dominate thinking instead of a cool head, has invariably led to a neglect of organization." [33] But organization, Sajhrir continued—with a reference to a remark made by Kautsky—was "the true weapon to be used by the Indonesian people in their struggle against capitalism and modern imperialism." [34]

Not only the neglect of organization, but also the politics of feeling so highly valued by Sukarno, received the censure of Sjahrir. Of the image of the beauty of Ibu Indonesia (Mother Indonesia)—her lovely landscape, the fruits that nourished her

[30] "Nampaklah perbedaan didalam hakekat dan didalam tudjuan pekerdjaan." See S. Sjahrir, *Pikiran dan perdjuangan* [Thought and Struggle] (1947), pp. 27f. This brochure is a reissue (unfortunately not in chronological order) of Sjahrir's articles in *Daulat Rakjat* from 1931 to 1934.

[31] S. Sjahrir, *Pikiran,* p. 26.

[32] DBR, p. 202, note: "Sebelum partai ini mulai menjusun, ia keburu didjatuhi palang-pintu." (This was in December 1932.)

[33] S. Sjahrir, *Pikiran,* p. 57.

[34] *Ibid.,* p. 62. Sjahrir quotes *Die neue Zeit,* 1904, No. 28, p. 36.

children, etc.—that was conjured up again and again by Sukarno at his rallies so as to stir up nationalist feeling, Sjahrir coldly remarked: "Mother Indonesia as a mystical experience lies outside the realm of practical politics." [35]

Another, more serious charge made by Sjahrir was against the effort for unity at any price, by which Sukarno's attempt in that direction had been condemned to failure from the start.

This striving for unity, [Sjahrir wrote] meant a crippling of *Realpolitik*. It had inhibited the work of the party, and the losers had been the masses, since the PPPKI had strictly forbidden its members to attack one another. "Brotherhood" was honored, and thus the feeble moderates, the profiteers who cooperated with the bourgeoisie, were the recipients of rank and power in the movement for freedom. They joined so enthusiastically in the chant of unity (which in fact hitched the people to the wagons of the bourgeoisie), that even from the PNI, the party of the proletariat, there came such orders as to "go and join some party, it doesn't matter which. Preferably a party that is a member of the PPPKI." [36]

Thus from the position taken by Sjahrir the "difference in underlying character" between the two nationalist parties becomes clear. For the PNI-Baru, the idea based on the theory of the class struggle occupied the foreground, namely that only among the revolutionary elements of the people—the exploited masses—had the struggle for freedom any chance of success. In the Partindo, on the other hand, as in the old Partai Nasional, obviously more was expected from the idea of racial conflict, of the Brown Front that Sukarno had proposed and to some degree realized—for all its inefficacy—in the PPPKI.

But still more is evident from Sjahrir's position than the "difference in the underlying character" of the two parties. Sjahrir returned to Indonesia as the representative of another world. In Holland, as he later wrote in his autobiography, he had "felt at home." [37] And in his writings he soon showed that he also felt at home in European thought. His acute analyses, his unsparing criticism of whatever he deemed worthless, and

[35] Sjahrir, *Pikiran*, p. 32.   [36] *Ibid.*, p. 41.

[37] See the diary he wrote in exile (1934–38), which appeared, under the pseudonym Sjahrazad, as *Indonesische Overpeinzingen* (1945), p. 161.

the unsentimental logic with which he argued, brought a totally different style to political discussion in Indonesia during the fall of 1931. He expected no more from the "solemn brotherhood" than he did from the resentment against the white rulers. He could be completely detached, and could discuss the psychological aspects of the struggle for Indonesian independence with the dispassion of an outside observer.[38]

Sukarno, as the contrast with Sjahrir's manner of thinking makes clear, operated in another mode. What Sjahrir had identified and condemned as a crucial hindrance to the movement, namely the striving for unity at any price, was for Sukarno the driving force behind both thought and action. Sjahrir soberly and openly declared after analyzing the movement: "PPPKI policy is the outgrowth of nebulous [mystical] thinking and weakness of spirit." [39] Sukarno, on the other hand, after the impotence of the PPPKI had already become clear, still proudly described it as "a part of my life." [40] Likewise, despite the manifestation, following his arrest and trial, that unity had been a failure, he took it for granted that the drive for unity would once more be resumed. Nor would he be content with reuniting the hostile brothers. At the Indonesia Raya Congress, Dr. Sutomo had declared: "You all should know that what Bung Karno understands by unity is not simply the unification of the PNI-Baru and the Partindo but rather the unity of the entire people, of the Partai Indonesia, Budi Utomo, Persatuan Bangsa Indonesia, and other parties. Is that not true, Bung Karno?" Bung Karno thereupon replied, "Yes!" This answer was received by those present with stormy applause.[41]

It was thus a matter of course that in April 1932, when the idea of reviving the PPPKI was discussed, the task was assigned to Sukarno.[42]

[38] Sjahrazad, *loc. cit.*, p. 175.

[39] Sjahrir, *Pikiran,* p. 44: "PPPKI politik ialah ta' lain dari politik jang timbul didalam semangat ngalamum, semangat lembek."

[40] *Bintang Timur,* February 27, 1929 (IPO 1929, No. 10, p. 287).

[41] I. Supardi, *Bung Karno,* p. 18.

[42] IPO 1932, No. 18, p. 280. When Sukarno submitted his reorganization plan for the PPPKI in the fall of 1932 (for details see Pluvier, *Overzicht,* pp. 65f.), despite his having dropped the requirement of

To Sukarno, who in working for unity could feel that he was completely at one with the popular will—at the time of the dispute with Sjahrir he published a newspaper significantly entitled *Fikiran Rakjat*, "The Thought of the People"—unity meant more than it did to Sjahrir, who could regard it only as a strategic means. Indeed, it had been Sukarno himself who, in what Sjahrir regarded as the height of irony, had again and again urged those at his meetings to join any party, it didn't matter which—preferably one of the member associations of the PPPKI.[43]

Sukarno saw unity—the harmonious coexistence of different Indonesian parties, whatever tactic they followed and whatever their goals—as bringing about at last a restoration of the order that had been destroyed in Indonesia by outsiders. In January 1928, after the establishment of the federation, he had declared: "We Indonesian nationalists are often given exhortations and told about the wonderful order under European leadership. But we want no sham order, we want the real thing." [44] It was for this reason that he proudly spoke of the PPPKI as "a return to ourselves," that he called upon the masses to join some party of the federation, and said it was a part of his life. It was for the same reason that Tjokroaminoto had once fought for unity in the movement.

This way of thinking—to aim for synthesis, compromise, Mufakat, for harmonious coexistence within their own traditional order—was peculiarly Javanese. So was the protest against powers that would make no accommodation with the indigenous order, but tried to destroy it. Against these enemies, these "demons," thinking based on synthesis was of no help. For this reason, the Javanese from time immemorial had taken

---

Mufakat, from which the membership had already dissociated themselves in May 1931, noncooperative and cooperative parties were still represented equally. However, the important parties, PNI-Baru and Partai Sarekat Islam Indonesia, avoided the new Congress of the PPPKI in May 1933 (IPO 1933, No. 19, pp. 299ff.).

[43] See, for example, SRI, February 15, 1928; IPO 1931, No. 43, p. 158; DBR, pp. 109f.

[44] SIM, No. 2, p. 58.

refuge in the magical and irrational—in spells and incantations, Djimats, the expectation of a miracle or of foreign assistance, and so on.

This was just as true of such modern Javanese as Tjokroaminoto and Sukarno. For Sukarno it no longer consisted in the magic words "Pantjasana" or "Tjondobirowo"—however often he might cite them—but rather in such modern slogans as "In unity is strength," "No sacrifice is wasted," or the dialectical assertion of their own power, along with the hope of foreign assistance or, if all else failed, of divine aid.[45]

Sutan Sjahrir, like Hadji Agus Salim—who in 1921 had forced the break between the Sarekat Islam and the PKI—and like Mohammed Hatta, was not Javanese but came from West Sumatra (Minangkabau). In analyzing the movement he could not overlook these irrational elements in Sukarno's leadership of the struggle: "For some years we have operated according to the modern way, through political parties, but still we meet all too often with ways of thinking that are based on a belief in Djimats and the Holy War, not only among the great mass of the people but also among the prominent leaders of the movement."[46]

Whom could he have meant by this except Sukarno? Was it not known that he was in the habit of fasting so as to increase his powers?[47] From this comparison of Sjahrir's and Sukarno's ways of thinking, it is understandable why Sukarno's attempt at unification was doomed to fail. The split among the nationalists had not grown, as Sukarno believed, out of a "misunderstanding"; rather, there really was, as Sjahrir declared, a "difference of underlying character." In the two parties, two different ways of thinking opposed one another, a "European" and a "Java-

[45] The long, tedious quotations from books of European scholars and journalists which Sukarno introduced in his defense speech were also nothing other than "assurances." There is no perceptible effort to analyze a single one of the authors for his own sake. *Pembela Islam* correctly remarked in its December 1930 issue that the nationalists had made Western professors their prophets (IPO 1930, No. 51, p. 471). The author of this criticism was in all probability Mohammed Natsir.

[46] Sjahrir, *Pikiran*, pp. 56f.

[47] Djojopuspito, *Buiten het gareel*, p. 57.

nese." Their outstanding representatives were Sukarno and Sjahrir, neither one of whom any longer understood the other. Sjahrir did not understand Sukarno's striving for unification; Sukarno did not understand that the gap was in fact unbridgeable.

When, after eight months of intensive effort, Sukarno was forced to announce the collapse of his drive for unification, he declared:

I do not deny the existence of minor differences over principles and tactics, but these differences are not so great or fundamental as to become grounds for division from one another. I would even assert that there are minor differences among particular groups within every party, that there is a relatively militant and a more conciliatory wing in every party.

For this reason I worked tirelessly to bring unity, tirelessly I soothed the overwrought, tirelessly I worked to get rid of misunderstandings. As one of the leaders of the Marhaens,[48] I saw that it was my task to achieve unity, my task to restore the organization of the Marhaens, my task to attempt whatever might be attempted, placing the success or failure of my efforts in the hands of Allah. I have often seen people smile, saying that of course everyone would like to have unity. But who among them, I would ask, has really tried to bring it about? [49]

It was obvious that Sjahrir and his group had not, for the simple reason that they knew they could accomplish more through their own organization than by means of a nebulous unity which they themselves found laughable.[50] Why should tensions between a moderate and a radical wing, which Sukarno believed he could see everywhere, be provoked at all if they could so easily be avoided?

They had no feeling that unity was a task, as Sukarno did.

[48] On the term Marhaen, see "Marhaenism," below.

[49] "Maklumat dari Bung Karno kepada kaum Marhaen Indonesia [Declaration of Bung Karno to the Marhaens of Indonesia]," August 1932 (DBR, pp. 167f.).

[50] Hatta, for example, made this ironic comparison: Persatuan (Unity) was sought, but Persatean (small pieces of meat skewered together for roasting) was at hand. Daulat Rakjat, April 20, 1932 (IPO 1932, pp. 241f.).

Quite the contrary! Sukarno's reference to Nanggala, the miraculous Indonesian weapon, and to "misunderstandings," sent them back to their own arsenal, and to a display of European weapons. Thus, in an article "On the Question of Unity," Sjahrir confronted Sukarno with the statement of a Dutch socialist, Henriette Roland-Holst: "The fanatical adherents of unity do not understand that the restoration of formal, organizational unity, even supposing that to be possible under today's conditions, would still not end internal disunity." [51] Likewise he quoted Karl Liebknecht: "Unity as a mere slogan is a will-o'-the-wisp, a self-delusion or a fraud. Only through relentless criticism will there be enlightenment; only through unity of conviction, aim, and will can there be the strength to create the new world of socialism"—or, for us, our country's freedom, Sjahrir added as he translated the quotation from the German.[52]

This brandishing of weapons by the spokesmen of both camps was only one more evidence of the fundamental difference whose existence Sukarno had thought he could deny. In Indonesia at this time there were a "European" and an "Indonesian" party. Sukarno's entry into the Indonesian party could have surprised only the uninitiated.[53] For those who had taken up Sjahrir's challenge and had analyzed the movement, Sukarno's reasoning was sufficient: that he had joined the Partai Indonesia because of his right to determine for himself where he could serve the Indonesian people best.[54]

Sukarno promptly took over the Bandung branch of his new

---

[51] Sjahrir, *Pikiran,* p. 51.   [52] *Ibid.,* p. 53.

[53] On the discussion of Sukarno's entry into the Partindo, see Pluvier, *Overzicht,* p. 51; also *Indonesia Merdeka,* Vol. 10, No. 1–3 (October 1932), pp. 31ff. Sukarno had already let it be known that he would join the Partindo, however, in the autumn of 1931 (IPO 1931, No. 50, p. 358). When he worked for unity, he assumed the guise of objectivity, but at the Partindo's first Congress (May 1932) he praised Mr. Sartono publicly for founding the new party; see IPO 1932, No. 20, p. 305. Even the name Partindo originated with Sukarno (IPO 1933, No. 49, p. 767). There was never a question of joining the PNI-Baru, which had of course been founded in opposition to Sukarno himself (he was even denied entrance to a meeting of its members; IPO 1932, No. 27, p. 23).

[54] "Maklumat," DBR, p. 169.

(or old) party, and at the next Congress, in April 1933, he was officially elected as the first chairman of the Partindo—a function he had performed, however, almost since his entry into the party in the summer of 1932.[55]

Marhaenism

Marhaen: The New Common Denominator

Whatever question there may have been of which of the two parties Sukarno would join goes back to the term "Marhaen."

It was a word that dominated political discussion in Indonesia beginning about 1932. Before then it had been virtually unknown.[56] Politically interested circles first heard it in Sukarno's defense speech, when he declared that Indonesian society, because of having been for centuries under the domination of imperialism, was typified by the little man: "It is a society made up largely of little men who are peasants, laborers, traders, seamen—in short, they are all Kromos and Marhaens, they are all little people.[57]

Until the end of 1930, the usual expression for the "little man" had been "Kromo." Beginning with the propaganda of the PKI, however, it was often used to refer to the proletariat. This forced Sukarno to cast about for a new name. During a walk one day he met a rice farmer who worked his own field, using his own tools, and who, as Sukarno later argued, was thus clearly no proletarian (since he did not sell his labor), but nevertheless lived in a state of poverty. Sukarno asked him his name. Marhaen, the peasant replied. Then and there, as Sukarno later recounted it, he was inspired to use this name to portray the suffering people of Indonesia.[58]

Sukarno had the great opportunity for such a portrayal in the

[55] See "Colijn-Nota," on the later arrest of Sukarno, in *Handelingen der Staten Generaal, Tweede Kamer,* 1933–34, II, Aanhangsel, pp. 25f.

[56] See the comment by the "omniscient" editors in IPO 1932, No. 18, p. 271.

[57] *Indonesia Menggugat,* p. 138.

[58] Thus Sukarno explained the origin of the term Marhaen in a speech in 1957. It appears, translated into English by Claire Holt, in *Marhaen and Proletarian* (1960), p. 7.

courtroom, where he not only gave a picture of their condition but also told the judges how the Partai Nasional had taken its cue from those who constituted the people:

In a society almost entirely made up of Kromos and Marhaens, we of the PNI . . . must likewise carry on a policy that is Kromoist and Marhaenist. . . . We cannot hope to defeat imperialism by going into competition with it, by trying to build up a "self-containing" national economy, as is happening in India. We can defeat it only by the action of the Kromos and the Marhaens, through nationalist mass action on the grandest scale. Therefore we seek to mobilize a force of millions from the masses, to direct the energies of Indonesian intellectuals toward organizing the masses. . . .

"*Of* the masses, *with* the masses, *for* the masses!" This must be our motto, and the motto of all Indonesians who would fight for the well-being of their land and people.[59]

Sjahrir, in the first article he published after his arrival in Indonesia, took over this entire passage from Sukarno's defense speech, explaining that in the PNI-Baru this program would be put into effect "perhaps more consistently and more radically" than it had been even by the old PNI.[60]

Thus Sjahrir still believed he was acting in the spirit of Sukarno at the time he accused the Partai Indonesia, whose statutes did not lead unequivocally to mass action, of an "offense against the spirit and the promises of the PNI." [61] It was only after Sukarno himself appeared that Sjahrir learned he had actually been deluding himself. In a later discussion of Sukarno's statement that imperialism necessarily led to the impoverishment, the "Marhaenization" of the people, and that to this there was only one answer—namely, mass action—Sjahrir significantly added, "That was the heart of Sukarno's defense speech, whether he intended it to be or not." [62]

According to Sjahrir's interpretation, Marhaenism thus meant concentrating on the masses and on the masses alone. All

[59] *Indonesia Menggugat,* p. 144.   [60] Sjahrir, *Pikiran,* pp. 6f., 12.
[61] *Ibid.,* p. 10.
[62] *Ibid.,* p. 33: "Pangkal pokoknja pembelaan Sukarno, disengadja atau tidak, adalah demikian itu."

other groups were a hindrance to the freedom movement and were to be strictly avoided. This was in fact not what Sukarno, the inventor of Marhaenism, had intended. At the trial he had spoken out clearly in favor of cooperation with the national bourgeoisie. But, because the bourgeoisie was still powerless, the movement was first of all directed toward the masses.[63] In Marhaenism he believed he had found a formula that encompassed "practically the whole of Indonesian society." If, for example, "small tradesmen" were already included, the door was then also opened for others, since Sukarno regarded himself not as the spokesman of one group alone but, as he declared at this time, "as representing the whole Indonesian people." [64]

Looking to the masses was for him—unlike Sjahrir, who saw in them the vehicle of the revolutionary spirit—the need of the hour; they represented just then the only potent force. But he had attempted to include in the masses as many groups as possible, for the unity of the people came first; this was Marhaenism.

As a result of Sjahrir's outspokenness, Sukarno now felt compelled to define his new common denominator more exactly. This necessarily led him to give more attention to Marxist thought.

Marhaenist Principles: Socio-nationalism and Socio-democracy

Not long after his entry into the Partai Indonesia, Sukarno published an article, "Political and Economic Democracy," [65] in which he warned the Marhaens not to look for a copy of the democracy practiced abroad, the form of democracy that was being propagated everywhere. It would not assure the well-being of the Marhaens, since at best it secured only political rights, while economically the masses continued to be in want.

In setting forth his reasons, he first gave a textbook account of

[63] De Locomotief, September 9, 1930, p. 22.

[64] Suara Umum, January 8, 1932 (IPO 1932, No. 1, p. 19).

[65] "Demokrasi-politik dan demokrasi-economi," Fikiran Rakjat, October 28 and November 4, 1932; see also DBR, pp. 171ff. On the dates, see IPO 1932, No. 45, p. 306.

European history according to the communists [66]—namely that
in Europe during the eighteenth century the aristocracy were
attacked by a "new class," the bourgeoisie, and were finally
overthrown "with the help of the masses." The masses, who had
been won over by the slogan, "Liberté, fraternité, egalité," had
been granted political rights with the establishment of parliamentary democracy, so that they could themselves send representatives to parliament. But they had been deprived of their
just reward, since in all lands where there is parliamentary
democracy, "capitalism prospers and takes control; in all those
lands the people live without happiness, in misery and
want. . . ."

Sukarno referred to Jean Jaurès, who was "no communist,"
quoting long passages from a parliamentary address made by the
socialist leader in 1893, discussing critically the economic impotence of the workers: what help was it to the workers that they
could overthrow ministers, that they could reign as kings in parliament, when at the same time they could be turned out into
the street by their bosses, and thus without warning their entire
existence could be seriously endangered? "Is this the 'democracy' that is so revered? No, this is not the democracy that we
are to copy; this is no democracy for the Marhaens of Indonesia.
For this is mere parliamentary democracy, mere political democracy. Economically it is no democracy at all." [67]

The opinion of Jean Jaurès, which fits so neatly into Sukarno's anti-Western prejudice, played a dominant role in all
his subsequent ideas concerning the Indonesian state. Again
and again he brought forward these statements from the year
1893 as the clinching argument against the system of parliamentary democracy,[68] as if nothing at all had changed at a distance

[66] Cf. the argument in Tan Malaka, *Massa-actie* (1926; reprinted 1947),
pp. 39f. That Sukarno had made eager use of this is demonstrable; see
Indisch Tijdschrift v. h. Recht, CXXXIII (1931), 636ff.

[67] DBR, p. 173.

[68] To mention only two separate occasions, in 1941 in the article
"Demokrasi Politik dengan demokrasi Economi = Demokrasi sosial [Politi-
cal Democracy and Economic Democracy Equals Social Democracy]"
(DBR, p. 589), and in 1945 in his address, *Lahirnja Pantjasila, The Birth
of Pantjasila* (1952), p. 27.

first of forty and later of fifty years. And indeed even in 1893 the standpoint represented by Jean Jaurès had already become highly questionable.

Karl Kautsky, whom Sukarno otherwise readily cited as an authority,[69] had declared around the same time that to see parliamentarism as representing the interests of the bourgeoisie alone "*had* a certain justification when Rittinghausen conceived his idea of direct popular legislation; it now has it no longer. For between then and now lies a period of the most prodigious advance by the proletariat." [70]

"Then" in Kautsky's terminology was 1850; "now" was 1893. Sukarno thus delivered his verdict against parliamentary democracy when for nearly half a century it had already been recognized by the European working class as a promising system for representing their interests. What could more clearly document Sukarno's vehement one-sidedness and his refusal to cope with actual conditions? He was only looking for opinions to support him in his unyielding judgment of the West. His statement at the end of the same article—"One need not be a communist to see that 'democracy' in those countries is only a bourgeois democracy" [71]—was, viewed objectively, simply not true. All the conclusions Sukarno had drawn up to the present about the "uselessness" of parliamentary democracy are therefore in great measure questionable.

Viewed subjectively, on the other hand, the picture of a West infected with capitalism was of great value for Sukarno. Out of the contrast he could paint for the Indonesian Marhaens a splendid future, and at the same time portray the struggle against the West as a Holy War. The idea of class struggle, which he was now obliged to take up—so as to argue the neces-

[69] See his attack on the Social Democrats in Chapter III, above. In his speech of defense as well, Sukarno quoted long passages from Kautsky's *Der Weg zur Macht* (1909) and *Sozialismus und Kolonialpolitik* (1907); see *Indonesia Menggugat,* pp. 47, 90f., 114f., 134, 150ff., 158.

[70] Karl Kautsky, *Parlamentarismus und Demokratie* (1893), p. 110. Kautsky's italics.

[71] DBR, p. 175. "Orang ta' usah mendjadi kommunis buat melihat bahwa 'demokrasi' negeri-negeri itu adalah demokrasi burdjuis sahadja."

sity of a more equitable social order—could thereby be further subordinated to that of racial conflict.

To achieve in Indonesia a society without oppressed classes, according to Sukarno, it was not enough that the Marhaens, who were to fight for it, should be "bourgeois revolutionaries," with independence as their final goal. They must be "social revolutionaries," and they must not rest until the happiness of all, of the entire Indonesian community, had been realized. To this striving Sukarno assigned a name he had newly coined— "Socio-nationalism" or "Marhaenist nationalism." [72]

The first description of Marhenist nationalism bore unmistakable traces of the dispute with Sjahrir, an echo of whose previous criticisms could be heard as Sukarno expatiated: "Socio-nationalism does not originate in 'feeling,' . . . in a 'lyrical state of mind,' but is based on social conditions as they are. Socio-nationalism . . . is not a nationalism of 'clouds' and 'incense,' it is not a nationalism 'floating in the air,' but one that stands with both feet on the ground of society." [73]

Sukarno was having to pay dearly, it appeared, for the step out of the "air" of "Eastern nationalism" and onto the "ground of society." He was having to deal for the first time with the split within the army of fighters for freedom which up to then he had so carefully avoided. In the same article he wrote: "Marhaenist nationalism rejects every bourgeois measure that might bring about the ruin of society." [74]

But whoever wished to equate this with a declaration of war against Indonesia's own bourgeoisie was soon to learn better from Sukarno himself. Shortly after the article appeared on November 26, 1932, Sukarno declared in Jogjakarta, the center of Javanese aristocracy, that the Partai Indonesia wanted no class struggle, it asked only that everyone—whether intellectual or not, whether high-born or low—unite in the cause of freedom. [75]

Sukarno may himself have felt that a basic declaration had

[72] DBR, p. 174.   [73] *Ibid.*, pp. 174f.

[74] *Ibid.*, p. 175: "Nasionalisme Marhaen menolak tiap tindak burdjuisme jang mendjadi sebabnja kepintjangan masjarakat itu."

[75] IPO 1932, No. 48, p. 354.

become necessary, and he now provided one in an article, "Indigenous Capitalism?" [76] After a brief Marxist analysis of capitalism, which necessarily led, he asserted, to the pauperization of the masses and to worldwide ruin, and which must therefore be rejected "by every man with logical principles," he posed the rhetorical question of whether indigenous capitalism was also to be rejected if it could be of use in the fight against imperialism. The answer promptly followed: "With conviction . . . I answer yes, we must also reject capitalism in our own people. We must be against an 'ism' that contributes to the pauperization of the Marhaens." [77]

But Sukarno was just as firmly opposed to the belief that the rejection of capitalism must be pushed to its logical conclusion even during the struggle for independence:

Does this mean that we are to be hostile to every well-to-do Indonesian? Not at all. We struggle not against the people but against the system. And not every well-to-do person engages in capitalism. Not every well-to-do person is rich because he has exploited other persons. Not every well-to-do person avails himself of means of production such as I have just explained in brief. . . . And not every well-to-do person follows or espouses the ideology of capitalism, the spirit, the thought of capitalism. In short, not every well-to-do person is a general, a sergeant, or a soldier of capitalism!

And finally, do our principles mean that we must emphasize the class struggle? By no means! We nationalists put our emphasis on the national struggle.[78]

From this argument it is clear that Sukarno would greatly have preferred to leave out the class struggle altogether. But since a just social order could not otherwise be achieved, he put off the social-revolutionary aspect of Socio-nationalism until after the "bourgeois-revolutionary" stage ended, with the win-

[76] "Kapitalisme bangsa sendiri?" in *Fikiran Rakjat,* end of November and beginning of December 1932 (IPO 1932, No. 49, p. 368; reprinted in DBR, pp. 181ff.).

[77] *Ibid.,* p. 182: "Dengan tertentu disini saja mendjawab: Ja, kita harus djuga anti kepada kapitalisme bangsa sendiri itu! Kita harus djuga anti isme jang ikut menjengsarakan Marhaen itu."

[78] *Ibid.,* p. 182f.

ning of independence. Sukarno at that time liked to speak of independence as a "golden bridge." Before this "golden bridge" had been attained, the Marhaens were to be concerned only that the command of the movement did not slip from their hands. But the united front, the race struggle, had precedence over the class struggle.

Once the "golden bridge" had been crossed, the way would open out in two directions: one leading to a world of happiness and well-being for the Marhaens, to a classless Marhaenist society, the other to a world of misery and tears. "Woe to you, Marhaens, if the chariot of victory should take the second way, if it should roll into a world of Indonesian capitalism and of an Indonesian bourgeoisie! So be vigilant, Marhaens! Take care to hold fast the reins of the chariot of victory in your hands." [79]

Once the "golden bridge" had been crossed, the time would have come for the social-revolutionary struggle. Then the building of a just social order could begin. And this could be achieved only once capitalism had finally been driven out. Sukarno had held fast with astonishing consistency to the position he had taken in 1921, when he proposed that the Sarekat Islam, once the "proper condition" had been arrived at, should fight on for the destruction of capitalism. [80] The goal of this struggle was what he now called "Socio-democracy," a system that did not serve the interest of minorities, as in his opinion parliamentary democracy did, but rather one "that seeks an order both political *and* economic, an order both of land *and* of livelihood. Socio-democracy is democracy both political *and* economic." [81]

Once again Sukarno was motivated by the striving for order. In the nationalist phase, the idea of a return to oneself could be seen as a positive element as opposed to the negative rejection of Western nationalism and the Western voting system. Similarly, there could be set against the deprecation of parliamentary democracy the wish for that true order which, in the Javanese view, was threatened with destruction not simply by

---

[79] Cf. *Mentjapai Indonesia Merdeka* [Toward Indonesian Independence], a brochure published March 1933; republished, Djakarta, 1959; reprinted in DBR, pp. 257–325. The citation is from DBR, p. 315.

[80] See "Sukarno's Early Political Views," in Chapter II, above.

[81] DBR, p. 175. Sukarno's italics.

the foreigners but by their political system as well. Thus parliamentary democracy was likewise rejected because it was not Indonesian but foreign, because it aimed not toward synthesis but toward decisions. Sukarno favored instead a solution such as he had hit upon, for example, for the advisory council of the PPPKI, in which, because of the requirement of Mufakat, all groups were equally represented.

Marhaenism and Marxism

Because of their Marxist ring, the ideas behind the Marhaenistic principles of "Socio-nationalism" and "Socio-democracy" call for an analysis of the Marxist content in Sukarno's Marhaenism.

"Every Indonesian who practices Marhaenism is a Marhaenist": so went the last of nine theses on Marhaen and Marhaenism that were advanced at a congress of the Partai Indonesia in July 1933, and which not long afterward were set forth and elaborated by Sukarno.[82] Thus every Indonesian was "Marhaenist"

---

[82] Published in *Fikiran Rakjat* under the title "Marhaen dan Proletar [Marhaen and Proletarian]," with a comment by Sukarno, in July 1933; reprinted in DBR, pp. 253ff. The significant nine theses of the Partindo are reproduced here word for word:

(1) Marhaenism, that is Socio-nationalism and Socio-democracy.

(2) Marhaen, that is the Indonesian proletarian, the poor Indonesian peasant, and other Indonesians who are poor.

(3) Partindo uses the word Marhaen and not Proletarian because the term Proletarian is already included in the term Marhaen and because the word Proletarian can also mean that the peasants and other poor people are not included.

(4) Because Partindo is convinced that other poor Indonesians also must become participants in the struggle for independence, it uses the word Marhaen.

(5) In the struggle of the Marhaens—the Partindo is convinced of this—the proletarians take over the most important part.

(6) Marhaenism is the principle, calling for a social structure and order that serves the Marhaens in every respect.

(7) Marhaenism is also the method of struggle in order to achieve this social structure and order, and therefore it must be revolutionary.

(8) Marhaenism thus is a method of struggle as well as a principle, which has as its goal to drive out every kind of capitalism and imperialism.

(9) Every Indonesian who practices Marhaenism is Marhaenist.

who was prepared to cooperate in building a just social order. In this way not only was the idea of class struggle avoided, but also individuals were left free to cooperate in the struggle of the poor and oppressed for a better future, whatever their social and economic position; this was true even for the propertied class. The article just cited on the question of indigenous capitalism had observed, instructively enough, that "not every well-to-do person follows or espouses the ideology of capitalism." Thus it was the option of every Indonesian to decide for himself what he would do. His material means were overlooked, and the question of where he stood took on an ethical character.

But this thinking was not only not Marxist, it was plainly anti-Marxist. The followers of Marx, no matter how they interpreted his teaching, made no attempt to do away with the basic assumption that "it is not the consciousness of men that determines their existence; rather, the existence determines the consciousness." But with this realization, as Lenin put it, "the search for motivating ideas in human history was at an end." [83]

It could already be observed during the nationalist phase that Sukarno did not know how to deal with the materialistic foundation of Marxism. By his arbitrary separation of speculative philosophical materialism from historical materialism, he had been able to restore a God-creator in place of matter, and had thereby transgressed a no less hallowed dogma. F. Engels, for example, had written in his *Ludwig Feuerbach:*

Which is primary, spirit or nature? . . . The answers the philosophers gave to this question split them into two major camps. Those who asserted the primacy of spirit over nature, and thus ultimately took for granted, in one form or another, the creation of the world, made up the camp of idealism. The others, who regarded nature as primary, belong to the various schools of materialism.[84]

Sukarno belonged to none of the various schools of materialism. From the start, no matter how Marxist his behavior often was, he had belonged in the idealist camp—as he did even now,

[83] Lenin, *Karl Marx* (1914); cited here from the Dutch edition (1933), p. 16.

[84] Marx and Engels, *Selected Works* (Moscow, 1958), Vol. II, p. 370.

in believing that his Marhaenist nationalism had both feet squarely grounded in society.

Sukarno's driving force was the idea of unity as it had been expressed in Javanese philosophy for centuries. It allowed him again and again to work toward a synthesis of everything that could be integrated with the indigenous order. It is this constant striving for synthesis that identifies Sukarno as an idealist. Marx, for example, hated synthesis: "When Aristotle denounces synthesis as the basis of all error, he is altogether correct," he wrote in an essay during his student days.[85]

Thus, whereas Marxist theory developed on the basis of exact antitheses, Sukarno held fast to his synthesis, even at a time when he felt especially close to Marxism. The word "Marhaen" itself offers the best proof of this. In the third thesis it was stated that Partindo used the word "Marhaen" and not "proletarian" because proletarians were included under the former "and because the word 'proletarian' could also mean that the peasants and other poor *are not included.*"[86]

That he thus went beyond Marxism, Sukarno was fully aware. But he believed he could nevertheless rely on the prophecies of Marxism. In his commentary he referred especially to the fifth thesis, that the proletariat must play the leading part in the struggle of the Marhaens: "This is what I call modern, this is what is essential. Because the proletariat at present are more up to date in their thinking, they as a class are more directly affected by capitalism. . . . Their opposition has greater value, their worth as fighters is greater than that of all other groups."[87] But fighting ability was not the only thing that interested Sukarno; there was still another reason for the central position of the proletariat among the Marhaens: "They [the proletariat] . . . are, according to Marx, a 'social necessity,' and the victory of their ideology later is a 'historical necessity,' a historical must. . . . Well, if this teaching of Marx is correct, the fifth of the nine theses is also correct."[88] In other words, with the thesis

[85] Blumenberg, *Karl Marx in Selbstzeugnissen,* in Rowohlts Monographien, No. 76 (1962), p. 21.

[86] See note 82 (3), above. Italics added.   [87] DBR, p. 254.

[88] *Ibid.,* p. 255.

that the workers had the major role in the struggle of the Marhaens, Sukarno believed he also had a claim to the victory foretold by Marx. For him the central position of the proletariat in the struggle of the Marhaens was a magical formula, which as the fifth of nine points stood exactly at mid-point, and as a result its magical function was further enhanced.

Marxism, for Sukarno, gave not only proof of the depravity of capitalism and of imperialism but also hope for their defeat. For this reason he believed in its prophecies: he believed in the irreconcilable antithesis between capital and labor, "because by reason of this antithesis, the fate of the workers lies in the hands of the workers themselves." [89] He believed in dialectic, for "dialectic requires that capital, at one pole, be overcome by labor, at the other." [90] He shifted these prophecies to the Indonesian freedom movement, for this was no mere "construction" but rather a product of society, of nature itself, and therefore invincible:

As though it possessed secret powers, as though it had an elixir of life, as though it were under the influence of the spells of Pantjasana and Tjondobirowo, . . . even so the movement, which upholds nature and is upheld by it, cannot be overcome; rather, it grows more and more overwhelming. Like nature itself, it cannot not, it *must* achieve its goal! [91]

For Sukarno, Marxism was the assurance of victory; accordingly, it assumed the central position in his Marhaenism. But it was only one element of Marhaenism; around it were gathered other elements—nationalism, belief in Allah, the struggle for total unity—and each of these other ideas was basically anti-Marxist. For Sukarno, however, this was no obstacle, since in the term Marhaenism he had found a new synthesis, just as he

[89] See the article "Bolehkah sarekat sekerdja berpolitik? [Ought Labor Unions to Be Politically Active?]" (DBR, p. 233): "Bahwa karena adanja antitese ini, nasib kaum buruh adalah didalam genggaman kaum buruh sendiri."

[90] *Ibid.*, p. 235: "Dialektikpun memestikan bahwa kutub modal nanti dikalahkan oleh kutub kerdja."

[91] "Mentjapai Indonesia Merdeka," DBR, p. 280. Sukarno's italics.

had previously found it in "Eastern nationalism," which was as broad as the air that gave all creatures room to live.

In March 1933, writing on the fiftieth anniversary of the death of Karl Marx, he expressed the synthesis as follows: "Nationalism in the Eastern world has been wed to Marxism; it has become a new nationalism. . . . It is this new nationalism that now lives among the Marhaens of Indonesia." [92]

The Marhaenist Party

Sukarno saw in a party with strict discipline, whose top leadership would be granted near-dictatorial powers, the appropriate instrument for binding together the divergent elements included under the concept of Marhaenism. Sjahrir and Hatta both favored genuine democracy within the party; the charge that the party leadership had acted "dictatorially" in dissolving the old PNI had been one of the reasons for founding the PNI-Baru. Sjahrir had also declared at that time: "The spirit of a mass party can only be democratic. No other spirit may be active in the party, and we must be on our guard, so that no other spirit can make its way into the party, otherwise the party spirit is lost." [93]

Even the communist Tan Malaka had insisted on democracy within the party, and on the yielding of the minority in controversial questions.[94] Sukarno, on the other hand, asserted:

At its core the party may not be democratic. . . . The democracy that is permitted at the core of the vanguard party is no ordinary democracy. Abroad, the democracy of the vanguard party goes by the name of democratic centralism: a democracy which gives the top leadership the power to punish every deviation, to expel any member or any section of the party that may endanger the struggle of the masses.[95]

Thus Sukarno's ideal was an all-powerful top party leadership ("Putjuk Pimpinan"), which could decide what was Marhaenist

---

[92] "Memperingati 50 tahun wafatnja Karl Marx [In Remembrance of the 50th Anniversary of the Death of Karl Marx]," DBR, pp. 220f.

[93] *Pikiran,* p. 8.　　[94] Tan Malaka, *Massa-Actie,* p. 51.

[95] "Mentjapai Indonesia Merdeka," DBR, pp. 305f.

and what was not. At the same time he added that he did not want the centralism of a dictator, although he gave no more precise explanation of just what he understood by "top leadership." The term could be interpreted in such a way that this centralism left the door open to a dictatorship of the party.

But Sukarno was not a man to carry strict party leadership to its logical conclusion, as Lenin had done after the break with the Mensheviks, and to build for himself a power apparatus which would grasp the reins at the critical hour. Although he had never given up the dream of one single party, which would first win freedom and later bring about Socio-democracy, again and again the revolutionary élan had been extinguished by his passion for seeing as many groups as possible represented in the party.

And so it was, once again, in the Marhaenist phase. Sukarno called for democratic centralism so that his Marhaenist party—which nevertheless every Indonesian who considered himself a Marhaenist could join—would be able to function. Whereas Lenin had used centralism to purge his party and to free it from all elements that might hinder its course,[96] Sukarno began by using it to enlarge his party, and thus concerned himself especially with the very groups Lenin had expelled first, the sympathizing fellow-travelers. Thus over and over again he was finally forced to use the centralized leadership to arrive at a settlement.

And thus Sukarno's referring to discipline as a vital principle of the vanguard party ("Partai Pelopor") was more the wish-fulfillment of a leader repeatedly disappointed by his comrades' lack of discipline than a description of actual conditions in the Partai Indonesia. Such remarks as that "a discipline hard as steel, which mercilessly penalizes every member who dares to offend against it, is one of the vital principles of the vanguard party" had a radical sound and were radical in theory; in practice, however, they were simply not feasible because of the heterogeneous structure of the party. Sukarno might succeed in forming a few "shock troops" among the youth, who had sworn

[96] Cf. G. v. Rauch, *Geschichte des bolschewistischen Russland* (1963), pp. 25ff.

themselves to an unconditional obedience [97]—but in general the radicalization was limited to stirring up an atmosphere of Holy War among the masses.

This was Sukarno's style, and he was convinced that by constant propagandizing about the people's misery, the party could gradually arouse dissatisfaction and stimulate a readiness for struggle among the people. That a radicalization of the people could be achieved through agitation alone was Sukarno's own private opinion; but once again he had at hand an authority who gave sanction to his style of leadership in the struggle. He quoted Liebknecht: "Pauperization becomes an occasion of radicalizing the masses, *but only if* the masses do not passively endure the growing pauperization." [98] Therefore, by means of propaganda and of drawing attention to suffering so as to set the Bandjir of the masses in motion, radicalization was possible; Liebknecht had said so—except that Liebknecht had not said so. In a footnote, Sukarno cited the German text: "Pauperization becomes an occasion of radicalizing the masses, *but only because* the masses do not passively endure the growing pauperization." [99] What was causal for Liebknecht, for Sukarno was conditional. Thus he could continue, "For this reason with the suffering that now exists the vanguard party can already . . . transform the entire mass into a surging sea of radicalism." [100]

Sukarno's careless handling of evidence has already been indicated, and it has been emphasized that at bottom he was concerned only with substantiating his own opinion.[101] Therefore it is useless to ask whether he would have changed his party's tactics if he had correctly understood what Liebknecht was saying. If Sukarno had discovered his error, he would have been

[97] "Colijn-Nota," *loc. cit.,* pp. 25f.

[98] In "Mentjapai Indonesia Merdeka," DBR, pp. 311f. The words in italics are "Tetapi hanja kalau."

[99] *Ibid.,* p. 312. Italics added. The German original reads: "Die Verelendung wird zu einer Ursache der Radikalisierung der Massen, aber nur deshalb, weil die Massen die wachsende Verelendung nicht passiv ertragen."

[100] *Ibid.*

[101] See "The Struggle for the Antithesis," in Chapter III, above, on his misunderstanding of Kautsky.

able to find another authority who advocated turning to the masses.

Besides, Sukarno was drawn toward the masses. To renounce open display for the quiet training of a revolutionary cadre, as Sjahrir and Hatta (who had returned to Indonesia in the summer of 1932) had begun to do in the PNI-Baru, had little attraction for Sukarno. He needed the applause of the masses for self-assurance; he needed the atmosphere of a crusade, since for him the idea that the people still yielded apathetically to their fate was unendurable. And so he chose to lead the Marhaenist party into the field of agitation. Because its radicalism was thus inevitably drained away in bold speeches, instead of a "surging sea of radicalism" it only stirred up passions that were soon to ebb.

Bharata Judha (Part Two)—
the War That Recognizes No Truce

Even in the midst of the debate with Sjahrir, Sukarno had announced that he was turning once again to the masses. In April 1932, when his future was discussed in the press, a letter he wrote to the editor of *Bintang Timur* recalled his statement, "Bung Karno is too much a man of action to trust in theory alone." [102] And in August 1932 he declared to the Indonesian Marhaens, with no less self-consciousness, that he had joined Partindo so that "now it can be seen where Bung Karno stands." [103]

Once again Sukarno drew the masses into the struggle. Within one year, between August 1932 and August 1933, 20,000 members were to flock to the Partindo; whereas in the same period, the membership of the party of the "Europeans," Sjahrir and Hatta, stood at 1,000 members, a figure it had already reached before Sukarno's release from prison.[104]

[102] IPO, No. 13, pp. 192f.

[103] DBR, pp. 169: "Kini orang 'bisa melihat dimana Bung Karno duduk.'"

[104] The figures on membership are from J. Th. Petrus Blumberger, *Politieke partijen en stroomingen in Nederlandsch-Indië* (1934), pp. 22f. That the masses had behaved circumspectly up to the time of Sukarno's

In November 1932 an event took place in the ranks of the PNI-Baru that moved Sukarno once more to expound in detail his theory of struggle. At that time Mohammed Hatta, who had taken over the chairmanship of the PNI-Baru after his return to Indonesia in the summer of 1932, was invited to become a candidate for the Dutch parliament from the Onafhankelijke Socialistische Partij in Holland, and he accepted without hesitation.

This provoked a great sensation in Indonesian nationalist circles [105] for next to Sukarno Hatta was by reputation the noncooperator par excellence. For years Hatta had set forth the guiding principles of noncooperation in *Indonesia Merdeka,* providing Sukarno—who had already become acquainted with the idea through Tjokroaminoto and the NIP—with the theoretical weapons for his campaign.[106] And now Hatta had declared himself ready to sit down in a parliament with the oppressors!

After the event became public, the Partindo distributed a leaflet with the December 10, 1932, edition of *Persatuan Indonesia,* warning the Indonesian people against Hatta, who had now been unmasked.[107] Although Sukarno later publicly dissociated himself from this pamphlet, it raised an issue between the parties of the "Indonesians" and of the "Europeans," on which as a matter of principle he believed he could not maintain silence. He now saw suddenly endangered the antithesis, the unbridgeable antagonism between Sinis and Sanas, from which for years he had derived his confidence of victory, since of course victory was promised to the party of the oppressed. Again he took refuge in the dialectic method:

It is this opposition of interests which leads to the conviction that Indonesia Merdeka could not be achieved if we did not carry out

---

reappearance in the movement is evident from the report to the Governor General, "Inlandsche beweging op Java" by Kieviet de Jonge, November 13, 1931. See *Politieke Mededeeling* II, November 18, 1931, in the Gobee collection.

[105] Cf. IPO 1932, No. 50, pp. 387ff.; No. 52, pp. 419ff.

[106] Sukarno repeatedly referred to articles written by Hatta in *Indonesia Merdeka* (most of which appear in M. Hatta, *Verspreide Geschriften*).

[107] IPO 1932, No. 50, p. 388.

the policy of noncooperation. . . . Noncooperation is a living principle; it means we are not to work together *with the masters in any area of politics,* but rather conduct *a war with the masters that recognizes no truce.*[108]

Hatta had disavowed this war that recognized no truce. He had at first even brushed aside protests with the statement that in principle noncooperation was not antiparliamentarianism—which amounted to anarchy. Sukarno objected that it would be anarchy to refuse a seat in one's own parliament, but not to avoid the parliament of the oppressors. He referred to the Sinn Fein movement in Ireland, which had likewise boycotted the English parliament and—as the name indicated—put Sinn Fein ("we ourselves") into the foreground.[109]

Hatta replied that Westminster was not The Hague and Ireland was not Indonesia. Ireland had not been a colony but rather a part of the kingdom of England. The Irish representatives had been elected by the Irish people themselves, but since in Westminster they were always voted down, they had returned to their homeland and made "Sinn Fein" their slogan. They had thus been driven to this step by considerations of *Realpolitik.* Thus the "Irish kris" that Sukarno had hurled came back at him like a boomerang.[110]

In an attempt to fend off the returning kris, Sukarno worked himself into a totally irrational position. Without dealing at all with Hatta's main argument, on the differing conditions in Ireland and Indonesia, Sukarno harped on the "positive force" of the Sinn Fein in bringing about the preconditions for a life of freedom. He quoted Sir Arthur Griffith, the father of the Sinn Fein movement, who [he said] had issued the summons: Forget the English people, work as if there were no English people, do not live in expectation of Great Britain's kindness, which does

[108] See the article, "Sekali lagi tentang Sosio-Nasionalisme dan Sosio-Demokrasi [Once Again Socio-Nationalism and Socio-Democracy]" (IPO 1932, No. 51, p. 400; DBR, pp. 187ff., esp. 189f.). Emphasis in original.

[109] DBR, pp. 189f.

[110] Hatta's reply is reprinted in Sukarno's article, "Djawab saja pada saudara Mohammed Hatta [My Reply to Comrade Mohammed Hatta]," from early 1933 (DBR, pp. 207ff.).

not exist, but believe in your own selves. Forge the weapons of the spirit, the only weapons that can break the shackles of your slavery. All this Hatta had "deliberately concealed" when he described the Sinn Fein movement "as mere *Realpolitik.*" But Hatta of late had been generally very much taken with *Realpolitik.*[111]

Sukarno had strayed so far from reality that he could make *Realpolitik* the grounds of reproach against Hatta. But through Hatta's behavior over the question of candidacy for the Dutch parliament, the difference between the "Europeans" and the "Indonesians" was once more glaringly exposed.

The noncooperation of the PNI-Baru was not a war that recognized no truce. It was much more an expression of confidence that the Dutch government would give the nationalists scope for the evolutionary development of their people. Hatta had regarded the proposed candidacy for the Dutch parliament as an honor; after having spent more than a decade in Holland, he could no longer regard the Dutch as unwanted outsiders. He was, along with Sjahrir and all the members of his PNI-Baru, a fervent nationalist, but like Sjahrir he was also "a Dutchman at heart, in the sense that he looked on the colonial masters not really as a foreign and hostile element but rather in about the same way a left-wing socialist regarded the Dutch government, with the unconscious assumption of many common norms."

This admirable characterization, which is Sjahrir's,[112] and which might also have been applied to himself as well as to most members of the PNI-Baru, once more brings into focus the difference from those who assumed no similar norms, the propagandists of the war that recognized no truce. Sukarno and his followers sensed the foreign and hostile element most deeply. They hoped for help from abroad because they expected none from the colonial power, and they clung to the principles which promised that it would some day arrive—such as the Marxist antithesis, which was most clearly expressed in noncooperation.

This was what Sukarno attempted to make clear to Hatta: "Noncooperation is not only struggle, it is also a principle of that struggle: and to this principle of that struggle we must

[111] *Ibid.,* p. 210.   [112] Sjahrazad, *Overpeinzingen,* p. 173.

adhere as closely as possible." [113] In his group, as Sjahrir later put it, noncooperation was "cultivated as a religion." [114]

This was demonstrated once more at the beginning of 1933, shortly after the dispute with Hatta. Because of the reproach made public in the dispute, that the method of provocative noncooperation was futile, Sukarno felt compelled to vindicate himself.

In an article significantly titled "Cannot Noncooperation Bring About Any Mass Action and Consolidation of Power?",[115] he made an unmistakable effort to conjure up the power of the "sacred principle." After a swipe at Gandhi, whom he again accused (as at the end of 1928) of not drawing upon the spirit of radicalism that animated noncooperation, Sukarno contrasted the Indonesian variant of noncooperation with the Indian:

Our noncooperation is not based on belief in the Ahimsa, on the teaching, "Do not resist evil." . . . Our noncooperation . . . entails activity and radicalism—radicalism of spirit, thought, and action, radicalism in every attitude, external as well as internal. This radicalism rejects all passivity, does not accept an attitude of "Keep still, make no attacks," but demands a militant posture. We may not assume the attitude of "Keep still, make no attacks"; we must leave home behind, must be on our way, so that we may launch the attack on all the enemy centers!

This was the call to Djihad, to the holy war, which no longer recognized any *Realpolitik*. Whoever within the ranks began to have doubts was unmasked as an apostate or considered a traitor.[116]

[113] DBR, p. 213: "Perkara non-kooperasi bukanlah perkara perdjuangan sahadja, perkara non-kooperasi adalah djuga perkara azas perdjuangan. Azas perdjuangan inilah jang harus kita pegang teguh sebisa-bisanja."

[114] *Overpeinzingen,* p. 178.

[115] DBR, pp. 193ff.: "Non-cooperation tidak bisa mendatangkan massa-aksi dan machtvorming?"

[116] Thus, for example, the Partindo forbade its members to read the newspapers of the PNI-Baru (see Hatta's complaint in *Daulat Rakjat,* February 1, 1933; IPO 1933, No. 7, p. 105); a respected editor received a threatening letter when he criticized Sukarno (IPO 1933, No. 47, p. 738); and so on.

"Leaving home behind" for the "war that recognizes no truce" was first seriously implemented in February 1933, after a long period of theoretical disputes. At seventeen different places in Central Java alone, Sukarno staged great rallies in which, according to a pamphlet issued at that time, 89,000 persons were "aroused." [117]

Or were they? Once more Sukarno had to prove himself in writing, for never before had doubts concerning his kind of campaign been more evident than this time around. Of the seventeen rallies only four—less than 25 per cent—ended in a normal way. All the others were broken up by the police either before or during the speeches, and then not even because of radical pronouncements such as could be found in Sukarno's essays at the time; no, even a harmless statement from him was enough to cause the guardians of order to step in and dissolve the meeting. Thus, for example, at Tjilatjap: "The Partindo wishes to enlighten the people"; at Kebumen: "The people must be one like Rama's army of monkeys"; at Ambarawa: "Let your spirit catch fire, Marhaens, so that we may be free"; at Semarang: "The Partindo is an enemy of capitalism and imperialism"; at Batang: "Indonesia can be free if the Marhaens are of one mind." [118]

This capricious intervention by the police showed how oppressively narrow a sphere of action was permitted Sukarno by the new master in the land, Governor General de Jonge, as compared to Governor General de Graeff. In his speeches there was no trace of good will toward the nationalists. In his view, on the contrary, it was deplorable that certain persons in the country had made the economic crisis an occasion for disturbing public order and chasing after political concepts; the government for its part therefore had to intervene occasionally—this was all he had to say of the nationalist movement when he spoke before the Volksraad in June 1933. [119]

But in Holland the man entrusted just then with forming a

[117] See the foreword to *Mentjapai Indonesia Merdeka* (also reprinted in DBR, p. 257).

[118] Cited from *Adil,* March 6, 1933 (IPO 1933, No. 19, p. 148).

[119] *De Locomotief,* June 15, 1933.

government was H. Colijn, who years earlier had declared unremitting war on the Indonesian movement. The demand made in 1928 by his much-quoted book—"So that there can be no misunderstandings, we should intervene immediately and unequivocally when the bounds of the permissible are exceeded" [120]—had given rise in Indonesian circles to references to an ultracolonial or "Colijnial" policy. Now the old fears were reawakened, and there was new alarm about the future of the movement.[121] But for Sukarno, to whom Colijn had already given thorough attention during a visit to Indonesia in 1928—in fact, the call for immediate intervention had been meant for him [122]—there could be no retreat.

Although in June 1933 a government decree had already forbidden membership in the Partindo or the PNI-Baru to all public employees, under penalty of dismissal,[123] and although after Colijn's election as Prime Minister the police began to intervene even more ruthlessly at its meetings,[124] the Partindo at its congress in July 1933 resolved to continue the Djihad. A new grand tour, this time in East Java, was to be launched in August, and on a certain day "simultaneous action" was to be taken by all branches.[125] But in fact this was never to occur.

On the night of August 1, 1933, after having been free for exactly nineteen months, Sukarno was again arrested. From the beginning there was no doubt that this time exile was in store for him.[126]

A few weeks later Colijn, who had temporarily taken over the

[120] H. Colijn, *Koloniale vraagstukken*, p. 34.

[121] Cf. IPO 1928, No. 38, p. 574; No. 40, p. 3; No. 41, p. 33; also IPO 1933, No. 24, pp. 367ff.; No. 25, pp. 383ff.

[122] For example, in the reference cited here, Colijn objected to "the noise of cocks that believe they can make the sun rise with their crowing" —a reference to Sukarno's frequently used metaphor, "The day does not dawn because the rooster crows, but the rooster crows because the day is dawning." See, for example, SIM, No. 2 (January 1928); also DBR, p. 41. For further statements by Colijn on Sukarno, see *Vraagstukken*, pp. 26ff.

[123] IPO 1933, No. 27, p. 415.   [124] *Ibid.*, No. 30, pp. 462f.

[125] IPO 1933, No. 29, pp. 455f.

[126] See the comment in IPO 1933, Nos. 31, 33. For more on Sukarno's arrest, see *De Locomotief*, August 1, 2, and 3, 1933.

office of Minister for the Colonies along with the premiership, explained to the Dutch parliament, in answer to a question on what had led to the arrest, that immediately after his release Sukarno had once again thrust himself forward "in a provocative manner." After the attempt at unification had failed, he had succeeded more and more in infecting the Partai Indonesia with his "revolutionary ideas," and this infection had spread to other parties. Thus Sukarno had engaged in "activity marked by defiance," and finally had even begun training "shock troops" who had to take a vow of unquestioning obedience to the party leadership. Also, he had repeatedly violated press regulations.

The authorities had taken every opportunity to make clear to Sukarno "that this performance could not go on any longer and that, if he persisted, he would inevitably come to grief. Despite all these warnings, however, he did not subject himself to even the slightest moderation." When the "simultaneous action" was planned, they had struck at last.[127]

The chronological link between Colijn's premiership and Sukarno's arrest cannot be ignored. The grounds for arrest cited by Colijn were deliberately played up; no disturbances were to be expected—there were no rumors as in 1929; it could not be said in 1933 that Sukarno had any great influence on other parties; and finally, Sukarno had displayed an "activity marked by defiance" ever since 1926. But for Colijn—as for Sukarno, his opposite number—objectively valid grounds were superfluous, since the verdict had been arrived at beforehand. For Colijn it was certain "that the performance could not go on any longer," and this opinion was undoubtedly shared by the incumbent Governor General de Jonge.

Thus to Sukarno, who had drawn no lessons from the experiences of the nationalist phase and could not decide upon a new style in leading the struggle, it had already been demonstrated in the Marhaenist phase that in the "war that recognized no truce," the provocative noncooperation he proposed had not the slightest hope of success. The torch he held out did not show the way out of the darkness—as he had proclaimed after his return

[127] "Colijn Nota," autumn 1933, in *Handelingen der Staten General, Tweede Kamer,* 1933–34, II, Aanhangsel, pp. 25f.

from prison in 1932—but only shed light on himself, the bearer of the torch. Thus his fame as the hero of the freedom movement had continued to grow despite the obvious failure of the attempt at unification; the hope of the masses was fixed on him because he was the only one who knew how to give them hope.

The Fall of an Idol

End of the Myth of Noncooperation

Sukarno had already spent more than three months in prison when the inconceivable occurred. Like a bolt from the blue, the news rocked the movement that the Dewa, the idol of the non-cooperators, had renounced the principle of noncoopera-tion.[128] No one wanted to believe it, but the executive committee of Partindo had to acknowledge that Sukarno, in a letter from prison, had announced his resignation from the party, because he no longer agreed with its principles.[129] From the entire Indonesian press, both right and left, there now arose a cry of indignation, which made clear for the first time the regard in which Sukarno had come to be held by everyone, whether or not they agreed with him politically.[130] Up until then

he had been the motor, the driving force of the left-oriented movement; it was he above all others who had sowed the spirit of nationalism in all classes of the people and in all parts of the land. It was he who had demolished the crumbling walls that divided the various groups of the people from one another: Javanese, Sumatran, Ambonese, Menadonese, etc., Marhaens and nobles greeted him as their champion. For them he was Bung Karno and nothing more. They did not see his leftist tendencies, they saw in him only the prophet of freedom. In him was the rallying point of all the feelings and longings that ruled in the hearts of the Indonesians.

This estimate was written not by a partisan of Sukarno but rather by the cooperation-minded Dr. Sutomo.[131] Ungrudg-

[128] Thus, for example, *Pemandangan,* November 21, 1933 (IPO 1933, No. 47, p. 738).

[129] IPO 1933, No. 47, p. 733.

[130] Cf. the detailed comments in IPO 1933, No. 47, pp. 735–43; No. 48, pp. 749–53; No. 49, pp. 765–70; No. 50, pp. 781–87.

[131] In *Suara Umum* (his newspaper), February 20, 1934 (see IPO 1934, No. 9, p. 132).

ingly he acknowledged Sukarno's merits, despite having been continually overshadowed by him as he carried on so much quiet, constructive work. To be sure, Sutomo's description referred only to the period up to Sukarno's release from prison, and thus only to the nationalist phase of Sukarno's activity. Later, according to Sutomo, it became evident that he had not risen to the great task, that he was "inwardly sick," and some of his admirers had begun to have doubts and had turned away from him.[132]

Those who had merely believed in Sukarno's lucky star, who had once supposed that "one on whom God's blessing falls will surely bring about a miracle" [133] had begun to have their doubts. When it became clear that Sukarno had not brought about the unification of the nationalists, in such circles the doubts and the inner estrangement began, and they hit upon the explanation that Sukarno had come out of prison a "sick man." That they had conjured up for themselves a false picture of Sukarno's accomplishment before his arrest, that the split which took place during Sukarno's imprisonment had been the result of a nationalist phase that had already become a myth—of such things, in these circles that measured greatness in terms of obvious success, no one was aware.

But those who—as Sukarno's old friend and teacher, Tjipto Mangunkusumo, wrote in a letter from exile, after Sukarno's release from prison—"burned incense before him and strewed flowers in his path," [134] not only believed in Sukarno's lucky star; more than that they saw in him the Ratu Adil who had vowed to lead them to the promised land. They carried pictures of him as Djimats,[135] wrote threatening letters whenever their Dewa, even with the best intentions, was criticized,[136] and so revered Sukarno that Hatta in the summer of 1932 was led to remark that the deification of leaders could only hurt the movement.[137] For these followers, even after Sukarno's release from prison, there was no doubt and no inner estrangement; Sukarno was for them indeed "the rallying point of all the feelings and

[132] *Ibid.*   [133] IPO 1932, No. 1, p. 66.
[134] IPO 1934, No. 3, pp. 37f.   [135] IPO 1933, No. 50, p. 783.
[136] IPO 1933, No. 47, p. 738.   [137] IPO 1932, No. 40, p. 232.

longings" that stirred their hearts. For them the news that Sukarno had renounced the sacred principle of noncooperation
was more than the abandonment of an illusion. For them a
world was in ruins, since—to use the word with which *Persatuan Indonesia,* long Sukarno's own newspaper, headed its
editorial on November 30, 1933—the Impossible had occurred.[138]

Was it any wonder that schoolchildren now tore down Sukarno's picture from the wall with sticks, that adults, in their
anger over what had happened, ripped up their cherished por-
traits of Sukarno? [139] Was it any wonder that the "Hosanna" of
the Indonesia Raya Congress (in January 1932) was now followed by a "Crucify him" such as had never before been heard
in the Indonesian movement? Even those who had had no part
in the worship of Sukarno, but who had warned against idolizing him, felt themselves betrayed. Hatta wrote of Sukarno at
this time:

It was none but he who forced the Partindo onto the field of agitation and implacable demonstrations, whose aftermath must now be
borne by the entire leftist movement. . . . It was not yet ten
months since Sukarno had beaten his breast and cried out that noncooperation excluded cooperation with the masters in every field,
and had called for unremitting struggle. Now he was the first to
give in. It was a Sukarnoist tragedy, without precedent in the history of the world.[140]

Was it really that? Yes, if Sukarno had apologized to the colonial government, as Hatta said he had,[141] he could prove a
"lack of character." But was the abandonment of the principle
of noncooperation proof that Sukarno was "no revolutionary
and still less a radical," as Hatta, when he came to speak again of
the incident, believed he could establish? [142]

Hatta, the realist who condemned iconoclasm as childish, and

[138] IPO 1933, No. 49, pp. 765f.

[139] *Ibid.,* No. 48, p. 752; also No. 50, pp. 781ff.

[140] *Daulat Rakjat,* November 30, 1933 (IPO 1933, No. 49, p. 767).

[141] This was confirmed by Hatta in a conversation with the author in
New York on September 13, 1968.

[142] IPO 1933, No. 50, pp. 782ff.

who insisted that no one must fall under the sway of anger and disappointment, was obviously not free of it himself when he declared, "The reasons for Sukarno's action are of no concern to the revolutionaries." [143] But those very reasons could have demonstrated that Sukarno was never more radical, never more revolutionary, than at the moment when he divorced himself from his own cherished principle. A sober reconstruction of events that were often overlooked by the polemics adds up to the following picture: [144] In the preliminary inquiry, Sukarno was interrogated about the purpose and aim of the planned mass action. As he had done before, during his trial Sukarno vigorously denied that he had intended to stir up a revolt. No one believed him. To the same question at a later interrogation, he again replied that he planned no revolt, and that if the government still chose not to believe him, he was ready to prove it through cooperation, even by sitting in the assembly.

This "conversion" on the part of Sukarno was at once reported in a note to the Governor General, and Sukarno brought his statement to its logical conclusion by announcing his withdrawal from the Partindo, on the grounds that he could no longer declare himself in agreement with the principles, direction, and activity of the movement, and by asking to be released as chairman of the party.

A few days later, while the reaction within the Indonesian movement was exploding with such vehemence, a new interrogation of Sukarno took place, one that went quite unnoticed by the public. He was allowed to answer questions with only a yes or no. Out of this interrogation, the *Locomotief* declared on the following day, "nothing came which lends credence to the recently reported conversion." [145] A "conversion" in the sense given publicity by the Dutch had thus not taken place. Sukarno had not become a friend of the Dutch. He had "converted" only from his cult of principle.

---

[143] *Ibid.*

[144] The account that follows is based on a comparison of Indonesian press comment in IPO and Dutch comment in *De Locomotief* during the fall of 1933.

[145] *De Locomotief,* November 24, 1933, p. 18.

What had driven Sukarno to this decision, which he so well knew would be unpopular? Here no more than a conjecture can be attempted. There are no new arguments that might shed light on this dark hour for Sukarno and that were not already known in 1933. There is only a certain distance in time from that passion-filled era.

Sukarno had always been—despite the radicalism he put on for show—essentially unstable. He felt sure of himself so long as he drew support from the jubilant masses and could feel himself one with the "will of the people." Whether this "will" really existed or was first suggested to the people by Sukarno was at bottom of no importance. Dr. Sutomo's enthusiastic estimate convincingly illustrates how Sukarno during the nationalist phase could justly regard himself as spokesman of the "whole people" because of the sympathy he encountered in those of all classes. His nationalism "as broad as the air" offered everyone a basis for working together. Thanks to the absence of the communists from the political stage, there was no group that really opposed Sukarno's efforts toward unity.

Imprisonment was a severe test for Sukarno. He suffered from his solitude, even though he could work during the day and use the library in the evenings.[146] But he could take comfort from the sympathy of the people and from knowing that he was regarded by all as a hero and martyr. He still felt in unison with the people, and this kept up his confidence.

It was only after his release from prison, after the homage had evaporated, that Sukarno for the first time felt isolated. For the first time he was no longer considered the representative of the entire Indonesian people. He saw his magical weapon, his Nanggala, the drive toward unity by glossing over the existing differences, quite deliberately rejected by some of the nationalists and condemned in thinly veiled terms as harmful.

Sukarno now became unsure of himself, the more since this time he could not proceed according to his proved formula and

146 See the letter, "Keadaan dipendjara Sukamiskin, Bandung [Conditions in Sukamiskin Prison, Bandung]," May 17, 1931 (DBR, pp. 115ff.). Sukarno worked by day in a room where notebooks and similar things were made. On his loneliness, see note 24, above.

banish the new opponents to the camp of the Sanas. Even if they were "Europeans" in thought, their goal was the same as his—Indonesia Merdeka, freedom for Indonesia. The immediate result was that Sukarno's own uncertainty spread to the movement, and some of the people "began to doubt" him, as Dr. Sutomo later observed. And yet the Marhaenist phase was his truly heroic period, when he tried for the first time to forge the movement into a weapon.

Despite all the mythical glorification, in the period of the old PNI the movement had never been a weapon. Certainly the party had swept the Indonesian consciousness across the land like a wave, so that at the time of Sukarno's trial the term "Indonesia" was taken for granted, whereas before he appeared on the scene it had existed only in the thinking of a few leaders. But even in 1930 this "Indonesia" was still no more than a vision, and nothing had yet been undertaken to make it real.

In order to be able to make this "Indonesia" a reality, in order finally to lend force to the movement, Sukarno arranged a marriage between "Eastern nationalism" and Marxism. It was not easy for him to take away from his own national bourgeoisie, who had pampered him up to then, the hope for a place "later on"; but in his Socio-democracy there was no place for them—and it was in this that the doubts of the group around Sutomo had their origin. From then on Sukarno sought in Marxist theory the certitude which the unison of the "whole people" could no longer give. The cult of principle reached its zenith in the sanctifying of noncooperation, the modern magical formula, the Marxist antithesis that promised the Marhaens —and Sukarno—the final victory over capitalism and imperialism.

It was a flight into unreality, for Marhaenism, which in theory stood "with both feet on the ground of society," lacked the necessary preconditions: the dissatisfied masses, insisting upon their rights and conscious of their power. The momentary aspiration that Sukarno had stirred up in his "war that recognized no truce" would subside as abruptly at the end of a speech as it had flared up at the beginning.

There were moments when Sukarno recognized the hopelessness of his action, especially after he had seen the alternative provided by Hatta, Sjahrir, and their colleagues. His doubts were not concerned with his own actions, however, but with the ability of the Indonesian people: "Where then are our great Buddha statues, our *Mahabhratas,* our Homers, our Dantes, our cathedrals, our temple of Peking?" he asked a friend in the spring of 1933, and then went on: "We can do nothing but copy, we are not capable of originals, not capable yet. It will probably still be a long time before the nationalist movement means anything." [147] At another time he even admitted that he would have the moral courage to become a cooperator if he could be convinced of the advantage of cooperation.[148] This would certainly have been a difficult undertaking, given Sukarno's personality. He knew all too well that his talent lay in agitation rather than in working quietly. After his return from the Congress at which it had been decided to continue the Djihad, he sighed over the "abnormality" of his life.[149]

These statements demonstrate that Sukarno had become unsure of himself. And with the second imprisonment he had only become more clearly aware that there was no chance of success and that his previous principles were questionable. He could no longer feel himself borne up by the sympathy of the whole people.

What finally drove him to his decision is unknown. Even if, in addition to realizing the senselessness of his kind of campaign, it had been the hope of mitigating his sentence (an idea that cannot be dismissed, since he abandoned his old warlike attitude *before* the announcement of the verdict) at bottom makes little difference. That Sukarno dared to renounce the sort of campaign that he had made his own, and thus to dislodge himself from the pedestal on which he had been placed in the hearts of his followers, was his *first revolutionary deed.* For the first time, after decades of Bharata Judha, Wajang fashion, Sukarno the realist had triumphed over the Dewa, over Sukarno the idol.

[147] *Bintang Timur,* November 24, 1933 (report by Sanusi Pane, a friend of Sukarno); IPO 1933, No. 47, p. 741.
[148] *Ibid.*   [149] IPO 1933, No. 47, p. 742.

The members of the Partindo carried on the shadow battle without their idol for one year more. It was a year of difficulties.[150] Then they too yielded to *force majeure,* and on December 1, 1934, they abandoned the rigid principle of noncooperation. It was still to be used in the future as a tactical weapon, but even then it proved ineffective. The self-dissolution of the Partindo on November 18, 1936—exactly three years after Sukarno's memorable decision—brought to an end the noncooperation movement in Indonesia.

Nor did the "European" party, the PNI-Baru of Hatta and Sjahrir, escape the same fate. Hatta's belief that the colonial government would give a chance for inconspicuous efforts to educate the people in the absence of a crusading atmosphere proved to be a fallacy. On February 26, 1934, one week after Sukarno sailed into exile, Hatta and Sjahrir were arrested; later they were exiled to Boven Digul, an infamous spot in the jungles of New Guinea.[151] Thus they received a severer sentence than Sukarno, who, possibly on account of having abandoned his old principles and withdrawing from the Partindo, was assigned to live on the island of Flores.[152] They, the tacticians, were regarded by Governor General de Jonge as more dangerous than Sukarno, to whom the representative of the Dutch crown at this time believed he could apply the judgment, "dangerous but stupid." [153]

[150] For details, as well as a good survey of the subsequent course of the movement, see J. M. Pluvier, *Overzicht,* pp. 60ff.

[151] On Sukarno's departure, see *De Locomotief,* February 19; on the arrest of Hatta and Sjahrir, *ibid.,* February 26 and 27, 1934.

[152] See Hatta's statement in February 1968 at an anniversary celebration of the PNI-Baru, as reprinted in *Harian Kami,* February 16, 1968, p. 4, and confirmed by Hatta in a conversation with the author on September 13, 1968.

[153] D. M. G. Koch, *Om de Vrijheid* (1950), p. 115.

V

The Islamic Phase
(1934–1941)

Sukarno and Islam up to 1934

In Tjokroaminoto's Sarekat Islam, during the years while Sukarno witnessed the association's growth as a member of the household of its chairman, the propagation of Mohammed's teaching had only a secondary importance. Not until the radical left wing had split off, and party discipline had been introduced, did Islam become dominant in the party program of the Sarekat Islam—a development that was made manifest as its Pan-Islamic character came more and more to the fore, giving notice that the nationalist period of Indonesian Islam belonged to the past.

Sukarno, who had remained a member of the Sarekat Islam throughout the period of the split—but was now strongly influenced by the NIP in Bandung—thereupon announced his withdrawal from the association.[1] However, this did not mean that Sukarno, who in his own early articles had called for "the strengthening . . . of Islam in Indonesia,"[2] now regarded Islam with indifference or even with "disdainful arrogance."[3]

[1] Letter from Endeh, October 17, 1936 (DBR, p. 342).

[2] See "Sukarno's Early Political Views," in Chapter II, above.

[3] H. J. Benda believes he must come to this conclusion in his emphatic separation of Moslems from "secular" nationalists. He sees in Sukarno the representative of the Westernized nationalist, who confronted Islam "with an attitude of disdainful arrogance, which was quite clearly derived from, and very similar to, prevalent Western attitudes" (Crescent, p. 59; also note 57). However, the series of articles "Digul dan Mecca," which Benda introduces among others as proof, come not from Sukarno, as is wrongly stated in Benda's source (H. Bouman, Beschouwingen, p. 47),

He was much too well aware of the "fighting worth" of Islam for his projected Brown Front, as was shown at length by his appeal for unity in 1926.

In the attempt to gather the multitude of Indonesian associations into one federation, Sukarno first hitched his wagon once again to the Sarekat Islam. He edited a nationalist section for its periodical, *Bandera Islam*, and thus in his own fashion worked against the Pan-Islamic tendency of the association. Nor was his campaign for nationalism in the Sarekat Islam during those years without success. In 1929 the party adopted a resolution changing its name to Partij Sarekat Islam Indonesia (PSII).[4]

However, this "retrogression" did not take place without prior disputes. Hadji Agus Salim, who had at first greeted Sukarno's appearance in the movement with benevolence, came to believe he detected a leaning toward idolatry in Sukarno's ecstatic depictions of the beauties of Ibu (Mother) Indonesia. In the summer of 1928, on the basis of various quotations from a speech made by Sukarno, he pointed to the dangers dormant in nationalism, describing as well a number of misdeeds that had been committed, "especially in Europe," in the name of nationalism.

This, Salim declared, was what took place when men were in the possession of a religion which in reality enslaved them. Such were the dangers of idolizing Ibu Indonesia for her beauties, her riches, and other material goods. But the real homeland, as Salim set out to prove by means of quotations from the Koran, was loyalty to the commands of Allah. Things in themselves were worthless; only if they were regarded as gifts of Allah could their true meaning become manifest.[5]

Sukarno was not at a loss for an answer.[6] He flourished his

---

but from Dr. Sutomo. See IPO 1930, No. 38, pp. 442ff.; also Chapter III, notes 5 and 6, above.

[4] See also Wertheim, *Indonesian Society in Transition,* p. 220.

[5] The article by H. Agus Salim ("Tjinta bangsa dan tanah-air [Patriotism and Nationalism]" appeared in *Fadjar Asia* and was reprinted in SIM, No. 9 (August 1928), pp. 216ff.

[6] Sukarno's reply appeared in the same issue of SIM (No. 9, pp. 223ff.), under the title "Kearah Persatuan [Toward Unity]," and is reprinted in DBR, pp. 109ff.

magic weapon, the drive toward unity, and uttered an "Alhamdulillah (God be praised)" that the PNI was permitted to occupy the front line in this battle for unity. He declared that the chairman of this party (himself, in other words) let pass no opportunity of calling on the people to join any party, and in this he saw "proof that the PNI does not place itself above other parties." [7]

This, however, Hadji Agus Salim had by no means asserted. He had only spoken generally of the duty of exploring and remaining loyal to the will of Allah, "so that we do not, in the stress of passion, stray from the right path . . . ," thereby indirectly complaining of an absence of inner humility.[8] There could have been no better evidence of the correctness of this veiled criticism than Sukarno's egotistical vindication, which completely missed the point of the problem.

The charge that nationalism might contain latent dangers was emphatically rejected by Sukarno. Hadji Agus Salim, he said, "forgot to mention," that Indonesia did not subscribe to aggressive European nationalism; he knew that Sukarno preached a nationalism which was "not concerned with material but with spiritual gains," that Eastern nationalism differed greatly from Western nationalism, for "our nationalism . . . makes us God's 'instruments' and leads us to a 'life of the spirit.' " [9]

For Sukarno this mystical formulation, bolstered by a reference to many other "Eastern nationalists," among them the "advocate of Islam," Mustapha Kemal (!), was sufficient proof that his nationalism was not "founded on worldliness" or "enslaved by matter."

Sukarno was not at this time a follower of Islam. What knowledge he had of it had been acquired so as to be able to take part in the discussion, and was largely based on Lothrop

[7] DBR, p. 110: ". . . suatu bukti, bahwa PNI tidak sekali-kali meninggi-ninggikan diri diatas partai-partai jang lain itu."

[8] SIM, No. 9, p. 219.

[9] DBR, pp. 112f.: "Nasionalisme kita adalah nasionalisme, jang membuat kita mendjadi 'perkakasnja Tuhan' dan membuat kita mendjadi 'hidup didalam roch.' " Sukarno here referred especially to Bipin Chandra Pal.

Stoddard's *The New World of Islam*—in which the "new world" attracted him more than Islam for itself.[10] Nevertheless, Sukarno's fundamental religious feeling at this period cannot be overlooked. For example, he described the PNI as "religiously neutral," *not* in the sense of the communists who totally denied God, but in order to make it possible for all schools of belief to gain admission to the party.[11]

In this sense, Sukarno himself was "religiously neutral." His basic religious feeling, which was not tied to any dogma, allowed him access to all cults, including Marxism, in accordance with the ancient Javanese belief that "all things are one." Sukarno was not a Moslem, he was a Javanese.

But he was never known to attack Islam. Even at those meetings where he criticized the backwardness of certain Islamic traditions, and where, for example, he attacked the polygamy sanctioned by Islam—in the emancipated woman, "released from her enslavement," he hoped for a valuable partner in the struggle for freedom [12]—he was conscious that in such matters he was at one with Islamic reformers in other lands.[13] And in certain ways he always remained close to the Islam with which he had grown up. As an engineer, for example, Sukarno worked in his spare time at designing a great mosque that was to become a center for the followers of Islam in Java and a symbol of their own value as opposed to the West and "its religion." [14] As a

[10] Sukarno had not gone more deeply into the problems of Islam before 1934. His many comparisons with Islamic movements in other than Asian lands as proof of the "fighting worth" of Islam were taken from the book by Lothrop Stoddard, which appeared in 1921.

[11] See "The Weapons of the Partai Nasional Indonesia," in Chapter III, above.

[12] See his article, "Congres kaum Ibu [Women's Congress]," SIM, No. 13 (December 1928; in DBR, pp. 99ff.); also "Marhaen dan Marhaeni [Marhaen and (feminine) Marhaen]," *Fikiran Rakjat*, July 1933 (DBR, pp. 245ff.).

[13] See, for example, Lothrop Stoddard, *The New World of Islam* (1921), pp. 258ff.

[14] A. Vandenbosch, "Nationalism and Religion in Indonesia," *Far Eastern Survey*, XXI (1952), 182f. Vandenbosch bases his report on an Indonesian bulletin from the year 1952; no evidence was found in contemporary sources.

Moslem Sukarno had once warned, for all his "neutrality," against the advance of Christian missions in the Indonesian archipelago.[15] And finally, as a man who in prison had failed to become a superman, Sukarno received consolation in his loneliness from the study of certain Islamic writings.[16] This led, after he had been released from prison and had acquired books about Islam—among them an English translation of the Koran [17]—to the ever more frequent use in his speeches of "Insja Allah (God willing)."

Likewise, in his attempt to unify the nationalists he placed the responsibility for its success in the hands of Allah.[18] But after that attempt proved vain, Sukarno turned with new zeal to Marxist principles, which appeared more promising of success. He hit upon a comparison with nature; just as nature *"must* achieve its goal," so the movement, "which upholds nature and is upheld by it," would certainly arrive at its goal.[19]

Yet the reliance on nature proved just as fruitless as the reliance on Allah, or earlier, on the word of "Eastern nationalists" or Western scholars. The new arrest brought an end, for a time, to magical tests and verifications—a time in which, as Sukarno later recalled, "the majority of my statements had a mystical ground, a religious basis which, although it had not clearly been formed into a religion, nevertheless already pointed clearly in that direction." [20]

Sukarno's Preoccupation with Islam in Exile (1934–1941)

The "Conversion" on the Island of Flores

Sukarno's departure on February 17, 1934, for Endeh, his place of exile on the island of Flores, was a journey into soli-

---

[15] H. Bouman, *Beschouwingen,* p. 52. Bouman cites "Sedjarah Pergerakan Indonesia," 1929–30, p. 140, which was not available to the author.

[16] Letter from Endeh, October 17, 1936 (DBR, p. 342).

[17] IPO 1932, No. 3, p. 42.

[18] I. Supardi, *Bung Karno,* p. 15; also "Maklumat," DBR, p. 168.

[19] See "Marhaenism and Marxism," in Chapter IV, above.

[20] Letter from Endeh, October 17, 1936 (DBR, p. 342).

tude. The area of the harbor had been tightly sealed off when, accompanied only by the closest members of his family (his wife, Inggit Garnasih, whom he had married after the divorce from Tjokroaminoto's daughter, a stepdaughter, and his mother-in-law), he boarded the ship that would take him into exile.[21] For him, accustomed to being at the center of public attention, this departure from Java was the first foretaste of the life of complete solitude that now awaited him. Never was his assertion of three hundred years' colonial exploitation of Indonesia to appear more questionable than during his first weeks on the island of Flores, where hardly a trace of the civilization he so appraised was to be found.[22]

Along with the outward solitude came an inner desolation: the idol of the Javanese was shunned by the frightened people of Flores. At first, Sukarno later recalled, "only two or three" had had the courage to visit him.[23] There also came back to him the collapse in the prison cell of all his previous theories, the recollection of the "dark hour" and the angry reaction of his adherents after concluding that he had let them down. Here he would have read for the first time the detailed reports that caused him to experience once more the total bitterness of his fall. And as he had done before, once again in the hour of loneliness Sukarno turned for refuge to Islam.

Sukarno's moves toward Islam can be traced with ease thanks to his letters to A. Hasan, the sympathetic leader of the Persatuan Islam (Islamic Unity) in Bandung.[24]

[21] Nasution, *Riwajat*, pp. 22f., 59. On Sukarno's departure, see *De Locomotief,* February 19, 1934, and IPO 1934, No. 9, p. 135.

[22] Of the island of Flores, the *Geillustreerde Encyclopaedie van Nederlandsch-Indië,* edited by G. F. E. Gonggrijp, published in the year of Sukarno's exile (1934), said that the government "only in recent years has been more intensively concerned with this area" (p. 309).

[23] Sukarno's editorial on the feast of Lebaran, "Kilatan Djiwa [Spiritual Light]," in *Asia Raya,* October 10, 2602 [1942], p. 1, which recalled this period. His circle of acquaintances later grew to include about forty persons.

[24] A. Hasan had founded in Bandung a reform movement, which had come to similar conclusions independently of other such movements in Islam—without, however, leaving the grounds of orthodoxy, as the Ahmadijah in India, for example, had done. Koran and Hadith as sources

In his first letter, dated December 1, 1934, Sukarno began by asking for books so that he might study Islamic problems more thoroughly, but went on to a subject that was being hotly discussed in the Moslem world: the veneration of Sajids. He objected that the cult of the descendants of the Prophet bordered on polytheism, and remarked that those who supposed there was an "Islamic aristocracy" were in error, since "there is no religion with a greater emphasis on equality than Islam." [25]

Sukarno had not arrived at this conclusion after a thorough study of Islam, much less a critical comparison of Mohammed's teaching with that of the founders of other religions. Rather, in his very first "Islamic letter" it came *a priori*, as had his deprecation of "Western nationalism" in 1926 and, in 1932, his rejection of parliamentary democracy.

But after this statement, Sukarno no less irreverently took Islam to task. In the second letter, dated January 25, 1935, he began to question one of the chief pillars of Islam, the Hadith [26]—not any special traditions, but rather the canonically recognized collections of Al-Buchari and Muslim. These Sukarno himself had not yet read; but he already agreed with the opinion "of an English Moslem" that Buchari had included "weak Hadith," which was largely responsible for the decline of Islam, the "outmodedness" and the "impurity" in its teaching.

And he also declared war on Islamic law, "for in everyday practice, the Islamic community is completely dominated by this law, so that the law overwhelms the belief." [27]

---

of understanding remained inviolable. See G. F. Pijper, "De Ahmadijah in Indonesia," in *Bingkisan Budi* (1950), for a brief characterization of Hasan's school (p. 248). In 1937 Hasan published Sukarno's letters as a brochure under the title *Surat-surat Islam dari Endeh* [Islamic Letters from Endeh] (DBR, pp. 325ff.).

[25] DBR, p. 325: "Tiada satu agama jang menghendaki kesama-rataan lebih daripada Islam."

[26] Hadith—"sacred traditions" from the sayings of the Prophet or members of the original community, later made binding for Moslems— together with the Koran are the foundation of the laws. See Th. W. Juynboll, *Handbuch des islamitischen Gesetzes* (1910), pp. 12ff.

[27] DBR, p. 326: "Sebab dalam praktek sehari-hari, ummat Islam sama sekali dikuasai oleh 'wet' itu, sehingga 'wet' mendesak kepada 'dien.'"

In the next letter (March 26, 1935), Sukarno returned to the Hadith. Having been informed meanwhile that the collections of Buchari and Muslim he had requested were not yet obtainable in a language he understood—Sukarno did not know Arabic—he asked that further efforts be made, for

I consider the study of the Hadith to be very important, because, according to my deepest conviction—as I wrote in one of my earlier letters—the Islamic world became backward because many persons "carried out" weak and false Hadith. Because of such Hadiths, the teaching of Islam was enveloped by mists of conservatism, of superstition, heresies, anti-rationalism, and so forth, although there is no religion simpler or more rational than Islam.[28]

Why did Sukarno wish to study the Hadith if his opinion of it was already determined? To this question only one answer is possible: he was looking for evidence to support his opinion. As he made use during the nationalist period of the remarks of "Eastern nationalists" that confirmed him in his anti-Western prejudice; as during the Marhaenist period he used the literature of Marxism at will; so here too he wished to make a tool of Islam, and with it to support his subjective opinion.

What did Sukarno understand by Islam? In the first letter he had stated that no religion gave greater emphasis to equality; in the third, he said that no religion was simpler or more rational; and in the eighth and eleventh letters, Sukarno had found the formula which, according to his view, summed up the positive features in three words: "Islam is progress." [29]

The question that had been so carefully formulated by the reformist school in Aligarh (India)—"Is Islam hostile to progress?"—a question which that school believed it could answer in the negative,[30] was for Sukarno no longer a question. Islam was "progress," and everything that stood in the way of that progress was "paralyzed," "unclean," "heresy," and so on.

It is noteworthy that after the third letter, Sukarno no longer criticized the Hadith. Perhaps Hasan had told him in the mean-

[28] DBR, p. 327.   [29] *Ibid.*, pp. 334, 340.

[30] See the statement of Khuda Bukhsh: "Is Islam hostile to progress? I will emphatically answer this question in the negative" (cited in Stoddard, *loc. cit.*, p. 31).

time what heresy he was committing when he made such remarks as, "It is my deep conviction that we can give no absolute
value to the Hadith." [31]

But Sukarno's anger at the paralysis of Islam remained, and
was now directed at new opponents, the Taqlid[32] or the Fikh[33]
generally. "If one reflects more deeply"—Allah's irreverent new
zealot observed in the fourth letter—"then the book of Fikh
has become the hangman of the soul and spirit of Islam." [34]

This was the book that for more than a thousand years had
determined the daily course of Islamic life, that for a thousand
years had been the guidepost of the Islamic community, respected in equal measure by scholars and by laymen. But
Sukarno stated in his eighth letter from Endeh, "For a thousand
years, Islam has stayed behind the times." [35]

The "centre need of Islam," explained Sukarno, who liked to
embellish his letters with Anglicisms, was a radical reform. For
him it was not enough to attempt to reach only gradual agreement on new questions, as happened, for example, at the Pales-
tine Congress in the summer of 1935. Sukarno criticized this
congress because it had "not tried hard enough." [36] In his opinion, Islam was "progress"; therefore it was incomprehensible to
him that the congress did not fling open the windows at once to
let fresh air blow into the musty chambers of Islamic orthodoxy.

He took even more harshly to task the Kijais [37] and Ulamas [38]

---

[31] DBR, p. 327: "Adalah saja punja kejakinan jang dalam, bahwa kita
tak boleh mengasihkan harga jang mutlak kepada hadits." For Hasan's
opinion on this, see note 24, above.

[32] Taqlid—the adoption of the opinion of another among the four
Fikh schools in certain questions on which one's own legal teaching offers
insufficient information—is thus not independent interpretation. Literally,
it is "proofs with authority." See Juynboll, *Handbuch,* p. 31.

[33] Fikh is legal teaching.

[34] Letter of July 17, 1935 (DBR, p. 328): "Ja kalau difikirkan dalam-
dalam, maka kitab-figh itulah seakan-akan ikut mendjadi algodjo 'roch'
dan 'semangat' Islam."

[35] "Seribu tahun Islam ketinggalan zaman" (*ibid.,* p. 334).

[36] Cf. the fifth letter, September 15, 1935 (DBR, pp. 329f.).

[37] Kijai, a religious teacher on Java. See, for example, G. W. J. Drewes,
"Indonesia, Mysticism and Activism," in G. E. von Grunebaum (ed.),

in his own country who did not have the slightest "feeling" (*sic*) for history. Although they could recite the Koran correctly, their knowledge of history as a whole amounted to nothing. At most they were acquainted with a part of the Tarich,[39] but this could not withstand the test of "modern science" (*sic*).

Next we hear from the adherent of the Marxist interpretation of history, who could give so detailed an account of European history in materialist terms, that the Dar ul Islam was so backward not because of any economic factors that were lacking but because of the absence of spiritual drive. The genius of Islam was dead since its followers had ceased to draw directly upon the sources of the Koran and the Hadith.[40] But even drawing upon these sources was not enough. In order to understand the will of Allah correctly, a broad general education was necessary. "By Allah! The science of Islam is the knowledge of the Koran and Hadith plus general knowledge." [41] Therefore, they should rush to catch up with the times. The great period of the first Caliphs must not become an immutable law for the Islamic community; it could only be interpreted as a historical stage in the process of history.

He did not tire of criticizing the backwardness of Islam and of castigating its sins of omission.[42] Had it been forgotten, he asked repeatedly, that the law recognized not only the terms "haram" (forbidden), "makruh" (objectionable), and "fard" (obligatory), but also "mubah" (permitted) and "djaiz" (valid), which were used far too little? The great Caliphs should be an example; they had caught the spark from the same sources that were still available today:

Unity and Variety in Muslim Civilization (1955), pp. 284–307, at the end of which Drewes discusses the Kijai (who in Java enjoys great respect because of his knowledge of Ngelmu [mysticism]). See also Clifford Geertz, "The Javanese Kijai: The Changing Role of a Cultural Broker," in *Comparative Studies in Society and History,* II (1959/60), 228–49.

[38] Ulama, an Islamic scholar or teacher.   [39] "Chronicle of Islam."

[40] See the seventh letter, December 14, 1935 (DBR, pp. 332f.)

[41] Ninth letter, April 22, 1936 (DBR, p. 336): "Demi Allah! Islam Science adalah pengetahuan Qu'ran dan Hadits plus pengetahuan umum."

[42] Cf. the letters of February 22, 1936, and August 18, 1936 (DBR, pp. 334, 339f.). On the individual terms, cf. Juynboll, *Handbuch,* pp. 59ff.

But what have we absorbed of the Word of Allah and the Sunnah of the Prophet? Not its spark, not its flame . . . , but the ashes, the dust, the asbestos . . . ashes that have the form of Islamic mouthings and Islamic piety without devotion; its ashes, so that they can only murmur the Fatihah [the introductory Sura of the Koran] and the confession of faith, but not its fire, which continues to flame from the end of one period to the end of another.[43]

This image of taking fire originated not with Sukarno but with his eloquent authority Jean Jaurès, who, however, had been referring not to Islam but to socialism. Jaurès had declared before the French parliament that the socialists had taken over the fire of the democratic ideal, whereas the liberals had kept only its ashes.[44] Sukarno had merely given the fire a new source.

Was it a new source for Sukarno as well? He believed that his fundamental religious feeling, his vague belief in a Creator-God, had meanwhile become "Islam." In his last letter from Endeh, dated October 17, 1936, he wrote:

In these letters a part of the change in my soul is sketched out, *a soul that was* only *superficially Islamic* has become a soul that is *convinced of Islam,* a soul that was aware of the existence of God but did not yet know God became a soul which every day faced HIM, a soul that philosophized much about belief in God but did not *believe,* became a soul that daily rendered homage to HIM.[45]

That during his intensive studies of Islam Sukarno would have experienced a sort of conversion was almost to be expected, in view of his characteristic engagement in the matter, as well as the outward and inner loneliness on the island of Flores. Moreover, in his philosophy of progress, that curious mixture of social dynamics with conformity to historical laws and with economic and spiritual driving forces, there was a place for a Creator-God from the start.[46] Besides the letters

[43] Letter of August 18, 1936 (DBR, pp. 340f.).

[44] The speech of Jean Jaurès was also quoted by Sukarno in his essay "Mendjadi guru dimasa kebangunan" [Becoming a Teacher in the Time of Awakening]," which possibly was written only after the outbreak of the Pacific war, and which is reprinted in facsimile in the appendix to DBR (p. 625).

[45] DBR, p. 342. Sukarno's emphasis.

[46] See "The 'Misconceptions,' " in Chapter III, above.

from A. Hasan, the association with Christian missionaries on Flores, whom Sukarno cultivated at this time,[47] would also have contributed to the strengthening of his concept of God.

In view of Sukarno's belief in progress, the victorious advance of the first Caliphs, who had seized the "fire," was without doubt a proof that this God had revealed himself in his creation through the Prophet. The closing of the "Bab el Idjtihad," the Gate of Knowledge, the denial of further interpretation of the sacred sources and modern research into the Word of Allah— and on the other hand the "final" fixation of this Word in inviolable laws—must have seemed to Sukarno to be a crime. The book of ethics must have become for him the "hangman of the spirit and soul of Islam"—of Islam as Sukarno understood it.

But Islam does not mean "progress"; Islam means devotion, submission—submission to the laws and the will of Allah as revealed to his Prophet on Mount Hira. But this was not what Sukarno learned on Flores. His urge toward reform, which appears quite understandable in view of the paralysis of the Islamic world, drove him in his demands to go far beyond those limits which were still respected even by Moslems favorable toward reform. This was soon to become obvious in Sukarno's attempts to modernize Indonesian Islam.

The "Modernization of Islam" in Benkulen

In February 1938, Sukarno's banishment was mitigated. Benkulen, on the southwest coast of Sumatra, was assigned as his new place of residence; here, within certain limits, he could move about freely.[48] He was also allowed to join a Moslem association, the Muhammadijah, which had branches throughout the Indonesian archipelago.

The Muhammadijah—founded in 1912 by Kijai A. Dahlan, who sympathized with the Egyptian reformism of Mohammed

---

[47] Letter of September 15, 1935. See also "Separation of State and Religion," in Chapter VI, below.

[48] Nasution, *Riwajat*, p. 60. The author is further indebted to two conversations with Professor G. F. Pijper, on February 19 and October 11, 1963, at Amsterdam. See also the article, "Ik stond er bij" (not available to the author), by D. v. d. Meulen, in *Nieuwe Stem*, January 1964.

Abduh—had developed by now into Indonesia's largest organization. It took care to remain aloof from all political agitation, and assigned great value to the mission of Islam within Indonesia.

G. F. Pijper, who at the end of the 1930's was "Advizeur voor Inlandsche Zaken," knew the Muhammadijah from years of personal observation, and before Sukarno's transfer to Benkulen—which was made in response to his suggestion—had studied the methods of the reform association in this particular province, publishing the results in an informative essay. [49] Out of his isolation in Flores and out of circles in which the practice of Islam was still entirely orthodox—insofar as he had contacts there—Sukarno now entered a world into which reformist ideas had already found their way. But there the Muhammadijah advanced slowly, true to its fashion, in winning over and instructing individuals, providing them with literature, and thus gradually doing away with practices which were not compatible with Mohammed's teaching. Outside Java the Adat, the customary law, which obstructed the reform movement everywhere, was still so strong that a way other than that adopted by the Muhammadijah would hardly have succeeded. Nevertheless, even in Benkulen there were still numerous sources of friction between the administrators of the Adat and the promulgators of reformist ideas.[50]

Sukarno launched himself into this new surrounding with a display that immediately returned him to the center of attention. At a meeting of the Muhammadijah at the beginning of 1939, Sukarno walked out with his wife because a Tabir, the veil-like curtain used to separate the women from the men, had been hung in a corner of the hall. Sukarno had previously told the council of the Muhammadijah that he regarded this curtain as a sign of the enslavement of woman, which had been neither required nor wished by Allah or the Prophet.

As he had hoped, this protest by Sukarno raised a great stir in the Indonesian Islamic community. Thus, for example, a corre-

[49] "Nieuwe godsdienstige denkbeelden in Benkoelen," in G. F. Pijper, *Fragmenta Islamica* (1934), pp. 159ff.

[50] *Ibid.,* pp. 176ff.

spondent for *Pandji Islam* was sent especially to Benkulen to interview Sukarno about the incident.[51] Asked during the interview whether he did not know that the curtain had become an Adat at Muhammadijah meetings, especially in Benkulen, he declared that of course he knew it, but joining the Muhammadijah did not mean that he agreed with everything that was practiced by the organization. He wished to serve Islam, but the curtain was not Islam. Sukarno continued:

I want to become a motor of evolution. World history shows that there is a constant struggle and a constant dialectic between old and young, orthodoxy and evolution, between conservative and modern. . . . I know there may be many, yes, even very many Moslems who would declare that my opinion about the curtain for the women is wrong; but that is orthodoxy, what else? [52]

Sukarno had found a new field of action in his "war that recognizes no truce." Because war against the aliens was forbidden to him, the restless "pupil of the historical school of Marx"—as he proudly styled himself in this interview [53]—carried his concept of a continuing dialectic from the political into the religious arena. Not, however, that in so doing he abandoned the larger goal of freedom from Western domination. Wherever the opportunity presented itself, Sukarno in his "Islamic" phase also held to the great antithesis.

He doubted, for example, that parliamentary democracy was the ideal political system for Islam; in his opinion, it lent itself to a "much more perfect form of government." [54] He rejected the Ahmadijah—however much he agreed with its rationalism as well as with its demands for a new interpretation of the Koran—not only because it made a cult of its founder, Mirza Gulam Ahmad, but also "because of its leaning toward English imperialism." [55] Even in the interview on the issue of the cur-

[51] The interview appeared in *Pandji Islam* in the spring of 1939 under the title, "Tabir adalah lambang perbudakan [The Curtain is a Symbol of Enslavement]," and is included in DBR, pp. 349ff.

[52] DBR, p. 350.

[53] *Ibid.*, p. 351: "Saja adalah murid dari Historische School van Marx."

[54] Letter from Endeh, September 15, 1935 (DBR, pp. 329f.).

[55] See the letter to *Pemandangan*, November 25, 1936 (DBR, p. 346).

tain, Sukarno did not forget to explain that he favored the separation of the sexes as required by the Prophet. "I reject their association in the Western manner." [56]

It was only the curtain that hid the women, which was degrading, that had to go. Sukarno's urge to reform may have been reinforced on this point by another motive. "Bung Karno has an eye for a pretty face," observed a contemporary Indonesian novel,[57] and it was later evident that he had glimpsed such a face in spite of the Tabir. Fatmawati, his third wife, whom he married in the summer of 1943, was from Benkulen.

However, for Sukarno the curtain was not only a symbol of the enslavement of women or an obstacle to seeing them; it was, as became clear from Sukarno's further exaggeration of this issue,[58] a welcome means of gaining public attention. Sukarno himself declared quite openly at this time, "I like very much to 'make a fuss.' Only by 'making a fuss' can the public be shocked so that they will awaken and begin to be interested in a problem." [59] The topic in which Sukarno wanted to interest the public was his idea for a general modernization of Islam, which he subsequently aired in *Pandji Islam*.[60]

Just as there was continual change in all things, declared Sukarno with an allusion to Heraclitus, so in the teachings of a religion there was a continual "panta rei." The doctrines themselves did not change; God's word and the Sunnah of the Prophet did not change; but the knowledge of men about them was subject to continual alteration. Therefore, new interpreta-

---

On the activity of the Ahmadijah in Indonesia generally, see G. F. Pijper, "De Ahmadijah in Indonesië," in *Bingkisan Budi* . . . , pp. 247ff.

[56] DBR, p. 350.   [57] Djojopoespito, *Buiten het gareel*, p. 57.

[58] See his open letter to the executive committee of the Muhammadijah in the spring of 1939, "Minta hukum jang pasti dalam soal tabir [I Ask for a Final Settlement of the Question of the Curtain]" (DBR, pp. 353ff.).

[59] "Saja suka sekali 'membongkar.' Hanja dengan tjara 'membongkar' orang bisa mengeweg-eweg publik supaja ia bangun dan memperhatikan sesuatu soal." See "Saja kurang dinamis [I Am Not Dynamic Enough]" (DBR, p. 447).

[60] Under the title "Me'muda'kan pengertian Islam [Modernization of the Understanding of Islam]"; reprinted in DBR, pp. 369ff.

tions and corrections of the old perceptions must again and again be made.

This new interpretation was now being carried on everywhere "with passion," after the centuries-long paralysis of Islam caused by the closing of the "Bab el Idjtihad"; and in Indonesia too it was time to begin with a "rethinking of Islam." Only then would Indonesian youth, whom the Islamic movement up to then had so unfortunately failed to reach, return to the fold. On the other hand, the fact that the young held themselves so strictly aloof was proof that "something" was wrong with Indonesian Islam. For, as Sukarno argued in support of this opinion (by modifying a well-known proverb), "Whoever would have the future, must have the youth." [61]

Islam could flourish again—Sukarno continued, with a reference to Farid Wadjdi [62]—only when its adherents respected freedom of spirit, of knowledge, and of understanding. The intellectuals too could demand reconsideration and did not need to swallow everything that did not satisfy their critical sense.

For his subsequent statements Sukarno offered authoritative support by referring to Ameer Ali, author of *The Spirit of Islam,* a work highly valued by Moslem intellectuals everywhere, which he had procured for himself while still in Endeh.[63] He quoted from it as follows: "The elasticity of laws is their great test, and this test is pre-eminently possessed by those of Islam. Their compatibility with progress shows their founders' wisdom." From this sentence, after translating it into Indonesian, Sukarno concluded with great satisfaction that "Islam can be compatible with all progress because its laws are 'like rubber'—so says Sir Sayid Ameer Ali. And these words of his are true." [64]

It may sound incredible, but the statement thus cited by Sukarno is not in Ameer Ali's book. The words Sukarno put

[61] DBR, p. 372.   [62] *Ibid.,* p. 374.

[63] Letter of September 15, 1935 (DBR, p. 331).

[64] DBR, p. 375: "Islam bisa tjotjok dengan semua kemadjuan karena hukum-hukumnja 'septerti karet,' *begitu* Sir Syed Ameer Ali berkata. Dan perkataan beliau ini adalah benar."

into the mouth of this eminent authority were in fact his own. Though the earlier illustrations that had been bent to fit, for example those from Kautsky [65] or Liebknecht,[66] might be accounted for as errors in translation, in this instance it was clear that Sukarno had made Ameer Ali his authority by having Ali proclaim his own opinion.[67]

This description of the Islamic laws as "like rubber," which strikingly recalls the description of his Eastern nationalism as "broad as air," and his Marhaenist version of Marxism, became the point of departure for Sukarno's proposal for a modern in-

[65] See "The Struggle for the Antithesis," in Chapter III, above.

[66] See "The Marhaenist Party," in Chapter IV, above.

[67] Because Sukarno, in quotations or references, gives no citation other than the name of the book (or, often, only of the author), the passage on which Sukarno's "quotation" is based could be found in Ameer Ali, *The Spirit of Islam* (London, 1922), only after a long search. In a chapter on "The Status of Women in Islam," Ali, attempting to explain the passage in the Koran that allowed polygamy, remarked that this was a matter of a particularly wise decree, concerning uncivilized and civilized peoples: if among uncivilized peoples polygamy was necessary for the care of women who were otherwise often unprotected, so in civilized lands Mohammed's teaching, "If you cannot deal equitably and justly with all, you shall marry only one" was valid. Then Ali remarked, "It must be remembered that *the elasticity of laws is the greatest test* of their beneficence and usefulness. And this is the merit of the Koranic provision. It is adapted alike for the acceptance of the most cultured society and the requirements of the least civilized" (*loc. cit.,* pp. 229f.). Accordingly, perhaps, monogamy could later be introduced in Islamic states by a consensus of the Ulamas, Ali went on after a brief discussion of the legal aspects, and then declared: "As remarked already *the compatibility of Mohammed's system with every stage of progress shows their founder's wisdom.* Among unadvanced communities, polygamy, hedged by all the safeguards imposed by the Prophet, is by no means an evil to be deplored" (*ibid.,* p. 231). For Ameer Ali, the matter here was the quite special one of polygamy, which according to him could be adjusted *only* by the Ulamas. Sukarno's generalization so as to describe all Islamic laws as "like rubber" called for a fabrication, and the central clause of his "quotation"—"*and this test is pre-eminently possessed by those of Islam*"—is just that (in addition, the clause is notable for its peculiar English). This was translated into Indonesian by Sukarno as "and this elasticity applies especially to the laws of Islam." That is, he surely wanted to add, "This *elasticity* is pre-eminently possessed by those of Islam."

terpretation of Islam. Certainly that was what Ameer Ali hoped for. The question was only, who was competent to interpret Islam anew? And here the views of Ali and Sukarno were widely divergent.

For Ameer Ali, the Mutazelites, the Islamic scholars of the early centuries of Islam, were the great example. They had delved into Islam in constant awareness that the perfection of all knowledge was the acknowledgment of divine truth. They had recognized that without the knowledge of God, all theories were doomed to founder. For Ali, only those who continually walked, as they had, in the footsteps of their Master and of his immediate successors, were authorized to attempt a new interpretation of the Koran and Hadith.[68]

Sukarno, on the contrary, dared to say "we"! His "most important conclusion" after a survey of the conditions of Islam in other lands was, "Let us, if we are not to rebel against the times, take hold of rationalism and make it our guiding star in the consideration of Islam. We shall lose nothing; rather, we shall benefit." [69] He could refer to the highest authority: Allah himself, and the Prophet, again and again had issued the challenge: "Why do you not think?" "Why do you not meditate?" "One word of knowledge is worth more than the recitation of a hundred prayers"—and so on.[70] If these commands were followed, the "outlook" (sic) of Islam would gradually alter, in its fundamental concepts as well as in the details of its knowledge. He was not calling for Islam to be given up; on the contrary, a reform of the Fikh doctrines was likewise in the interest of Islam itself. However, Sukarno's urge to reform was not limited to the book of Fikh: "We must interpret every sentence of the Koran, every statement in the Hadith, every word from the history, in the light of the true spirit of Islam." [71] Sukarno then proceeded

[68] Ameer Ali, *The Spirit of Islam,* pp. 416ff.　　[69] DBR, pp. 398f.

[70] These quotations were not discovered one way or another by Sukarno, but were common property in the reform literature on Islam. See L. Stoddard, *The New World of Islam,* p. 28, and A. Ali, *Spirit,* pp. 360ff., in which whole catalogues of such teachings from the Koran and Hadith are collected.

[71] DBR, p. 400.

immediately to show how the new interpretation was to be carried out:

Let us not look at the letter; let us look at the spirit, the soul of the letter. . . . In this way we can free Islam from the controversy over the letter, that is, the casuistry of the Faqih. In this way, we can think independently, comment independently, interpret independently, guided only by the one compass, the spirit of [true] Islam.[72]

For most Indonesian Moslems, who tended to be quite conservative, the unthinkable had occurred. Koran and Hadith, the sacrosanct foundations of belief, were to be newly interpreted, without regard to "the letter." Was this independent thinking, investigation, and interpretation still guided by the "spirit of Islam," or was it in reality independent even of that spirit? To this question, after Sukarno's praise of rationalism, the answer was not hard to find.

Sukarno's article, whose intention was an effort toward modernizing Islam in Indonesia, was taken as a challenge by Indonesian Moslems. One of these "independent" interpretations was exactly what they had been waiting for; and it came in an article Sukarno wrote in April 1940 for the birthday of the Prophet. He gave the title "Society in the Age of the Camel and Society in the Age of the Airplane" to his observations,[73] which he prefaced (and concluded) with a parable: One day his stepdaughter Ratna Djuami came to him complaining that the dog had drunk from a bowl at the well. He had advised her to wash the bowl thoroughly with soap and creolin. But his daughter hesitated, and finally she asked: But had not the Prophet commanded in such a case that the bowl be washed seven times over, one of those times with earth? He had answered that in the time of the Prophet there had been no soap or creolin, so that he could not yet have commanded the use of either one. Whereupon, Sukarno continued, the face of his daughter had brightened.

To a clever young Moslem scholar, Mohammed Natsir, whom

72 *Ibid.*

73 "Masjarakat onto dan masjarakat kapal udara" (from *Pandji Islam,* April 22, 1940; DBR, pp. 483ff.).

Sukarno had repeatedly praised for his learning, this seemingly innocent parable gave an opportunity of pointing out the dangers of freethinking in the field of religion.[74]

To begin with, Natsir did not deny the utility of thought detached from tradition. He acknowledged that by independent thinking faith could be strengthened and much of the superstition that clung to religion could be eliminated without great difficulties. A free intellect would open the windows of the study and let in the fresh air. But, Natsir went on, this gust of fresh air could become a storm, which would throw everything in the study into confusion and which could also shake the foundations of religion. "Freedom without discipline produces terrible confusion; freedom without authority is anarchy." [75] A man who believed he could solve all mysteries with his intellect was in reality no longer using his free intellect, but was chained by a modern Taqlidism which bore the name of rationalism.

In the same manner as Ameer Ali, Natsir portrayed how the Mutazelites had exercised their rationalism, namely "in the search for God." He referred to Kant—and who did not recognize him as a great thinker? But Kant too had denied that all problems could be solved by "pure reason." And finally Professor Farid Wadjdi, to whom Sukarno owed his ideas of freedom in thought, interpretation, and investigation, had likewise not advocated free thought. Farid Wadjdi had declared that in questions of faith, there was no place for the purely rational; he had cited Mohammed's declaration that questions of belief were to be left to him; in worldly matters, on the other hand, men of the world knew more than he.

This was the compass by which the Moslems set their course: strict obedience in questions of faith; in worldly matters, a scrutiny of tradition and only then a free decision.

Following this statement of principle, Natsir addressed him-

[74] Mohammed Natsir, "Sikap Islam terhadap Kemerdekaan Berfikir [The Attitude of Islam toward Free Thought]," appeared in *Pandji Islam* (April–June 1940) following Sukarno's article, and was reprinted in Natsir, *Capita selecta I* (1954), pp. 206ff. On Sukarno's evaluation of Natsir, see DBR, pp. 326, 336.

[75] Natsir, *loc. cit.,* p. 210.

self to Sukarno's parable.[76] Using the same terms, he put before him the way a true Moslem in Sukarno's place would have behaved. He would not have allowed the opportunity to pass of explaining to his child *why* the Prophet had given his command: first the look backward, then the look forward, even if soap and creolin were the outcome. Sukarno's answer, on the other hand, proved that he formed his opinion quite freely, without at all concerning himself with religious significance.

Soap and creolin were only the beginning. Another day, others would come and ask: "Why, when water is lacking, take earth, as prescribed, for the ritual cleansing before prayer? Take perfume; it is more hygienic, though Mohammed could not have recommended it because at his time there was no perfume. . . . Finally what we get from pure reason is not an interpretation of religion but a liquidation of religion. The 100-per-cent freethinker sets his limits himself. He wants to change everything, he wants to criticize everything, he wants to demolish everything—except the freethinker himself." [77]

Mohammed Natsir, like Sutan Sjahrir, Hadji Agus Salim, and Mohammed Hatta—all of whom energetically opposed Sukarno's deliberate simplifications *in order to find a common denominator*—came from West Sumatra, which could be regarded as a kind of opposite pole to syncretistic Java.[78] Just as

---

[76] *Ibid.*, pp. 218ff.   [77] *Ibid.*, p. 223 (cf. also p. 226).

[78] A detailed investigation of this matter, which by 1921 was already being discussed in the Indonesian movement, would be of interest. See the statement by the chairman of the Young Sumatran Association, Amir, on July 31, 1921, that the Javanese were more interested in philosophy, and were thinkers and dreamers, whereas the Sumatrans were more sober and had more understanding of practical politics and of the economy (IPO 1921, No. 32, p. 254). The more pronounced tendency toward individualism among the Sumatrans is also emphasized by D. de Vries, *Culturele aspecten in de verhouding Indonesië-Nederland* (1947), p. 91. In stressing this point, however, the author does not intend to set up the thesis of a fundamental difference between the Javanese and the Sumatrans generally, as might be concluded from J. M. van der Kroef's critical remarks on the German edition of this book in "Sukarno, the Ideologue," *Pacific Affairs*, XLI (1968), 248–50. The writer is well aware of the attraction of a sober political style for Javanese intellectuals, especially those who went abroad to study or later recognized the alter-

ruthlessly as Sjahrir had criticized Sukarno's ideas not quite a decade before, Natsir now exposed the deficiencies in Sukarno's version of Islam. It was basically the same charge that had been made against Sukarno in 1928 by Hadji Agus Salim—of a lack of devotion, a lack of "submission," a lack of "Islam."

It is to be emphasized that Sukarno had not entered the ranks of the Indonesian Moslems as a hypocrite. He believed in Allah, performed the Salats (prayer exercises), and observed the fast in the honest conviction that this was "Islam." But he was fired as well by the doctrine of social progress, and this awareness gave him no rest and indeed no choice but to assume for himself the role of Prophet and, contrary to all orthodoxy, to proclaim his own message of salvation—that "Islam is progress."

Sukarno regarded the God-given endowment of intellect as an absolute gift without any obligation in return. Unlike the Mutazelites of the first centuries or Ameer Ali and Natsir in his own time, who had first to "inquire into" the new knowledge, Sukarno brought that knowledge with him when he began to occupy himself with Islam.

What would have occurred if Sukarno had attempted an independent interpretation of the Koran and Hadith is easy to guess. His investigation of the spirit behind the letter, as seen in his interpretation of Ameer Ali's book, including his invention of additions for the missing parts, allows little doubt to arise that the outcome would have been at least a new religion—if not a liquidation of religion, as Natsir believed was to be feared.

Meanwhile, however, new developments attracted Sukarno's attention. The Second World War had broken out, and its further course, even from Sukarno's place of exile, was more and

---

native presented by Sjahrir, Hatta, and others. On the other hand, the Javanese cultural environment certainly had some impact on Sumatran politicians, especially those who had lived in Java since their early youth —as, for instance, the West Sumatran Muhammad Yamin. It should be noted, however, that even Yamin had little understanding of what is here regarded as essential to Javanism, namely the drive for unity. By the end of the Dutch rule, Yamin was regarded in the Indonesian movement as "de eeuwige scheurmaker," the eternal factionalist. Cf. Pluvier, *Overzicht*, pp. 112–13.

more to dominate his interest. His preoccupation with Islamic reforms thus was ephemeral. For him it was a way to continue his struggle, to awaken the people, to arouse their fighting spirit. He was not concerned with an Islamic revival as were Natsir, Salim, and Hasan. And thus his intervention in Islamic affairs was rejected by the reformists, whereas the orthodox— the main target of Sukarno's criticisms—remained untouched, and in time were even to show some interest in his syncreticism.

VI

Sukarno's Development to Late 1941

The Synthesis of Nationalism, Marxism, and Islam

In the young Sukarno's earliest political opinions there was already a discernible effort, though at that time still unconscious, toward a synthesis of the three currents by which he was influenced—nationalism, Islam, and Marxism. In 1921, for example, he announced: "Once the proper conditions come into being and our own parliament . . . is achieved, the Sarekat Islam must still not end its activity, but must continue to act for the strengthening of democracy and of Islam in Indonesia, and for the destruction of capitalism." [1]

The two decades that followed saw no further basic changes in Sukarno's view. What in 1921 had still been vague and uncertain was by degrees more exactly defined. "The proper conditions" and "our own parliament" became "Indonesia Merdeka"—independent Indonesia; Sarekat Islam became the Partai Nasional Indonesia (1927–30) and later the Partindo (1931–33). But in style both successor parties resembled the old Sarekat Islam, whose "breadth" allowed space for all currents. During the period of the PNI this breadth went by the name of "Eastern nationalism," during the period of the Partindo by the name of "Marhaenism."

The orientation toward nationalism, Marxism, and Islam remained constant, although the estimate of Islam underwent some variation. Throughout the period under consideration

[1] See "Sukarno's Early Political Views," in Chapter II, above.

they were regarded primarily as natural allies in the struggle against colonial domination. By 1926 these three strands, nationalism, Islam, and Marxism, were already so interwoven that Sukarno's articles from the autumn of that year seriously denied the existence of fundamental differences among them. Such points of friction as that between Moslems and Marxists over the position of religion were reduced to "misunderstandings." For Sukarno, historical materialism did not exclude a Creator-God, and in his opinion the early Islamic community came very close to the ideal communist society.

It was a curious coincidence that after having entered the Indonesian independence movement, as he did with this series of articles, Sukarno was to ally himself one by one with each of the three currents, nationalism, Marxism, and Islam, in three distinct phases.

During the period from 1926 to 1930, the nationalist idea with which Sukarno had become more closely associated among the warriors, the Ksatrijas in Bandung, clearly occupied the foreground. In the Partai Nasional Indonesia, as in the Indonesian federation PPPKI, the particular object in view was the inclusion of all Indonesians and their disengagement from outsiders. As common ground Sukarno offered an "Eastern nationalism" that was "broad as the air," and his tireless efforts for agreement among individual schools of thought bore fruit. He achieved a sense of unity such as had never before existed in an archipelago hitherto united only by the colonial administration. It is undeniably to his credit that in three years the Indonesian idea had become a matter of course in the independence movement.

Immune to attack from any quarter—bearing in mind the self-elimination of the Communist Party in 1926—Sukarno, the necromancer of unity, reigned as an uncrowned monarch over a "state within a state" until that reign was forbidden by the colonial authorities.

The second phase, after his release from prison and until his exile (1932–33), was dominated by Marxist slogans. From the criticism of the "European" Indonesians Sjahrir and Hatta, it had become evident that the "state within a state" was not enough to lend force to the desire for independence. Now Sukarno sought a weapon in Marxist writings, and he believed he had found it in Socio-nationalism. As a new principle he offered Marhaenism, in which the proletariat was to take the central position—but no more than the central position— together with what he hoped would be as many other Indonesian groups as possible. During the nationalist period, Sukarno had played now and then with Marxist theory as a means of securing his position in dialectic fashion. Once the unity of the people, which had sustained him up until then, no longer existed because of the split in the movement, Marxist theory became something more for Sukarno. He ferreted out its principles and adhered to them because they alone were able to nourish the hope of victory against the common enemy. The principles themselves were accorded a cult-like reverence, just as in the first phase nationalism had often been described as the fulfillment of a divine mission.

Then followed the period of exile and of preoccupation with Islam, the profession of belief in Allah and his Prophet. But just as the underlying religious mood had not been completely eliminated in the earlier phases, so now the Marxist belief in progress was not abandoned by Sukarno. Because he regarded Islam as identical with progress, he needed only to disclose the "misunderstanding" that had caused the backwardness in Islam. This misunderstanding was the "throttling of rationalism" and a literalistic credulity in the observance of the law. But in reality the Islamic laws were "like rubber"—or so Sukarno set out to demonstrate—and thus here too he had found the broad foundation he needed for accommodating nationalist and Marxist ideas within Islam.

Thus Sukarno embodied all three currents, nationalism, Marxism, and Islam, *as he understood them,* during each phase. Each, his nationalism, his Marxism, and his Islam one after another occupied the foreground and stood respectively for the categories of space, time, and depth in the edifice of Sukarno's thought. Now they were no longer separable; they had been fused into a solid synthesis. In the summer of 1941, Sukarno himself totted up the account:

There are men who say Sukarno is a nationalist; others say he is no longer a nationalist but a Moslem; and others, again, say he is neither nationalist nor Moslem but a Marxist; and finally there are still others who say he is no nationalist, no Moslem, and no Marxist, that he is a man with his own opinions. This latter group declares that if you want to call him a nationalist, he does not agree with what is commonly called nationalism; call him a Moslem, and he expresses opinions that do not accord with the opinion of many Moslems; call him a Marxist—he performs his prayer exercises; say he is no Marxist—he is "mad" over Marxism. . . . What is this Sukarno? Is he a nationalist? A Moslem? A Marxist? Readers, Sukarno is—a mixture *of all these isms*.[2]

"All things are one": such was the Javanese philosophy of earlier centuries, which had been able to assimilate cultures of the most heterogeneous origin, insofar as they turned out to be adaptable and did not attempt to disturb the Tåtå, the indigenous order. The same view dominated Sukarno the Javanese, who had become the point of convergence for all the modern currents which, in his opinion, were able to restore the real order after its destruction by the invaders. It so dominated him that he regarded himself as a mixture of "all these isms" at a moment when tactics did not count because he was in exile, far away from the movement.

As one who had always called for the unity of nationalists, Marxists, and Moslems, and who had constantly sought a common denominator for them all, he had himself become that unity. At the end of the article, that summer of 1941, he declared: *"I am a convinced nationalist, a convinced Moslem, a convinced Marxist. My heart overflows with the synthesis of these three currents, and for me it is a mighty synthesis."* [3]

Preliminary Ideas on a Future Indonesian State

The Useless Parliamentary Democracy

No less old than his "mighty synthesis" was Sukarno's detestation of capitalism. Once independence had been achieved, he

---

[2] "Sukarno—oleh Sukarno sendiri [Sukarno, by himself]," June 14, 1941. With this article Sukarno introduced himself as a new contributor to the journal *Pemandangan* (DBR, pp. 507ff.; cited here, *ibid.*, p. 508).

[3] DBR, p. 513.

wrote at the age of nineteen, the Sarekat Islam must not cease to struggle against capitalism; "What good is our own government if it is directed by adherents of capitalism and imperialism?" [4]

This antipathy to capitalism had deepened in the decades that followed. All the suffering and misery in the world were attributed to capitalism, and in those years of wild agitation it and imperialism, which in Sukarno's opinion was the inevitable consequence, were again and again represented as Enemy Number One. Sukarno first carried his anticapitalist attitude to its logical conclusion at the beginning of the 1930's, when he took from the native bourgeoisie the hope for "something later." Until independence their cooperation was desired. But in Marhaenist Indonesia there was no longer a place for native capitalism, or at any rate for a system that would make its dominance possible.

For him, parliamentary democracy was such a system. It not only offered capitalism temporary advantages but also guaranteed that it would continue. And of this, for him, excerpts from a parliamentary speech made by Jean Jaurès in 1893, along with more recent communist interpretations, were sufficient evidence. It was therefore ruled out as a possible form of government for the Indonesia of the future, so far as Sukarno was concerned, by the beginning of the 1930's. His mistrust of it was only strengthened by subsequent developments in Europe.

In his opinion, fascism was the logical consequence of a mature capitalism, which could no longer tolerate the free competition secured by parliamentary democracy, but required a police state for the protection of its interests. This development had proceeded most rapidly in Germany and Italy; but for Sukarno it was certain that other nations with parliamentary democracy could not escape a similar fate. In England and America, the signs of crisis could already be detected, "although the decline [of capitalism] there is not yet so acute that it is necessary to bring out the whip." [5]

[4] See "Sukarno's Early Political Views," in Chapter II, above.

[5] From "Fasisme adalah politiknja dan sepak terdjangnja Kapitalisme jang menurun [Fascism is the Politics and Activity of Capitalism in Decline]" (DBR, pp. 589ff., 601): "Tetapi turunnja itu belumlah begitu mendesak, sehingga perlu main tjambuk."

This opinion dating to the autumn of 1941 shows that Sukarno's old prejudice had undergone no change during the years of exile; and in other statements from this period, parliamentary democracy was likewise rejected on principle.[6] Political rights, as guaranteed by parliamentary democracy, were not sufficient for the happiness of the people, so long as economic equality was lacking. Even the political rights were questionable, for the propertied classes of course dominated all the channels of propaganda, which in turn guaranteed a majority of the seats in the parliament. And finally, private property was protected by parliamentary democracy. Although parliament might legislate a cow into a horse, it could not attack private property, and inequality in social status was guaranteed as a result.[7]

The Indonesian concept of democracy was different. It adhered to Musjawarat, a general exchange of views among the interest groups represented in the nation, leading ultimately to Mufakat, the consensus. And this spirit was reinforced by Islam, which emphasized equality and consultation for everyone.[8]

Thus through all the years of exile Sukarno had held fast unshakably to the "Indonesian version" of democracy that he had first put into practice in the federation in 1927, and which was to be guided by the principle of Mufakat. If it had since been abandoned as a weapon in the battle for freedom, it was still a political ideal.

In 1933, he had attempted to present as one of Sociodemocracy's goals an agency representative of the entire people, which was to be as comprehensive as possible, even though he still made no more precise statements about the manner in which it would function. The rule of the people must be assured in all sectors, political, economic, and cultural. All larger

---

[6] "Bukan perang Ideologi [It Is Not a War of Ideologies]," 1940 (DBR, pp. 361ff., 365f.); "Beratnja perdjuangan melawan Fasisme [The Difficulty of the Struggle Against Fascism]" (DBR, pp. 547ff., 549f.); and especially "Demokrasi politik dengan demokrasi economi-Demokrasi sosial [Political Democracy and Economic Democracy Equals Social Democracy]" (DBR, pp. 579ff.).

[7] "Demokrasi politik" (DBR, p. 586).

[8] "Indonesia versus Fasisme," 1940 (DBR, pp. 457ff., 458).

industries and their profits must benefit the entire people; there would be no more privileged classes. "The political-economic republic of Indonesia is the reflection of harmony among the people, cooperation among the people, and equality among the people." [9]

So as to be able to achieve this ideal of a "true order," the Marhaenist party would have to intensify the idea of equality in its struggle for freedom: "the spirit of Gotong-Rojong too must be implanted in the hearts of the masses, so that the masses, who for centuries have been infected by the sickness of individualism, can begin from now on to become 'new men' who will regard themselves as 'men of the community,' who will constantly put the general welfare ahead of everything else." [10] Gotong-Rojong was the voluntary mutual help which in Java, as in other parts of the Indonesian archipelago (Tolong-Menolong) had been employed for ages in house-building, harvesting, clearing land, and so forth. With the emphasis on this concept and the divorce from the "sickness of individualism," the separation of "Eastern" from "Western" concepts was all but complete.

The idea of Permusjawaratan, of a general consultation with perpetual concessions from the various sides so as to arrive at Mufakat, has as little in common with Western ideas of a debate entailing clear arguments and a final decision by the majority, as the idea of an individual losing himself in the collective, in Gotong-Rojong, has with the liberal ideas of freedom and individuality.

But this was precisely the goal of Sukarno, who otherwise put such stress on progress. He believed that with what in Western terms seems to be a step backward, he could make the great step toward the future, toward a classless society, and that he could thus circumvent the hated capitalism which he believed to be rooted in liberalism.

It was this system of "Indonesian democracy," which he had

[9] "Mentjapai Indonesia merdeka [Toward Indonesian Independence]" 1933 (DBR, p. 321): "Politiek-economische-Republiek Indonesia adalah gambarnja satu kerukunan Rakjat, satu pekerdjaan-bersama daripada Rakjat, satu ke-sama-rasa-sama-rataan daripada Rakjat."

[10] *Ibid.*, p. 322.

already ingeniously worked out by the end of the 1920's, that Sukarno put into practice in Indonesia at the beginning of the 1960's.

Separation of State and Religion

In his attempts to modernize Islam, Sukarno had not failed to refer to the example of Turkey. In a forty-page article he tried to make clear to the Islamic community in Indonesia that the measures of the Young Turks, in particular Kemal Ataturk's separation of religion and state, had been basically a "liberation of religion." [11]

After a detailed account of the Young Turks' economic and political motives for separating religion from the state, Sukarno set forth with barely concealed approval the particular steps toward secularizing the Turkish state in the 1920's: the end of the sultanate (1922), the end of the caliphate (1924), and the declaration of religion to be a private matter (1928).[12]

True Islam, Sukarno stated, associated various conditions with the caliphate, two of which were particularly important: first, the Caliph was to be *elected* by the Islamic community; second, the Caliph must be in a position to protect the entire Islamic community. The first, however, had been in effect for only twenty years, following which election had been superseded by dynasties. And the second condition had likewise no longer been fulfilled after the thirteenth century. Not elected and lacking in authority: it was thus that the Caliphate had survived the centuries, as a shadow of what it had really been meant to be. What was still worse, religion had for centuries been made the "tool of politics." Only through the measures brought about by the Young Turks had it been given back to the community. Furthermore, he argued, this had been a necessary development:

The separation of religion and state was not begun by Kemal and his colleagues. No, this separation was the conclusion of a process

[11] "Apa sebab Turki memisah agama dari negara [Why Does Turkey Divide Religion from the State?]," 1940 (DBR, pp. 403ff.). In this article Sukarno draws with especial partiality on Halide Edib Hanoum, *Turkey Faces West.*

[12] "Apa sebab" (DBR, pp. 433ff.).

that had gone on for decades and for centuries, it was the result of a social necessity which in the time of Suleiman I, four hundred years ago—Suleiman the Lawgiver!—had already forced the state to issue a code of law outside of the laws of Islam.[13]

Thus, the secular state was a historical necessity. Even the possibilities opened up by the formula "Islam is progress" were not enough to replace it. And Sukarno in this case did not place the decision on the propriety of Kemal Ataturk's action in the hands of Allah: "Only the history of the days to come can be the judge of this." [14]

For Sukarno, the thought that the conservative Ulamas should dominate political decisions was unendurable. For this reason alone he looked upon the separation of religion and state as indispensable. On the other hand, he looked forward quite seriously to a reinvigoration of religion, once it had a chance to develop freely.[15]

One final consideration played an important role in Sukarno's thought. Whoever argued for the unity of state and religion, and wished to make the Islamic law the law of the state, he noted in another context,[16] ought to bear in mind the Christians and other religious communities. They would naturally not agree to an Islamic constitution. What, then would happen to them? The ideal of democracy admitted of no possibility other than the separation of religion and state; the alternative— an Islamic state—could only mean a "dictatorship over minorities." [17]

However critically Sukarno confronted the West, he never went so far as to give Christianity itself a share in the responsibility for undesirable developments in Europe. Secretly he admired the activity and drive of the missionary societies he had been able to observe—as he had observed while he was in exile on the island of Flores, for example, the untiring work of the

---

[13] *Ibid.,* p. 442.

[14] *Ibid.,* p. 445: "Jang dapat mendjadi hakim baginja hanjalah sedjarah kelak kemudian hari."

[15] DBR, pp. 404f., 440f., 443, and many others.

[16] "Saja kurang dinamis [I Am Not Dynamic Enough]," 1940 (DBR, pp. 447ff.).

[17] *Ibid.,* p. 452.

fathers at the Steyler Mission, as a result of which he revised the unfavorable views he had once held of the missions.[18] In one of his letters, he wrote of the Catholic missionaries:

> I have respect for their devotion to their work. We often condemn the missions—but what do we do to spread and strengthen Islam? That the missions develop Roman Catholicism is their *right,* and we may not condemn or complain of it. But *we,* why are *we* lazy, why are *we* negligent, . . . why have *we* no wish to be zealous? . . . It is right for Islam to be ashamed.[19]

In these statements, Sukarno implicitly expressed the idea that the Christian community had appropriated the "fire" whose extinction in the Islamic community he so deeply regretted. If progress was the criterion of belief, then Sukarno had to grant a high value to Christianity, even though he had once described the Church as a bulwark of the propertied classes.

In his series of articles entitled "Modernization of Islam," Sukarno had briefly treated the development of Christianity and had concluded, drawing upon Ameer Ali, that after the councils of the fourth century and the expulsion of Arianism, rationalism had been killed by Catholic dogma. Only after the protests of Luther and Calvin had the Catholic Church become aware that the free study of the sciences and philosophy did not necessarily lead to apostasy. After those protests, it too had undergone a reform, and now appeared to an outsider more liberal than the reformed churches themselves. He hoped that Islam would likewise experience such a period of awakening.[20]

On religious questions, Sukarno was tolerant. This tolerance was not limited to the "possessors of Scripture," but embraced Hinduism and Buddhism as well. That his own mother, a Balinese, had been raised as a member of the Brahman caste in the Hindu religion, might in itself have been a decisive obstacle to the young Sukarno's becoming a Moslem fanatic, had it not been for the influence of the cultural syncretism of Java and of the ultimate wisdom of Javanese mysticism, that "all things are one." In his speeches Sukarno was fond of bringing up compari-

---

[18] See "Sukarno and Islam up to 1934," in Chapter V, above.
[19] See letter of September 15, 1935 (DBR, pp. 330f.). Emphasis Sukarno's.
[20] DBR, p. 396: "Me'muda'kan perngertian Islam."

sons from the most varied religions and cults; Buddhist, Islamic, and Christian images frequently appeared in kaleidoscopic sequence.

From all this it is easy enough to conclude that Sukarno, even in the period of intensive preoccupation with Islam, did not lean toward an Islamic state. As one who strove constantly for synthesis, for whom "dictatorship over minorities" was always odious, he declared in 1940, when he took a stand on principle concerning the question of an Islamic state: [21] certainly it was no matter of "one sentence on a piece of paper"—as he styled the constitution—whether a state was really Islamic or not. Democracy offered possibilities enough for translating the spirit of Islam into legislation. If the laws of Islam were not yet acceptable to a popular representative body, then that only proved that the people were not yet an Islamic people. And so there must be propaganda until the parliament "overflowed" with Islamic delegates, for then the state by itself would assume the character of an Islamic state, even without the statement in the constitution.

An Islam, on the contrary, that could exist only when protected or supported by the state was no Islam. Therefore, it was better and "more manly" for the challenge of democracy to be consciously acknowledged: " 'Good, we accept the separation of state and religion, but we will inflame the whole people with the fire of Islam, so that all the delegates in parliament will be Moslems, and so that all the decisions of the parliament will be filled with the spirit and the soul of Islam!' " [22] It was here that Sukarno had found his ideal solution: agreement on the constitution was made possible in principle for all groups, all schools of thought, and all divisions of the people. If the Moslems wished to demand a special position because of their high proportion in the islands (about 90 per cent), that was open to them. But this meant intensive education, it meant awakening the people from their indifference. Finally, the separation of state and religion offered the guarantee that in its attempt to catch up with the times, the state did not always have to reckon with a veto by a council of Ulamas relying on orthodox laws.

In the spring of 1940, as he worked out a "modernization of

[21] "Saja kurang dinamis" (DBR, pp. 447ff.).   [22] *Ibid.*, p. 453.

Islam" from his desk in Benkulen, Sukarno had little trouble in arriving at this solution to what he described as the "difficult problem" of the relation between religion and the state. To realize the ideal of an Islamic state, he declared toward the end of the article, the expert in matters of religion was not enough: "The realization of this ideal requires a statesman." [23]

The moment that was in fact to demand a statesman had meanwhile drawn nearer, as he may at this time have guessed. Exactly five years later, Sukarno was to stand before a committee dealing with a constitution for the Indonesian state, and to repeat the ideas set forth here almost word for word. After bitter disputes over that "one sentence on a piece of paper," he was finally able to win. This scene marked the end of a new phase in Sukarno's struggle for Indonesian independence—the time of cooperation with the Japanese occupying power, to which we shall now turn our attention.

[23] "Saja kurang dinamis" (DBR, p. 454): "Melaksanakan itu ideal lebih memerlukan 'keahlian kenegaraan.' "

PART THREE
UNDER THE BANNER OF COOPERATION:
SUKARNO'S STRUGGLE FOR
INDONESIAN INDEPENDENCE DURING THE
JAPANESE OCCUPATION (1942–1945)

VII

Arrival of the New Masters

Waiting for Japan

Sukarno and Japanese Imperialism up to
the Outbreak of War in the Pacific

When the Netherlands was occupied by German troops in
May 1940, the Dutch colonial government was virtually isolated. All its efforts in the colony were now directed toward
maintaining the status quo.

Declarations of loyalty on the part of the Indonesian nationalists were accepted as a matter of course. All aspirations toward
a future autonomous status within the Dutch empire, which for
years had been advanced in the form of petitions, were now put
on ice after a pattern established in 1918, by the appointment of
a commission of investigation.[1]

The final opportunity of demonstrating the slightest willingness to oblige Indonesian groups willing to cooperate was thus
wasted by the colonial regime. With appalling consistency, from
the rise of the nationalist movement to the end of colonial rule,
that regime had throttled every wish for a real partnership and
delivered proof after proof for the correctness of Sukarno's the-

---

[1] The reference is to the so-called Visman-Commissie, which was to
"investigate more closely" the wishes of all groups of the population; in
reality, however, it was nothing more than a delaying tactic. In it, experts
on the Indonesian movement such as D. M. G. Koch were deliberately
passed over in preference to employees who first had to become acquainted
with the material (conversation with Professor G. F. Pijper on October 17,
1963). For a general account of developments that cannot be discussed
here in more detail, see Pluvier, *Overzicht,* pp. 167ff.; also the recollections
of a member of the Visman Commission, W. F. Wertheim, in *Nederland
op den tweesprong* (1946), pp. 6ff., as well as J. de Kadt, *De Indonesische
tragedie: Het treurspel der gemiste kansen* (1949), pp. 17–41.

ory that nothing was to be expected of it. Thus it played out the role of the Kaurawas perfectly to the end.

The Indonesians, after having attested their loyalty in May 1940, were disillusioned and made no secret of their anger. In the autumn of 1940, after the newspapers had carried the declaration of a Japanese minister (Kobayashi) that, if Japan intended to extend its influence to the East Indies, it would be dependent on the support of the Indonesian people,[2] Thamrin dared to refer publicly in the Volksraad to the conclusions that had been drawn from Kobayashi's statement, namely that once again they had begun looking forward to the coming of the Japanese.[3]

The colonial power was less indifferent to this theme—the probing questions of the chairman at Sukarno's trial on how Sukarno's party would behave in the event of Japanese aggression may be recalled—than it was to the wishes of the nationalists. Only a few weeks later, on January 6, 1941, Thamrin was arrested on charges of subversive activity,[4] along with the old fighter for freedom, Douwes Dekker, who in 1913 had already proclaimed the slogan, "Free from Holland." The affair took on a tragic note when Thamrin, while still in detention pending investigation, died suddenly of a heart attack.

In the Indonesian press, these incidents gave rise to agitated discussion. Even Mohammed Natsir, who was otherwise not uncritical of the nationalists, defended them against the suspicion that there was "Wang Ching-weiism" in Indonesia. "If their speeches sound critical, that is certainly much better than if they were to remain quiet and secretly plan revenge." [5]

Sukarno was one of those who remained quiet. From him af-

[2] Mohammed Natsir, "Gapi-Komisi Visman" (in *Cap. Sel. I*, p. 346), an article dated March 1941, in which he quotes Kobayashi's statements.

[3] See "The Hour of Djajabaja," below.

[4] Cf. S. L. van der Wal, *De Volksraad en de Staatkundige Ontwikkeling van Nederlands-Indië*, Vol. II (1965), p. 590.

[5] "Pendirian politik M. H. Thamrin [The Political Standpoint of M. H. Thamrin]," January 1941 (*Cap. Sel. I*, pp. 333ff., esp. 336). See also the article by Natsir, "Adalah Wang-Ching-Weisme di Indonesia? Tidak sahut kita [Is There Wang Ching-wei-ism in Indonesia? No, We Answer]" (*ibid.*, pp. 339ff.).

ter May 10 there was not so much as a syllable of commiseration with Holland's fate—as there was, for example, from the true Ksatrija Tjipto Mangunkusumo, who since 1927 had been continuously in exile, but who in May 1940 nevertheless publicly called for a burying of the hatchet and for once more taking up the "old hobby," the struggle for independence, only after the liberation of the Netherlands,[6] and who informed Sukarno accordingly.[7]

But Sukarno maintained his silence. Even when, in the spring of 1941, the then Advizeur, Dr. Pijper, visited him and held out the prospect of a return to Java if he would write pro-Dutch articles, Sukarno's only response was that he would make known this "inducement" to the Indonesian movement, so as to show "where Bung Karno stands," as he had put it in 1932.[8]

Since the trial, his conviction that war would break out in the Pacific had gone unchanged. For him, now that the "competence of Marxism in political, historical, and social questions" had been proved anew, as Sukarno believed he could conclude from the outbreak of war in Europe,[9] it was only a question of time, given the active propaganda of the Japanese, until the war in the Pacific, already prophesied for so long, finally broke out. Sukarno must have guessed that it would not be much longer, for the article "Sukarno, by Himself," published in June 1941, contained the remarkable sentence, "Formerly I was devoted to the theory of Marxism; now it has become a part of my inner satisfaction." [10]

This "inner satisfaction" prevented Sukarno, in his anti-fascist articles of the time, from judging events in Asia as harshly as he did those in Europe. So, for example, a stand against Japanese actions in China is completely absent. Only once did he even mention that war was being waged in China,

6 See Natsir's article, "Dr. Tjipto membela sikapnja [Dr. Tjipto Defends His Attitude]," July 1940 (Cap. Sel. I, pp. 318ff.).

7 Sutan Sjahrir, Out of Exile (1949), p. 220.

8 Conversation with Professor Pijper, October 17, 1963, in Amsterdam. See also Asia Raya, September 30, 2604 (1944), p. 1.

9 "Sukarno—oleh Sukarno Sendiri" (DBR, p. 511).

10 Ibid.: "Dulu saja tjinta kepada teori Marxisme itu; kini mendjadilah ia sebagian dari sajapunja kepuasan djwa."

and this was in a quotation cited to show how many allies England could gain for herself in Asia by a consistent policy of granting independence.[11]

Soon afterward, in the summer of 1941, Sukarno even described the Japanese Army, which for years had been waging an aggressive war of the most undisguised sort, as a "self-defense force." [12] At about the same time he wrote, in an article entitled "Fascism Is the Politics and Activity of Capitalism in Decline": "Anyone who has ever studied Marxism knows that the true emblem of the [fascist] state is the club. In Germany, the state has truly transformed itself openly into a cudgel; in Italy it is the same; it could be said that even in Japan it is the same." [13] The modifying clause "it could be said"—like his remark in 1929 that although Japan was imperialistic, it must decide whether it wished to choose the side of a West that was hastening toward its decline, or of the rising East,[14] was an expression of uncertainty over how he should react to the phenomenon of an Asiatic imperialism which squared so little with the pure image of the East. Out of a flood of anti-fascist articles during this period, this was until recently the only one known in which Sukarno permitted himself even a muted criticism of Japan.[15]

[11] See the article, "1,000,000,000 Extra," a review of Fritz Sternberg's article, "One Billion Extra," in *Asia,* 1941 (DBR, pp. 541ff.).

[12] In "India Merdeka—dapatkah ia menangkis serangan [Can an Independent India Withstand Attack?]" (DBR, p. 569): "Tenaga pertahanan-diri seperti misalnja Japan."

[13] "Fasisme adalah politiknja. . . ." (DBR, p. 601).

[14] See "Trust in Foreign Assistance," in Chapter III, above.

[15] Further critical remarks by Sukarno on Japanese fascism ("This moral evil is not of the whites alone [sic]. Japan, too, has this lust for power") can now be found in an article quoted by Sukarno in his *Autobiography as Told to Cindy Adams* (1965), p. 146. According to Sukarno, this article was published in *Pemandangan* in July 1941. It has not been reprinted in DBR, and thus far the author has not succeeded in obtaining a copy or in locating further evidence. The same applies to the series of articles in *Ilmu dan Masjarakat,* mentioned by Takdir Alisjahbana, *Indonesia: Social and Cultural Revolution* (1966), p. 170, in which "before the war" Sukarno "expressed his sympathy with National Socialism." Thus the interesting question of whether there was a change in Sukarno's attitude toward fascism, and of when it occurred, must for the time being remain unanswered. In 1940–41, however, he was quite outspoken in his criticism of "the Hitlers and Mussolinis of the world."

This strangely ambivalent attitude toward Japanese imperialism strengthens the impression that Sukarno had literally looked forward to the outbreak of the Pacific war. He had already indicated how he imagined the Indonesian nationalists would act in the event of a Japanese invasion as long ago as 1930, when he declared: "Suppose there were hostility between one Asian people and, for example, English imperialism. I would then hope that this Asian people would receive help from other Asian peoples." [16] Since then this view had hardly changed. Although Sukarno had become more intimately acquainted with the dangers of fascism, the war was the only chance to drive Western imperialism, still the archenemy, out of Asia. It was not necessary to support fascism directly; nevertheless, they had a common enemy. In August 1941, he cited Nehru, who had said: "Even if the Indian people do not agree with Nazism and fascism, even if the Indian people recognize the evil of Nazism and fascism, . . . they will surely part company with the English. They have no wish to help the English in the present war." [17]

Sukarno took the same position [18] when the Netherlands Indies responded to the Japanese attack on Pearl Harbor on December 7, 1941, with a declaration of war. It is possible that at some time he had expressed anti-Japanese sentiments in private conversation, but he had never done so in public statements, as had the "European" Indonesians who recognized "common norms." After the outbreak of war in December 1941 Hatta wrote from exile an article in which he called for struggle against the Japanese. For him, there was no difference between European and Asian imperialism: "If we are convinced that Japanese aggression endangers our ideals, then we must resist

[16] See "The Trial of Sukarno," in Chapter III, above.

[17] See "1,000,000,000 Extra" (DBR, pp. 544f.). Nehru's article (here translated from the Indonesian) appeared in *Asia* under the title, "The Parting of the Ways."

[18] The data on Sukarno given in this paragraph are based on a critical examination of the source materials, not yet released for publication, in the Rijksinstituut voor Oorlogsdocumentatie at Amsterdam. The author is especially indebted to the chronicler of these events, Mr. A. G. Vromans. He would also thank the then Adviseur, Professor Pijper of Amsterdam, for additional data.

Japanese imperialism. Even if we believe that Japan will probably win, it remains our duty to come to the defense of our endangered ideals. It is better to die on one's feet than to live on one's knees." [19]

From Sukarno, who had already declared in 1929 that the Pacific War would hasten the coming of freedom,[20] such an appeal would have been unthinkable. The colonial government may have perceived the difference between the nationalists. Whereas Hatta and Sjahrir were flown back to Java in the final hour before the Japanese invasion,[21] Sukarno was not permitted to return to Java.

Even an urgent request by the Resident of Benkulen to the Governor General, in mid-February of 1942, to have Sukarno sent back to Java because he feared "unfortunate results" from his encounter with the Japanese—who had already landed on Sumatra—was not granted. Thereupon Sukarno was transferred from southern Sumatra to Padang (Central Sumatra). Apparently this was to prevent his initiating revolutionary activity immediately after the occupation in an area where he already had many acquaintances. Because at this time the Dutch, for their own part, still counted on early relief from the Allies, Sukarno's transfer to an unfamiliar province shortly before the capture of Benkulen probably seemed to the Resident the safest measure he could take.

The conjecture that Sukarno was to have been interned in Australia from Padang [22] is false. Although such a plan had once been discussed in the Raad van Indië, there was no legal pretext for carrying it out. On the basis of the "exorbitant rights" under which Sukarno had been exiled, the sentence could be passed on to Indonesians only within the archipelago. The assertion that Sukarno himself had repeatedly and urgently

[19] *Pemandangan,* December 22, 1941; cited in B. H. M. Vlekke, *Nusantara* . . . (1945), pp. 396f. (The chapter entitled "War Comes to the Indies" has been completely eliminated from the 1959 edition.)

[20] See "Trust in Foreign Assistance," in Chapter III, above; also Sukarno, *Autobiography,* p. 146: "This war . . . I had calculated would bring my dreams full circle."

[21] Sjahrir, *Out of Exile,* pp. 225ff.

[22] As given by Nasution, *Riwajat,* p. 60.

sought to be evacuated to Australia [23] is the product of a campaign of defamation instituted after the war, and there is not the slightest evidence for it either in contemporary Dutch sources or in Sukarno's basic attitude.

There was talk of evacuating the "European" nationalists, above all Mohammed Hatta,[24] who was to continue to propagate democratic ideals from Australia. But by the time this step was seriously considered, it was already too late. On March 1, 1942, the Japanese landed at various points in Java, and a week later the island was officially in their hands.

The Hour of Djajabaja

In the summer of 1941, Sukarno was not alone in his "inner satisfaction," which made him certain that war would soon break out in the Pacific. The Indonesian people believed with the same intensity in the coming of the Japanese. For them, the expectations did not rest on the "competence of Marxist theory" concerning political questions, but rather, as in 1929, on the prophecy of Djajabaja, in which he had foretold the arrival of small yellow men from the north. From Sjahrir's records it becomes clear how deeply rooted the Djajabaja legend was even in Bandaneira, far away from Java, how intently people looked forward to the fulfillment of the prophecy even before the outbreak of war, and how they saw the Japanese as potential liberators.[25]

More than any statement of principle, the futile attempts of Hatta and Sjahrir to counteract this popular superstition showed how far removed from the people they had become. Sjahrir's comments in exile—"We often did not understand one another, the people and I; I was too abstract for my people, too 'Western'; I stood beyond their capacity to comprehend. And they for me were often too dull, they made me doubt by their animosity and their misunderstanding, they made me angry and

[23] H. J. H. Alers, *Om een roode of groene Merdeka* (1956), p. 47; D. Wehl, *The Birth of Indonesia* (1948), p. 10.

[24] Sjahrir, *Out of Exile*, p. 233.

[25] Sjahrazad, *Overpeinzingen*, pp. 100f. 120, 136, 160f., 166f.; also Sjahrir, *Out of Exile*, pp. 218f., 232f.

impatient with their petty failures" [26]—were borne out by his critical view of the Djajabaja myth, which had been gaining ground since 1940, just as they had been ten years earlier by the uncomprehending rejection of Sukarno's striving for unity. If Sukarno was often clearly the inferior of Sjahrir (as he was of Hatta, Salim, Natsir, and others) in objectivity as well as in detailed information, nevertheless he was much more closely united to the thoughts and hopes of the people. Their common "waiting for Japan" was further evidence of this.

After the statement by Kobayashi in the autumn of 1940, that should Japan extend its sphere of influence to the East Indian islands, it would need the help of the native people, the speculations began to be revived again, especially on Java. Soon an acrostic in Indonesian, based on the name Kobayashi, was circulating: "*K*oloni *O*rang *B*elanda *A*kan *J*apan *A*mbil *S*eantero *I*ndonesia (Japan will take the entire Dutch colony of Indonesia)." [27] As the outbreak of the Pacific war came near, the rumors flew thicker still, so that after the attack on Pearl Harbor the police were finally no longer feared, and it was openly declared: "The prophecy of Djajabaja will be fulfilled; the period of white rule is over." [28]

The approaching Japanese played the role for which they had been destined by Djajabaja to perfection. They dropped pamphlets over Java that read:

We announce to you the arrival of the Japanese Army. The Japanese Army will land in Indonesia in order to [*sic*] fulfill the prophecy of his majesty Djajabaja. . . . Remember: his majesty Djajabaja said, yellow men will come out of the north to liberate the Indonesian people from the slavery of the Dutch. Look for the yellow skins.[29]

[26] Sjahrazad, *Overpeinzingen,* pp. 34f.

[27] So Thamrin declared in the Volksraad in the fall of 1940; see Pluvier, *Overzicht,* pp. 183.

[28] Sjahrir, *Out of Exile,* pp. 232f.

[29] Quoted in I. J. Brugmans, H. J. de Graaf, A. H. Joustra, and A. G. Vromans, eds., *Nederlandsch-Indië onder Japan'sche bezetting; gegevens en documenten over de jaren 1942–45* (1960), pp. 98f.

By such clever propaganda the Japanese could only feed Indonesian hopes. And when they were finally able to take Java without serious resistance within the first eight days of March 1942, the Japanese were accorded a welcome such as they had certainly not expected. "A frantic atmosphere of welcome ruled the entire region of the East Indies," the Japanese Admiral Maeda, who during the occupation was to acquire great prestige in the eyes of the Indonesian nationalists, later recalled.[30]

There is no doubt that the Japanese had "his majesty" Djajabaja to thank for this welcome. For a century and a half his prophecy of the liberation of the Javanese by the army of the Prince of Kling had lain dormant in popular consciousness. Since the rise of Japan as a world power, hopes had shifted to the northeast, and with the propagation of the Indonesian idea, the entire archipelago had come to be included in the liberation.

Tjokroaminoto's Sarekat Islam, as well as Sukarno's Partai Nasional Indonesia, had unwittingly fed popular superstition, which in a time of crisis could become a political factor of first importance. The Sarekat Islam had learned this in the so-called "Section B" affair in 1919–20, and so had the PNI exactly ten years later, when there were rumors of an uprising.

If, at such a moment, the control of the movement slipped from the hands of the charismatic leaders—first Tjokroaminoto and later Sukarno—and they were punished for "crimes" they did not commit, Djajabaja was able to avenge them: he gave them, along with the crown of martyrdom, a kingdom in the hearts of the masses, and so it would be this time.

A matter that did not interest the Japanese,[31] but that was

[30] Rijksinstituut voor Oorlogsdocumentatie, Indische Collectie (RVO-IC 005302).

[31] *Untuk apa sekarang Nippon berdjuang,* a question-and-answer manual issued by the Japanese military government in 1944, asked laconically (Question 15; p. 9), "How did Djajabaja's prophecy go 600 years ago?" According to the answer, "It was prophesied that a great king, riding on a white horse, would free the Indonesian people." It was then explained, so that no misunderstanding could arise, "By the king on the white horse is meant His Highness, the Tenno Heika."

very closely observed by the Indonesian people, was the second part of the prophecy—that after a "year of corn" the yellow men from the north would return to their islands. Already in 1943, versions of Djajabaja circulated in Java which gave details about the end of yellow rule.[32] Thus the Japanese were regarded from the beginning as guests whose days were numbered. This part of the prophecy was also emphasized by Dutch propaganda about Djajabaja in radio broadcasts from America —without, however, paying attention to the "final" statement, (at least at this time), that the sons of the fatherland would later take the government into their own hands.[33]

The people knew better than the Japanese, and also than the Dutch, what Djajabaja meant. Therefore, public interest was focussed on the reappearance of the man who for a decade and a half had embodied the Ratu Adil idea and who in great measure owed his fame to this popular belief: namely Sukarno.

A Japanese inquiry into the popular mood at the beginning of 1943 observed: "His name is on the lips of all, whether they know him or not; Indonesians of all groups are concerned about him." And after describing the expectations of the various groups, the report went on concerning the people generally: "They speak of rumors such as that 'Sukarno will be king of the archipelago' and that 'the Japanese will appoint him Governor General.' But they have not the faintest notion of politics." [34] Sukarno had no need to fret, as Sjahrir did, about a lack of contact with the people. Eight years of exile could not diminish his reputation. From the moment he made his confident return under the new masters in the summer of 1942, he was once more the focus of hope and anticipation.

[32] One such version was given to the archives of the RVO in Amsterdam by Dr. H. J. de Graaf.

[33] See W. F. Wertheim, *Nederland op den tweesprong* (1946), p. 15. Professor C. C. Berg reported to the author that he had had trouble explaining to the Dutch prisoners in the internment camps that the prophecy did not provide for any "return of the whites." However, some versions of the prophecy had also once more taken this very possibility into account.

[34] Beppan Report, February 15, 1943 (RVO-IC 008223f.)

Before Sukarno's return to the movement can be depicted, however, the occupation policy of the Japanese for Indonesia must be briefly considered.

General Guidelines of Japanese Occupation Policy up to September 1944

The exaggerated expectations of the nationalists with respect to "liberation," which the Japanese themselves had encouraged, received a severe setback a few days after the occupation of Java.[35] Although at first the red-and-white flags of Indonesia had actually been dropped from Japanese airplanes, a decree issued only fourteen days after the occupation outlawed the wearing or display of the Indonesian colors. A further order forbade any discussion, organization, speculation, or propaganda about the political organization or administration of the country.

At that point the widespread game of choosing cabinets that had been engaged in by Indonesian newspapers came abruptly to an end. And finally, in May 1942, the Indonesian nationalists were given to understand that they would make themselves ridiculous in the eyes of other nations if they continued to refer to "Indonesia" in a political sense: it was nothing other than an ethnological term.

Instead, on the birthday of the Tenno (April 29) the Japanese proclaimed a strange new creation under the name of the Triple A (Tiga A) Movement, from three initial letters in "Japan, the leader of *A*sia, the protector of *A*sia, the light of *A*sia." It might more correctly have been called the "Triple J Movement," since it was clearly concerned not with Asia but only with Japan. It evoked no popular response. Soon such

[35] Cf. the following in H. J. Benda, "The Beginnings of the Japanese Occupation of Java," *Far Eastern Quarterly,* XV (1956), 541ff. G. Pakpahan, *1261 hari dibawah sinar Matahari Terbit* [1261 Days Under the Rays of the Rising Sun] (1947), Chapter I, gives an excellent account of the arrival and first actions of the Japanese. For the first laws, see the brochure published by the military government in June 1942, *Undang-undang dari Pembesar Balatentera Dai Nippon Nr. 1–20* [Laws of the Commander in Chief of the Japanese Army, Nos. 1–20.].

ironical versions as "Awas Armada Amerika (Beware the American fleet)" were in circulation.[36]

Thus after scarcely two months' occupation, the suddenly awakened nationalism had again been choked off, and along with it the genuine enthusiasm for cooperation with these "liberators."

Certainly the Japanese had hardly expected that the masses would be so easily decoyed. The military regime had first of all to observe the policy guidelines that had been worked out to some degree for particular regions that were to be occupied before the outbreak of the war.

These guidelines provided [37] for giving independence to the Philippines promptly, and for holding out at least the prospect of independence to Burma. For the Netherlands Indies, on the other hand, all political considerations were made subordinate to a plan for the economic exploitation of the area. Here the Japanese hoped to have a minimum of difficulty and even contemplated retaining the Dutch experts. The promise of greater participation by Indonesians in the government, and the incitement of a hope for possible independence after the war, were believed to be a sufficient concession to the interests of the Indonesians.

Moreover, in organizing the occupation the Japanese destroyed Indonesian unity. Java received its own command (the Sixteenth Army); Celebes, Borneo, and the entire eastern region of the archipelago, were placed under the Navy, which was frequently at odds with the Japanese Army and which had its command in Makassar (Celebes). Finally, Sumatra fell under the administrative area of the Twenty-Fifth Army, based in Singapore. Thus for the *first time* a policy of divide-and-rule

[36] See, for example, G. W. Overdijkink, *Het Indonesische problem; de feiten* (1946), pp. 22ff.; also Pakpahan, p. 13ff.

[37] Cf. W. H. Elsbree, *Japan's Role in Southeast Asian Nationalist Movements 1940–45* (1953), pp. 13ff.; also M. A. Aziz, *Japan's Colonialism and Indonesia* (1955), pp. 99ff. ("Plans for Indonesia"), and Nishijima Shigetada and Kishi Koichi, *Japanese Military Administration in Indonesia* (1963), pp. 103ff. Elsbree has obviously examined Japanese documents; Aziz depends primarily upon the testimony of the Japanese before the military court set up in Tokyo after the end of the war.

was deliberately imposed on the archipelago, which had been embraced by the administrative unity of the Netherlands Indies for some forty years.

The Japanese war aim of a "Greater East Asia Co-Prosperity Sphere" was also to be given an ideological basis in particular countries. Guidelines were laid down for freedom "correctly understood" and "incorrectly understood." Western liberalism and communist ideas were to be destroyed, and the idea of an East Asian community emphasized instead. Only within the framework of the Co-Prosperity Sphere was freedom possible, and such a freedom was "different from an independence based on the idea of liberalism and national self-determination." [38]

Nevertheless, the Japanese did have an interest in winning over leading personalities with influence among the masses, and every possible effort was to be made in this direction. On the other hand, those not prepared to abandon Western ideas, and those opposed to the Japanese, were to be "eliminated." [39]

Thus the only concession to the Indonesians was to offer participation in the government and to stir up hopes for a "correctly understood" freedom after the war, but without any binding promise. Broadly outlined, these were the occupation policies in effect from the spring of 1942 to about May 1943, with certain tactical options left open.

But after the beginning of 1943, when the advance of the Japanese had been checked, they became increasingly interested in Indonesia's natural resources. In addition, by holding onto the Netherlands Indies they intended to secure a valuable pawn for possible peace negotiations. From then on, the notion of future independence was pushed more and more into the background. Whereas preliminary steps toward independence for the Philippines and Burma were taken in January 1943, at a secret meeting in May 1943 Tokyo decided to "incorporate" the Indonesian archipelago into the territory of Japan.[40]

Up to this moment, the possibility of independence after the war had still been left open even by the Tokyo government. But after the spring of 1943, any such hope was systematically

[38] Elsbree, *Japan's Role*, pp. 26f.   [39] *Ibid.*, pp. 38, 40f.
[40] *Ibid.*, pp. 47f.

undermined. Official statements referred only to Java or the "southern regions (Daerah Selatan)" and the "Indonesian idea" was completely eliminated. Up until September 1944, when because of the unfavorable course of the war Tokyo decided to change its attitude toward the Indonesians, these guidelines were fully in effect.

The measures taken by the military regime in Java accurately reflected the directives worked out in Tokyo. If a certain attitude of good will toward the nationalists is observable up to about April 1943, after May 1943 there was an increasingly open ruthlessness toward all Indonesian interests. The nationalists, who up until then, under Sukarno's leadership, had voluntarily cooperated with the Japanese, were thus gradually forced to reconsider their attitude. The crisis that arose moved toward a climax in the spring of 1944, and led in August 1944 to the nationalists' first real success. For the occupation power, this opened up new perspectives, in that summer of 1944, for a struggle that had long appeared hopeless.

We shall now turn our attention to this struggle for partnership, with all its hopes and its disillusionments.

VIII

The Struggle for Partnership
(March 1942–August 1944)

Sukarno's Decision to Cooperate with the
Japanese Occupation

The decisive meeting between Sukarno and the Japanese took place on March 17, 1942, in Bukittingi, the home town of Sjahrir and Hatta, where Sukarno had been taken from Padang to meet Colonel Fujiyama, the first military commander of Minangkabau. Some years later he described this first meeting in detail.

At the entrance to the Ngarai canyon, overlooked by the Merapi and Singgalang volcanoes, the Japanese colonel inquired whether, since as a patriot Sukarno certainly desired the independence of his fatherland, he was aware that it could only be achieved through cooperation with Dai Nippon (Greater Japan). He thought it over, Sukarno went on, and then:

Alhamdulillah—Allah be praised, there is no God but he—gave me a sign. There at the entrance to the Ngarai, I answered, Yes! Indonesia's independence can only be achieved by cooperation with Dai Nippon. At the entrance to the Ngarai, I became aware that the lifeline of Indonesia lay in Asia; the goal and purpose of the war in Greater East Asia became plain to me; it became clear to me how false is the anti-Japanese propaganda of the Allies.[1]

---

[1] See *Asia Raya* (AR), the only newspaper appearing continuously from April 29, 2602 [1942] to the end of the war (more precisely, until September 7, 1945), issues for November 13, 2604 [1944], p. 2, and September 8, 2604, p. 3. For more details on this "enormously important meeting," at which Sukarno decided to cooperate with the Japanese, as he now recalls it, see his *Autobiography*, pp. 159–62.

For a long time during the Japanese occupation Sukarno's speeches were censored, as will be shown presently. Therefore, care is required in interpreting them. It is not possible, however, simply to write off all his anti-Allied statements and to conclude with Kahin that "according to his instructions from the Japanese he attacked the Allies." [2] Sukarno's fundamentally anti-Western attitude, which he had cultivated for two decades, required no reinforcement from the Japanese. Even after censorship was lifted, the Allies remained Enemy Number One. Rather, Sukarno's praise of the Japanese is to be taken with a grain of salt; but here too it will become clear that, despite strict censorship, Sukarno knew how to say exactly what he wanted to, often in language quite bluntly critical.

The "entrance to the Ngarai," which he so often invoked in describing his first meeting with the Japanese, became for Sukarno (who liked to look for symbols before decisive actions) [3] the entrance into a new phase of his struggle, the beginning of the struggle for Indonesian independence under the Japanese occupation. One year later, he declared in Djakarta to an audience of 200,000, "We are now pursuing the struggle, we are now participating in the Bharata Judha, we are now making sacrifices too." [4] With this allusion to the decisive battle of the legend, Sukarno made it clear that he had again taken up his old struggle against the West.

He had to wait patiently for a few months more, however, before he could initiate his planned cooperation with the Japanese. Soon after the occupation, various young Indonesians had already addressed to Lieutenant General Imamura, the first Saiko Sikikan (Commander in Chief) on Java, a petition to free Sukarno. Imamura later recalled that he had thereupon sent an airplane to Sumatra to fetch the "Doctor," even though he had been warned from Singapore that Sukarno was a secessionist

[2] Kahin, *Nationalism,* p. 108.

[3] Thus, for example, the establishment of the PNI occurred on July 4, 1927. This was a kind of appeal to the American independence day; the similarity of the days was frequently invoked, as for example in SIM, No. 7–8 (July 1928).

[4] AR, March 12, 2603 [1943], p. 1.

and that the Sixteenth Army would one day regret its decision.[5]

But Sukarno's return to Java was not to be accomplished so promptly or so gloriously. In June, two members of the Triple A Movement, which had been founded in the meantime, went to Sumatra to establish a similar movement and to arrange for Sukarno's release.[6] Soon afterward it was announced in *Asia Raya* that Sukarno had first returned from Padang to Benkulen to close up his household there, and had then traveled on to Palembang, where he was awaiting permission to return to Java.[7]

Four more weeks passed before Sukarno's arrival in Java could be reported. On July 9, 1942, after a stormy voyage in a small motor launch that took four days and four nights, he arrived in Java with members of his immediate family. There he was met by a few companions of years gone by—among them Mohammed Hatta, in whose house later that night Sukarno also met Sutan Sjahrir. What was discussed on that first evening is recorded by the latter.

Sukarno—called "Abdul Rahman" by Sjahrir in his autobiography—had appeared to be "strongly affected" by the Japanese successes. However, according to Sjahrir, "he regarded them as pure fascists, and felt that we must use the most subtle countermethods to get around them, such as making an appearance of collaboration. He furthermore considered the future far from promising, *because* he thought the war with Japan would last at least ten years." [8]

The question is whether Sjahrir had correctly interpreted the opinions of Sukarno. In Sukarno's own account of the meeting [9] there is no evidence that he recommended "the most subtle countermethods to get around them," or that he believed the future to be "far from promising." If Sukarno believed the war "would last at least ten years," this could be interpreted as meaning that he found the future quite promising, since what

---

[5] H. Imamura, "A Tapir in Prison," RVO-IC 002460, p. 123.

[6] AR, June 9, 2602 [1942]; also Pakpahan, *1261 hari*, p. 16.

[7] AR, June 13, 2602 [1942].

[8] Sjahrir, *Out of Exile*, p. 246. Emphasis added.

[9] Sukarno, *Autobiography*, pp. 173f.

Hatta and Sjahrir seemingly took for granted—namely that the reconquest of Java by the Allies would amount to a liberation—did not hold for him. Even if he regarded the Japanese as "pure fascists," a point that he might have stressed in order to avoid distrust on the part of his old opponents, this was not necessarily an obstacle to cooperation. "This is the chance we have waited for," he now claims to have exulted on that occasion. "Of this I am certain. The occupation will prove a magnificent opportunity to educate and ready our people." [10] And this, after all, had already been his intention in the late nineteen-twenties.

The different attitudes toward the West of Sjahrir and Hatta on the one hand and Sukarno on the other have been referred to often enough. Here they must receive brief mention once again; otherwise Sukarno's subsequent behavior could be misinterpreted. Sjahrir reports as well their clear understanding that the Japanese would attempt to capitalize on Sukarno's popularity, and that they had reached an agreement to extract political concessions in return. Thus for some months Sukarno had kept him informed of all his activities and asked for his opinion. For a time it appeared as though his idea of a national organization combining all classes of the people might have a chance of success. But then it became clear that the Japanese had quite different intentions. Under these conditions, efforts for loyal collaboration were doomed to fail. Thus there was no reason for Sukarno to continue to meet with him, "and I lost touch with him until just before the proclamation of our independence." [11]

These words of Sjahrir, who because of his own "unpopularity" could risk organizing an anti-Japanese resistance movement, unmistakably contain a subtle criticism. There would have been reason for further contact, especially after September 1944, if the two men had held similar views. It may be noted that in all these years Hatta had never lost touch with Sjahrir; as Sjahrir himself says, "He also received our reports and warned us when he heard that something was brewing on the Japanese side. From him I heard everything that took place among the Japanese and among the collaborating Indonesians." [12]

10 *Ibid.;* also pp. 156f.   11 Sjahrir, *Out of Exile,* p. 247.
12 *Ibid.,* p. 242.

Between Sjahrir and Hatta there was a meeting of minds, the "unconscious assumption of common norms" with the defenders of Western democracy, to quote Sjahrir's words once again. For Sukarno, however, this was no more true in 1942 than it had been in 1932.

Hatta, in his speeches during the Japanese occupation, was always able to indicate—either through subtle irony or by praise in the wrong place—that he had been practically forced by the Japanese to cooperate. Never did he lend himself to open attacks on the Allies. In the entire period, his attention was principally devoted to quiet work for the movement. For him, to cooperate with the Japanese, as Sjahrir once expressed it, was to bow before "force majeure." [13]

For Sukarno, on the other hand, this "force majeure" did not exist. From his own standpoint he behaved quite as consistently as Hatta and Sjahrir. For him, the Japanese occupation offered a unique opportunity to realize a long-cherished ideal that was not attainable under Western domination. "Nippon mengasih kans kepada kita (Japan is giving us a chance)," he said again and again in his early speeches.[14] In March 1943, after the death of Tjipto Mangunkusumo, his old friend and teacher, who at the cost of his own popularity never made a secret of his distaste for the Japanese aggressors, and who scorned all collaborators (with the single exception of Hatta),[15] Sukarno still attempted to "explain" to him, in a funeral oration, that the earlier phase of the struggle for independence was now closed and that a new period had begun "with new enthusiasm." [16]

Sukarno's reasons for cooperating with the Japanese were strong enough to whip up this "new enthusiasm":

1. *They had a common enemy.* If the Japanese directed their propaganda toward the elimination of Western liberalism and individualism, and if they emphasized the communal spirit, they would then have expressed Sukarno's innermost thoughts. During his exile, nothing in his rejection of Western ideals had

---

[13] Sjahrir, *Out of Exile,* p. 242; Pakpahan, *1261 hari,* pp. 14f.

[14] See, for example, AR, October 10, 2602, and December 7, 2602.

[15] Sjahrir, *Out of Exile,* p. 242.

[16] AR, March 13, 2603 [1943], p. 2.

altered. For him, liberalism, then capitalism, then imperialism, and then fascism represented a single line of development, and must be driven out of Asia by the unification of all forces. For this reason he had propounded his "inter-Asianism" for decades, never mind what form it might finally take. Even though he may have been skeptical of the Japanese war aim of a Greater East Asia Co-Prosperity Sphere led by Dai Nippon, for at least a part of the way they were following a common path.

2. *There was an opportunity to arouse the popular consciousness.* The part of the way they had in common was ideal for arousing and inflaming the people's readiness for struggle. The Japanese—especially after their military advance had come to a standstill—were dependent on the active help of the population for the defense of their "plunder." This called for intensive propagandizing among the masses, whose growing dissatisfaction with the new masters' Draconian measures could, under skillful direction, strengthen the pressure for independence to a degree previously unimagined. The very weapon that was essential to the Japanese could one day actually be used against them.

3. *There was an opportunity to build a united front.* Because of tactical considerations related to the war, the Japanese had been interested from the beginning in a unified popular organization. They saw it as the best guarantee of the smooth transmission of orders down to the Desas (villages) and, on the other hand, of quick recognition for complaints from below.[17] For years, building a united front had been Sukarno's dream, which had been destroyed for him not by the Dutch colonial power —as he was characteristically to assert in subsequent months— but rather by Sjahrir and Hatta. That both men, because of the circumstances, were now likewise interested in a national organization as inclusive as possible, was evident from the nocturnal conversation in Hatta's house after Sukarno had been released.

4. *There was an opportunity for agitation.* Mass agitation had always been Sukarno's forte. It was by openly challenging his opponent that he had won his reputation; underground work devoid of show, and the attendant necessity for intrigue

[17] The statement was made by H. Shimizu, Sukarno's constant "shadow" of 1942–45 (see RVO-IC 006584).

and attention to details, were impossible for him. He needed headlines, huge rallies, and the applause of the masses to be able to forge ahead in arousing the popular consciousness and building a united front. Only so long as he occupied the spotlight did force emanate from him. Only when he occupied the spotlight did his vanity and his capacity for leadership blend in the dazzling combination to which he owed his fame. Sukarno's weakness was inseparable from his greatness.

For these reasons, each of which inclined him toward cooperation with the foreign occupying power, it would not appear necessary to go into the question that was passionately discussed following the end of the war, of whether or not Sukarno had been a "real collaborator." [18] If by collaboration is understood identification with the goal of the foreign masters, then Sukarno was never a "collaborator"—never at any time in the three years. As he saw it, a Greater East Asia Co-Prosperity Sphere under Japanese leadership was no more desirable for Indonesia than dominion status within a Dutch empire.

Sukarno was, however, a cooperator, one who wished to work in genuine partnership with the Japanese; and this he did—as contrasted with Hatta, for example—from the beginning to the end of the occupation period.

The Time of Hope (July 1942–June 1943)

From Sukarno's Return to the Movement to the End of 1942

The press hailed Sukarno's return to Java with banner headlines and lead editorials. One of these announced:

Now Engineer Sukarno has returned to our midst. Now as the central figure, as the center of interest for all Indonesian movements, he will devote his entire strength to the realization of great ideals:

---

[18] For a summary of these discussions, see Aziz, *Japan's Colonialism* (1955), pp. 210f. Their polemic character and meager expertise make unnecessary a more detailed discussion of these writings. Even one expert on the Indonesians, J. de Kadt, in *De Indonesische tragedie* (1949), was ready to charge Sukarno with "betrayal of democratic principles" (p. 74) —proof that, like most observers, he associated Sukarno entirely with Hatta and Sjahrir.

to forging a spirit of unity and to leading the land in the direction of a Greater Asia. The Japanese too look to Sukarno for aid—aid that comes from a generous and joyful heart.[19]

And it had really been so. By their brutal suppression of the decades-old spirit of freedom, the Japanese soon transformed what began as sympathy into its opposite. Their Triple A Movement had met with no response whatever, and no respected Indonesian of importance accepted a leading position in it. Sukarno, warned by Hatta not to join the movement, tried initially to change it.[20] Finding that he could not succeed, however, he dissociated himself from it, and the "movement" was finally abandoned in November 1942. Sukarno was well aware that he could make demands in exchange for his cooperation, and this he did at once.

The Saiko Sikikan,[21] Lieutenant General Imamura, described in his memoirs the first meeting with Sukarno, which took place at the general's residence only a few days after Sukarno returned to Java.[22] Sukarno had asked what plans the Japanese had for the future for Indonesia. He was told that whether Indonesia received autonomous status within the Japanese empire, freedom as a member of an alliance, or complete independence, was a question that would be decided by the Japanese government and the Tenno himself; he had no say about this. It would no doubt be discussed only after the war, and until then the military regime would be in effect. But he promised Sukarno that the welfare of the population would be attended to, and that Indonesians would be able to share in governmental and administrative assignments.[23]

---

[19] AR, July 10, 2602 [1942], p. 1; also Pakpahan, p. 16.

[20] Sukarno, *Autobiography*, p. 174.

[21] Commander-in-Chief of the military in Java.

[22] Imamura's reference to May 1942 (RVO-IC 002460) is incorrect, as is Sukarno's statement that he was received by the Saiko Sikikan on the day after his return to Java (*Autobiography*, p. 175). On July 10, the day after Sukarno's return from Sumatra, however, a rather formal meeting took place in a school (see AR, July 11, 2602, p. 3). This was certainly no "coincidence," as *Asia Raya* had it, but whether it was prearranged on the part of the Indonesians or of the Japanese is difficult to guess.

[23] RVO-IC 002460, pp. 123ff.

Imamura had thus done nothing more than give Sukarno an account of the guidelines that were then still in force—to encourage a hope for independence after the war, and to promise more native participation in the government. Indonesia was still spoken of, and the conversation must have left Sukarno with the impression that the Japanese were genuinely interested in having his cooperation. When Nakayama, Imamura's adjutant and later Somubucho (Chief of General Operations), asked him about his readiness to cooperate, he took the liberty of making one stipulation. As Imamura himself recalled, Sukarno declared that he was willing to lead the people as the Japanese asked, "on condition that they would not work against him after the war." And the military government promised to give him every possible support.[24]

Sukarno's articles and speeches from this time indicate that at first he tried to institute a partnership on the basis of mutual respect and understanding. He made repeated comparisons of Bushido, the Japanese chivalric virtue, with the behavior of the Indonesian Ksatrija.[25] The Japanese knew that Sukarno would feel himself honored if they described him as a "true Ksatrija," [26] and that he would charge the Japanese with a lack of Bushido if he were to feel deceived by them.[27] Sukarno appears to have found some response to this appeal in his relations with Nakayama [28] as well as with Imamura. Imamura summed up his impression of Sukarno, who until his own departure from Java in November 1942, had repeatedly sought him out, as fol-

[24] *Ibid.* See also Sukarno, *Autobiography,* pp. 175f.

[25] See, for example, AR, September 7, p. 3; November 6, p. 1; December 9, p. 2; February 10, 2603 [1943], p. 2; also the article, "Djiwa ksatrija dan djiwa budak [The Spirit of a Knight and the Spirit of a Slave]" in the special issue of *Asia Raya* that appeared in September 1942 in connection with the six months' anniversary of the "liberation" of Java.

[26] "Kesan tentang Ir. Sukarno [Impression of Engineer Sukarno]," *Djawa Baroe* [New Java], I (1943), 6.

[27] For example, in December 1942 Sukarno accused H. Shimizu, chief of the Sendenbu, the Japanese propaganda department, of having no Bushido when the latter attempted to hold onto the leadership of a youth organization, which Sukarno had been promised would be partly his (RVO-IC 005132).

[28] See Chapter IX, below.

lows: "From these conversations I gained the impression that he was a man of iron resolve. All his thinking was centered on independence, and his passion for it would never desert him. He was a true gentleman. I admired him greatly, and encouraged him to make every proposal for the general welfare of the people." [29] No wonder that Sukarno felt encouraged in his actions by this trust and benevolence on the part of the highest official in the land, or that he became convinced that there was something to be gained from the Japanese more speedily than there had been under colonial rule.

Thus in September he even elicited from the Saiko Sikikan an official statement that "if present conditions do not yet accord with the ideals of the Indonesian people, the people are not to be disappointed, because at present we are still fighting for the common welfare of Asia. The people are to trust in the wisdom of his supreme majesty, the Tenno Heika." [30] Even in this, Imamura did not go beyond the guidelines laid down by Tokyo. But a new tone was discernible, which differed significantly from the harsh jargon of command during the first period. The Commander in Chief in Java let it be understood that he knew that the people expected more of the Japanese. This declaration, which was to "be made known to the entire people," was in sharp contrast to the usual tendency toward a one-sided glorification of Nippon, and was the first effect of Sukarno's appearance on the scene.

In the meantime, Sukarno had also sought contact with the people. In a spectacular tour through Java that began only a week after his return from Sumatra,[31] he had re-established links with most of the nationalist leaders from former days.

[29] RVO-IC 002460, p. 125. Sukarno, for his part, describes Imamura as a "true Samurai" (*Autobiography*, p. 175).

[30] On the occasion of handing over a painting made while the conversations between Imamura and Sukarno were taking place. (AR, September 19, 2602, p. 2). The meetings, during which the picture was painted, by Bezuki Abdullah, began on August 23 (AR, August 24, 2602, p. 2) and lasted until around September 9.

[31] See *Asia Raya* from July 16, 2602 to August 3, 2602. The following places were visited during the tour: Sukabumi, Bandung, Jogjakarta, Solo, Kediri, Blitar, Surabaja, and Semarang.

Everywhere he was greeted enthusiastically, and the Japanese officials traveling with him could hardly have failed to be impressed by the popularity which now blazed up anew, despite his eight-year absence from Java.

Then came Sukarno's entrance into the Moslem community. At first, there were regular announcements about which mosque he would visit to offer his Friday prayers.[32] Soon, at the request of the Moslems, he began giving little talks in which he told of his conversion into a "true Moslem," or took a stand on Islamic questions, such as that of Mohammed's ascension into heaven (Miradj). Sukarno did not forget to mention that in addition to the five pillars of Islam there were also duties of Moslems to the fatherland. His Islamic activity reached a climax on Lebaran (which in 1942 fell on October 10), an occasion for which he received a great number of invitations in various Moslem circles; he wrote the editorial in *Asia Raya,* and finally spent the holiday itself with the Muhammadijah, to whom he reported on his experiences in exile.[33]

But Sukarno was also able to reach the Christians. He appeared at the opening of an assembly hall for the Christian community as the representative of the Islamic community, and spoke of the "true position" of the Moslems toward the Christians as well as of the bond between the two communities in national questions.[34]

Thus within a very few weeks Sukarno had been able once again to fix himself in the minds of the most varied groups of the population—so well that the gossip column of *Asia Raya* was already printing lampoons that compared the more modest activity of other Indonesians with a leader who always occupied the spotlight, and whose features were unmistakably those of Sukarno.[35]

[32] AR, August 11, August 17, August 26, September 2, and September 9, 2602, among many others.

[33] AR, October 10 and 11, 2602.

[34] AR, September 25, 2602, pp. 2, 3. Further details on Sukarno's speech were not provided. He apparently stressed the idea of tolerance. Sukarno was also present at a celebration of Christmas (AR, December 23, 2602, p. 2).

[35] See the column "Sambil lalu [In Passing]," by Odji, in November.

But Sukarno needed the spotlight. Extraordinary though it may have seemed when he asserted on the very day he returned from exile that with ten inspired youths he would stir the whole world to revolt, holding up his own youth as an example,[36] or when a few weeks later he assumed before the Japanese General Imamura the role of "spokesman for all the people of Indonesia," [37] or when at a reception arranged by him for highly regarded popular leaders who had been unceasingly active for decades he expressed joy that he now had important comrades in "my struggle," [38] or when he declared at a large rally, "The eyes of all the world, even in London and Washington, are upon this event," [39] the self-aggrandizement that can be so embarrassing in retrospect often had exactly the opposite effect at the time the words were spoken. It produced an atmosphere of "Führer befiehl, wir folgen Dir," of absolute trust, and gave him the support he needed to lend force to his demands upon the Japanese.

Never, during the period under consideration here, did Sukarno attempt to misuse this trust for the increase of personal power; the interests of the people, or what he saw as those interests, were given absolute primacy. His constant exertions for unity in the movement were, for example, in striking contrast with the actions of Hitler, who in and after Landsberg willfully sowed disunity in the party in order to strengthen his own position. For all the similarity of the two men in their influence over the masses, their campaign methods, and their demagogic talent, Sukarno was never intentionally ruthless but always conceived of himself as a spokesman of the people. It is interesting to note a remark in the spring of 1943 by a high-level Japanese employee flatly denying that Sukarno had the qualities of a "great leader" because he had never once kept a dossier on the sins of his co-workers, and permitted subordinates to associate with him without any particular show of respect.[40]

When the figure of "Uncle Kisut" was used to refer to Sukarno, there were protests from readers (AR, November 6 and 9, 2602).

[36] AR, July 11, 2602, p. 2.　　[37] AR, September 10, 2602, p. 2.
[38] AR, November 5, 2602, p. 2.　　[39] AR, December 9, 2602, p. 1.
[40] RVO-IC 005136.

From an objective standpoint, Sukarno was actually correct when he referred in the autumn of 1942 to "my struggle." He had overcome the reserve of Ki Hadjar Dewantoro, the Suardi Surjaningrat of earlier years, who in the years since 1923 had established an extensive school system with his Taman Siswa, and who by working away inconspicuously had done an immense amount to develop a national self-awareness; and he had also won the cooperation of Kijai Hadji Mas Mansur, long the chairman of the Muhammadijah. He had brought the two to Djakarta, where, together with Sukarno and Hatta, they formed the "Four-leafed Clover" (Empat Serangkai), which was later to become the nucleus of effort toward a new, purely Indonesian movement.[41]

From its inception this new movement was in sharp contrast to the Triple A Movement, which was abandoned at the same time.[42] The official inauguration of the new movement was planned for the anniversary of the "awakening of Asia," celebrating the Japanese attack on Pearl Harbor. However, when December 8, 1942,[43] actually arrived, it remained merely a proclamation.

At the mass meeting that had been staged, after two Japanese had spoken of forming a new popular organization, Sukarno declared, with his usual lack of modesty: "On this day *I* announce the birth of a new people's organization, a new people's movement whose leadership has been assigned by the military government to *me*, Mohammed Hatta, Ki Hadjar Dewantoro, and *Kijai* Mansur." [44] Unfortunately, Sukarno went on, time did not permit a detailed description of the organization, so today he would speak only of the basic character of the movement. As its chief feature he emphasized that through it the entire Indo-

[41] On the origin of the "Four-leafed Clover," see AR, October 6, 7, 27, 28, and 30; November 5, 2602 (1942).

[42] On Indonesian dissatisfaction with the Triple A Movement, see Nishijima and Kishi, *Japanese Military Administration in Indonesia*, pp. 336ff., 344f.

[43] The difference in the date from that regarded in the West as marking the outbreak of the war—December 7—stems from the placing of the international date line in the Pacific.

[44] AR, December 9, 2602, p. 2.

nesian people (non-Indonesians were not to be included in the organization), both old and young, nobles and Marhaens, Moslems and adherents of other faiths, were to be forged into a unity.[45]

And so once again—as with each earlier advent by Sukarno into the movement (in 1926 and in 1932)—the idea of the united front took first place. Now for the first time the plan appeared to have support from all sides. The Moslems, represented by K. H. Mansur; the "European" nationalists, represented by Hatta; and the nationalists concerned with preserving the indigenous culture, represented by Ki Hadjar Dewantoro—all joined forces with Sukarno, who, moreover, commended the Japanese for promising their full support "without any wish to intervene in the organization and its operation."

Always before—Sukarno declared, falling back on the old legend—the colonial regime, through its poisoned policy of divide-and-rule, had been able to hinder the unity of the movement. Today the military government itself was interested in the achievement of a united front. Formerly, a conflict of interest with the colonial power had existed; it had been preferable to be exiled or hanged rather than cooperate with it. But today there was a community of interest between the Japanese and the Indonesian sides: "For that reason we now cooperate with the government and the government cooperates with us. Long live the cooperation between Japan and Indonesia!" The new movement was to become a driving force in that cooperation. It was to forge the Indonesian people into a strong nation, capable of becoming a full-fledged member within the family of Asian peoples and of supporting to the full the war now being waged by Dai Nippon. As Bambang Tutuka—here Sukarno went back to the realm of Javanese myth—had been plunged into the boiling crater of Tjandradimuka and become hardened, to emerge from his ordeal as the invulnerable Gatotkatja, so now the Indonesian people were being seethed and hardened in the cauldron of war, in order to emerge from it invulnerable, as a stout people able to resist every attack.[46]

Toward the end of 1942, Sukarno's idea of how cooperation

[45] *Ibid.*   [46] *Ibid.*

with the Japanese would function was clear enough. The new organization was to do its best to stir up and mobilize the people, free of foreign interference; in exchange for this privilege, the Japanese were to be given support in their conduct of the war. Even though the circumstance that up to December 8, 1942, no authorization for the new movement had yet arrived from Tokyo, may have dampened Sukarno's optimism, during the first six months he had nevertheless known how to make it clear to the new masters that a movement unilaterally emphasizing Japanese interests could not succeed, and that the war effort they desired could be expected only from a relation of partnership.

Beginning of the Putera Movement

Permission for the new movement was extraordinarily long in coming—a sign that in Tokyo, where the Indonesian independence movement had obviously been underestimated, there was anything but satisfaction with the course of events. Sukarno, who in his speech on December 8, 1942, had declared that the new organization would begin its activity on January 1, 1943, had to announce on December 31, 1942, that the launching of the movement had been postponed because "preparations have not been completed." [47]

The new year began with further disappointments. Although Prime Minister Tojo, in a speech before the Japanese Diet on January 28, had announced the future independence of Burma and the Philippines, at the same time he had spoken of Indonesia as the "southern regions" and thereby deliberately treated the lands of Sumatra, Malaya, and Java as territories completely divorced from one another, territories whose inhabitants, Tojo proclaimed, were to "be treated as our own children" if they remained loyal to the regime. [48] But Tojo had also pronounced an undisguised threat to the "southern regions." Those who refused to comprehend the true ideals of Dai Nippon would have to reckon with severe measures.

Sukarno was far from happy over the delay in the permission

[47] AR, December 31, 2602, p. 1.
[48] AR, January 30, 2603 [1943], p. 1.

and the paternalistic admonitions Tojo had directed at the southern regions. He had no intention of dealing with either the unwelcome embrace ("as our own children") or the threat except on his own terms. In an article on the anniversary of the fall of Singapore (February 15), he wrote: "Every form of colonization is destructive. Always, colonization lays waste and brings catastrophe to the land and people who are colonized. Their riches, their culture, their love of life, their courage are all destroyed, all laid waste." [49] To forestall possible Japanese suspicions, he added the remark that he had seen it all with his own eyes in Benkulen, where not only the Dutch but also the English had long upheld colonial interests. But it would have occurred to an Indonesian who read between the lines that here, for once, the cliché phrase "Western colonialism" had not been used; instead, the blame was put on "every form of colonization." And upon closer examination, further hints can be found—for example, in referring to the destruction of culture. Even in his most violent attacks against Holland, Sukarno had not charged it with the destruction of Indonesian culture, but rather with the opposite—with inhibiting progress through an exaggerated concern for the old culture.

But the Japanese attempted to bring about a rapid Nipponization. In every issue of *Asia Raya* there was language instruction in Japanese. Japanese textbooks, Japanese official terms, and Japanese holidays were introduced, as well as the duty of bowing in the direction of the Japanese court, which the Indonesian Moslems regarded as blasphemy, and harsh corporal punishment, which deeply offended the sensitive Indonesians.[50] All this was a telling demonstration of Tojo's pledge to treat the Indonesians as their own children—and of the proposal that was gaining favor in Japan, of annexing the East Indian islands.

Sukarno's first reaction showed that he was not willing to let himself be reduced by the Japanese to the status of a puppet. Moreover, he knew that the war had taken a critical turn. Stalingrad and Guadalcanal had fallen, or—as the phrase went

---

[49] "Tiap-tiap pendjadjahan merusak," AR, February 15, 2603, p. 1.
[50] Sjahrir, *Out of Exile,* p. 247; also Benda, *Crescent,* pp. 122ff.

in *Asia Raya*—because of a new strategy, had "been temporarily relinquished."[51] But once the aggressor's attack had been brought to a halt, as Sukarno himself had taught in 1941, there could only be an unending retreat.[52]

The Japanese must have perceived that a further concession to the nationalists was now required. About a week after Sukarno's condemnation of every kind of colonialism, it was announced that the movement would be launched in March. This news came as such a surprise that Hatta promptly interrupted a trip through Java and returned to Djakarta.[53]

The new movement was officially inaugurated on March 9, the anniversary of the "liberation of Java." Its title revealed the twin tasks the movement would have to fulfill. For the benefit of the Japanese it was called "Pusat Tenaga Rakjat (Center of the People's Strength)," to indicate the mobilization of the people's energies that was likewise desired by the occupying power. For the benefit of the Indonesians, on the contrary, its name combined the first two letters of the three words, *Pu-te-ra*—and "Putera" was the Indonesian word for "son." In a speech on March 9, Sukarno declared quite openly that this name reminded every Indonesian that he was a Putera of Ibu (Mother) Indonesia, and had the duty to serve her for as long as the blood still flowed in his veins and as long as he still felt life within himself.[54]

Given this definition, there could be no mystery as to which of the two tasks of the Putera had the greater significance for Sukarno. Indeed, he referred unmistakably to the delaying tactics of the Japanese, using words that gave the lie to all previous

[51] AR, February 6 (Stalingrad), and February 10 (Guadalcanal), 2603 [1943].

[52] See his article of August 1941, "Beratnja perdjuangan melawan Fasisme [The Difficulty of the Struggle against Fascism]," DBR, pp. 547ff. The thesis of the turning point and the inevitable retreat originates, however, not with Sukarno himself, as might be supposed from the article, but with Ernst Henri, whose book, *Hitler Over Russia* Sukarno had previously reviewed in an article, "Djerman versus Rusia, Rusia versus Djerman [Germany against Russia, Russia against Germany]" (DBR, pp. 515ff.).

[53] AR, February 23, 2603, p. 2.   [54] AR, March 9, 2603, p. 1.

announcements that the preparations had not yet been completed. "My brothers," he declared to the nearly 200,000 persons who had assembled from all parts of Java, "from December 8 of last year until this day, we have all trod, as it were, on burning coals, as though we could wait no longer for the time to come when this movement might begin its work. . . ." [55] But Sukarno had also brought along a proof of the "good will of the Japanese." By some means he had extracted from them—as he had in September from Imamura—a declaration that could be read to the people. "The Japanese military government," Sukarno announced, "declares that Nippon has subdued the Dutch and not the Indonesians. Nippon does not intend the subjugation of Indonesia; Nippon did not come here to oppress the Indonesian people of Java." [56] None of the 200,000 listeners, aside from Sukarno and the Japanese officials themselves, knew that this declaration had not come from the Japanese. From the Japanese came only the statement that Nippon had not come to this land to oppress the inhabitants of Java.[57] Thus on their own part the Japanese had adhered strictly to the line that still referred only to Java and completely denied the all-Indonesian aspect. Accordingly they must have listened with a good deal of consternation to Sukarno's expansive way with quotations—with which the reader is already sufficiently acquainted from his Marxist and Islamic studies—before the crowd that day. It was impossible to disown Sukarno's "quotation," for in so doing they would have branded themselves as colonialists.

Sukarno, as becomes evident here, up until then had played a completely independent role. The Japanese, who in a radio broadcast from Tokyo at the beginning of March had introduced him to all the world as the leader of a movement for the creation of a "new Java," [58] had come up against an opponent who seemed to be a match for them. He, whose name had once again been "on everybody's lips," was for them the key to reach-

[55] AR, March 12, 2603, p. 1.   [56] *Ibid.*

[57] Speech of Gunseikan (Chief of the Military Government) Okazaki before the Indonesian Moslems, AR, March 4, 2603, p. 1.

[58] AR, March 6, 2603, p. 1.

ing the masses. To snub him publicly or to write him off would have unmasked their true intentions and stiffened popular resistance. He had truly, in the phrase that was now recalled by *Asia Raya,* become the "central figure." [59] However, his political gains thus far were small. Tokyo had not allowed the "Indonesia Raya" or the use of the red-and-white flag, as had been requested by the Indonesian leaders. They were not even permitted to call the movement Putera Indonesia.[60]

In March 1943, Java had a visit from Aoki, the Japanese minister for Greater East Asian Affairs. Admiral Maeda, the Japanese Navy's liaison with the Sixteenth Army, who at the time had already met with the Indonesian leaders, later recalled that Sukarno and Hatta strongly pressed Aoki, now that a promise of independence had been made to the Philippines and Burma, to make Indonesia the same pledge. Aoki had agreed to convey the wishes of the Indonesians to Tokyo.[61]

And although the decision was being made in Tokyo for annexation rather than a pledge of independence, Sukarno plunged with great élan into this newest activity, the Putera movement. It was greeted with high expectations among the populace, aside from the Prijajis, the old bureaucratic nobility who feared for their privileged status.[62] It was assumed that the military government would gradually be superseded by the Putera.[63]

At the head of the movement stood the Pemimpin Besar, the "Great Leader"—to use the resounding title that Sukarno had been given—and next to him stood three deputies, the three other members of the "Four-Leafed Clover," Hatta, Mansur, and Dewantoro. From an advisory council (Madjelis Pertimbangan), on which some Japanese also sat, the top leadership received advice and suggestions for building up the movement. This council was to meet every three months.

The interim working program of the Putera consisted of

[59] Editorial by Sukardjo Wirjopranoto, AR, March 8, 2603, p. 1.
[60] Cf. Nishijima and Kishi, *loc cit.,* pp. 349ff.
[61] RVO-IC 006901 and 006931ff.
[62] RVO-IC 005798 (Beppan-Report).
[63] Pakpahan, *1261 hari,* pp. 27ff.

eight points, which were: (1) to lead the people to a strong sense of duty and responsibility in the new society; (2) to destroy the influence of America, England, and Holland; (3) to participate in the defense of Greater East Asia; (4) to educate the people to bear, physically and psychologically, all the hardships brought about by the war; (5) to contribute to a deepening of mutual knowledge between the Japanese and Indonesian peoples; (6) to promote the learning of the Japanese language and to provide for the dissemination of the Indonesian language; (7) to give the people a new self-assurance and to strengthen their determination; (8) to contribute to the dissemination of knowledge concerning health and popularization of sport for physical fitness.

In every province and in the regencies, subsections were to be established whose chairmen were to meet together once a year for a general Permusjawaratan.[64]

The following weeks were devoted to putting together the sections of the Putera. Every day there was news of this in the press, and in Djakarta itself work was soon under way on a Putera headquarters, in which four bureaus (organization, cultural affairs, propaganda, and public health) were to be housed. Sukarno was in his element. In an article, "Putera Has Begun Work," published on March 12, he self-confidently announced that he was asking for just one month's patience. Once the main office had been made ready and opened, he would call the leaders of the subsections to Djakarta, where he would give them further instructions. "To put it more plainly, I will not have everyone working according to his own ideas. Everything must be done in accordance with my instructions." [65]

Sukarno believed that he was soon to realize his old dream of a mass organization built up according to the principle of leadership that he had developed for the first time all of ten years before.[66]

The formal opening of the main office of the Putera took place on April 16, with the inevitable flourish of propaganda.

[64] For details on the structure and organization of the Putera, see AR, March 11, 2603 [1943]; also Nishijima and Kishi, pp. 352ff.

[65] "Putera berdjalan," AR, March 12, p. 2.

[66] See "The Marhaenist Party," in Chapter IV, above.

Sukarno declared in his speech that he would never forget what Colonel Nakayama, Imamura's former liaison officer and later Somubucho (Chief of General Operations) had said to him on the day of his return from Sumatra: "The foundation of all cooperation is mutual understanding." This sentence would become the motto of cooperation between Putera and the military government, for "Indonesia knows the wish of Dai Nippon, and Dai Nippon knows the demand of Indonesia. On this basis alone will cooperation be fruitful." [67]

After an extended statement of gratitude to the "elder brothers" from Japan, he attempted a final appeal to their vanity:

You "elder brothers" are sons of a people who have a great deal of experience in how a people can become strong. In this we as yet have no experience. Therefore we, the leaders of the Putera, expect as much advice as possible from the elder brothers. For we, the Indonesian people, likewise wish to become a strong nation. We wish to become a strong member of the new community which you are now bringing into being in Asia. We will follow the advice of the elder brothers. We trust Dai Nippon. For advice and help we offer our heartiest thanks. And now I come to a close. The blessing of Allah Subhanahu Wata'ala on the Putera, Dai Nippon, and Indonesia, and on the cooperation between Dai Nippon and Indonesia.[68]

Sukarno's appeal to the "elder brothers" for cooperation in the form of a prayer was fitting, just as the recall of Colonel Nakayama at this point was likewise not a coincidence. Nakayama had been ordered back to Japan at the end of March, and had been replaced by Yamamoto,[69] whose completely different feeling toward the nationalists was to become evident

[67] Literally, "On this basis certainly the cooperation will be the most fruitful [Dengan dasar jang demikian pastilah pekerdjaan-bersama itu mendjadi subur-sesubur-suburnja]." The threefold phrasing has the tone of an incantation, which can best be conveyed by the modifying "alone" and was doubtless understood in this sense by the readers.

[68] AR, April 16, 2603, p. 1.

[69] Yamamoto Moichiro came to Java at the end of March with the rank of colonel, and there became Somubucho (AR, April 1 and April 3, 2603); in August 1943 he became General, and in the fall of 1944 he took over the post of Gunseikan—that is, he became chief of the military government in Java.

following Sukarno's speech. In this first appearance before the Putera, Yamamoto, who embodied Japan's new attitude toward Indonesia, did not hesitate to describe the Indonesians as "natives" (Penduduk Asli), to speak merely of Java rather than of Indonesia, and to offer the following two-point summary of his "suggestions" to the Putera: (1) The aim of the Putera to organize all the people's efforts "means nothing more than to work for final victory in the war for Greater East Asia." (2) Because all the work of the movement was closely connected with the military government, "the decisions and plans of the military government must be exactly carried out by the leaders." [70] Such rudely sobering words had not been heard from the Japanese since Sukarno's reappearance in the movement. In fact, the appearance of Yamamoto in Indonesia heralded a new era in the relations between the Japanese and the Indonesians. Hatta, who made the final speech at this inaugural celebration, said with his own peculiar irony that they were happy to work toward realizing the ideal of "Asia for the Asians," for the sake of which they must also "swallow bitternesses." [71]

From then on Yamamoto, who after his first tour through Java expressed satisfaction over "how well the employees carry out the orders of the government," and who was happy "over the eagerness to learn Japanese," [72] proceeded once more to cut down, step by step, the area of influence the nationalists had been able to take over in the time of Imamura and Nakayama.

Yamamoto later declared that he had concluded upon his arrival in Java that the Putera had become a sort of independence movement. Thereupon he had "reversed" this aspect of the movement, and he could recall that its leaders "were very much displeased with me." [73]

Although news that sections of the Putera had been established continued to arrive from various cities of Java, the truth was that, after a few promising weeks, its great day was already past. The expansion of the Putera in Java was the end of the time of hope for the nationalists, rather than the beginning of pressure against the Japanese occupation forces, as the history of

[70] AR, April 16, 2603, p. 1.   [71] Ibid.
[72] AR, April 15, 2603, p. 1.   [73] RVO-IC 004344.

the Putera up to the end of 1943 has hitherto been regarded almost unanimously in the literature on the Japanese occupation.[74] Benda alone has referred to the ability of the Japanese, while on the surface fully supporting the Putera for propaganda reasons, to limit its real influence from the beginning by obstructing plans for establishing sections in the countryside.[75]

Benda's interpretation is the one to be adopted here, with a single addition. Originally—when the Putera was inaugurated, and during the first four weeks of its activity—the Japanese presented scarcely any obstruction to the movement. Maeda later testified that authorizing the Putera movement had been an "emergency measure" to meet the urgent demands of the nationalists and to give scope to their drive for action, "since the position of Tokyo on the future of the archipelago was not yet settled." [76] Once the decision had been made by Tokyo, in May 1943, to "incorporate" Indonesia into the Japanese empire—a decision that Yamamoto unquestionably anticipated at the time of his departure for Java—the Putera was doomed to insignificance.

One of Yamamoto's first measures was to bring the press entirely into line. *Asia Raya* found itself obliged to apprise its readers, in boldly spaced type, of his belief that "government and press must be one." [77] Next came a closer censorship of speeches. Whereas Sukarno had previously been able to say what he pleased, in more or less outspoken terms, he was now forced to make use of subtler methods. Yamamoto later testified concerning the period that followed: "Sukarno had little influ-

[74] See Kahin, *Nationalism,* pp. 107ff.; Elsbree, *Japan's Role,* pp. 87f.; K. de Weerd, *The Japanese Occupation of the Netherlands East Indies* (1946), p. 33. De Weerd's unpublished work dates to just after the war, and is based on interviews and an examination of Japanese documents. His source material has now been collected in RVO-IC at Amsterdam and has been used in the present work. A completely different opinion appears in Aziz, *Japan's Colonialism,* p. 214; the author believes, for example, that he can conclude from its program "that the Japanese directly profited from the Putera"!

[75] *Crescent,* p. 140, also notes.

[76] RVO-IC 006931f.; cf. also Pakpahan, *1261 hari,* pp. 29f.

[77] AR, April 15, 2603, p. 1.

ence because he was under strict censorship, about which he often complained bitterly. His speeches were all examined beforehand, and this he did not like." [78] Sukarno was soon able, however, to convey the nature of this new situation. On the birthday of the Tenno (April 29), he told so improbable a story about the reasons for his exile that his listeners and readers must certainly have understood that he was not speaking freely.

He had once spoken, he said, with an Indian by the name of Mota, about a visit to Gandhi followed by a trip to Japan. The English had learned of this conversation and reported it to the Dutch colonial authorities, whereupon he was arrested and exiled. This curious opening was followed by a statement that cast doubt on Yamamoto's belief that Sukarno was under "strict control." Sukarno went on, "But in my heart I have vowed that, when I am again free and unfettered, then I will continue my fight against modern imperialism"; [79] and this meant that Japan, for the time being, was included.

Although at the opening of the Putera's headquarters Sukarno still called earnestly for the advice and help of the "elder brothers," by the time the advisory council was installed at the end of May 1943, he appeared to have revised his expectations. "I implore the help and counsel of Allah Subhanahu Wata'ala for the Madjelis Pertimbangan of Putera and for myself; I ask the Indonesian people for their prayers and all possible support. Amen, Amen, ja Rabbal Alamin." [80]

On June 17, when the speech by Tojo at the eighty-second session of the Japanese Diet was published in Java, hope flared up anew that perhaps Tokyo might still prove ready for a concession. Tojo had declared that in the future opportunity to take part in the government would be given to particular peoples in the southern regions, according to their abilities, and this was to come about with particular speed in Java, in fulfillment of the wishes of the inhabitants.[81]

[78] RVO-IC 016902; also Sukarno, *Autobiography,* pp. 178f., obviously following Kahin's interpretation (*Nationalism and Revolution in Indonesia,* p. 108).

[79] AR, April 30, 2603, p. 2.   [80] AR, May 27, 2603, p. 2.

[81] AR, June 17, 2603, p. 1.

In a radio address to "all Asian brothers," Sukarno asked, as though Tojo had already promised independence, whether the brothers everywhere in Asia knew what Tojo's speech meant? "Indonesia, formerly annexed by a small country in Europe, now returns to the company of the Asian peoples." Ecstatically he invoked the blessing of Allah on the samurai sword of Dai Nippon. He vowed that the brothers in Burma, China, Thailand, India, and the Philippines, together with Indonesia, would rally with all their strength to Japan's struggle, whose aim, once its ideal of Hakko Ichiu had been realized, was to liberate the great Asian family of peoples from the influence of Western nations.[82] And in a speech at a mass meeting in Djakarta, he continued his extravagant praise of Dai Nippon. Once again Sukarno compared Japan's war aim, which he described here as the Hakko Ichiu (Brotherhood of Nations), with that of the Allies, as set down in the "lying document, the Atlantic Charter." In it had been asserted the wish to defend democracy. But they had never consulted their own people before declaring war; and besides, the English and American workers had never enjoyed any of what they called "democracy."

He had come back to his old theses, especially as he spoke of the "lie" of the Western powers about wanting "to defend the rights of all peoples." He portrayed colonial domination by the whites in the fiercest terms, recalling how the English, during the First World War, had spoken of self-determination and had been unmasked by the bloodbath of Amritsar. After dwelling at length on the sufferings of Indonesia, he ended by declaring that the revolt of all Asian peoples against England and America "is nothing other than a spark from the fire of God's own vengeance." [83]

At this time Sukarno's speeches against the Allies began to take on the inflammatory manner that was reminiscent of Goebbels. His notorious jingle, "Amerika kita seterika, Inggeris kita linggis (We will wipe out America and liquidate England)," used for the first time on April 29, 1943, occurred after

[82] AR, June 21, 2603, p. 1.
[83] AR, June 25, p. 1; June 26, 2603, p. 2.

that in many speeches, to which it made a rousing finale as he called on his audience to stand and repeat the verse with their fists clenched.[84]

Not to be overlooked in such slogans for stirring up the masses is the idea of demonstrating to the Gunseikanbu (military government) something that might be phrased as follows: "Only I, Sukarno, am in a position to influence the masses to do what you wish; so do not try to meddle in my following." On the other hand, it cannot be denied that Sukarno began to identify himself more with the side of the Japanese and more than ever to regard their war as Indonesia's. This was the period in which he lost contact with Sjahrir. During a trip through Java for the official installation of the Putera sections, he had been enthusiastically greeted at Bandung by 100,000 persons. After ending his speech, he returned to the speakers' platform and as a special bonus announced to the crowd the news that had just come in, of how in the Solomon Islands an enemy fleet had been devastatingly defeated "by us." [85]

Soon afterward, on July 7, Prime Minister Tojo paid a surprise visit to Java. In a hastily arranged meeting, Sukarno again thanked him for his statement before the Diet, as well as for coming "to Indonesia," which had never previously been visited by a head of government, but only by ministers for the colonies. Then Sukarno actually declared:

Your Excellency, our loyalty to Dai Nippon is greater and greater, we are more and more convinced that the present war of Dai Nippon for Greater East Asia is a holy war that will give Asia back to the Asian peoples, that will give the Asian countries back to the individual peoples, and that will join all these countries into one family with a common well-being, under the leadership of Dai Nippon.[86]

Tojo did not allow himself to be disconcerted by Sukarno's plea to "give back" Indonesia, since—like the colonial ministers mentioned by Sukarno—he had traveled to a "colony," as it had

[84] See, for example, AR, April 20, 2603, p. 2; July 5, p. 1; October 26, 2603, p. 1.

[85] AR, July 5, 2603, p. 1.

[86] *Djawa Baroe,* Vol. 1, No. 14, pp. 12f.; AR, July 8, 2603, pp. 1, 2.

now become by official decision in Tokyo. He had therefore not come to "Indonesia," but rather, as he said in his speech, to the "southern regions"; he did not speak of the "Indonesian people" but of the "natives of Java." Although he repeated the promise he had given a few weeks before, of participation in the government, he added that he hoped it would be understood that the "real goal" of Japan was to devote every effort to supporting the Japanese Army, subordinating all economic and cultural activity to the efforts of the regime, and contributing "in this way" to bringing the new Java into being. This was his message to the inhabitants of Java.[87]

Tojo's sobering statements temporarily put an end to hopes for a concession on the part of Tokyo to the nationalists' wishes, hopes that had lately been maintained only by artifice. The months that followed were marked by a humiliation such as had never in its history been experienced by the Indonesian population.

The Period of Humiliation
(August 1943–February 1944)

"The First Step toward the First Step"

On August 1, 1943, the first steps toward people's participation in the government were announced in Java, and on August 2 they appeared, with a detailed commentary, in *Asia Raya*. The measures, in the words of Harada,[88] the new Saiko Sikikan, were to serve the inhabitants of Java in becoming "inwardly and outwardly one with Japan and the Japanese." They provided for establishing a Central Advisory Council (Chuo Sangi-in) in Djakarta and similar councils on the provincial level (Sangi-kai). Their task would be "to make suggestions to the government and to answer questions from the government."

---

[87] *Ibid.*

[88] Lieutenant General Harada had come to Java on May 25, 1943, and remained as Commander in Chief of the Sixteenth Army until the end of April 1945 (AR, May 25, 2603, p. 1; April 27, 2605, p. 1). A partial list of the commanders and responsible officers in Java from 1942 to 1945 appears in the first section of the Bibliography.

In addition, a few capable inhabitants of Java were to be installed in various offices of the military regime as advisors (Sanyo).

Hypocritically—having himself made the suggestions in response to an order from Tokyo [89]—the Somubucho Yamamoto declared before representatives of the press:

Although these first measures are not yet fully in agreement with the declaration of Prime Minister Tojo at the eighty-second session of the Diet, they are nevertheless to be regarded as a first step by the government toward further, far more generous prospects. For this reason, this first step will be a test of the inhabitants. If they work willingly and loyally at this first opportunity, more generous measures will certainly follow.[90]

Yamamoto could scarcely have given more unmistakable evidence of the macabre game he intended to play with the nationalists. On the same day that the permission "to answer questions" in the future was made public, notice that Burma had received its independence also appeared in the press. For the Indonesians, independence was more remote than ever. For some months the name "Indonesia" had been consistently eliminated from official usage, and the idea of a "partnership" with the "natives" of Java was of interest only insofar as it might directly profit the occupying power.

Sukarno was now in a difficult position. He began his official speech of thanks with the significant remark: "As is known, I have already many times expressed the happiness of the Indonesian people at the declaration of Prime Minister Tojo before the eighty-second session of the Diet." [91] All enthusiasm had vanished; the "thanks" to the military government were sheer irony. During a new trip through Java, [92] however, Sukarno must have been on the lookout for suitable members for the Central Advisory Council, since the first disappointment

[89] RVO-IC 005838/39. The times given in the source (Saito) are not reliable; it is impossible to conclude from that source, as does Aziz (*Japan's Colonialism*, p. 215), that Yamamoto had informed Sukarno about the measures before they were announced from Tokyo.

[90] AR, August 3, 2603, p. 1.   [91] AR, August 2, 2603, p. 2.

[92] AR, August 10, 2603.

about Tokyo's plans left him with no choice but to play the game; he was already too much involved to do otherwise. In a second comment on the Central Advisory Council, he said, "We must distinguish the reality of today from the possibilities of the future,"[93] and he never gave up quoting, at the least opportunity, Yamamoto's statement that the first measures were "not yet fully in agreement with the declaration of Prime Minister Tojo."

He did so in his first speech as Gicho—Chairman of the Central Advisory Council—a post to which he had been nominated and appointed in mid-October, at the initial meeting of the forty-three-member advisory group.[94] "If we wish to obtain more," he continued, "then we must clearly understand the conditions we have to fulfill." The present measures had been described by the military government itself as "the first step" toward the fulfillment of Tojo's promise. But he himself had said, in the presence of the Japanese Prime Minister, "that his promise is the first step toward what is desired by the Indonesian people."[95]

Thus Sukarno, shorn of all illusion, gave expression—not as direct criticism, which was no longer possible since Yamamoto had appeared on the scene, but nevertheless unmistakably—to what he really thought of the Japanese measures. All the same, a "first step toward the first step" had to be taken, for "the goal that is the same for all of us . . . will not be reached if we are not zealous, if we do not apply ourselves wholly, are not ready for sacrifice, do not understand the present war, do not support the present war up to the winning of victory."[96]

On the following day a statement appeared in *Asia Raya* that "the whole people will pray for their Bung Karno, that he may successfully pass his test and obtain a position of importance for the Indonesian people."[97] If any doubt remained concerning

---

[93] *Djawa Baroe,* Vol. I, No. 18 (September 15, 2603), p. 4.

[94] Two candidates were suggested in secret ballot, one to be nominated by the Saiko Sikikan. Nothing was made known of the exact result of the ballot (AR, October 17, 2603, pp. 1, 2).

[95] AR, October 17, 2603, p. 1.   [96] *Ibid.*

[97] AR, October 18, 2603, p. 2.

the status of the Central Advisory Council, this vanished on the opening day of the first session. Among other things, the delegates had to stand and listen to the question of the Saiko Sikikan: "In what way can practical help be given to the Japanese Army by the people?" [98] This "significant question," which had to be answered within the next four days, again emphasized the words of the Gunseikan (Chief of the Military Government),[99] who on the eve of the opening session had declared: "The purpose of setting up this Central Advisory Council is purely and simply a strengthening of the military government, so that it can work more efficiently." [100]

The course of the sessions of the Council, which from then on had to report every three months to receive and answer a similar question from the Commander in Chief, cannot be explored any further here. Suffice it to indicate that in time the Council developed in a direction not originally anticipated by the Japanese, and placed more emphasis on the interests of the Indonesian population than they could in the long run have desired. The Japanese had hoped to rely on the Mufakat of respected Indonesians (of whom the committee was largely composed),[101] to give greater weight to their attempts at exploitation.

The harsh manner in which the Japanese sought to influence the sessions of the Council, and the fact that it was allowed no criticism whatever of the government's measures, might lead one to conclude after superficial consideration that even the impotent Volksraad (VR) far surpassed it in importance.[102] It

[98] *Ibid.,* p. 1.

[99] On Japanese titles and commanders on Java, see the first section of the Bibliography.

[100] AR, October 17, 2603, p. 1.

[101] The members are identified in AR, October 16, 2603, p. 1. Among them—in addition to the "Four-leafed Clover" were many old comrades-in-struggle of Sukarno, including Mr. Sartono, Mr. Budiarto, Oto Iskandar Dinata, R. Rooseno, Mr. Sujudi, Dr. Samsi, and Mr. Iskaq, among others. See also, B. R. O'G. Anderson, *Some Aspects of Indonesian Politics under the Japanese Occupation* (1961), 10, note 18.

[102] Aziz, *Japan's Colonialism* pp. 220f. Even Benda defends this view (*Crescent,* p. 251, note 28).

may be recalled, however, how painfully little the Indonesian nationalists were able to achieve in the VR in the entire twenty-three years of its existence, despite the privilege of criticism and (after 1927) the so-called co-legislative function. Quite aside from the government's not being bound by the decisions of the VR, because of the heterogeneous structure of that body and the multiplicity of groups represented, some with widely divergent interests, the nationalists could never achieve a majority in the VR.

And here the Central Advisory Council begins to take on significance: it was composed exclusively of Indonesians. Even though an entire staff of Japanese observers was constantly present, the opportunity to set up roadblocks against oppression was never to be ignored. Therefore, behind decisions by the Council which appear from without to serve Japanese interests exclusively, there was often an explanation having a distinct social character, and aimed at reducing, rather than adding to, the burdens placed on the population by the war.

Finally, it may be noted that to most nationalists an emphasis on work, increased productivity, and even forced labor itself were only to be welcomed; for all of them, directly or indirectly at some time in their struggle for freedom, had reached the point where the general lack of interest in organization and a reluctance to cooperate actively had caused them to despair. This widespread disinterest had been the chief enemy of the nationalists during the colonial period, and at the return of the colonial masters would be the latter's trump card. Indeed, at one time they had concluded from the lack of a general urge to be independent a "volonté générale" in favor of their presence.[103] The cooperation that was equally desired by the military regime and by the nationalists now offered a stronger assurance of building up a public awareness of the Indonesian idea.

And if forced labor finally provoked resentment, so much the better, since in that event the nationalists would be the sole beneficiaries and could confront the Japanese with stronger de-

[103] An express reference to Rousseau's "contrat social." See W. F. Staargaard, *Oost en West in Nederlandsch-Indië* (1928), pp. 33ff.

mands. These considerations should also be taken into account in interpreting the decisions of the Central Advisory Council; they recur in every one of Sukarno's speeches from that time.

The cooperating nationalists were prepared to support the Japanese not only with labor but also with military aid. In the autumn of 1943, Sukarno's old comrade-in-struggle Gatot Mangkupradja—one of the four defendants in the trial of 1930 —asked the permission of the military government to form units of Indonesian volunteers and have them trained by the Japanese. What the Dutch colonial government had always refused, for fear of possible consequences, was at once accepted by the Japanese, who because of the Allied counteroffensive now had to prepare for the defense of their conquered territories.[104] In an impassioned speech, Sukarno called on heaven and earth as witnesses "that we serve our fatherland by pouring out our blood in the war for Greater East Asia. . . . Every enemy who later attempts to infringe on the position of our people will be liquidated, if only the entire Indonesian people are filled with the military spirit and the spirit of heroism." [105] It was not only for "now," the war for Greater East Asia, but above all for what would be "later," that they had a weapon in their hands. And "every enemy" included the Japanese as well, if they dared to infringe on Indonesia's position once the period of building up public awareness had been completed.

The authorization of Indonesian volunteer units, the Peta (Defenders of the Fatherland),[106] was more than a "first step toward the first step." It was above all proof that the Japanese, when they found themselves in trouble, were ready to make further concessions, and thus justified continued cooperation

104 AR, October 2 and 4, 2603. On Gatot Mangkupradja's proposal, see his article "The Peta and My Relations with the Japanese," in *Indonesia*, No. 5, (1968), pp. 105ff.

105 AR, November 10, p. 2. Sukarno's speech on November 3, 1943, "Djadilah banteng [Become Wild Buffaloes]," was reprinted in installments from November 5 to 10.

106 Peta = *Pembela Tanah-air* [Defenders of the Fatherland]. On the early history of Peta see G. J. Pauker, "The Role of the Military in Indonesia," in J. J. Johnson (ed.), *The Role of the Military in Underdeveloped Countries* (1962), pp. 185ff.

with them, even at a time when they showed no willingness whatever to make concessions in the political field.

The Visit to Tokyo: Medals, Not Promises

On November 8, hundreds of marching youths gathered before Sukarno's house to volunteer for the Peta. But they had to disperse, for Sukarno was about to make a journey.[107] For the first time in his life, he would be leaving Indonesia—along with Hatta and a representative of the Moslem community, Ki Bagus Hadikusumo—to convey to Tokyo (or so it was said officially) the gratitude of the Indonesian people for being allowed to participate in the government.[108]

But what had really led the Japanese military government to send Sukarno, Hatta, and Hadikusumo to Tokyo? The temporal proximity of the "Greater East Asia Conference" that just had been held in Tokyo on November 5 and 6, 1943, and at which closer cooperation between Japan, Manchukuo, China, the Philippines, Thailand, and Burma had been agreed upon (East Asia Charter),[109] cannot be overlooked. There had been no representation, official or unofficial, of Java—not to mention Indonesia—and it is probable that this situation had led Sukarno to a resolute confrontation with the military government.

The military government may already have realized that Sukarno had been put into a difficult position because of the total exclusion of Indonesia from the conference. They must have understood that if Sukarno's popularity were to decline, the prospects for increased cooperation by the people would likewise diminish, and they undoubtedly believed that in the unofficial visit to Tokyo they had found an acceptable middle course. For one thing, Sukarno could then present his troublesome demands (for permission to use the Indonesian flag and anthem) in person; for another, they surely hoped that on the spot he would be impressed by the Japanese war effort, and also that his hopes for a pledge of independence might perhaps be bought off with personal honors.

---

[107] AR, November 8, 2603, p. 2.   [108] AR, November 15, 2603, p. 1.
[109] See, for example, M. A. Aziz, *Japan's Colonialism*, p. 217.

To such things, the Japanese knew, Sukarno was not immune —as proof of which, they had put him at the head of every organization and every committee, each with an imposing title. In August 1943, directly after the announcement of the disappointing "first measures," they had brought Fatmawati, who was to be his third wife, from Sumatra to Java, where the marriage then took place quietly on August 22.[110] Could this have been a mere coincidence? And now, after the Greater East Asia Conference, they proved it again at Tokyo. When Sukarno, Hatta, and Hadikusumo were personally received by the Tenno on November 16, the Tenno shook only Sukarno's hand.[111] The day before, when the three Indonesians had been decorated with the order of the Holy Treasury, Hatta and Hadikusumo had received the award of the third class, whereas Sukarno himself received the seldom-bestowed award of the second class.[112]

Nevertheless, Sukarno did not permit himself to be distracted from the main purpose of his journey. He met four times in all with Prime Minister Tojo,[113] and—it is reported by various Japanese sources—pressed him strongly for a promise of future independence and for permission to use the Indonesian flag and anthem.[114] But Tojo remained adamant, and Sukarno was obliged to begin the journey back to Indonesia without the promise. Meanwhile, however, the three Indonesians were to be conducted on a fourteen-day tour of Japan, where they were shuttled from religious shrines to armament factories, before their departure for Java on December 3 was announced.

In an early interview, Sukarno still appeared very much impressed, above all by the "extraordinarily high honors"—which, however, he interpreted from the first as an expression of regard for the Indonesian people of Java. In addition, the tremendous activity and self-discipline of the Japanese had made an impression. No sacrifice was regarded as too great in order to realize the ideal of the Greater East Asia Co-Prosperity Sphere. Finally, there had also been the opportunity to become acquainted at close range with the "spirit of Japan," and to observe the spiri-

---

110 RVO-IC, Soekarno file, not numbered.
111 Pakpahan, *1261 hari,* p. 41.   112 AR, November 17, 2603, p. 1.
113 On November 14, 16, 17, 21.   114 Elsbree, p. 49; RVO-IC 005870.

tual influence on the present generation of the ancient religious shrines: it was a "holy spirit, inhabited by a will of steel." [115]

A few days later there was a press conference [116] devoted to the same theme. Again Sukarno strayed off into abstractions; he spoke of the brotherhood of the Japanese and Indonesian people, referred to their common veneration of ancestors and regard for family ties, and suggested in conclusion that from the similar appearance of the two races it could be deduced that "southern blood" must flow in the Japanese. Hatta,[117] on the other hand, was more specific. Since he had been in Japan in 1933, he was able to draw a concrete parallel between the situation then and in the present. He emphasized the great development of heavy industry, and was especially concerned with its meaning for the Asian area *after* the war, where Sukarno's interest in everything concerned only its utility *for* the war.

Sukarno and Hatta, who had shared the same experiences there, thus brought home quite different impressions of Japan. For Sukarno, who was obviously impressed (a quantity of photographs reveal more than any words), it was the "spirit," the "activity," the "self-discipline," the "will of steel," the "complete unity between home front and battlefront"; [118] from

[115] AR, December 5, 2603, p. 1.

[116] AR, December 8, 2603, p. 3.

[117] Kahin reports that the Japanese military government had sent Hatta, whom they considered unreliable, to Japan so that he could be taken into custody by the Kempeitai, but that the mistaken award of the Order of the Holy Treasury protected him from the clutches of the Kempeitai (*Nationalism,* p. 107). This story, however, although no doubt indicative of Hatta's relation to the Japanese, can hardly be credited. The arrival of the three Indonesians was officially announced before (!) the award of the medal (AR, November 15). If there had really been a plan to arrest Hatta, there would have been an opportunity in Tokyo between November 13 and 15—especially since the Indonesian delegation was accompanied by two Japanese, who could easily have explained the "misunderstanding" in Tokyo. That the visit was announced only after the delegation arrived in Tokyo was no sign of "lack of interest" (Aziz, *loc. cit.,* p. 218), but a matter of wartime tactics; Tojo's visit in July had likewise not been announced.

[118] See also Sukarno's article, "Nippon dimasa perang [Japan in Wartime]," *Djawa Baroe,* No. 24, p. 9.

Hatta (who in the photographs appears always reserved and critical) came such sober observations as that liberalism no longer existed, that industry had quadrupled, and that the development of heavy industry offered a good chance for the subsequent industrialization of Southeast Asia.

The same difference—between a propensity for slogans and a concern with detail—had caused Sukarno and Hatta to follow different paths in 1932. Since 1942 it had developed not only that they got along well, but that in their diversity they were an excellent complement to one another. What Sukarno as an agitator was able to bring about in the way of a following and a consensus, even with the Japanese, Hatta was able to organize and direct through quiet work in committees. Thus the cooperation of Sukarno and Hatta that grew out of the force of circumstance proved a happy one for Indonesian interests. Although they had different opponents—for Sukarno it was Western imperialism; for Hatta, Japanese fascism—their single goal of independence could level all differences, and thus unite them firmly at moments when that goal was threatened.

Sukarno must have become more clearly aware that this goal was threatened once the glow of the flatteries, the receptions and decorations in Tokyo had faded. He had brought back nothing aside from the medal of which *Asia Raya* noted, on the day after the award, that it was bestowed only on "state employees" who had rendered important services.[119] But an employee of the Japanese empire Bung Karno had no wish to be. A few days after his return from Tokyo, he declared at a mass meeting that although he had met in Japan with the friendliest treatment and with evidence of the highest respect, what had moved him most deeply had been to set foot once again on his native soil and to stand before his own people. At that moment he had become aware that for him there was only one thing—to "suffer with the people, rejoice with the people, die with the people." [120]

[119] AR, November 17, 2603, p. 1.   [120] AR, December 9, 2603, p. 2.

Divide and Rule, or Mobilize All Forces? (November 1943–February 1944)

Even as Sukarno and his companions sojourned in Japan, the Japanese, who now increasingly called for more effective popular participation in building defense installations, in manufacturing arms, and in the wretched labor brigades (Romushas) which were sent to the theaters of war, were casting about for a new instrument for reaching the man in the Desa.

The Putera had not developed into such an instrument. It had not been able to set up any sections in the countryside; and after Yamamoto, early in the summer of 1943, had "reversed" its tendency to become an independence movement, it had devoted itself more and more to social tasks. Toward the end of the year, the only thing about it that still appeared effective was the "Body for the Aid of the Heroes" (Badan Pembantu Pradjurit), which had been proposed at the first session of the Central Advisory Council and had been organized by Putera, and which was concerned with the plight of Romushas, forced laborers, and war volunteers and their families.[121]

Nothing could have been further from the intentions of the Japanese than to support such a tendency. Accordingly, they turned to look for another partner that offered the possibility of reaching the masses, and they found it in Islam. Benda has set forth the reasons that led the Japanese gradually to devote more attention to the Indonesian Kijais and Ulamas, whose authority extended down to the village level. He has traced in detail the path of the Masjumi (Association of Indonesian Moslems),[122] which was founded on November 23, 1943.[123]

This united front of Indonesian Moslems undoubtedly contributed in the long run to the strengthening of Islam in Indonesia. Whether this is what the military regime intended, however, is questionable. Benda's conclusion, that Islam won prestige in connection with the establishment of the Masjumi,[124]

[121] AR, October 22, 2603, p. 1; December 31, 2603, p. 1.
[122] The Indonesian name in full is *Madjelis Sjuro Muslimin Indonesia.*
[123] *The Crescent and the Rising Sun,* pp. 105ff.   [124] *Crescent,* p. 153.

would not appear to be borne out by a demand that amounted to an ultimatum, calling upon the Islamic parties, which had hitherto gone their separate ways, to unite,[125] or by the harsh tone that was subsequently used by the military government in dealing with the Moslems.

K. H. M. Mansur, for years chairman of the Muhammadijah and the representative of the Indonesian Moslems in Sukarno's "Four-leafed Clover," declared in his initial statement about the Masjumi: "Without abandoning the teaching of Islam, we must [now] try to adjust our way of life and views to the new era and to bring them into harmony with it."[126] These words expressed not enthusiasm but a genuine concern for religion, since it was obvious that the Japanese were engaged in nothing other than the manipulation of religion for their own purposes. The goal and intent of the association, as stated in the program of the Masjumi, was to consolidate the ties among all the Islamic associations of Java and Madura, "so that the entire Islamic community may give aid and exert its energies toward realizing the Greater East Asia Co-Prosperity Sphere under the leadership of Dai Nippon, as truly accords with the will of Allah."[127] Why, aside from the desire to reach the masses, the Japanese decided on this forced merger of orthodox and reform movements, is best explained in a declaration by the chief of the Sendenbu (Propaganda Section) of the military government, who later said of the founding of the Masjumi, "The reason was that the Kijais were trying to involve themselves in politics, and the Japanese did not like it."[128] This "involvement in politics" could certainly have referred as well to the Putera, in which K. H. M. Mansur played an important role. By the erection of a centralized organization, the Japanese hoped to establish better control over the practices of the religious teachers in the countryside, and to prevent them from stirring up internal resistance against the "infidels" who worshiped a man as a god.

If the Japanese really intended, as Benda's thesis has it, to play off the Moslems against the "secular" nationalists, and ac-

125 See the governmental declaration in AR, November 24, 2603, p. 1.
126 AR, November 24, 2603, p. 2.   127 AR, December 21, 2603, p. 1.
128 RVO-IC 006583 (H. Shimizu). See also Pakpahan, 1261 hari, pp. 34f.

cordingly permitted greater influence to the former while cur-
tailing the influence of the latter,[129] then the tone with which,
during the ensuing months, the Ulamas and other representatives of Islam were summoned to Djakarta for instructions in
the "holy war," is not the only thing that would be surprising.[130] There would have had to be, first of all, a reason for the
Japanese policy of divide-and-rule, as there would have been if
what is contended by Kahin and others, that by the end of 1943
the Putera had become a threat to the Japanese position,[131]
had any basis. But it has been pointed out by Benda himself
that activity by the Putera had come to a standstill toward the
end of 1943, after which that organization had been unable to
exert any real influence.[132]

Finally, stirring up an internal struggle between various
groups—if one assumes with Benda that for years there had
been a strong rivalry between "secular" nationalists and Moslems [133]—could have indicated that the Japanese wished to
gain time. But this motive, which was to be significant at the
beginning of 1945, when passions could scarcely be kept under
control,[134] is out of the question for the end of 1943. Because
the course of the war had become increasingly critical for the

[129] See, for example, *Crescent*, pp. 152f., 156f.

[130] See *Asia Raya*, January to July 1944, *passim*. Only the naming of
K. H. Hasjim Asj'ari as Shumubucho (Chief of the Office for Religious
Affairs)—a purely token matter—on August 9, 1944, can be regarded as a
concession by the Japanese to the Moslems (Pakpahan, *1261 hari*, p. 69).
All previous measures, including the publication of *Suara Muslimin Indonesia* and *Sinar*, served mainly for purposes of indoctrination. See, for
example, the ironic comment of Hamka, whom Benda otherwise is fond
of citing as an authority, and who wrote in AR, April 4, 2604 [1944]:
". . . this newspaper [*Sinar*] is very useful to explain to the Kijais the
circumstances and the goal of the war for Greater East Asia and at the
same time simplifies efforts to make demands known to them."

[131] See "The Beginning of the Putera Movement," above.

[132] *Crescent*, p. 140.

[133] This thesis pervades Benda's entire book. In its extreme form, it
cannot be agreed to here. Frequently there appeared to be less rivalry
between nationalists and Islamic reform movements than between reformist and orthodox-minded Moslems themselves.

[134] See Chapter IX, below.

Japanese, every possible effort had to be undertaken to mobilize the efforts of all the people: according to the New Year's message of the Saiko Sikikan for 1944, "The Army, the government, and the people must be one." [135] But this would have meant the cooperation of as many groups as they could reach; and therefore nothing would have been further from the Japanese than a policy of divide-and-rule and the fomenting of internal quarrels.

Thus after the creation of the Masjumi, the four princes who, in keeping with the tradition of the Dutch, had been granted a certain autonomy in their principalities,[136] were summoned to the palace of the Commander in Chief of the Sixteenth Army, where they were "advised" to "exert all their strength toward fulfilling their important task." At the same time, the ties between their courts and the corresponding representatives of the military government were to be "strengthened." [137]

Then, at the beginning of the new year, came the decisive step toward a total harnessing of forces, with the announcement of a new mass movement under the command of the Japanese military government. It later received the Japanese name "Djawa Hokokai" (Javanese People's Service Association). The authorizing order to the Saiko Sikikan, published on January 9, 1944, made it known that all segments of the population were to be included in the new movement. A majority of previous organizations were to be amalgamated into it, among them the Putera—which had formerly, according to a very ambiguous commendation, "directed all its energy to strengthening the community of the Javanese people." [138]

Precisely the opposite was envisioned for the future. From now on it was no longer the popular interest but rather that of the military government that was to take priority. The initial

[135] AR, January 1, 2604 [1944], p. 1.

[136] The four principalities in Central Java (the so-called "Vorstenlanden") were Surakarta, Jogjakarta, Mangkunegara, and Pakualaman. They had been officially permitted to handle their own administration during the Japanese occupation period as well. On the course of affairs in Jogjakarta, see Selosoemardjan, *Social Changes in Jogjakarta* (1962), pp. 41ff.

[137] AR, December 2, 2603, p. 1.

[138] AR, January 9, 2604, p. 2. On the reluctance of the Putera and the population about this step, see, for example, Pakpahan, *1261 hari*, pp. 48, 51f., also Nishijima and Kishi, pp. 393ff.

measure was to set up at once what were called Tonari Gumis (Neighborhood Assistance Units) in the countryside, made up of from ten to twenty households each, so as—it was said ironically—"to realize the spirit of Gotong-Rojong [the Indonesian tradition of mutual help]." [139]

With this enforced mobilization of the rural population a new problem came to the fore—the question of who would lead the rural population as the Japanese envisioned. In the principalities, districts, subdistricts, and villages, only one authority, aside from the Ulamas, was available to the Japanese for conveying orders—the Prijajis, members of the venerated administrative class, who during the colonial period had very often worked against the nationalists.

If the Japanese now seized upon these Prijajis, it was first of all simply because there was no other choice. It is impossible to share Benda's opinion that they did so as a further means of promoting their policy of divide-and-rule and of limiting the influence of the nationalists.[140] As the months went by, there was as little sign of increased prestige for the Prijajis as for the Ulamas—in fact, quite the reverse. At the time the new measures were launched, there was repeated mention of the "promotion and transfer" of large numbers of Prijajis,[141] who, after this shift away from their own localities, were regarded as hardly more than civil servants for carrying out the orders of the Japanese.[142]

[139] AR, January 12, 2604, p. 1.

[140] *Crescent,* pp. 154f., 156f. For the article by Anwar Tjokroaminoto, "Siapa menang [Who Will Win?]," cited by Benda to support his thesis (on the strengthening of the prestige of the Prijajis), see AR, April 6, 2604, p. 2, in which Tjokroaminoto quotes "saddening" opinions from the people that hint at a victory by the Prijajis over the nationalists. The article does not permit one to conclude that there was a similar intention on the part of the military government. Rather, this is made unlikely at the opening of the same article when Tjokroaminoto writes that the Prijajis, as was known, had been sent in *to begin with* ("buat langkah permulaan"), in order to get the Djawa Hokokai moving. In other words, they were treated as a stopgap, since the Japanese undoubtedly distrusted them above all because of their bondage to the colonial masters.

[141] See, for example, AR, January 15, 2604, p. 3; January 28, p. 1.

[142] Cf. W. F. Wertheim's opinion, cited in Benda, *Crescent* (p. 265, note 18), which regards the function of the Prijajis in the same way.

It has been necessary to discuss Benda's intriguing theory of a deliberate game played by the Japanese for the purpose of weakening the nationalists by strengthening rival forces, since Benda has thus far been the only one to analyze at all closely the relations between the Indonesians and the Japanese throughout the occupation period.[143] His account conveys the impression that the nationalists acquiesced in such a game and in effect sanctioned the way their influence had been lessened.[144] It will become clear, however, that in their plan for harnessing all forces the Japanese could not have done without the cooperation of the nationalists, to whom in the period of their so-called impotence they made the most momentous concession, namely permission to found the Barisan Pelopor (Pioneer Corps), described by Benda himself as "an organizational weapon of first importance." [145] This was in fact granted not, as Benda reports, *after* a significant change in Japanese policy toward Indonesia "in late September" of 1944,[146] but as early as August, at a time when, in Benda's view, "the area of nationalist activity had been considerably narrowed." [147]

The Protest of the Nationalists and Its Consequence (February–August 1944)

With the ruthless measures taken by the military regime toward the end of 1943 and at the beginning of 1944, and their one-sided emphasis on Japanese interests, the Indonesians who were willing to cooperate, and Sukarno as their head, were obliged to re-examine their position if they did not wish to lose the trust of the people.

As early as the second session of the Central Advisory Council (January 30–February 3, 1944), at which drastic rules of conduct were handed down to the delegates by the military govern-

[143] The research of M. A. Aziz, *Japan's Colonialism and Indonesia* (1955), deals too little with the reactions of the Indonesians. Aside from the work of Benda, a more detailed investigation is available only for the period from September 1944 to August 1945; see B. R. O'G. Anderson, *Some Aspects of Indonesian Politics under the Japanese Occupation, 1944–1945* (1961).

[144] Benda, *Crescent*, pp. 154, 156f., 164, 167f.   [145] *Ibid.*, p. 178.
[146] *Ibid.*   [147] *Ibid.*, p. 168.

ment,[148] it was evident that they were not inclined to cooperate in producing the enthusiasm that had been called for in the proposals of the military government. In answer to the request of the Saiko Sikikan—who had again asked practical measures for mobilizing the population [149]—two committees were formed in which the interests of the government and of the population were kept carefully separate. Suggestions for strengthening defense preparations were taken up in the first committee; in the second, on the other hand, there were suggestions for increased food production. And Sukarno did not fail to mention in his closing address that the government was interested "most especially in the results of the first committee." [150]

Nor did he content himself with this ironic observation. He also appealed to the government for confidence. After an extraordinary speech to the delegates on the confidence the military government had placed in the people, he added that the population likewise trusted the government. This was a "glorious synthesis," such as had never been experienced in a long colonial history—"We trust the government and the government trusts us." And he closed the appeal, which had been directed much less toward the delegates than toward the representatives of the government, with the words: "Bear this in mind, that there is no more shameful behavior than a breach of trust." [151]

The same theme recurred in a radio address which Sukarno made on the following day, February 4, 1944. After declaring that there had been no relation of trust with the Dutch colonial government because they had had different goals and a synthesis had therefore not been possible, he asked his listeners: "Why must partnership with a power that wishes to colonize or that is imperialistic fail? Why must it miscarry or be without results? Because all attempts at colonization carefully avoid placing any

---

[148] They were always to keep in mind what could and could not be done; they were to be brief and not to put their own knowledge on display; they were to engage in no criticism of government measures, "so as to have a good name among the people"; etc. (AR, January 31, 2604, p. 1).

[149] See the text of the questions in AR, January 19, 2604, p. 1.

[150] AR, February 4, 2604, p. 1.   [151] Ibid.

trust in our people!" Everyone knew that this could only refer to the Japanese, and Sukarno immediately pointed out what would happen in the event of a breach of trust:

Because of their distrust, we likewise felt obliged not to put our confidence in the Dutch government. Because of their distrust, we too became distrustful, and our earlier movement began with passion to undermine the position of the Dutch government. From the moment the Dutch government withheld its trust, it began to totter. The feeling of distrust toward the Allies was the beginning of their fall from the throne, and it is the feeling of trust that will bring about a new reconstruction in our land.

The final clause of the final sentence was Sukarno's concession to censorship. But it cannot erase the impression that it was really intended to read, "and the feeling of distrust will bring down the Japanese in our land. . . ." Sukarno's preliminary clause had been too careful not to call forth this conclusion automatically.

Later in the speech, which was significantly entitled, "Forming Destiny by One's Own Efforts," [152] Sukarno spoke at length concerning the two functions of the present war: it destroyed and it built up, it had its "antithesis" and its "synthesis" —for "in the midst of this war the peoples of Asia are weaving their own destiny"—and his listeners must have understood that the hour had now also arrived for Indonesia. Therefore, he went on, it was necessary that all forces be mobilized under the leadership of Dai Nippon. But not *for* Nippon—and it is typical of Sukarno's position that regardless of censorship he could say, "Our entire enthusiasm in this vast struggle must be directed by us toward one goal, that of securing a happy future *for ourselves.*"

On the day that saw the publication of this final section of Sukarno's speech—which appeared in installments [153]—more detailed information about the Djawa Hokokai, the "Javanese People's Service Association," the announcement of which had aroused Sukarno's distrust, was also published.

---

[152] "Menenun nasib dengan tenaga sendiri." This radio address, made February 4, 1944, was reprinted in AR, February 5–8, 2604.

[153] *Ibid.,* February 8, 2604

In structure it resembled the Putera. Once again, a number of sections were to be set up and coordinated with a head office (Chuo Honbu), and the occupant of this head office, as in the Putera, was to be Sukarno. Once again he had been given an imposing new title, that of Chuo Honbucho, in addition to having been named during the autumn as Sanyo (adviser) to the Chief of General Operations (Somubucho), and to being called Gicho as chairman of the Central Advisory Council. But despite all this profusion of Japanese titles, Sukarno was not chief of the Djawa Hokokai. Looming above him was the military government, which issued the orders, and the officials under him were likewise controlled by Japanese. Sukarno was thus only an organ for the execution of orders, shackled from above as well as below.

But since it was he who was the focal point of the movement, all the unpopular measures of the People's Service Association were linked with his name, and this tarnished his reputation. It began to be said for the first time that he was a "lackey of the Japanese," [154] and the more perceptive were sympathetic because "his position was deplorable and difficult." [155] Yet these very months were Sukarno's truly heroic period, during which his old fighting spirit once again revived.

First of all, the Djawa Hokokai was not the place from which he could exert pressure in his struggle for partnership and the recognition of Indonesia. That place, as will be shown presently, was the much-maligned Central Advisory Council. But the Djawa Hokokai was not worthless to him either. It gave him the opportunity to travel all over Java, an opportunity of which he made extensive use in March and June of 1944,[156] and which is in itself sufficient to cast doubt on the thesis concerning the limiting of the nationalists' influence. No such opportunity for public exposure was given either to the Masjumi or to the Prijajis.

Moreover, the Djawa Hokokai offered an opportunity for agitation not only against the Allies but also against the Japanese. Thus in March 1944 an announcement calculated to at-

---

[154] RVO-IC 006524-35, a report by a member of the Beppan staff.
[155] Pakpahan, *1261 hari*, p. 54.   [156] AR, March 22ff., May 30ff., 2604.

tract the masses to a gathering at which Sukarno was to speak proclaimed:

Speeches can be heard on the radio. But if we are able to see the speaker for ourselves, everything becomes much clearer, for we witness the feelings that are reflected in the face of the speaker. Do his words come from the heart or are they only lip-service? We can decide all this if we are there in person! Right? Find out tomorrow at Ikeda Square.[157]

This was undoubtedly an appeal to popular discontent, a signal to be on the alert for hidden meanings; and those who came did not go away disappointed. They first heard the Saiko Sikikan, letting it be known that he had heard Sukarno's appeal for trust as he thanked the population publicly for their trust in Japan.[158] Immediately afterward, Sukarno delivered a speech containing such statements as, "Once Allah has resolved to destroy a nation, then its cannons, its torpedoes, its airplanes, its fortifications, and all its weapons are useless. God destroys no power that has not transgressed." He had said this here, he went on, so that it might be heard by the Dutch who were in Australia, England, and America, and who wished to return to Indonesia. But Sukarno said it also for the Japanese who sat next to him on the platform; indeed, another sentence that came near the end of the speech could likewise have been designed for them: "Before the curtain has fallen on the war for Greater East Asia, we too, the Indonesian people, will have proved to the whole world that we can fight like a tiger to defend our homeland and our people." [159] The audience, alert for hidden meanings, could easily have detected a warning against the Japanese hunger for territory in such statements, which clearly stood out from the otherwise monotonous attacks against the Allies. At moments when Sukarno was displeased with the Japanese, he left it to his audience to decide who was the opponent. In times of censorship, this was his secret weapon, which never failed to be effective. The Japanese might have recalled on that day, March 9, an event that had occurred scarcely

---

[157] AR, March 8, 2604, p. 1.   [158] AR, March 10, 2604, p. 1.
[159] AR, March 10, 2604, p. 2.

three weeks earlier—the first sizable rebellion, Moslem-engineered, by the rural population against the Japanese occupation.[160]

Yet neither agitation nor travel through Java—however urgently Sukarno needed these to keep popular good will for himself—brought concessions from the Japanese. To accomplish this there was only one way—to delay the orders for an increase in popular activity, thereby forcing the Japanese to restructure the Djawa Hokokai and giving the nationalists the influence they demanded.

Even though the Djawa Hokokai built up its branch organizations with astonishing speed all over Java, the movement at first totally failed to produce the effect the Japanese hoped for. In April 1944 this led the Saiko Sikikan once again to call together the Central Advisory Council and to put before the delegates the question of how the duty of participating in the "holy war" and of increasing their zeal could be made clear to the inhabitants.[161]

This gave Sukarno an opportunity to question the collaboration of the Prijajis,[162] which he had viewed with skepticism from the beginning, and to stress the need for a genuine popular leadership. Thus even at this time it was evident that the Chuo-Sangi-in (Central Advisory Council), described up to now as simply a tool of the Japanese and at this particular time as the scene of lofty and "condescending and haughty 'lectures' "

[160] *Asia Raya*, March 8, 2604, p. 2, carried a detailed report of the revolt in Tasikmalaja on February 18, 1944, in which the leader of approximately 500 rioters was officially described as "insane." That this riot was directed by Moslems also goes against the thesis that the policy of the Japanese toward Islam was valued by the Moslems as a gain in prestige . . . See also the statement by Mansur before the Central Advisory Committee in May 1944, that the Moslems felt they were "still hindered" in the practice of their religion (AR, May 2, 2604).

[161] AR, April 25, 2604, p. 1.

[162] See his comments in AR (March 1, 2604, p. 2), casting doubt on the ability of the Prijajis to lead the people. The same ideas were also evident in a radio address, "Melatih diri [Train Yourselves]," given April 19, in which Sukarno was still attempting to move the Prijajis with a call to a stronger union with the people (AR, April 20, 21, 22, 2604).

by the Japanese military government,[163] could become a weapon for the nationalists.

This occasion saw a remarkable change in the phrasing of the oath which Sukarno customarily took on behalf of all the delegates before the session began. Whereas the two previous oaths (in October 1943 and January 1944) had referred only to the delegates' obligation to discuss the wish of the military government and to coordinate all forces for achieving the final victory,[164] the oath taken at the third session of the Central Advisory Council (May 8-11, 1944), concerned the "responsibility" they bore as members of the Council, and the phrase on the final victory was eliminated! [165] The Japanese took note of this at once. Hastening to interpret the "responsibility" in their own way, they declared it was entirely fitting that the members of the Central Advisory Council should feel "responsible" for bringing the aid of the population to a satisfactory outcome.[166]

A closed session of the Council then dealt with how more collaboration by the people could be obtained, and nearly every one of the twenty-two speakers brought up the necessity of installing "genuine leaders." Mr. Iskaq, Sukarno's old colleague from the beginnings of the Study Club in Bandung, put it this way: "We, as leaders of the people, must guide the people and trust in their powers and abilities in all matters." [167]

And so the reply to the Saiko Sikikan—after a notably protracted complaint about the low level of popular awareness concerning the significance of the war that was being fought— recommended "forming at once a Barisan Pelopor (Pioneer Corps) in the Djawa Hokokai, to be composed of mature young men who fully understand the duty of achieving final victory and are ready to offer themselves for the struggle, in whatever way may be required." [168]

Just how the delegates envisioned these pioneers is shown more precisely in an article by Sukardjo Wirjopranoto. They were to set an example for the people in all matters; they were to strengthen the sense of responsibility among the population; they were to associate with people of all classes, peasants as well

[163] Benda, Crescent, p. 275, note 93.   [164] AR, January 30, 2604, p. 1.
[165] AR, May 8, 2604, p. 1.   [166] Ibid., p. 4.
[167] AR, May 11, 2604, p. 1.   [168] AR, May 19, 2604, p. 1.

as tradesmen, and thus contribute decisively to the formation of a new society, "in which individualism is no more." [169]

But this was exactly the program Sukarno had put forward more than ten years earlier for resisting the Dutch colonial power.[170] The similarity in organization (which was to be built up according to the leadership principle), form of activity (by penetrating the whole of Indonesian society), and stated aims (the strengthening of collectivism, the eradication of individualism), was most obviously expressed by the similarity of name: in 1933 the Partai Pelopor, in 1944 the Barisan Pelopor. The one difference was that in 1933 Sukarno had wanted this vanguard party to take up the struggle against the colonial power under the slogan of noncooperation; and the attempt had been a miserable failure. But now in 1944, under the slogan of cooperation with the ruling power, Sukarno's old program had a unique chance of success.

The Japanese, whom the nationalists were now pressing harder than ever for a promise of independence,[171] knew exactly what sort of weapon they would be putting into the hand of the nationalists if they granted this request. They were now being asked to grant what they had refused in connection with the Putera, namely a contact between the nationalists and the masses of which they would not be in control; and they knew that this opportunity would be used less to reinforce servitude than to promote the desire for independence.

Now they were faced with the disagreeable choice either of using a tool that assured the mobilization of the masses, with unpredictable consequences, or of having still to cope with an apathetic population. For weeks the Japanese put off a decision, until the event that finally turned the tide in favor of assuming the risk: the fall of Saipan, the important island link between the Japanese motherland and the "southern regions." In mid-July, after weeks of desperate resistance, out of which not a sin-

[169] "Barisan Pelopor dan persahabatan [The Pioneer Corps and Friendship]," AR, May 19, 2604, p. 1.

[170] In his essay, "Mentjapai Indonesia Merdeka" (DBR, p. 306). See also "The Marhaenist Party," in Chapter IV, above.

[171] RVO-IC 005803 (Maeda).

gle Japanese emerged alive, the island was securely in American hands.[172]

To Sukarno, the conquest of Saipan also came as a shock. He wrote at this time in an article entitled "Java—a Gigantic Fortress," [173] that the homeland could become a theater of war tomorrow or the day after; therefore from now on, every Indonesian, whether young or old, must adopt an attitude of determination:

If the enemy should dare press forward to this homeland of ours, then he must be met with every means at our command that can be used as a weapon, from the cannons and airplanes of the military government to the boiling water that is heated in the kitchen by little mother Sarinem. The entire island of Java must become an impregnable fortress against all powers, for we will not be subjugated again by imperialism. Every city, every village, every house— yes, every heart must become a fortress.

This article left no doubt that for him, even during his protest against the Japanese tactics, Western imperialism was still Enemy Number One. It was also known to the Japanese,[174] who in this time of uncertainty over what island the Americans might have chosen as the next target in their island-hopping strategy abandoned their resistance to the formation of the Barisan Pelopor.

Thus at a Permusjawaratan of the Djawa Hokokai in late July 1944, Sukarno was able to be openly critical of the previous organization's ineffectiveness. If the Djawa Hokokai were compared with an army, he said, it was clear that thus far communications between the general and the soldier had not been what they ought to be. Many orders from above had not been carried out, and on the other hand, things had been done without authorization from above. The organization therefore needed pioneers who could be relied upon down to the last detail.[175]

An account of this meeting reported that the proposal to set

[172] Cf. the reports in AR, June 21–July 21, 2604.

[173] "Djawa Sentotai," Djawa Baroe, Vol. 2, No. 14 (July 15, 1944), p. 3; AR, July 22, 2604, p. 1.

[174] RVO-IC 006524-35 (Beppan).   [175] AR, July 25, 2604, p. 2.

up a Pioneer Corps within the Djawa Hokokai had "met with fervent approval." [176] In the weeks that followed, Sukarno's office worked out more precise details for the new organization, and on August 15 the installation of the Barisan Pelopor was at last officially announced.

The nationalists had thus achieved their first real success since the beginning of the occupation. At the very time when the lack of any concrete pledge from Tokyo made them appear especially impotent from without, they had succeeded in putting their hands on a weapon that could be dangerous to any opponent. This development, to which the military government finally gave its consent on August 10, 1944, was given impetus by the Allies' military successes in the Pacific area. But it would not have been possible without Sukarno's unending vigilance and his tenacity in adhering to the idea of partnership, which ended by placing the Japanese in a difficult position, since they had entered the war under the slogan of liberating the Asian peoples.

Now Sukarno had gotten the partnership even without a pledge from Tokyo, and with his own organization in hand, he was able to extend his influence down to the villages.[177] All the leaders and their subordinates in the Barisan Pelopor were Indonesian, as was Sukarno's deputy. The advisers, along with Hatta, Mansur, and Abikusno, included a single Japanese, whose influence under such conditions was barely perceptible. Officially, Sukarno was known to be under the command of the chief of the military government, and the military commanders had charge of the provinces. But the orders that mattered came from Sukarno, who had already built up the nucleus of his own command structure on his many trips through Java.

After the installation of the Barisan Pelopor on August 15, 1944, Sukarno was to have exactly a year, to the very day, under Japanese leadership, in which to exercise his influence as he chose.

[176] AR, July 26, 2604, p. 1.

[177] On the entire temporary organization of the Barisan Pelopor, see AR, August 15, 2604, p. 1.

IX

The Road to Independence
(September 1944–August 1945)

Sealing of the Partnership

The Promise from Tokyo

Sukarno was spared having to fight on two fronts—against the ever-advancing Allies and against the intransigence of the Japanese. On September 7, 1944, the totally unexpected news was received in Java of the declaration by Prime Minister Koiso, Tojo's successor after the fall of Saipan,[1] at the eighty-fifth session of the Diet "that the Japanese Empire [hereby] announces the future independence of all Indonesian peoples, and thus the happiness of the Indonesian peoples may be forever secured." [2] The note reading "The Navy withheld its consent," [3] which appears in the documents following this announcement, reveals the internal dissensions that preceded this promise from Tokyo. The Navy, which in the eastern part of the archipelago was not so strongly pressed by nationalist demands as the Sixteenth Army was in Java, was again and again to resist any further measures for the hastening of independence.

There was, however—at least in the fall of 1944—yet another

[1] AR, July 24, 2604, p. 1.
[2] The text appears in AR, September 8, 2604, p. 1. Kahin (*Nationalism*, p. 115) speaks of the "very near future," and B. R. O'G. Anderson, *Some Aspects of Indonesian Politics under the Japanese Occupation 1944–1945* (1961), p. 2, of the "near future" for the promised independence. These optimistic interpretations do not accord, however, with the formula "Kelak pada kemudian hari (later on, in the future)." See also the text given by Elsbree (*Japan's Role*, p. 51), who on the basis of Japanese documents translated the passage as "in the future."
[3] Elsbree, *Japan's Role*, p. 50.

[276]

Japanese authority that was to resist any show of generosity toward the wishes of the nationalists. This was the military government of Java itself. Although it knew the impatience of the nationalists, it believed that for the present, by making a general pledge of independence, it had given a sufficient token of willingness to cooperate, and for this reason it took no action on a much more generous offer from Tokyo. In fact, a week before the pledge was announced, the military government had been asked whether it would favor not only permitting the use of the Indonesian flag and anthem, but also the setting up within a short time of a committee to study the question of independence. The military government informed Tokyo that future measures ought to be focused on Java: first of all, a school ought to be established there in preparation for eventual independence, and "government participation" ought to be expanded.[4]

Thus, although Tokyo was already prepared to make a distinct concession because of the unfavorable course of the war, the military government in Java feared that if it were to do so, the enthusiasm might easily get out of hand, so that it could not be channeled into support of the war; accordingly, the military government tried to gain time.

Sukarno of course knew nothing of this grim move by the military government when, on September 7, he was abruptly summoned to the command headquarters from a work camp where he was serving as a volunteer.[5] In the presence of newspaper reporters, the Somubucho Yamamoto, who was certainly not without responsibility for reducing the concessions, read him the promise of the Japanese government. Sukarno turned pale, and was at first unable to say anything. Tears streamed from his eyes; he could not yet grasp what had happened. For years he had been working toward this moment, enduring humiliations and the biting scorn of those who believed they knew more about the Japanese.

---

[4] See the official report of the military government on the independence movement, RVO-IC 005870f.

[5] Cf. AR, September 8, 2604, p. 3, as well as the special issue of *Djawa Baroe* (Vol. 2, No. 18, September 15, 2604) containing many articles and pictures on the occasion of the announcement of future independence.

What must surely have surprised Sukarno most was the proclamation of independence for all of Indonesia, after years of total refusal by the Japanese to acknowledge its existence. But he had remained implacable about it, thus producing some odd situations—as, for example, when Prime Minister Tojo, on his visit in July 1943, spoke only of Java and Sukarno for his part spoke only of Indonesia. It was no doubt largely thanks to him that Tokyo's pledge had now admitted the all-Indonesian concept.

On September 8, 1944, representatives of all groups of the population made a hastily arranged visit for the purpose of thanking the Saiko Sikikan. When after the ceremony the Japanese Commander in Chief told Sukarno in broken Indonesian to "fight hard for the future of the Indonesian people," once again Sukarno lost his composure. He stood there sobbing helplessly, the man who was hated by the Dutch and feared by the Japanese because with an unerring instinct he had noted their weaknesses—the rigidity of the former and the constraints upon the latter—and despite all his "egregious errors" had again and again proved right in the end. As one who fought passionately, he likewise reacted with emotion.

Benda [6] has called into question the opinion of Elsbree, that after the pledge of eventual independence "a decisive change" can be noted in the tone of the speeches and declarations of the Indonesian leaders.[7] And so far as Sukarno is concerned, one may well ask, Why should there be? Regardless of censorship, he had been able to express his displeasure at all sorts of measures taken by the Japanese; and now that the promise he had so ardently desired had come to pass, he was unconstrained in honoring their willingness to cooperate. "Life or death with Dai Nippon until we are independent; life or death with Dai Nippon when we are independent": this became his new slogan in the days that followed.[8]

Sukarno was no less well aware, however, that the promise was not a purely altruistic act, but that the Japanese hoped thus

---

[6] *Crescent,* pp. 174f., 277 (note 11).   [7] *Japan's Role,* p. 81.

[8] He used it for the first time in his radio speech to the Japanese people on September 7, 1944 (AR, September 8, 2604 p. 2), and thereafter in nearly every public address.

to release new energies in support of their struggle. Of this the Saiko Sikikan had left no doubt when he declared, "Should final victory not be achieved, should Greater East Asia not become a reality, the Indonesian islands will likewise not receive their independence." [9]

The timing of the pledge must also have given him pause. Thus in a special session of the Central Advisory Council Sukarno declared quite openly that everyone knew the war had reached a phase in which the hour had come when the honor of the Asian peoples was at stake. "In so important and so *critical* a moment, the Empire of Dai Nippon has proclaimed the future independence of Indonesia. . . ." And so he set forth his new formula for a life-and-death struggle: "I, as a leader of the people, place the accent on the struggle for life and death, for it is a struggle that unnerves the enemy from without, while building the strength of the nation from within. *More important* than the fact that there has been a promise of independence. . . ." [10] He was thus under no illusion that further concessions by Tokyo were to be expected momentarily. But the time had to be utilized so that his people could finally move toward achieving independence through their own efforts.

This was the point of divergence for Japanese and Indonesian interests that up to now had run parallel. The material utility of the labor that was to be performed in the "life-and-death struggle" benefited the occupying power, whereas its ideological value in mobilizing the people served only Indonesian interests; for, as Sukarno declared, if there was to be enduring freedom, forces had to be mustered that could destroy any obstacle in the way to independence.[11]

Pantja Dharma—The Indonesians' Promise of Loyalty

Among those obstacles, in addition to the Japanese and the ever-advancing Allies, was yet a third. This was the threat of internal disintegration, the danger that groups sympathizing secretly or openly with the Allies might undermine or destroy

9 AR, September 8, 2604, p. 1.
10 AR, September 12, 2604, p. 2. Author's italics.
11 AR, September 12, 2604, p. 2.

Sukarno's idea of cooperation, and thus at the very last moment bring the successful outcome of a protracted humiliation into jeopardy.

In September 1944, that danger was still not very great. The Kempeitai was on the watch. Furthermore, the propaganda effect of being permitted to display the red-and-white flag of Indonesia along with the banner of the Rising Sun, and to sing the anthem "Indonesia Raya," had been considerable, producing a sudden resurgence in the low esteem into which the cooperators had fallen. Ki Hadjar Dewantoro, the venerable fighter for independence who during the period of humiliation had withdrawn after having first collaborated in the Putera, declared with relief: "Now the people need no longer doubt us, the people's leaders, or withhold their trust from us." [12] But the danger of new resentment, once the intoxication of the promised independence had worn off, was still to be reckoned with. Sukarno was aware that for some months there had been an amorphous resentment, that many were already looking to the Allies and would be averse to remaining openly on the side of Japan. Thus in September, turning to the delegates at the special session of the Central Advisory Council, he declared that he was a Moslem himself, and looked unquestioningly to Allah and the Prophet for guidance. But he also had a high regard for the teachings of Krishna in the *Bhagavad Gita,* calling on the hesitant Ardjuna to fulfill his duty without thought of loss or gain:

It was only by taking this stand that the Pendawas were able to defeat the Kaurawas. And I declare that only by taking such a stand can we ourselves smite the enemy and redeem the soil of the homeland. Let all of you gentlemen—nay, let me now say, comrades—let us all recognize our duty, let us do our duty, without thought of loss or gain.[13]

Sukarno did not identify the enemy more precisely here, knowing that his hearers had different opponents. But in his appeal to his countrymen, he once again employed as a weapon the myths he had virtually never used against the Japanese. Al-

12 *Ibid.*   13 *Ibid.*

though he had often likened the occupation to being plunged into the crater of Tjandradimuka, an ordeal from which the people were to go forth invulnerable as Gatotkatja, the image was more expressive of an inner necessity than of anything anti-Japanese. For the opinion of Kahin that Sukarno's speeches were "full of subtleties and double talk" which the Japanese had not understood but which had a meaning for the Javanese population,[14] little evidence can be found in the sources.

Sukarno avoided stirring up anti-Japanese sentiment by the use of examples from the myths because he saw nothing to be gained from an increase in popular discontent. Only in the final days before the Japanese surrender, when he was certain that the long "year of corn"—as the period of Japanese rule had been described—was drawing to a close, did he go back to his tested method of combat from the Dutch colonial period.[15] For Western imperialism had remained his chief enemy, and he never wearied of opposing the rumors that originated in Allied propaganda, in pamphlets and radio broadcasts. From his own guard, the Barisan Pelopor, which appeared increasingly powerful after the promise of independence,[16] he extracted an oath "to destroy not only the enemy but every person, regardless of nationality, who aids the enemy and hinders the realization of independence." [17]

A few days later, on October 29, 1944, the Americans landed on Leyte in the Philippines, and thus became an immediate threat to Indonesia. In his appeal for struggle on the side of Japan, Sukarno grew more emphatic:

Do all the comrades understand—are they deeply aware, so that it has penetrated their flesh and blood, to the very marrow of their bones—that independence for Indonesia can be realized only by the way of cooperation with Japan? I ask this here because I know that there are still many among our people whose ideas in this matter

---

[14] Kahin, *Nationalism,* p. 108.

[15] See "The Proclamation of Independence," below.

[16] See, for example, Pakpahan, *1261 hari,* pp. 79ff.; here it is reported how Sukarno, under pressure from the Barisan Pelopor, went to the Saiko Sikikan to demand for them the status of a militia.

[17] AR, October 18, 2604, p. 1.

remain unclear, who are still handicapped psychologically as a result of agitation against the Japanese in the time of the Dutch, or by spies at present—who are still intoxicated by liberalism, who make individualism an ideal, and do not want to participate in the war with all its burdens and bitterness.[18]

This last, although ostensibly directed at the intellectuals, no doubt referred above all to one man—Sutan Sjahrir, who had come to exert a widespread influence upon the students and was responsible for their isolation. Once again the movement threatened to split apart, for Sjahrir and his group did not take it for granted, as Sukarno did, that the Allies would once more give full scope to colonialism. For them the Japanese were still the archenemy despite any promise of independence, and they had already made this so clear even in the fall of 1944 that at the opening of the Central Advisory Council on November 12, 1944, the Somubucho spoke of hearing that there were groups, notably among the students, who flagrantly ignored their obligation to work toward independence, and gave their support only when the form of a future government was discussed. They were, he said, lacking in character and did not understand that independence concerned the whole people and not merely the leaders.[19]

During this same session, at Sukarno's urging [20] the Central Advisory Council passed a resolution that the "Pantja Dharma," the five duties of the Indonesian people, were to be regarded as a pledge of loyalty to the Japanese. As a result, in the months that followed there were stirrings of discontent among the Pemudas (older youth), not only with the Japanese but also with Sukarno, who had held fast unshakably to his idea of partnership with the occupying power until nearly the end of the war.

[18] AR, November 11, 2604, p. 2.   [19] AR, November 14, 2604, p. 1.

[20] AR, June 28, 2605 (1945), p. 1. The committee that formulated the Pantja Dharma was installed at the suggestion of Sukarno's old confidant, Mr. Sartono. Sukarno, who before then had participated infrequently in other working committees, took over the direction of the committee himself and probably had a strong influence on the wording of the promise of loyalty. See AR, November 17, 2604, p. 2; also Sukarno's articles, "Pantja Dharma," in AR, beginning on November 22, 2604.

The Pantja Dharma went as follows:

1. In this life-and-death struggle, together with the other peoples of Greater East Asia, we stand united with Dai Nippon and are prepared for sacrifice because this is a struggle in defense of right and truth.

2. We are laying the foundations of an Indonesian state that will be independent, united, sovereign, just, and prosperous, that will give credit to Dai Nippon and that will live as a faithful member within the circle of the Greater East Asian family.

3. We strive with unfeigned ardor for fame and greatness, as we guard and exalt our own civilization and culture, promote Asian culture, and bring its influence to bear on the cultures of the world.

4. We serve—in firm brotherhood with the other peoples of Greater East Asia—our own state and people with unshakable loyalty, and in continual accountability before Almighty God.

5. We struggle with ardent longing toward lasting peace throughout the world, a peace founded on the brotherhood of all humanity and one that conforms to the ideal of the Hakko Ichiu.[21]

The Time of Waiting (November 1944–April 1945)

Delaying Tactics of the Japanese

The Sixteenth Army, having correctly anticipated the reaction of the populace to the promise from Tokyo, was able at first to hold in check the sudden blaze of the Indonesians' desire for freedom, as expressed above all in the Barisan Pelopor,[22] with a hint at further concessions. But in the long run, as the Japanese may have perceived, vain promises were of as little use as the oath of loyalty; and now for the first time, toward the end of 1944, they had every reason to look for an ally against the nationalists. And it was here—or so they thought—that the

[21] AR, November 17, 2604, p. 1. Subsequently they were reprinted in a conspicuous place on the seventh of each month.

[22] Pakpahan, *1261 hari*, pp. 79ff.; AR, October 2, 2604 (the informative seven-point declaration of Chairul Saleh); also AR, October 3 and 18; and many other citations.

Masjumi, their own creation, which was a year old in November and had made considerable progress in that time, lent itself to their purposes. The military regime had been forced gradually to make real concessions to them, just as it had to the nationalists.[23]

While the Central Advisory Council at its sixth session, held from November 11 to 17, was recommending coordination among all previous organizations,[24] the members of the military government were doing exactly the opposite. When, on December 4, 1944, they gave the Masjumi permission to build up its own military organization, they had in effect placed in the hands of Indonesian Islam what could eventually become a weapon to be used by the more radical Moslems against the nationalists—a development that would indeed take place in Indonesia after the war.[25]

Political and military considerations no doubt also played a role in the decision of the military government to permit the creation of Hizbullah, the "Army of Allah," in order to strengthen the defenses of Java against an Allied invasion. But this was not its primary purpose, since according to the description of its tasks the Hizbullah was to be attached to the Peta— the "Defenders of the Fatherland," in training since 1943—only as a "reserve." For the Moslems, greater importance attached to the tasks described under Point Two: (a) the spread of the doctrine of Islam; (b) guidance of the Islamic community in obeying the laws of Islam; (c) the defense of Islam and of the Moslem community of Indonesia.[26]

The military government hastened to add that the Hizbullah was established not at its command but by the wish of the Islamic community itself; its character was wholly autonomous, and it was under the sole direction of the Masjumi.[27]

[23] Benda, *Crescent,* Chapter 7, pp. 150ff. Here, however, the nomination in August 1944 of K. H. Hasjim Asj'ari as Shumubucho (Chief of the Office for Religious Affairs) is regarded as the first real concession.

[24] AR, November 17, 2604, p. 2.

[25] On the significance of the Hizbullah, see Benda, *Crescent,* pp. 178f., 185.

[26] AR, December 4, 2604, p. 1.   [27] AR, December 5, 2604, p. 1.

Another extraordinary demonstration of regard for Islam was the sudden formation of a committee to establish a University of Islam.[28] Up until about November 1944, Islamic interests were often flagrantly neglected even in the courses for the training of Kijais and Ulamas—as is evident, for example, in the schedule of a course given between November 1 and 21, 1944.[29]

These measures taken by the military government may be seen as a conscious policy of divide-and-rule, such as Benda believed he could detect as much as a year before.[30] The Japanese, toward the end of 1944, were hoping to diminish the pressure from the nationalist side, in which the Moslems had a part (since they were also represented in the Central Advisory Council), by playing off the two groups against each other. For them a united front, as proposed in November 1944 in the Central Advisory Council, had become a threat, given the universal desire for independence. Now they clearly had reason to split the movement.

But neither the nationalists nor the Moslems would do the Japanese the favor of subordinating their common goal, independence, to an internal power struggle. In the fall of 1944 there was no genuine rivalry between the two groups. Sukarno observed after a tour through Java on October 21, 1944, "The internal unity between the leaders of the Moslems and the leaders of the nationalists is firm as a rock." [31] And Hatta, in classifying the population at the end of December 1944, decided on the following categories: (1) leaders; (2) Prijajis; (3) intellectuals; (4) tradesmen; (5) the people—peasants, urban workers.[32] Hatta—given his scrupulosity—would not have failed to distinguish among the leaders as "secular" nationalists and Moslems, if at the end of 1944 there had been reason to do so.

It thus seemed only natural that at the seventh session of the

[28] AR, November 23, 2604, p. 1.

[29] RVO-IC 006121. Of sixty classroom hours, only four were devoted to Islam.

[30] See the previous chapter.

[31] "Erat-seerat-eratnja." See AR, October 21, 2604, p. 2.

[32] AR, December 29, 2604, p. 2.

Central Advisory Council in February 1945, both nationalists and Moslems, who saw through the maneuver at once, repeated still more plainly their demand for unity between the two organizations. The argument for the proposal went as follows: "It can be said that up until now there have been two distinct movements, the Djawa Hokokai and the Masjumi. Although there is no disagreement between the two, it is possible that the firm unity necessary at this time may be weakened if the two organizations remain independent." [33] From this statement Benda believes he must conclude:

This was the first open and unmistakable warning to Muslim leaders that the exceptional role which Indonesian Islam had played under the aegis of Dai Nippon would be challenged by the nationalist leadership. The Islamic federation . . . was threatened with the loss of its autonomy. The Masjumi executive, as well as the Japanese authorities, met this first suggestion with silence.[34]

On this point, Benda's sharp insistence on the rivalry between Moslems and "secular" nationalists is open to question. He takes it for granted that the gradual concessions made by the Japanese to Indonesian Islam had necessarily added to the tensions between Moslems and nationalists on which he has placed such emphasis. This thesis—which has been temporarily adopted by Anderson [35]—is, however, not borne out by the evidence Benda cites.

The decision of the Central Advisory Council was by no means an "unmistakable warning" to the Moslem leaders, unless they warned themselves. Three noted leaders of the Muslims, K. H. M. Mansur, Wachid Hasjim, and Abikusno, had sat with five second-rank nationalists on the committee that worked out the proposal for combining Djawa Hokokai and Masjumi.[36]

---

[33] AR, February 27, 2605, p. 2.   [34] Benda, *Crescent,* pp. 183f.

[35] Anderson, *Some Aspects,* p. 15. For a different interpretation of Japan's approach to Indonesian Islam, see the same author's essay, "Japan: 'The Light of Asia,'" in J. Silverstein (ed.), *Southeast Asia in World War II: Four Essays* (1966), pp. 18–19.

[36] AR, February 26, 2605, p. 2. In addition to Mansur, Hasjim, and Abikusno, those on the committee were Sendjaja, Toha, Fathurrachman, Djamin, and Purubojo—none of whom were important nationalist leaders.

Clearly, this was not a declaration of war against the Moslems but a vote of no confidence by Moslems and nationalists on the use by the Japanese at the end of 1944 of the tactic of divide-and-rule, a tactic which only later was to have disastrous consequences. The Japanese of course did not react to the motion of the Central Advisory Council; the Islamic organization remained in existence, and came gradually to be dominated by more radical elements, who made use of the gift handed them by the Japanese and forged from it a weapon that would be used in the postwar conflict between Moslems and nationalists.[37]

The unwillingness of the Indonesians to be made into a partisan tool of the Japanese was emphasized by a revolt of the Peta in Blitar on February 15, 1945.[38] Now for the first time the military government in Java felt obliged to announce officially the "Committee for the Investigation of Indonesian Independence" that had been proposed from Tokyo in September 1944. This took place on March 1, 1945,[39] but two months were still to elapse before the committee was actually formed, on April 29, 1945, and the Japanese brought about another delay of four weeks before it finally convened for the first time on May 28, 1945.

These dates—announcement on March 1, installation on April 29, and opening session on May 28—are clear evidence of how grudging the Japanese were with their concessions. During this period the Americans moved from victory to victory in the Philippines; the island of Okinawa fell into their hands, enabling them to attack the Japanese homeland with squadrons of bombers; and finally, as the war in Europe came to an end with the unconditional surrender of Germany, it became possible to transfer further Allied units to the Pacific Theater.

That the Japanese, despite all these crucial developments,

[37] Benda's strong emphasis on the rivalry between nationalists and Moslems during the occupation period is probably due to this postwar development. Commenting on the tensions which he already saw at the beginning of 1945, he says, "These problems, as we know, have continued to beset Indonesian politics to this very day" (*Crescent*, p. 185).

[38] Pakpahan, *1261 hari*, pp. 108ff.; Anderson, *Some Aspects*, pp. 46f.; Benda, *Crescent*, pp. 182, 270 (note), 283; also Aziz, *Japan's Colonialism*, p. 228, and AR, May 19, 2605, p. 1.

[39] See AR for this date.

showed so little willingness to oblige and used every possible excuse for further delays, which in Indonesian eyes seemed endless, in the end seriously harmed the esteem in which Sukarno had been held, and considerably strengthened the impression that he was a spineless tool in the hands of the Japanese.

Sukarno between the Fronts

Sukarno's behavior during these months, as he ceaselessly upheld the "life-and-death struggle" at the side of Japan and the unpopular pledge of loyalty, the Pantja Dharma, and as he had the people recite it standing, at meetings,[40] would be difficult to understand if he himself had not seen the approaching Allies as his greatest enemy.

Given the widespread dismay over the ruthless exploitation carried on by the Japanese within the Peta, among the students, and in the populace as a whole, his position as intermediary with the Indonesian population would have allowed him to put more force than he did into his demands for a speeding up of the concessions. But his concern was not with stirring up sentiment against the Japanese; rather, it was with shaping a determined opposition against the West.

Whereas a "glorious synthesis" with the Japanese was possible because at least temporarily they and the Indonesians followed the same path, a compromise with the West was out of the question. "We must root out from our souls every thought of compromise with the opponent. There can be no compromise between justice and tyranny; there can be no more compromise between us and the enemy than there is between life and death." So he declared in December 1944,[41] and two months later Sukarno again said with fierce determination that should the Allies dare to land in Indonesia, the whole Indonesian people would fight against them on the side of the Japanese. The young people with military training would fight with guns, the rest of the population with other weapons of resistance, and the old men would murmur spells, until the English, the Americans, and the Dutch had been destroyed.[42]

---

[40] See, for example, AR, December 15, 2604, p. 1.
[41] AR, December 15, 2604, p. 1.   [42] AR, February 12, 2605, p. 2.

In this sense Sukarno's elite troops, the Barisan Pelopor, which had meanwhile extended their organization deep into the countryside, were determined to work among the population. In the decisions reached by a Permusjawaratan in February 1945, every sentence was an expression of vehement anti-Western feeling. A fight to the finish was declared not only against the obvious enemies, America, England, and Holland, but also against "Western ideology with its individualism and liberalism." In its stead, "Eastern ideology" with its spiritualism and the spirit of mutual help (Gotong-Rojong) was to be given all possible support.[43]

Because of this militant anti-Western attitude, Kahin believed he had to regard the Barisan Pelopor as a partisan tool of the Japanese.[44] But this the Barisan Pelopor was not—any more than its chief, Sukarno, was.[45] It accepted only the propaganda version of the war aims of the Japanese, the "liberation of the Asian peoples." Thus regarded, the Japanese were allies, and they were treated accordingly so long as they did not offend too obviously against the "partnership." Sukarno had let the Japanese know often enough that he regarded them solely as tools, as again and again he explained to the masses, in a manner anything but flattering to the Japanese, that Allah had sent them for the purpose of freeing the Asian world from Western imperialism.[46]

Moreover, each time the Japanese too obviously transgressed this "decree of Allah" and behaved like colonizers, Sukarno had made a protest: he had protested in 1943, when permission to found the Putera was delayed; he had protested the disappointingly small concession made by Tokyo in the founding of the Central Advisory Council; he had protested at the beginning of 1944, when the Japanese attempted to use all available forces

[43] AR, February 14, 2605, pp. 1, 2.   [44] *Nationalism,* p. 110.

[45] That the Barisan Pelopor was led by Sukarno escaped the attention of Kahin, who has regarded Sukarno's cooperation with the Japanese too much from the standpoint of tactics.

[46] To mention only a few notable occasions: AR, September 9, 2602, p. 3; March 9, 2603, p. 1; June 26, 2603, p. 2; January 1, 2604, p. 2; March 10, 2604, p. 2.

for themselves; and he did so now, once again, in the spring of 1945, as the delaying tactics of the Japanese became evident.

In mid-January 1945, Sukarno had garnered new hopes that there had been a sign from the Japanese when Foreign Minister Shigemitsu announced in Tokyo that his government looked forward eagerly to realizing the independence of Indonesia, since the policy of regard for the sovereignty of all nations laid down in the Greater East Asia Charter would thereby be fulfilled.[47]

But when it later became apparent, as it did on March 1, 1945, that in announcing the investigating committee the Japanese were once more seeking merely to gain time, he openly declared[48] that like everyone else he impatiently awaited the day of independence. But now "only" the investigating committee had been granted. "Why must there first be a wise and careful investigation of independence? For what reason? So that the independence of Indonesia—Indonesia which is so important and so rich, Indonesia the greatest booty of Asia, as the Americans once called it—so that the independence of Indonesia can be really strong, unshakable, and enduring." In other words, Sukarno was giving here what in his opinion was the reason why the Japanese did not set Indonesia free: its wealth. And now for the first time he also dared to question the absolute readiness for struggle, as he exclaimed: "Be prepared! Exert yourselves and concentrate all your energy. Train yourselves to defend the homeland, though it be with spears of sharpened bamboo. Let us shed as much sweat as possible in time of peace, so that little blood may be shed here once war begins."

The Japanese had to hear as well that independence was "no matter of a piece of paper," but a question of the "survival of the fittest"—that at bottom the Indonesians were not dependent on the fiat they had so carefully withheld. Sukarno ended this remarkable radio address with the old fighting slogan of the Indonesian independence movement: "Rawé-rawé rantas, ma-

[47] AR, January 23, 2605, p. 1.

[48] See the radio speech by Sukarno on March 2, 1945; reprinted in AR, March 3, 5, and 6, 2605.

lang-malang putung (Let nothing hinder you along your way; break through every obstruction)." [49]

But Sukarno went no further than this. At a time when the war appeared to be closing in on the islands, there could be for him no possibility of heroic protest against the Japanese. Caught between two fires, even though he tended to identify himself with the Japanese side, he had nevertheless to reckon with a changed attitude among the population. They sensed the approaching end of the "year of corn," as the period of Japanese occupation had been called. He was forced now and then to use aggressive language in order not to lose touch with the people, and in this way he had maneuvered himself into an unhappy position.

It may be deduced from the remarkably objective account of Pakpahan, who lived through the occupation period in Dja-karta, that at this time there was more and more grumbling among the people over the attitudes of their leaders. Pakpahan, who fully understood the hard-pressed position of the leaders, exposed as they were in equal measure to orders from above and pressure from below, nevertheless concluded in regard to the constant declarations of fidelity and loyalty to Dai Nippon:

> Truly, the deeds and the behavior of our leaders were extremely disappointing. They were none of them anything other than a means to an end or a tool in the hands of the Japanese government, which manipulated them as it chose. At last the question sprang forth from our hearts: How much longer can they take advantage of the name of the people and still call themselves leaders? Is it not their duty as leaders to defend the rights and the honor of the people, so that they are not ruled and abused by foreigners?
>
> Indeed, if they acted so by intention, if the rights and the well-being of the people were used for the realization of an ideal or as a political tactic, this we could understand. But there ought to have been limits. And when those limits were overstepped, then the

[49] This saying—apparently an order to Hanoman's monkey army from the Wajang literature—had already appeared on the title page of a brochure by Douwes Dekker, Tjipto Mangunkusumo, and Suardi Sur-janingrat, *Onze verbanning*, as early as 1913.

leaders ought to have resorted to measures to curb the abuse, even if
the consequences were a risk to themselves. For it is the duty of a
leader not to be a "trafficker in the rights and the honor of the people." [50]

Pakpahan made this pronouncement in full awareness of the
gravity of the accusation, and many at this period must have
thought as he did, especially in circles where there was no militant anti-Western sentiment. Pakpahan—a clergyman from the
Batak region of Sumatra—had obviously not recognized that
Sukarno was in dead earnest, for example, in preferring the Japanese occupation to the Dutch colonial period. This Pakpahan
regarded as simply too much. From his perspective, therefore,
he could not regard Sukarno as anything more than a partisan
tool in the hands of the Japanese. His account shows clearly how
difficult Sukarno's position was; for dissatisfaction was widespread among the intellectuals, who anticipated no further concessions from the Japanese. Thus Sutan Sjahrir found it an easy
task to organize the resistance of his underground movement
over the pledges of loyalty.[51]

Besides the delaying tactics of the Japanese and the angry
protests of his own people, there was yet a third burden pressing
on Sukarno: the Allied advance.[52] Since November 1943, the
Dutch in exile had left no doubt as to what was in store for Sukarno once Java had been reconquered.[53] In addition, the return of the whites threatened to be the beginning of a new
colonization. The Dutch had proclaimed this openly, and Sukarno—whose decades-old prejudice allowed no other conclu-

[50] G. Pakpahan, *1261 hari dibawah sinar Matahari Terbit* [1261 Days
under the Rays of the Rising Sun] (1947), p. 96.

[51] This is also clear from Pakpahan's notes. See *1261 hari*, p. 126.

[52] He expressed his relief when a British fleet—which was expected to
land on Java at the end of April, turned northward to join the battle
against the Japanese home islands. See "Matahari hampir terbit [The
Sun Has Almost Risen]," AR, April 30 and May 1, 2605.

[53] "We will know how to settle accounts quickly and thoroughly with
figures such as Ir. Sukarno." See *Oranje: Tijdschrift voor de Nederlandsche en Nederlandsch-Indische gemeenschap in de Zuid Pacific,* Vol.
II, No. 8, p. 18.

sion—could see the Americans and the English only as their helpers.

For this reason, even now, when he was forced to meet the popular will halfway, he held fast to the unpopular Pantja Dharma. In a speech echoing the old ideals from the earlier years of the period of struggle, he declared that even though his people did not know how long the war would last and what sacrifices Indonesia still had to make, "nevertheless, we fight on with determination at the side of Dai Nippon, in the same life-and-death struggle with Dai Nippon. Why? Because we understand nationalism as being from God and for God. Because we hunger for independence, and for us that independence is truth and justice; truth and justice are defended by Dai Nippon, and God is always on the side of truth and justice." [54] Once again Sukarno sought refuge in God. His disagreeable position at this period appears to have left him no other way out. The secret of how, despite that position, he nevertheless succeeded in giving consolation and hope to his people, was his alone. For example, on March 9, 1945, the day of the "liberation of Java," columns of people who had been rounded up for the celebration had to wait for hours on an empty stomach, first in pouring rain and then under a scorching sun, before the ritual began. Sukarno alone appeared to know what must be going on in the minds of the masses gathered in the square. "Believe me," he cried out, "in an independent Indonesia no Indonesian will go hungry, every Indonesian must and shall be fed." These words were accepted as a sign by the hungry people.[55] Even if a few here and there had begun to have doubts of Bung Karno, and to feel oppressed by his preaching of total war, the hope for a better future was still centered in him. They sensed that he was not the "trafficker in the rights and the honor of the people," [56] even though often they did not understand him.

[54] See the radio address on March 7, 1945, entitled "Setia kepada tjita-tjita [True to the (Old) Ideals]," in which the ideals of a just social order for Indonesia were developed as in earlier years; AR, March 12, 13, 14, 2605.

[55] Pakpahan, *1261 hari*, p. 106.

[56] The epithet, "Pendjual hak dan kehormatan bangsa," was also put in quotation marks by Pakpahan. This charge was undoubtedly made in

The Time of Testing (May–August 1945)

Sukarno's Role in the Committee for the Investigation of Indonesian Independence

On April 30, one day after the announcement of the composition of the Committee for Investigation of Indonesian Independence,[57] the Japanese heads of the bureaus of general operations, in whose domain the question of Indonesian independence fell, met in Singapore. And here for the first time Nishimura, the representative of the Sixteenth Army, urged emphatically "that there is no way to win the confidence of the people but to go through with independence." [58] With this, the period of deliberate delay was over, and the actions of the nationalists, who since April 25 had been able to publish their own journal,[59] were no longer so restricted as before. This new development was underscored by the visit Sukarno was able to pay at the end of April to the sphere of influence of the Japanese Navy in Makassar (on the island of Celebes).[60]

For a while after his return from Celebes, little was heard of Sukarno. This was due in part to the sudden death of his father,[61] but also to the tasks connected with the formation of the investigating committee (hereafter to be referred to under its Indonesian initials BPKI).[62] Thus in those days, he must have

---

Indonesian circles during the spring of 1945, notably by the Prijajis, who feared for their position in the new state. See the pamphlets by M. Slamet entitled *Japanese Machinations,* issued between the autumn of 1945 and the spring of 1946.

[57] AR, April 29, 2605, p. 1. For a detailed comment on the composition, see Anderson, *Some Aspects,* pp. 18ff.

[58] RVO-IC 005872 and 059330. Nishimura had taken up his duty as Somubucho with the Sixteenth Army in December 1944.

[59] *Indonesia Merdeka* (published by Djawa Hokokai) appeared biweekly, on the 10th and 25th of each month.

[60] On this subject see AR, May 4–7, 2605, and *Indonesia Merdeka* (Dj. H.), No. 2. On the diminished opposition of the Japanese Navy, see Anderson, *Some Aspects,* p. 12.

[61] AR, May 8 and 19, 2605.

[62] The Indonesian name is "Badan Penjelidikan Kemerdekaan Indonesia."

been working on the speech that was to become the foundation of the new Indonesian state, and was in later years to make known Sukarno's name far beyond the boundaries of Indonesia. This was his speech on the Pantja Sila, the "five basic principles" of the Indonesian state, or the Indonesian *Weltanschauung*.

This speech was given by Sukarno—who this time, obviously by his own wish, so as to be able to play a more active role, did not take over the chairmanship of the committee [63]—on June 1, 1945, the final day of the first session of the BPKI, which had begun on May 28. It was the absolute climax of the session, and its impact on the sixty-two delegates from all groups of the population was obvious. In it Sukarno declared that the future Indonesian state was to be founded on five principles: (1) nationalism, (2) internationalism (or humanitarianism); (3) democracy (in the sense of Mufakat, consensus); (4) social justice; and (5) belief in one God.

The arguments and ideas set forth by Sukarno will be discussed presently in greater detail.[64] Here let it be noted only that the speech gives no hint of opposition to Japanese domination, as may all too easily be gathered from the prefatory notes of Indonesian editors to various later editions of the speech, all emphasizing the "strict censorship" and the "flagrant contrast with the spirit and character of the time." [65] If Sukarno and the other Indonesians expressed their ideas openly within the BPKI, this was not "high treason" [66] but the express wish and intent of the Japanese,[67] who hoped just then that the committee would become embroiled in fierce debates and time be gained thereby.

[63] AR, April 29, 2605, p. 2; also Anderson, *Some Aspects,* p. 19. On the recommendation of Sukarno and Hatta, the chairmanship of the BPKI went to Dr. Radjiman, a veteran of the independence movement, who had been present already at the first congress of Budi Utomo in 1908.

[64] See below, Chapter XI.

[65] See the foreword to *Het ontstaan van de Pantjasila* (1952), p. 3, and to *Lahirnja Pantjasila—The Birth of Pantjasila* (1952), p. 9.

[66] See, for example, Carl Weiss, *Sukarnos 1000 Inseln* (1963), p. 40.

[67] See the statement by Yosio Ichibangase, the Japanese Vice-President of the BPKI, RVO-IC 005851.

But thanks to the transcendent role played by Sukarno in the meetings, this wish of the Japanese was not to be fulfilled. After the first session of the BPKI, which was restricted to more general subjects, it was recommended that the sixty-two delegates take up in detail in their own provinces the following themes, concerning which resolutions would then be passed at a further session: (a) the form of the government of the future state; (b) the territory; (c) the problem of nationalities; (d) economic and financial policy; (e) defense; (f) education; (g) a draft constitution; (h) the place of religion in the state.

The statement given by Ichibangase, the Japanese Vice-President of the BPKI, in November 1945,[68] suggests that the Japanese believed these themes would offer enough material for dispute to ensure extended discussions by nationalists, Moslems, and Prijajis, as well as the various segments of the population.

But at the next session of the BPKI, from July 10 to 17, it became apparent that the immense labor could be completed within a single week. Here the preliminary work that had been performed in the meantime was clearly evident. And on the decisive question, the position of religion in the state, this preliminary work was above all Sukarno's doing.

Following the same argument as in the article written from exile in Benkulen in 1940,[69] Sukarno in his Pantja Sila speech had proposed that through intensive propaganda for Islam the Moslems should make the Indonesian parliament a place in which, through a general Mufakat, the laws of Islam could become laws of the state, if such laws were desired. Also as in 1940, he mentioned that the Indonesian state must exist "for all," and that special rights must be granted to no segment of the population at the expense of any other. No expression of protest came from the Moslems in the BPKI, but it was generally perceived that the successful conclusion of the investigations, which were thereupon to be forwarded to Tokyo for appraisal, depended on whether the decision was for an Islamic state or a secular state.[70]

Before the first meeting of the BPKI the Japanese military

[68] RVO-IC 005850.   [69] See above, Chapter VI.
[70] See "Agama dalam Indonesia merdeka [Religion in Independent Indonesia]," *Indonesia Merdeka* (Dj. H.), No. 3, May 25, 2605, p. 3.

government had declared that its attitude on the place of religion in the state amounted to "a blank sheet of paper." This Benda regards as marking the end of Japanese support for the Moslems against the "secular" nationalists. He believes that the statements of the Moslem leaders, who at this time put the unity of the nation above everything else, are a result of this new situation.[71] The present investigation indicates that the tensions between Moslems and nationalists in the occupation period were not as severe as Benda thought them to be. The desire for unity invariably came first with the various schools of thought. Therefore the statement of the Masjumi leader Wachid Hasjim, that "what we need most of all at this time is the indissoluble unity of the nation," [72] requires no further comment at this point. It shows, however, that the Moslems, even when the fate of the Islamic state, their ideal for decades, was at stake, were in principle ready to compromise.

And the nationalists did not permit this question to come to a vote, which they could have won easily since they had a clear majority in the BPKI. They too sought a compromise, in order to find a common solution along with the Islamic movement which would enable everyone to be in favor of the Indonesian state. For this reason a special committee was installed, with Sukarno as chairman, in which nationalist and Islamic interests were represented equally.[73] This committee worked out the compromise. In the so-called Djakarta Charter, the preamble to the Indonesian constitution,[74] the Pantja Sila were designated

[71] See Benda, *Crescent,* pp. 188f. Anderson (*Some Aspects,* pp. 20f., 26) goes beyond Benda in his belief that the composition of the BPKI must be seen as hopelessly biased against Islamic interests. It should be noted, however, that in the crucial committee that worked out the preamble to the Constitution, Islamic and nationalist interests were represented equally. See note 73, below.

[72] *Indonesia Merdeka* (Dj. H.), No. 3 (May 25), p. 3; also cited in Benda, *Crescent,* p. 189.

[73] Its members were Sukarno, Hatta, Subardjo, Yamin, Wachid Hasjim, Muzakkir, H. A. Salim, Abikusno, and Maramis.

[74] Cited in Anderson, *Some Aspects,* pp. 27f. See also Muhammad Yamin, *Proklamasi dan konstitusi Republik Indonesia* [The Proclamation and Constitution of the Republic of Indonesia] (1951), p. 17. But Yamin,

the basis of the future state and the observance of the Islamic laws was made obligatory only for those professing Islam. Nevertheless, at the second session of the BPKI there was still heated discussion of this formula, in which the nationalists who insisted on the compromise came to the verge of defeat. After heated debate that went on through an entire night, the Moslems were granted the further concession that the President of the state was to be a Moslem.[75]

The next morning Sukarno, in tears, begged the assembly to give its Mufakat to this solution, and in the end Moslems and nationalists responded unanimously to his fervent appeal. The only ones refusing consent to this solution, reached in true Indonesian spirit, were four representatives of—the Chinese.[76]

The outcome was a brilliant victory for Sukarno and for the idea he had defended since 1927—that only unanimity among all schools of thought could open a way acceptable to all Indonesians. And not only the solution of the question of state and religion in the preamble to the Indonesian constitution, but also the constitution itself, markedly reflected Sukarno's views from earlier times.

Although in 1945 most of the members of the BPKI rejected a state that followed the Western pattern of parliamentary democracy, and all sides gave priority to the indigenous Indonesian system of Permusjawaratan and Mufakat,[77] for decades no one had so clearly defined this idea as Sukarno, who even in 1927 had given this foundation to the PPPKI,[78] and who since

---

who himself had a part in working out the Djakarta Charter, gives a text from which all Japanophile passages have been expunged, and even asserts (*ibid.*, p. 16) that the document was a rejection of fascism.

[75] RVO-IC 005852f. (Ichibangase). Anderson (pp. 30ff.), using other sources; also J. H. A. Logemann, *Nieuwe gegevens over het ontstaan van de Indonesische grondwet van 1945* (1962), as noted in the bibliography. Logemann makes use, as does Anderson, of Notonagaro, *Pembukaan undang-undang dasar 1945* (1957), a work not available to the author.

[76] RVO-IC 005853. In addition to the four Chinese, one Menadonese also submitted a supplementary proposal. No evidence for the abstention of the delegates of the Chinese minority can be found, however, in Muhammad Yamin, *Naskah persiapan undang-undang dasar 1945* [Documents on the Preparation of the Constitution of 1945] (1959), p. 396.

[77] Logemann, *Nieuwe gegevens,* pp. 703ff.

[78] See above, Chapter III.

then had held fast unshakably to the principle of representing all sides.

Many constitutional proposals were submitted, and on July 11, 1945, these were turned over to a committee, once again under the chairmanship of Sukarno. The lawyer Supomo undertook to work out the final draft of the constitution in detail.[79] It remained for him to translate the decades-old political ideas of Sukarno into legal terminology.

The highest authority was vested in a People's Congress (Madjelis Permusjawaratan Rakjat), which was to meet every five years, and in which as far as possible all major classes and segments of the population were to be represented. It was to elect the President, who would hold nearly unlimited power for a period of five years, and who was responsible only to this People's Congress. An ordinary parliament (Dewan Perwakilan Rakjat) was to have a mainly advisory function, as had the earlier Volksraad and the later Central Advisory Council. The President was not bound to follow its recommendations; however, this advisory parliament was to be represented at full strength in the People's Congress, and thus to have a share in the highest authority. The President was to appoint the ministers, who were to be responsible to him alone.

Thus all power and responsibility were centered in the President: "He must be the true leader of the nation and of one mind with the whole people" (Supomo).[80] This had been the goal of Sukarno's "centralized democracy" or "democratic centralism," as he had formulated it in 1933. His idea of a *Führerstaat* had crystallized during the Japanese period; [81] in both the Japanese military government and his own organization, the Barisan Pelopor, he had been able to observe the effectiveness of directly transmitted orders. In a time threatened by conflicts

[79] Logemann, *Nieuwe gegevens,* pp. 694f., 703ff. Logemann speaks of "Supomo's theory of the state."

[80] *Ibid.,* p. 706.

[81] In 1940, Sukarno in an article, "Indonesia versus Fasisme [Indonesia against Fascism]," was critical of *Führerprinzip* and *Kadavergehorsam.* See DBR, pp. 457ff. In 1933, however, he came close to these principles in demanding full powers for the leadership and rejecting democracy in the ranks of the party. See "The Marhaenist Party," above.

with Western powers, a strongly centralized state structure appeared to Sukarno the best guarantee of its ability to function.

Hatta, in accepting the *Führerstaat*, demanded that certain rights (freedom of association, assembly, and speech) be guaranteed. Here his basically liberal attitude also came into play. On the other hand, Sukarno, who spoke only of the "poison of liberalism" and the "sickness of individualism," was a determined opponent to the granting of liberal rights, in particular the freedom to form associations.[82] He saw that the chance had finally come to realize his decades-old dream of a unified popular movement. At each of his entrances into the movement, 1926, 1932, and 1942, it had been his chief concern to bring about the unity of all groups. That was the heart of his concept of Marhaenism, and—as will be shown presently—the main concern of his Pantja Sila speech. The desire for unity ruled him as an internal force, which in 1927 had driven him to found the first Indonesian federation, in 1932 to make a desperate attempt at unifying the divided nationalists, in 1942 to form the "Four-leafed Clover," and to organize the Putera movement, in which all schools of thought were included. He also looked to this unified popular movement for the reconstruction of a just social order once the state had been established. He saw the unhampered right of association as a threat to this development—quite correctly, as would be demonstrated a few months later.[83]

Among other important decisions by the second session of the BPKI between July 10 and 17 were the preference by a great majority for a republic, on the question of the form of the state, and, in the territorial question, for the idea of a Greater Indonesia. The entire archipelago—not only the Dutch colonial empire, but also the British and Portuguese possessions in the archipelago—was to form the territory of the future Indonesian state.[84]

Sukarno showed himself as well to be an ardent advocate of

[82] Anderson, *Some Aspects*, p. 32; also Yamin, *Naskah*, pp. 292ff.

[83] See below, next Chapter.

[84] Anderson, *Some Aspects*, p. 29; Logemann, *Nieuwe gegevens*, pp. 702f.

the idea of a Greater Indonesia. He spoke of having once thought of a Pan-Indonesia including the Philippines, but these islands had meanwhile become an independent state. However, he held fast, as did the majority of the delegates, to the inclusion of the Malay peninsula: he had, he said, received countless letters from Malayans pressing for inclusion as part of Indonesia. But more important for Sukarno than the wish of the Malayans must have been the further argument that for Indonesia it was vital to have the Straits of Malacca firmly in hand, since the proximity of Malaya to Sumatra could easily be an unending threat to Indonesia's security.[85] This argument reveals Sukarno's old anxiety over continued exposure to the influence of British colonial policy in the Southeast Asian area, which even led, following the establishment of the state of Malaysia, to open threats of war.

A few weeks after this session of the BPKI Marshal Terauchi, the Japanese Commander in Chief for Southeast Asia, refused to recognize these extensive territorial claims. Sukarno, who had been invited to his headquarters with Hatta and Dr. Radjiman, thereupon declared—possibly under pressure from Hatta—that he accepted the boundaries of the former colonial empire of the Netherlands Indies as the limits of the future Indonesian state.[86]

It was only a few days after his return from Saigon that the old dream of an Indonesian independence, without the participation of the Japanese, and indeed even against their will, for the first time became a reality. But this is to anticipate a development for which the way was paved outside of the conference rooms, one that spread like wildfire and gave a powerful impetus to independence: the angry protest of the Pemudas, the Indonesian youth groups, against the Japanese masters and against what they saw as the procrastination of their own leaders.

[85] Yamin, *Naskah,* pp. 204ff. Sukarno—in contrast to Hatta—had defended the Greater-Indonesian idea even in the presense of Marshal Terauchi at Saigon. See RVO-IC 005857.

[86] RVO-IC 005857. See also Anderson, p. 62.

Sukarno and the Pemudas

The revolt of the Peta in Blitar in mid-February 1945 was the signal for a rising spirit of protest, concealed at first but gradually more and more outspoken, among the Pemudas, the Indonesian youth groups, against the Japanese occupation power. Even though in the first months the press carried no report whatever of the uprising in Blitar, rumors of the event and of its leader Suprijadi, for whom the Japanese searched in vain to the very end of the war, soon spread all through Java.[87]

Prominent Indonesians were summoned to sit in on the investigation by the Japanese military tribunal, since the Japanese were very well aware of the widespread resentment. Sukarno himself was forced to make a statement about the event. He declared that he regretted what had happened because the actions had been irresponsible and lacking in foresight, and thus could be a danger to Indonesian interests. But he trusted in the clemency of the Japanese, and hoped those involved would receive light sentences.

In Sukarno's attitude, expressed in carefully chosen words, Pakpahan saw an attempt "to avoid too close an association with any party," [88] thus indicating that here Sukarno was caught between opposing forces. Sukarno held inflexibly to this middle position during the months that followed, when he was under increasing pressure from the Pemudas. By so doing he eventually prevented a revolt which, given the Japanese Army's state of full alert, would have led to a catastrophe and destroyed all Indonesian hopes at one stroke.

Moreover, there was nothing Sukarno feared more than the shifting of forces that was quietly taking place. By continuing to preach the Pantja Dharma, and by writing a pamphlet, in May 1945, that once more justified in detail the "five duties" and the call to "life or death with Dai Nippon," [89] he was first of all at-

[87] Pakpahan, *1261 hari,* pp. 108f.   [88] *Ibid.,* p. 110.

[89] "Menudju Indonesia Merdeka" [Toward an Independent Indonesia]." It was reprinted in *Pradjurit* ["Hero"], which was published by the Djawa Hokokai every fourteen days, beginning in August 1944, and which served to stir up the fighting spirit of Indonesian youth until the end of the war.

tempting to halt the gradually increasing sympathy for the Western powers. The charge often heard at this time, that the "older leaders" favored the Japanese side out of their own interest, was finally made in public by Sutan Sjahrir, who during these months came more and more into prominence.[90] On the other hand, Dr. Radjiman, later president of the BPKI and a veteran of the freedom movement since the founding of Budi Utomo (1908), defended the "older leaders": "In our opinion it is clear that if the Pendawas Bima and Ardjuna support their elder brother Prabu Darmakusuma, who has a pure [holy] intention, then Bima and Ardjuna are also pure, and both are free of self-interest. It is these two who will wipe out the Kaurawas." [91] The language of myths had sprung up again.[92] It was used by the leaders not against the Japanese but against the importunate youth. The "Kaurawas" remained the archenemy. They had to be wiped out. The Pemudas were told that Bima and Ardjuna—possibly a reference to Sukarno and Hatta, who were included under the term "older leaders"—were on the side of justice and thus had no base motives.

The Pemudas, however, also had recourse to the myth; and whereas the "older leaders" drew upon the *Mahabharata,* they chose the *Ramayana.* An article from this period, provocatively entitled "Liberation of the Fatherland," asserted that when the [doomed] hero Kumbakarna decided to join the struggle against a power many times stronger, it was by no means in order to defend the "elder brother" Dasamuka. For the latter had refused to give back the "abducted goddess Sita":

Now it is perhaps clear that Kumbakarna by no means conducted his battle with the intention of justifying the deeds of his elder brother. No! That was not what impelled him to go willingly to his

[90] Cf. AR, March 16, 2605, p. 1, for Sjahrir's opinion of the "New Life Movement," planned during March 1945. A new movement could not be called to life, he said, unless the leaders themselves renewed their lives and gave a clear example by abandoning their own interests. See also Pakpahan, p. 126.

[91] *Pradjurit,* No. 16 (May 15, 1945), p. 10.

[92] See, for example, *Pradjurit,* No. 10 (February 15, 1945), pp. 25f., in which cooperation with the Japanese is compared with the *Ramayana.*

death in opposing an enemy who was many times stronger. It was the struggle for his homeland, for his fatherland. And it was to protect the honor of his ancestors, because he felt the blood of Ngalangka flowing in his veins.[93]

More clearly than all the resolutions taken by the Pemudas at the time, these words expressed what was at stake for them. They were ready to fight against the Allies, not on the side of the Japanese but only for their fatherland, and they wanted that fatherland to be a reality before joining in the fight against the vastly greater strength of the enemy. It was a rejection of Sukarno's slogan, "Life or death with Dai Nippon," as confirmed in the Pantja Dharma, a rejection of the idea that the Japanese were the defenders of justice. Thus viewed, the passionate demands of the Pemudas for immediate independence, which in June and July 1945 were raised quite openly,[94] became understandable.

At first, by appealing to their sense of duty, Sukarno tried to remind the Pemudas that freedom could not be achieved simply by singing the national anthem but only through struggle and sacrifice. Indonesia did not want a sham freedom but a genuine sovereignty, as it had also been formulated in the Pantja Dharma.[95] But by mid-June 1945, at the eighth session of the Central Advisory Council (June 18-21), Sukarno had to hear his old comrade-in-struggle Ki Hadjar Dewantoro say "that the reputation of the leaders is ruined in the eyes of the people." [96]

Sukarno now risked falling into a dangerous isolation.[97] The

[93] Subagijo I. Notohidjojo, "Kemerdekaan Tanah-air," *Indonesia Merdeka* (Dj. H.), No. 6 (July 10, 1945), pp. 5ff.

[94] *Indonesia Merdeka*, No. 4 (June 10)ff.; AR, from about May 24, June/July, *passim*.

[95] See the title page of *Indonesia Merdeka*, No. 3, May 26; also AR, May 29, 2605, p. 2. Anderson's opinion (*Some Aspects*, p. 54) that Sukarno "contradicted himself" when he made use of the Pantja Dharma even after the Pantja Sila speech, cannot be accepted. The Pantja Sila were valid for the future Indonesian state; for the relation between Indonesians and Japanese, the Pantja Dharma were still fully valid after June 1.

[96] AR, June 19, 2605, p. 2.

[97] A symptomatic scene occurred at the beginning of May, when Sukarno returned to Java from his trip to Makassar. It is obvious from the photograph that his call of "Dai Nippon Banzai" (to be spoken with arms

argument he had previously used to justify cooperation with the Japanese—that the Japanese were the chosen instrument for liberating the peoples of Asia—now became, as for the first time the possibility of actual independence was hinted at in the committee sessions, a popular laughingstock. It must have come as a total mockery of partnership when, on March 12, it was suddenly reported first that Japan intended to give independence to Annam, Cambodia, and Laos, and then, a day later, that Annam had declared its independence and had been recognized by Japan.[98] It was clearly stated in the newspapers that the Philippines and Burma had also received their independence, with no long-drawn-out preparations, and the Japanese had likewise set up their regime on the island of Java without preliminary investigations. Accordingly, Indonesia ought to be given its freedom without delay.[99]

What use was it for Sukarno to declare, as he did in his Pantja Sila speech of June 1, 1945, that the Indonesians were overimpatient for freedom, like a bridegroom who could not wait for the wedding, even though the household furnishings had not yet been procured?[100] The Pemudas were miles ahead of him, and they were soon calling even for a struggle against the Japanese. It could not be understood otherwise when on July 3 the once strictly censored *Asia Raya* carried the statement: "The Indonesian Pemudas do not want to build on filthy ground; rather, they want to clear away the filth before the proud and firm new structure arises." But three weeks later Sukarno was still proclaiming his belief in the rightness of the Japanese side in the war, and in the obligation to support them.[101]

It was clear at this time, when various outlying territories of Indonesia were already occupied by Allied troops, that there was a profound division between Sukarno and the Pemudas. They attempted to remind him of his old slogan, "Whoever has the youth, has the future."[102] Sukarno had already once before re-

---

raised, and then repeated), went all but unnoticed by any of the bystanders (AR, May 7, p. 1).

[98] AR, March 12 and 13, 2605.   [99] AR, June 9, 2605, p. 1.

[100] *Lahirnja Pantjasila—The Birth of Pantjasila* (1952), pp. 13ff.

[101] AR, July 21, 2605, p. 2.

[102] *Indonesia Merdeka* (Dj. H.), No. 7 (July 25), p. 14.

versed this saying, after the dialectic manner he so delighted in: "Whoever has the future, has the youth." [103] According to this saying, during these months there would have been no future for him.

If Sukarno had made greater demands of the Japanese, he could now have been sure that the majority of the population were behind him. The Pemudas not only waited, but were burning with eagerness to back up such demands with force. But there was the risk that all the pent-up energy and radicalism might explode in the "wrong direction"—and this was what Sukarno feared. He wanted to save that radicalism for the conflict with the NICA,[104] who had long since given notice that they would soon appear from their territories in New Guinea.

So he used all his energy to prevent the growing anti-Japanese sentiment from exploding. There was only one way to do this—by drawing the youth into a greater share of responsibility. In June, as pressure by the Pemudas hardened, Sukarno had his old confidant Sartono bring forward in the Central Advisory Council the proposal to found a unified popular movement, with strong participation by the youth organizations, that would incorporate all existing organizations.[105] In this way the old dream of unity could be realized, and at the same time the youth could be offered a new field of activity. In contrast to the spring of 1945, when the military regime still opposed the wish for a unified popular movement, it now gave its consent without particular difficulty.[106]

As before with the Putera, a kind of "Four-leafed Clover" was formed, a steering committee in which all groups of the people were represented.[107] Sukarno said explicitly that this "New Movement (Gerakan Baru)" was different from all previous

[103] See, for example, "Mendjadi guru dimasa kebangunan [Becoming a Teacher in the Time of Awakening]," undated facsimile, DBR, pp. 611ff. The essay appears to have been written shortly before the outbreak of the Pacific war; it was not published, but was repeatedly used by Sukarno during the occupation period as basis of a speech. (AR, November 25, 2602, p. 2; March 26, 2603, p. 2; etc.)

[104] Netherlands-Indies Civil Administration.

[105] AR, June 22, 2605, p. 2.   [106] AR, July 2, 2605, p. 1.

[107] Sukarno, Hatta, Wachid Hasjim, and Wirnatakusuma were represented on the committee (AR, July 4, 2605).

movements during the period of the Japanese occupation, which had borne the "stamp of the military government." The present movement would be devoted exclusively to the interests of the people.[108]

When the military government still spoke of having certain "expectations" of the movement, the enraged delegates of the Pemudas walked out of the planning session.[109] During the crucial sessions of the BPKI in mid-July there were further delays. Only in the light of the events treated here can Sukarno's dominant role in this body be appreciated. Finally, on July 28, a Council of Leaders for the New Movement, in which all previously existing associations and military organizations were represented, was installed.[110]

At last Sukarno had reached the goal: one movement with all sides represented, his wish since the days of the split in the Sarekat Islam (1921), had been realized for the first time nearly a quarter of a century later. On August 3 the Council of Leaders held its first meeting in Sukarno's house and elected him head of the New Movement. Hatta said in a little speech that Sukarno, who had already stood so many times at the head of a movement, was now called upon "to fulfill the mandate of history" and to lead the people from their present misery into a happy future.[111]

As a first step, a great meeting of the youth organizations was called for mid-August in Djakarta. It appeared possible that the clarifying discussion would take place there and that the united front would be sealed. But events did not proceed that way. On that third day of August, the hour in which the "mandate of history" was to be fulfilled was closer than anybody then supposed.

The Proclamation of Independence

Meanwhile, in July an order had come out of Tokyo via Marshal Terauchi, the Commander in Chief of the "Southern Re-

---

[108] AR, July 2, 2605.

[109] Anderson, *Some Aspects,* p. 57. On the "expectations" of the military government, see AR, July 7, 2605, p. 1.

[110] AR, July 28, 2605, p. 1.   [111] AR, August 10, 2605, p. 2.

gions," to speed up Indonesian independence.[112] This led to the announcement on August 7 of a Committee for the *Preparation of Indonesian Independence.*[113]

Sukarno declared triumphantly that this was the "final step" on the way to independence. The Committee was, he went on, the first to be composed wholly of representatives of the Indonesian people. The end of its session would see the proclamation of independence. Freedom could only be guaranteed, however, "when every single foreign imperialism has been destroyed." And so—"Let us fight on. Our motto remains the same: Freedom or death. To the Japanese empire I express my most sincere thanks." [114] For Sukarno the time of "Life or death with Dai Nippon" was over. Ever since the meeting of the Council of Leaders on August 3, he had shown greater determination. On August 4 he had spoken openly in reply to those who were fearful of doubts among the leadership concerning Indonesia's own capacity for independence. "Truly there are no such doubts," was his answer to all those who might think thus.[115]

With his "most sincere thanks" to Japan after the announcement of the preparatory committee, Sukarno had extricated himself at last from a dangerous embrace. On the same evening he gave his "corn speech," with its allusion to the prophecy of Djajabaja that at the end of a "year of corn" the conquerors from the North would return to their own land. "Before the corn is ripe, Indonesia must be independent," he declared, with the sharp hint that his audience should give careful thought to the "mystery" of this sentence. Only now, since—as he put it— "Dai Nippon has already begun to recognize our independence," did he make use of the myth against the Japanese. This was evidence of his sense of responsibility—that he began to feed the hopes of the masses only when the moment had come for their realization.

But he could now also insist that there was no longer any

112 Anderson, pp. 33ff.; Elsbree, *Japan's Role,* pp. 93ff.; Aziz, *Japan's Colonialism,* pp. 246ff.

113 AR, August 7, 2605, p. 1. This date had already been set, and thus cannot be regarded as an effect of the bombing of Hiroshima (August 6).

114 AR, August 7, 2605, p. 1.   115 AR, August 6, 2605, p. 1.

reason to rebel against the Japanese. Japan itself had declared that out of the preparations would come the proclamation of the republic:

From this, my brothers—from the setting up of this Preparatory Committee—it is clear that the only remaining opposition to the independence of Indonesia comes from Allies—the Americans, the English, and the Dutch. Destroy this opposition, if you would taste the sweetness of Indonesia's independence, now ripe with promise.[116]

Sukarno had hardly ever been so vehement against the Allies, and in particular against the Dutch, as in the rest of this speech. From a contrast between the "freedom already recognized" by Japan and the establishment by the Allies of the Netherlands Indies Civil Administration (NICA), he plunged into a direct attack. The Indonesians did not want them, even though they promised mountains of gold; they must go back, back home to Holland. The Indonesians knew that behind their promises were stockpiles of bombs, explosives, and cannons, and that together with Englishmen, Americans, and Australians they had already attacked the Indonesian people, burned Indonesian villages, killed Indonesians, widowed the women and made orphans of the children. But they certainly also knew that the Indonesians were ready to die for their freedom. "Hundreds of thousands of Pemudas" had volunteered for suicide squads, and their slogan was "Freedom or death."

When Sukarno was able to speak without any censorship, he stirred up feeling against the Allies—a feeling that had intensified from year to year—to the boiling point. He remained consistently on the path he had taken, and was prepared to follow it to the end. It ought not to be thought that with the Preparatory Committee the struggle was at an end: "No, our struggle has only just begun." The intent of this sentence was rhetorical; but so far as Sukarno was concerned, it contained an indisputable truth. Over the last few years he had not struggled. He had resisted the Japanese; he had let them feel his reluctance and

[116] Radio speech on the evening of August 7, 1945. See AR, August 8, 2605, pp. 1, 2.

dissatisfaction, but he had never gone so far as to risk a break with them. All the while, the West had still remained his opponent.

Immediately after the announcement of the Preparatory Committee, Sukarno, Hatta, and Dr. Radjiman were flown to the vicinity of Saigon, where they were given more detailed instructions about the realization of independence by Marshal Terauchi.[117] On August 18 the Preparatory Committee was to meet for the first time under the leadership of Sukarno, and delegates from all parts of the former Netherlands Indies were to be present. No further statements were made about the date of independence. Sukarno later declared that it had been set for August 24.[118]

After the delegation returned to Java on August 14, Sukarno displayed a mood of high optimism. "In my recent radio address, I declared that Indonesia would be independent before the corn was ripe. But today I can declare that Indonesia will be independent before the corn blossoms." [119] It was in fact to come even more quickly than Sukarno predicted. Dramatic events awaited him.

The unwillingness of the Pemudas to wait any longer for the consent of the Japanese had reached a climax. In many circles the view prevailed that independence as a gift from Tokyo would debase and blemish the character of the Indonesian independence movement.[120] Sutan Sjahrir, Sukarno's adversary from the 1930's, was a strong proponent of this view.

[117] For details, see Anderson, *Some Aspects,* pp. 60ff.; H. J. de Graaf, "The Indonesian Declaration of Independence," *Bijdragen tot de Taal-, Land- en Volkenkunde,* CXVIII (1959), 305ff.; eyewitness reports, RVO-IC 005846 (Myoshi); and Hatta's, essay, "Legende en realiteit rondom de proclamatie van 17. Augustus," in *Verspreide Geschriften,* pp. 330ff.

[118] AR, September 3, 2605, p. 1.

[119] AR, August 14, 2605, p. 1. The translation given by Anderson (*Some Aspects,* p. 64)—"If I used to say, that Indonesia would only be free when the maize bore fruit, now I can declare . . ." is incorrect. Sukarno had never referred to Djajabaja before his radio speech (to which he here expressly refers).

[120] See, for example, A. Malik, *Riwajat dan perdjuangan sekitar proklamasi 17 Augustus 45* [History and Struggle over the Proclamation of August 17, 1945] (1956), pp. 16ff.

Sjahrir recalls [121] that he met with Hatta before the delegation left for Saigon and urged him to speak so forcefully on behalf of the Indonesians as to provoke open disagreement with the Japanese. The "convinced collaborators" would then be forced into open acknowledgment of the Indonesian cause.

There can be no doubt that this was aimed at Sukarno. And subsequent events served merely to underline Sjahrir's conviction that Indonesian independence could be salvaged only if it were accompanied by a revolt against the Japanese. While Sukarno and Hatta lingered in Vietnam, he led the Pemudas to expect that the moment for which they had waited so long would come in a few days. On the day after the delegation returned, Sjahrir sought out his old friend Hatta and urged him, with an allusion to the Japanese surrender, to proclaim independence. In this way Sjahrir hoped to pass over Sukarno completely. Hatta agreed to the plan, but objected "that a proclamation not made by Sukarno would have no great support"; whereupon they decided on trying to win over Sukarno.

Hatta first made the attempt alone—without success. Sukarno did not believe that the Japanese had surrendered, as was being rumored everywhere on that August 15.[122] Sjahrir himself then went with Hatta to visit Sukarno, whom he apparently succeeded in convincing of the necessity for an immediate proclamation, as he spoke of the angry bands of Pemudas who had already arrived in the city. At any rate, Sukarno gave his promise to make a proclamation of independence at five in the evening.[123]

However, at five in the evening nothing happened; and in the meantime Sukarno, along with Hatta, tried to get an official confirmation of the surrender from the Japanese. Admiral Maeda, the only friend of the Indonesian nationalists during the years of humiliation under the Japanese, promised to inform Sukarno as soon as he knew more details. Sukarno then sent word to the Pemudas that the declaration of independence

[121] Cf. Sjahrir, *Out of Exile,* pp. 253ff.

[122] Malik, *Riwajat,* pp. 20f. Sjahrir wrongly refers to August 14. For an exact chronology, see Anderson, pp. 65ff.

[123] Sjahrir, *Out of Exile,* p. 254.

would be postponed until the following day, August 16.[124]

The Pemudas reacted with fierce indignation. They decided to go ahead with the proclamation, if necessary without Sukarno and Hatta. But this Sjahrir was able to prevent: "It would bring us into opposition with our own people, and we could not allow that to happen under any circumstances." [125]

But there were other youth groups who now attempted by themselves to hasten things along; at their head were Chairul Saleh, Sukarni, Wikana, and Malik, who has described these events in a pamphlet.[126] At a private meeting they decided to force Sukarno and Hatta to make the declaration. There was a dramatic scene when their delegates confronted Sukarno late in the evening, and he flatly refused to yield to their demands. Wikana then declared, "If Bung Karno does not announce independence tonight, tomorrow there will be murder and bloodshed everywhere."

Sukarno, losing control of himself, rushed toward Wikana and exclaimed, "Go ahead and cut my throat, go on, drag me into a corner and kill me, no need to wait until tomorrow." [127] The Pemudas had not expected this. Subdued, they left without having achieved their purpose, on the advice of Hatta, who had meanwhile been summoned and who advised them to make the declaration on their own. Returning to their companions, they debated further and hit upon the idea of kidnapping Sukarno and Hatta that same night. So at four in the morning the two leaders were dragged from their beds and after a wild journey were brought to a barracks (Rengasdengklok), where they were to be subjected to further "force." But in reality the Pemudas themselves did not know what should be

[124] Cf. Anderson, *Some Aspects,* pp. 65ff.; de Graaf, "Declaration," pp. 311ff.; Hatta, "Legende," pp. 333ff.; A. Malik, *Riwajat,* pp. 35ff.; and Sidik Kertapati, *Sekitar proklamasi 17 Agustus 1945* [On the Proclamation of 17 August 1945] (1964), pp. 94ff.

[125] Sjahrir, *Out of Exile,* p. 255.

[126] A. Malik, *Riwajat.* His portrayal of the events, however, exaggerates the role of the Pemudas.

[127] See the account by Hatta, who witnessed the scene at first hand, in "Legende," pp. 338f.

done, and they sent a man to Djakarta to make contact with other groups.

This prank—which demonstrates the Pemudas' immaturity and makes it easy to guess what a catastrophe would have ensued if they had actually launched their planned revolt against the Japanese Army—ended on the evening of August 16, with the return of Sukarno and Hatta to Djakarta. On that night, at the home of Admiral Maeda, who had often provided the Indonesians with an opportunity for open discussion, and who after the promise of independence from Tokyo (in September 1944) had worked actively to prepare the youth of Indonesia for their future tasks in an Indonesian state,[128] the Indonesian declaration of independence was composed.

Now, after his experiences with the Pemudas, Sukarno was ready to agree that they could not wait any longer. Nevertheless, on the evening of August 16, accompanied by Maeda and Hatta, he sought out the Japanese chief of general operations to ask official permission to call together the Preparatory Committee, which by then had assembled in Maeda's house, ahead of schedule.

But Nishimura refused to make any advance in the date. He did not allow himself to be impressed even by Sukarno's hint that riots might very possibly break out. The Pemudas were to be informed that the Japanese Army was on guard and could prevent any attempted putsch.

Hatta then raised a decisive objection. He declared that the Pemudas' unrest should be looked at psychologically. The Allies might land any day, and the Pemudas were determined to fight,

---

[128] On Maeda's role in the Indonesian movement see the numerous interviews conducted by the Dutch with and concerning him following the end of the war (RVO-IC 006894-006902, 006931-33, 005802-06, 006825-29, 006076-89, 059397, etc.). There is nothing to indicate that the supposition made by Kahin (*Nationalism*, pp. 118ff.) is correct—namely that Maeda's activity was intended to strengthen a pro-Communist element, so as to win allies in Indonesia for an expected Communist rebellion in Japan. As early as 1945, Maeda had energetically defended himself against the charge that he had deliberately supported Communism: "Nobody who knows me will entertain the idea for a moment" (RVO-IC 006828).

"but only once they are sure that their death will serve the fatherland; they want to have a fatherland before they die." [129] To this, Nishimura gave no reply. Although he once more refused to grant official aproval of the meeting, he hinted that he could not object to a "tea party," such as Sukarno had finally proposed.[130]

In what proved to be a long "tea party," the form of the proclamation was hammered out, and once again a putsch, this one planned for midnight, was prevented.[131] Various groups had brought forward proposals that differed notably in the degree of their feeling against the Japanese. Sjahrir, who did not participate in the meeting at Maeda's house because he believed that the old ideals were being betrayed in the final hour, later remarked bitterly that all the passages in the proclamation that might have reflected the struggle of the Indonesians against the Japanese had disappeared from the final version.[132]

The final text of the proclamation read: "We, the people of Indonesia, hereby declare the independence of Indonesia. Matters concerning the transfer of power and so forth will be executed in an orderly manner and in the shortest possible time." Sukarno's original handwritten text still bears traces of the midnight struggle. At stake were the words "transfer" (pemindahan) and "executed" (diselenggarakan).[133] Perhaps the final version was reached by the method of compromise on which Sukarno placed so high a value. The more radical elements gave up their proposal to "seize" power, and the more moderate gave up the meek "endeavor."

This text, which was signed by Sukarno and Hatta in the name of the Indonesian people, was read to a small group of adherents at about ten o'clock on the following morning, August

---

129 RVO-IC 011155-57 (Hitoshi Nakamura, Adjutant to Nishimura).

130 Ibid. See also RVO-IC 005847 (Myoshi, Hatta's "shadow").

131 De Graaf, "Declaration," pp. 320f.

132 Sjahrir, Out of Exile, p. 258.

133 See O. Raliby, Documenta Historica I, Sedjarah dokumenter dari pertumbuhan dan perdjuangan Negara Republik Indonesia [Documentary History of the Origin and Struggle of the Republic of Indonesia] (1953), p. 4; also Anderson, pp. 84f.; Malik, pp. 53f.; Kertapati, pp. 113ff.

17, 1945, by a pale and tired-looking Sukarno. The Indonesian flag was then raised on a bamboo pole, and those present sang "Indonesia Raya" [134]

It was an unnatural and sobering occasion—this, the great moment for which Sukarno, along with Sjahrir and Hatta, the Indonesian leaders of earlier years, and the youth groups who had only recently come into prominence, had striven tirelessly, in continual readiness for sacrifice.

Sukarno, who in the first decade of his struggle for independence had tried so desperately to transform the anti-foreign sentiment that was latent among the people into a revolutionary fighting spirit, during those last months had been placed on the defensive by the volcanic force of that same spirit. His one-sided anti-Western attitude had given him the reputation of being a "lackey of the Japanese." This Sukarno had never been. He had at no time subordinated his goal, Indonesian independence, to Japanese interests. He had been constantly on the alert for a chance to realize his decades-old dream without open conflict. Throughout the entire period he had not only been the central figure of the movement, one who was decisive in setting the course of negotiations for future independence, but had also remained for the masses the symbol of freedom and of hope for a better future, even when he preached total war and made struggle at the side of the hated oppressor into a duty.

Nothing can more clearly demonstrate Sukarno's transcendent position in this period than the fact that not one of those who were dissatisfied with his leadership dared take it upon himself to proclaim independence. "It is certain that he was the hero of the people, the hero of the great masses." [135]

[134] On the background of the scene, see the illustrations in O. Raliby, *Doc. Hist.*, and Kahin, *Nationalism*, p. 136. For a brief speech made by Sukarno on this occasion, see Raliby, *Doc. Hist.*, pp. 13f.

[135] M. Cohen Stuart-Franken, *Van Indië tot Indonesië* (1947), p. 120.

PART FOUR
BEYOND THE "GOLDEN BRIDGE"

X

Summary of Sukarno's Role after the Proclamation of Independence

The Beginnings of the Republic

On August 18, 1945, the day after independence was proclaimed, the Preparatory Committee elected Sukarno by ac-
clamation as first President of the young Republic of Indonesia, with Hatta as Vice President. At the same meeting, a few
minor changes were made in the Constitution that had been
drafted during July 1945; the Japanophile passages were stricken
from the preamble to the constitution, and a clause was added
that gave sole responsibility to the President for a six-month
period, since the abrupt end of the war meant that the People's
Congress, which had been vested with the highest sovereignty,
could not be assembled.[1]

A Central Indonesian National Committee (Komite Nasional Indonesia Pusat—KNIP) was to sustain the President in
his work, and as soon as possible replace the Preparatory Committee, to which the odium of "made in Tokyo" still clung. The
members of this Central Committee were appointed by Sukarno and Hatta within a few days.

The establishment of a single party, a Partai Nasional Indonesia, was also agreed upon. On August 23, 1945, in his first
radio address as President,[2] Sukarno explained the difference
between the two projected organizations. Everywhere in the

---

[1] For details see Anderson, *Some Aspects,* pp. 195ff. For an eyewitness
account by Dr. Amir, a member of the Preparatory Committee, see RVO-
IC 009416ff.

[2] "Penggantian zaman dan kewadjiban kita [Our Duty and the Changing Times]," in O. Raliby, *Doc. Hist.,* pp. 17ff.

country, following the example of the KNIP, national committees were to be established in which the people as a whole were
to be represented. "Popular leaders from all groups, all schools
of thought, and all classes must be united in these national committees. The Prijajis, the Ulamas, the adherents of the nationalist movement, the Pemudas, traders, salesmen, etc.—all must
work together in these national committees." They were first to
apply their efforts to four tasks: (a) to express the people's will
to be independent; (b) to weld all classes into an indivisible
unity; (c) to ensure the people's security; (d) to sustain the
leaders in their effort to realize the ideals of the Indonesian people.

But the party was to become the motive force in every field of
the struggle; it was to defend the Republic, reinforce the spirit
of patriotism, and carry out economic and social measures for
putting the constitution into effect.

Thus Sukarno's first measures as President were an exact continuation of his old ideals. *One party*—this had been his ideal
ever since the split in the Sarekat Islam. The main idea of his
Partai Nasional in the 1920's, of his Marhaenist party in the
1930's, and finally of the Putera in the 1940's, had always been
the same: to embrace all political tendencies, thus avoiding the
tensions and open battles inherent in a multiparty system and
directing all energies toward one goal. Previously that goal had
been the achievement of independence. Now it became a question of striving to defend independence and to establish a just
social order.

As a young man in his twenties, Sukarno had described this
goal as the Sarekat Islam's task once it had "a parliament of its
own." As a man in his thirties, he had grappled more closely
with party organization, so as to be able to keep the multitude
of schools of thought (which were to be taken into the party)
under control. Thus he had called for "democratic centralism"
and for strictly disciplined subordination to the orders of the
top leadership.

As a man in his forties, he had shown by his efforts through
the "Four-leafed Clover" during the Japanese occupation period
(1942–43), and again through the Council of Leaders of the New

Movement (1945), what he expected this top leadership to be. The main currents of political activity among the people were to be represented in this leadership council, and were to arrive at a single unified decision.

Unity, for him, had thus remained the decisive force in all phases of his career, and now that the Republic had been proclaimed, he declared, "In these crucial hours the only attitude that can bring our nation into being is unity, unity, and once again unity."

The national committees, which Sukarno spoke of as an interim solution, were now for the first time to reflect national unity by representing the interests of as many classes as possible. Only thus could there be a realization of the idea of Permusjawaratan, of general discussion, which Sukarno had regarded ever since the founding of the first Indonesian federation in 1927 as the only possible form of genuine democracy for Indonesia.

Sukarno viewed the national committees as an interim solution because he hoped to be able eventually to alter the structure of the population as it then was and to transform it into a collectivist social order, which was to be based on the principle of Gotong-Rojong, of mutual help. This meant strict obedience to orders from above, in the national committees as elsewhere. Thanks to the unlimited powers granted the President by the Constitution, Sukarno was able to begin working at once toward realizing his old ideals. At the first session of the KNIP on August 29, 1945, it became clear what powers the body was intended to have, and the way it was, in accordance with the clause that had been added to the Constitution, to "sustain" the President. At the end of his remarks, Mr. Kasman Singodimedjo, the commander of the Peta, who had been first chairman of the KNIP, turned to Sukarno and declared that he was "ready to carry out the orders of the government." [3]

A few days later, on September 5, 1945, Sukarno formed a

[3] See Kasman Singodimedjo (ed.), *Negara Republik Indonesia* [The Republic of Indonesia] (1945), p. 20; also A. G. Pringgodigdo, *Perubahan kabinet presidensiil mendjadi kabinet parlamentar* [The Change from a Presidential to a Parliamentary Cabinet] (1955), p. 25.

cabinet that was responsible solely to himself,[4] and on September 10 he issued a decree that in the future the orders of the government of the Republic were alone to be obeyed.[5] A note from the Allies had made the Japanese military government responsible for maintaining the status quo, and thus it had refused from the beginning to support the Republic in any way whatsoever. Sukarno insisted at the time that he and Hatta, repeatedly through "person-to-person discussion," had arrived at a gentlemen's agreement for negotiating a gradual transfer of power into Indonesian hands.[6]

But the radical elements were not in favor of such a gentlemen's agreement; they felt cheated of their revolution and demanded an unconditional surrender of power. There had been widespread national enthusiasm at the time independence was declared; but by mid-September the long-suppressed resentment against the Japanese, who continued to withhold key positions from the Indonesians, had once again risen to a dangerous level.

Already there had been bloody clashes. And now that the Communist Party, illegal since 1927, had begun once more to agitate publicly, in an attempt to capitalize on the revolutionary climate among the Pemudas, a revolt appeared inevitable.[7] At a mass meeting held September 19 on the Koningsplein in Djakarta, 200,000 persons, most of them young, gave vociferous expression to their displeasure with the Japanese. Tan Malaka and his followers anticipated that a clash had thus become unavoidable, and the Japanese had well-armed troops stationed about the square, ready for whatever might happen.

At this critical moment, in which revolutionary sentiment had reached the boiling point, Sukarno once more demonstrated his astonishing power over the people. After weeks of preparations, Tan Malaka's effort petered out as a result of a

---

[4] For its composition, see Raliby, *Doc. Hist.*, pp. 33f.   [5] *Ibid.*, p. 34.

[6] See, for example, AR, August 30, 1945, p. 1, and September 3, p. 1.

[7] Thanks above all to the activity of Tan Malaka, who with the declaration of independence was once more at the center of things, and who once again demonstrated his fine instinct for revolutionary developments. For a description, see A. Malik, *Riwajat,* pp. 48ff.

speech lasting less than five minutes, in which Sukarno im-
plored those present to maintain discipline and return home
quietly. The government, he said, would defend the Republic
to the last gasp; the people must trust it to do so, and to prove it
they should disperse and leave the square at once.[8]

And this was exactly what took place: the crowd broke up
and went home. On the same day the instigators of the meeting
were arrested. One of them was Adam Malik, who in describing
the scene speaks indefatigably of the revolutionary spirit among
the masses, and thus only emphasizes what Sukarno had accomplished.[9] A few days later Yamamoto, probably still struck by
this demonstration of Sukarno's personal force, warned the
Allies not to underestimate Indonesian nationalism and above
all not to punish Sukarno and Hatta as war criminals. They had
cooperated with the Japanese, he said, merely in order to protect their countrymen and to advance the cause of Indonesian
independence.[10]

Sukarno Deprived of Power (Fall 1945)

On September 29, Allied troops under the command of a
British general, Sir Philip Christison, began landing on Java. In
his first statement Christison declared that the government of
the Republic would not be expelled; the British expected it to
carry on the civil administration in areas not occupied by British troops; that the British intended to meet the leaders of the
various groups and explain to them further; and that Christison
planned to win over the Dutch and Indonesian leaders to a
round table conference, which up to now had been decisively
rejected by the Dutch.[11]

There could have been no clearer refutation of Sukarno's
decades-long prejudice against the West—which in those days

[8] Raliby, Doc. Hist., pp. 35, 111 (photograph and comment). On this
event see also Anderson, Some Aspects, pp. 123ff.

[9] A. Malik, Riwajat, pp. 76ff. He makes every effort to represent Sukarno
as a lackey of the Japanese and a betrayer of the revolution.

[10] Anderson, pp. 120f.

[11] O. Raliby, Doc. Hist. (with English text), p. 47.

he adroitly concealed—than the British general's declaration. Instead of the expected incursion of a predatory imperialism, the British now even declared that they did not intend to tamper with "internal Indonesian affairs"; rather, they would use the troops only to evacuate prisoners of war, to disarm and repatriate the Japanese, and to ensure order.[12]

Sukarno declared that if only these goals were pursued, the Indonesian people would not hinder the Allies in their work.[13] At the same time he gave one of their correspondents an interview, following which the latter enthusiastically declared, "Lincoln is alive in Indonesia." Sukarno ("no doubt, he is the best man in Indonesia") had told him, he reported, that in three and a half years he had succeeded in founding a republic modeled on the United States, which was built on a democratic foundation. Now Indonesia only awaited recognition by the United States.[14]

Thus Sukarno was able quickly to adjust to the new relationships; and on the surface, his presidential cabinet may indeed have exhibited some similarity to that of the United States. But what was more important was that the Allies themselves appeared to be impressed by the Javanese population's desire for freedom,[15] and that they placed no serious obstacle in the path of Sukarno's attempt to obtain entry for Indonesia into the worldwide family of nations. On the contrary, they privately acknowledged the justice of the Indonesian cause and attempted to bring about a meeting between Sukarno and Van Mook, representing the Dutch, which took place in October; but the discussion was unofficial and achieved no results at all.[16]

Finally, the Allies had no intention of in any way altering Sukarno's position as President. During this time, nevertheless, it was critically weakened, as the result of a purely internal de-

[12] *Ibid*, pp. 36f.   [13] *Ibid.*, p. 43.

[14] Richard Straub, BBC, London, October 2, 1945; *ibid.*, pp. 47ff.

[15] For the reaction of the British and American press, see J. H. Boas, *Het Indonesische vraagstuk en de Britische pers* (1946), and J. F. Engers, *Het Indonesische vraagstuk in de Amerikanische pers* (1946).

[16] See, for example, the recollections of H. J. van Mook, *Indonesia, Nederland en de wereld* (1949), pp. 102f.; also O. Raliby, *Doc. Hist.*, pp. 56, 60, 62f.

velopment that once more brought into prominence a man whose rivalry with Sukarno following his appearance in the independence movement at the beginning of the 1930's had been given particular attention—namely, Sutan Sjahrir.

Sjahrir had remained aloof from the work of the young republic. Believing that independence had been betrayed by the drafting of the proclamation in the house of a Japanese admiral, he had set out on a trip through Java to ascertain the mood of the people and study the effects of the proclamation. To the ever sober and careful Sjahrir, what he found came as a surprise. He wrote:

The effect of the proclamation was tremendous. It was as though our people had been electrified. A majority of the Indonesian civil servants, administrators, police, and the military organizations immediately declared their support of the Republic. National strength and unity reached greater heights than anything we had known before.[17]

This impression caused him, and the groups under his influence, to declare their solidarity with the young Republic. He had been forced to recognize that Sukarno's close ties with the people had not been disrupted, regardless of all he had demanded of them, and that he was generally regarded as the true leader.

When in Java the lines had been drawn, despite the initially benevolent attitude of the Allies as well as the Indonesians, and the first street fights had taken place between the largely pro-Dutch Ambonese and the Republicans—a conflict that threatened to expand into open conflict with the gradually infiltrating Dutch troops—Sjahrir abandoned his noncommittal attitude, and in mid-October he joined a Working Committee newly formed from within the KNIP.[18] This Working Committee (Dewan Pekerdjaan) amounted to the first curb on the President's power.

In the KNIP, the announcement by its chairman, Kasman Singodimedjo, on August 29, that it was ready to carry out the orders of the government had met with no little consterna-

[17] Sjahrir, *Out of Exile,* p. 259.   [18] *Ibid.,* p. 263.

tion.[19] Its members had envisioned something else quite different in the way of "sustaining the President" until the People's Congress could be formed; and recognizing the danger in an absolute power responsible to no one, they had decided to use their own initiative. A member of the KNIP wrote in 1946:

The people's demand for democracy was not to be fettered, and so on October 7, 1945, a petition was signed by fifty members of the KNIP, urging the President to use his special powers to set up the People's Congress [Madjelis Permusjawaratan Rakjat] without delay. It suggested that until the People's Congress had been established, the members of KNIP be designated as members of the Congress.[20]

This urgent desire for a body to which the President would be responsible likewise dominated the second session of the KNIP, which was convened on October 16 as a result of the petition, and in which Sukarno did not participate. The proposal to form a Working Committee was made and then promptly issued as a decree by Hatta, who as Vice-President conducted the meeting. This, the famous "Decree X"—so called because the parliamentary secretary had no records at hand, an indication of the abruptness with which the decision was taken —contained the statement:

. . . the KNIP is to receive legislative power until the formation of the People's Congress and of the Parliament, and to participate in establishing the broad outlines of policy. It is further decreed that because of the critical circumstances, the day-to-day work of the Central Committee be performed by a Working Committee, which is to be elected from the KNIP and is to be responsible to it.[21]

This marked the beginning of the end of Sukarno's absolute power. Sjahrir, after being elected Chairman of the Working Committee on October 20, issued a statement on the rights and duties of the new body, stating, among other things, that as a participant in establishing broad outlines of policy, the Working Committee would cooperate with the President in developing those outlines, but would not have the right to intervene in

---

[19] A. G. Pringgodigdo, *Kabinet presidensiil,* pp. 24ff.   [20] *Ibid.,* p. 27.
[21] The "Maklumat X," with annotations, appears in A. G. Pringgodigdo, p. 27.

day-to-day policy; that legislative power would likewise be exercised jointly with the President; but that he alone was empowered to implement the laws.[22]

This covert and circumscribed separation of powers, although on the surface it still emphasized the power of the President, in fact decisively undermined it. Very soon it was evident that the "broad outlines" also extended into day-to-day policy. Only a week later, on October 27, 1945, a statement was issued, signed jointly by Sukarno and Hatta, that "through the acknowledgment of differing views, unity among us will be strengthened and the spirit of popular sovereignty will be consolidated." [23]

This was no longer the language of Sukarno, but that of Sjahrir and Hatta. It was exactly the same argument that Sjahrir had used against Sukarno's attempt in 1932 to re-establish the unity of the nationalists, at whatever price. Then as now, Sukarno had held the opinion that differing views ought not to be acknowledged but to be submerged within the unity of a single party. This was what he had emphasized once again in his speech of August 23 on behalf of one party. In October 1945, that party had not yet come into existence. Its debut had been postponed in favor of concentrating all energies on the regional national committees.[24]

But the "acknowledgment of differing views" could have but one consequence, and it was one that Sjahrir made public a few days later, on November 3—namely, permission to found political parties, and thus explicitly to criticize the one-party system as a violation of the principle of democracy.[25] Finally, on November 11, the ultimate step was announced by Sjahrir: the responsibility of ministers to Parliament.[26]

Thus within less than four weeks Sukarno had been reduced from an absolute ruler to a figurehead. The strongly centralized state that he considered necessary in order to complete the revolution had been changed, step by step, to a parliamentary democracy, a system that for two decades he had incessantly at-

[22] A. G. Pringgodigdo, *Kabinet presidensiil*, p. 29f.

[23] O. Raliby, *Doc Hist.*, pp. 519f.

[24] AR, August 29 and September 1, 2605.   [25] O. Raliby, p. 528.

[26] A. G. Pringgodigo, *Kabinet presidensiil*, pp. 73 (text), 76ff. (comment).

tacked for all sorts of reasons. He had labeled it inappropriate as a form of government for Indonesia because he saw it as a handmaid of capitalism, as guaranteeing the despotism of interest groups rather than the interest of the people.

In barely four weeks Sutan Sjahrir, along with other Indonesian proponents of liberalism, had swept aside Sukarno's old ideals of an Indonesian democracy based on Permusjawaratan and Mufakat. Thus it was entirely logical that Sjahrir on November 14, 1945, three days after the introduction of ministerial responsibility, should announce the resignation of the presidential cabinet and the formation of a parliamentary cabinet of his own. The statement by his government emphasized the responsibility of the ministers to Parliament (or for the time being, to the KNIP) and advocated the formation of political parties.[27]

Sukarno yielded to this deprivation of power and to the destruction of his long-held ideals without serious resistance because of the situation, which for him had become critical. The Dutch were under orders to have no official contact with Sukarno, since for them his role during the Japanese occupation was not a thing to be passed over in silence. Sukarno must have realized that in such circumstances, Sjahrir had become the man of the hour. In the fall of 1945, what came first was the preservation of the Republic.

It was not only his anti-Japanese past that made Sjahrir the logical negotiator with the Dutch. If anything were achieved, it could only be through presupposing certain "common norms," and for this Sjahrir was qualified. Moreover, unlike Sukarno he had no prejudice against the Dutch, and—again unlike Sukarno—he had the unique gift of being able to put himself completely into the position of another, as his writings repeatedly and astonishingly demonstrate.[28] He knew that a rigid attitude,

[27] *Ibid.,* p. 37f., 74f.

[28] See S. Sjahrir: *Pikiran dan perdjuangan; Indonesische overpeinzingen; Out of Exile;* and *Perdjuangan kita* [Our Struggle], a polemic dating to the autumn of 1945, in which he settled accounts with the "real collaborators" who during the Japanese occupation were out for their own gain.

such as Sukarno had originally adopted, meant that nothing could be achieved. By offering his hand to the former colonial power, he proved before all the world that the Republic was ready to negotiate, and in so doing greatly strengthened its reputation abroad.

In return for all this, the price Sjahrir demanded was high. He, the "Western" intellectual, insisted upon the Western form of government, which he had experienced in Europe and in which he believed. For him it embodied true democracy, just as for Sukarno true democracy was embodied in the Indonesian system that was his model. Now that system had to give way to the "acknowledgment of differing views," which was to set the course of politics in Indonesia over the next twelve years.

Return to the Indonesian System (1957)

Until 1949, when parliamentary democracy which had operated de facto in Indonesia since the fall of 1945 was made constitutional, the Working Committee was in control of Indonesian politics. During these years [29] the struggle against the Dutch colonial power, which sought by every means to reestablish itself in Indonesia, was predominant. In addition, there were internal conflicts with radical groups, notably with the communists, who attempted to stage a coup d'état in September 1948.

The action of the United Nations finally forced Holland to end its interference and to release the Indonesian leaders who had again been exiled at the end of 1948—Sukarno, Hatta, and Sjahrir, among others. There followed the Round Table Conference at The Hague (1949), which ended with the recognition of the "United States of Indonesia." And in August 1950 the unified republic that had been the goal of the struggle for freedom was at last established, through declarations of solidarity with the Republic by the various federal states the Dutch had set up artificially throughout the archipelago.

A detailed account of the position of the President as set forth

[29] For an excellent account of events after 1945, see Kahin, *Nationalism and Revolution in Indonesia* (1952). During the decisive years (1948–49), Kahin was himself in Indonesia. For this period his book is unsurpassed.

in the Indonesian constitutions of 1949 and 1950 can be dispensed with here.[30] It need only be emphasized that the President, as Chief of State, could in theory take no independent measures. The incumbent Prime Minister was completely responsible to Parliament for statements and actions by the President. Even in his role as Commander in Chief of the armed forces—the title deliberately altered by the Constitution to "Supreme Authority of the Armed Forces"—the President's orders were to be countersigned by the Minister of Defense. The only prerogative he was still able to exercise after 1950 was that of naming future cabinet "formateurs."

Sukarno's unhappiness over this straitjacket was soon evident, and again and again, most often in public speeches, he violated the Constitution that shackled him to Parliament. He had no thought of refraining from political statements, whether or not they were consonant with the official policy of the government in power. As early as 1951, this led to a request that he explain beforehand whether he was speaking as Bung Karno, the leader of the people, or as President of the Indonesian Republic— whether what he asserted was his private opinion or the official view of the Indonesian government.[31] Nor was this all. Official committees charged with inquiring into the position of the President directed that "President Sukarno should not make a practice of intervening in the conduct of state affairs; it must be remembered that the functions of the office of President are quite different from the activities of Bung Karno as the leader of a popular movement"; and so on.[32]

But the persons of Bung Karno and the President, although easily distinguishable on paper, were indivisible in practice. Nevertheless, in the retention of West New Guinea by the Netherlands, Sukarno had soon discovered a basis for carrying on his old campaign against imperialism and colonialism as

---

[30] See A. K. Pringgodigdo, *The Office of President in Indonesia as Defined in the Three Constitutions in Theory and Practice,* translated by A. Brotherton (1957). Pringgodigdo was for many years the Indonesian Secretary of Government.

[31] A. K. Pringgodigdo, *The Office of President,* p. 49.   [32] *Ibid.,* p. 51.

Bung Karno *and* as President,[33] since the incorporation of Irian Barat, as New Guinea was known in Indonesia, was likewise an interest of the Indonesian state.[34]

Moreover, Sukarno's antipathy to parliamentary democracy, which was to blame for his powerlessness, continued to grow. Gradually his loyalty to the constitution became questionable. In October 1952 he did reject a proposal by discontented army officers, who asked him to assume dictatorial powers or to introduce a triumvirate consisting of Hatta, Sultan Hamengkubuwono IX, and himself and to dissolve the Parliament. At that time Sukarno's position was still weak. He had only recently begun to look for allies among the parties favorable to his view that the Indonesian revolution was not yet completed, and had found some response from the reorganized PKI, the Murba, and the PNI. But he had met with strong opposition in the camp of the liberal Masjumi and of the Partai Sosialis Indonesia, led by Sukarno's old political opponents Mohammed Natsir and Sutan Sjahrir—both of whom, along with Hatta, believed that the aims of the Indonesian revolution had been achieved with the transfer of sovereignty.

Following the first general elections in 1955, which proved that Masjumi and the PSI had less support than had been imagined, Sukarno, openly backed by PKI and other opponents of Masjumi and the PSI, began to attack parliamentary democracy as he had done decades before. He held it responsible for the growing difficulties in every field—for political and economic crises, for corruption and dissidence, for agrarian unrest and religious fanaticism. In 1956 he even spoke of his desire "to bury the parties," more than forty of which had come into existence after Sjahrir's call for the founding of such parties in November

[33] For a description of one such propaganda trip by Sukarno for the recovery of West Irian, see J. F. Goedhart, *Een revolutie op drift* (1953).

[34] According to the agreement at The Hague (1949), the question of "West New Guinea" was to be settled within a year. For documentation of the discussions, see J. F. M. Duynstee, *Nieuw Guinea als schakel tussen Nederland en Indonesië* (1961). On general political developments in Indonesia from 1950 to 1957, see H. Feith, *The Decline of Constitutional Democracy in Indonesia* (1962).

1945. Trips to socialist countries in 1956 had strengthened Sukarno's previous conviction that only through guided democracy—the "democratic centralism" of the 1930's—could the goal of a just and prosperous society be realized. In his famous "Konsepsi," which was announced in February 1957, Sukarno pleaded for the formation of a Gotong-Rojong cabinet, in which the PKI was to be included as one of the major parties, and for the institution of a National Council, made up of all functional groups of the society (peasants, students, women, etc.).

Some four weeks later, on March 14, 1957, martial law was proclaimed to counter the spread of rebellion in the outer islands. This was a death blow to parliamentary democracy in Indonesia. Sukarno now could convoke the proposed National Council without difficulties, although the idea of a Gotong-Rojong cabinet including the PKI had to be dropped because of mounting opposition from all sides. In a speech in July 1957, commemorating the thirtieth anniversary of the PNI, Sukarno referred to the old ideals, to Marhaenism and Socio-democracy with their emphasis on collectivism and their disdain for liberalism. And as on earlier occasions it was clear to him "that liberal politics will not lead us to prosperity and social justice as it is stated in our constitution." Only by following the old principles could the spirit of Pantja Sila, the spirit of mutual help and of mutual tolerance, become effective. He himself, Sukarno declared, had not strayed by one step from the old ideals. "There are men who say Bung Karno has become a communist, especially since I have been to the Soviet Union and to China. But I am no communist; I stand by the Pantja Sila now as always; I am still the Sukarno of 1927." [35]

Two years later, in July 1959, after a revolutionary government of the defenders of liberalism had been crushed in Su-

[35] See his speech on July 3, 1957, at Bandung, which was given the title "Marhaen and Proletarian" by the translator, Claire Holt (1960; pp. 25, 27). For a detailed account of this period in Indonesian politics, see D. S. Lev, *The Transition to Guided Democracy: Indonesian Politics, 1957–59* (1966).

matra, Sukarno, backed by the Army, re-introduced by decree
the constitution of 1945, which gave him nearly unlimited authority as President.

Step by step—just as in the fall of 1945 the centralized state
had been "stolen" from him by the followers of liberalism—
Sukarno, fourteen years later, now drove parliamentary democracy out of Indonesian politics.

He formed a new cabinet, which after October 1959 was no
longer responsible to Parliament. In January 1960 he took control of all political parties, reserving the right to dissolve them if
he found it necessary. In March 1960 he ordered the elected
Parliament dissolved because it had refused to approve the proposed budget for 1960. Finally, in August 1960, came the first
suppression of political parties that refused to follow the path
proposed by Sukarno—the Masjumi of Mohammed Natsir and
the Socialist Party of Sutan Sjahrir. Hatta had already resigned
the office of Vice-President before this development, thus letting
it be known that he likewise declined to follow the path Sukarno had laid down.[36]

But for Sukarno a new phase of his old struggle to realize a
just social order in Indonesia had now begun. Side by side with
the expulsion of the liberal system, the Indonesian system was
being introduced.

March 27, 1960, saw the announcement of the formation of a
Gotong-Rojong Parliament as a body to advise the government,
representing nearly all elements of the population. On August
15 came the announcement of a People's Congress, which as the
sovereign authority of the state was to meet once every three
years. At the same time, Sukarno appointed the central council
of a National Front.

This National Front, which was to incorporate nationalist
(Nasionalis), religious (Agama), and socialist (Komunis)
groups, was given the name Nasakom after the respective initial

[36] Hatta had resigned in December 1956. For a discussion of his controversy with Sukarno, see J. M. van der Kroef, "Sukarno and Hatta:
The Great Debate in Indonesia," *The Political Quarterly*, Vol. 29 (1958),
238–50.

syllables. Thus Sukarno had a new term for his old desire for a single movement that would embrace all the political tendencies of the population.

Or was it a new term? Sukarno's political activity in 1926 had begun with an article, "Nationalism, Islam, Marxism," demonstrating the possibility of a synthesis among these three schools of thought. And now, in 1961, the same concepts were compressed into the single word Nasakom. By drawing upon the same political movements with which he had begun his struggle for freedom, now that he had returned to power he sought to take up the struggle to realize a just social order. There could be no more emphatic support for his assertion, "I am still the Sukarno of 1927."

The Sukarno of 1927, in his desire for unity, conceived the first Indonesian federation in which all factions, some of which were openly quarreling, would be combined into what was then described as a "state within a state." As a weapon against the colonial power that beset it, the value of this organization was nil. Its importance consisted solely in the equal representation of the various groups.

In the struggle for freedom, it appeared that to mobilize the people through systematic education, as Hatta and Sjahrir attempted to do, had a better prospect of success than Sukarno's exaggerated hopes for "unity," which hampered all action. But in an independent Indonesia, no longer beset by a colonial power, the question of whether under strict leadership the Indonesian system can succeed remains to be settled.

Sukarno's attempt to bring into existence a just and prosperous society has failed. His guided democracy, based on charisma and persuasiveness, depended heavily on the loyalty of PKI and the Army as the two best organized power blocs in the country. That loyalty, however, was dubious from the outset, since as contending political heirs both groups watched the activities of their antagonists with mounting distrust. Neither the raging struggle against imperialism nor Nasakom—in Sukarno's eyes the culmination of all philosophical concepts—could bridge the gap between these two powers and the mass organizations that had gathered about them. Thus Nasakom was an empty formula, just as the Pantja Sila were in the time of liberal democracy, when the respective parties acquired their own strength and refused to pour their ideologies into the "melting pot" devised by Sukarno in his drive for an all-embracing unity. Whenever Sukarno perceived the irrelevance of one formula, he produced yet another. In 1965 the most important of these were combined to make up the Pantja Azimat Revolusi, the Five Spells of the Revolution. But they were of no help to him either. The reason for his ultimate fall was not that he deviated from his old ideals and concepts, but rather that he refused to depart from them after their value had come into question.

XI

Conclusion: The Pantja Sila

Sukarno's Pantja Sila Address

Sukarno's address before the members of the Investigating Committee (BPKI) on June 1, 1945, in which he developed what he called the five pillars of the future Indonesian state, offered both Kahin and Benda—thus far the only scholars to attempt a portrait of the early Sukarno—a proof of their contentions. Kahin has characterized Sukarno as a man of synthesis; with this opinion the present study is in agreement, despite Kahin's differing judgment of Sukarno's attitude toward the West. Discussing the Pantja Sila in 1952, Kahin wrote: "Probably in no other exposition of principle can one find a better example of the synthesis of Western democratic [sic], Modernist Islamic, Marxist, and indigenous-village democratic and communalistic ideas which forms the general basis of the social thought of so large a part of the post-war Indonesian political elite." [1]

Benda, who in 1958 arrived at another judgment of Sukarno —as the spokesman of the "secular" nationalists, in rivalry with the Moslems [2]—concludes from the Pantja Sila speech that the attention Sukarno gave the Moslems on this occasion "testifies to the enormous strength which Indonesian Islam had attained in the most recent past" (1944–45). [3] But even before the outbreak of the Pacific war, Sukarno, using almost the same arguments, had called upon the Moslems to forego an Islamic state

[1] Kahin, *Nationalism,* p. 123.

[2] Benda, *Crescent,* p. 59. In more recent studies Professor Benda has dissociated himself from this view; see for example, H. J. Benda, "Tradition und Wandel in Indonesien," in *Geschichte in Wissenschaft und Unterricht* (1963), pp. 46–53.

[3] Benda, *Cescent,* pp. 189f.

for Indonesia.[4] And on closer examination every opinion and every argument of Sukarno appears familiar, as it does in this instance. *His speech is a classic summary of the political ideas he had developed up to 1945.* After a few introductory remarks about the need for their own philosophy of government, he told the members of the Investigating Committee: "Together we must seek a unified philosophical basis, a world view, on which we all agree. I repeat: agree." [5] Such was Sukarno's chief concern on that June 1—to offer to all delegates a philosophical system from which no one need withhold his consent.[6]

As the first principle or "pillar" of the state that was to be, Sukarno specified Indonesian "nationalism." This did not mean "nationalism in a narrow sense," he added at once; the state to be founded must be "all for all" or "one for all, all for one"— all, that is, who had earned a right to a homeland in Indonesia.[7] This recalls the year 1926, and Sukarno's attempt to find a common denominator for the various currents at work among the people. That common denominator was nationalism, but not— just as clearly as it was stated two decades later—nationalism "in a narrow sense"; rather, it was to be "broad as the air, with space for all living things and all that they need to live." Ever since that time the idea that it was "for all" had been continually emphasized. It was the idea that had led in 1927 to the Indonesian federation, with the requirement of Mufakat, so that the minorities might also have a voice; that had led in 1933 to the extension of the proletariat into Marhaenism, so that all classes of the people could join the Marhaenist party; and that in 1940 had led to the rejection of an Islamic state so

[4] "Saja kurang dinamis [I Am Not Dynamic Enough]" (1940); DBR, pp. 447ff. See also Chapter VI, above.

[5] See *Lahirnja Pantjasila—The Birth of Pantjasila* (1953), p. 18; also *Civics: Manusia dan masjarakat baru di Indonesia* [Civics: The New Man and the New Society in Indonesia] (1960), p. 295.

[6] Anderson (*Some Aspects,* p. 26), professes to see a "challenge" to the Moslems in Sukarno's remark that the composition of the BPKI showed Islam to be not yet sufficiently disseminated among the people. Nothing could be further from Sukarno. This was his old argument that Islam had not yet sufficiently "inflamed" the masses.

[7] *Lahirnja,* p. 19.

that no one would be deprived of his hereditary right to a home
in the Indonesian state. Officially this effort went under the
name of "nationalism"; in reality it always amounted to the
search for a united front.

In justifying his nationalism, Sukarno had once quoted the
definitions of Ernest Renan and Otto Bauer. In Indonesia,
meanwhile, geopolitical arguments for an Indonesian nationalism were more often used—not least as a weapon against the
Japanese occupation.[8] Even here, Sukarno taught that Renan
and Bauer had thought only of the community of men and not
of the soil they inhabited. To do this was necessary, however,
since "even a small child, when he looks at the map, can see that
the Indonesian archipelago forms a unit." On the map, he
noted, the island group was set off clearly from the continents of
Asia and Australia. And so it was in other parts of the world:
the Japanese islands, the Greek islands were all "created by God
as unities." Unity had been realized only twice before in Indonesian history: during the empires of Sriwidjaja (from the seventh to the thirteenth century) and of Madjapahit (from the
thirteenth to the fifteenth century).[9] Therefore, Sukarno further explained to the Moslems, the goal and content of Indonesian nationalism was nothing other than the realization of this
unity as willed by God.

One more group who, like the Moslems, opposed too strong
an emphasis on nationalism, was made up of delegates from the
Chinese minority living in Indonesia. These delegates were reminded by Sukarno that it was Sun Yat-sen himself who had
called him back to nationalism from cosmopolitan ideas in his
youth, through his San Min Chu I (Three Democratic Princi-

[8] See, for example, Sukarno's statements in May 1944 (AR, May 26,
2604, p. 1); also the essays of Muhammad Yamin on Indonesian history
in June 1944, in which one chapter is entitled "Geopolitik Madjapahit,"
and in which he did not fail to mention that the Japanese islands "also"
formed a unity (AR, June 5, 2604).

[9] Benda (Crescent, p. 216, note 58) based on this passage the assumption that Sukarno saw in Islam the "historic destroyer" of the great Indonesian past. For this, however, there is no evidence. See instead AR,
November 10, 2603, p. 2, in which Sukarno holds the luxury and wealth
of Madjapahit responsible for its decline.

ples). It has been questioned whether the influence of Sun Yat-
sen on the young Sukarno had indeed been so great as Sukarno
tried to make it seem when he needed the approval of the Chinese.[10] At this time, however, as he searched for a philosophical
system, the three principles of Sun Yat-sen—nationalism (Min-
tsu), democracy (Min-chuan), and socialism (Min-sheng)[11]—
may have exerted a stronger influence on him. It is quite possible that the San Min Chu I, which is repeatedly mentioned in
the Pantja Sila speech, was a model for the idea of Pantja Sila.

The second principle that Sukarno offered to the delegates
was "humanitarianism" (Kemanusiaan) in relations between
nations, which he also called "internationalism." Here, implicitly if not explicitly, the old distinction between "Eastern" and
"Western" appeared once again. His deprecation of chauvinism,
of "aggressive nationalism," and a reference to Gandhi's "My
nationalism is humanity" plainly tend in that direction. In
1926, using the same argument, Sukarno had opposed "Eastern"
to "Western" nationalism, adopting Pan-Asianism or Inter-
Asianism as an ally in the struggle against the West, so that in
the end a clear distinction between nationalism and internationalism was no longer possible.[12]

It may be that during the Japanese period he had put the
ideal of Hakko Ichiu (the brotherhood of peoples) in the place
of "Eastern" nationalism; this is indicated in such statements by
Sukarno as that "we must not only found a free Indonesian
state, but also strive to form a family of peoples from all nations," or that "we must strive for the unity and brotherhood of
the whole world." [13]

Whether as the Hakko Ichiu (without, of course, acquiescing
in the Japanese claim to leadership) or as "Eastern" nationalism, Sukarno's second principle contained the missionary urge
toward creating a new world, which is also a strong element in

[10] See "The School of Sarekat Islam," in Chapter II, above.

[11] For an interpretation of Sun Yat-sen's Three Democratic Principles
see H. Herrfahrdt, *Sun Yat-sen. Der Vater des neuen China,* Hamburg,
1948.

[12] See "Nationalism, The Common Denominator," in Chapter III, above.

[13] *Lahirnja Pantjasila,* p. 24.

Indian nationalism; [14] and it was directed primarily, as was India's message of salvation through humanitarianism, against a West "imprisoned in materialism."

That Sukarno regarded "world unity" as the highest ideal was, in view of his drive for unity, no longer surprising. In the microcosm of Indonesia, and thus also in the macrocosm, the genuine order willed by God could be reflected only in unity.

The idea of unity was likewise pre-eminent in his third principle, Mufakat, unanimous consensus, or "democracy." But this could be achieved only through representing all sides to a degree that would satisfy each one.

Like the first two principles, this idea can be traced back to the beginnings of Sukarno's political activity. As early as 1927, in the first Indonesian federation, he had sought genuine representation for all sides; and through introducing Mufakat as a requirement, he had also tried to guarantee minorities a genuine right to be heard. In his protracted struggle against parliamentary democracy, he had again and again emphasized the superiority of the "Indonesian system"; and during the Japanese occupation the idea of collectivism had become even stronger.

This idea appears in connection with Sukarno's passionate appeal to the Indonesian Moslems not to insist on an Islamic state, since the active cooperation of other religious communities would be made impossible. There were internal disputes all over the world—as he had observed in 1932, at the time of his attempt to unify the nationalists. But God had given man the ability to think, and thus Sukarno wanted to try to achieve the best possible policy for Indonesia by means of debate. Even one's daily sustenance was obtained only after the rice had been pounded and husked.

The result to which Sukarno looked forward was expressed in the fourth principle, that of "social justice" (Keadilan sosial). Nor did he neglect, once again, to speak of the uselessness of parliamentary democracy, once again drawing on the moldy arguments of Jean Jaurès dating to the year 1893. A dozen years

14 E. Sarkisyanz, *Russland und der Messianismus des vorderen Orients*, (1955), pp. 317ff.

had passed since his discovery in 1932 of that indictment, so perfectly tailored to his anti-Western prejudices against liberalism—which guaranteed political rights but hampered social justice—but Sukarno remained consistent. "If we seek democracy, then we do not need the democracy of the West but rather a general consensus; it brings life, it is a political and economic democracy, and it can bring about social justice." [15]

It becomes clear once again just here that the West was not included by Sukarno in his struggle for a synthesis. Although his nationalism and internationalism (humanitarianism) had originated out of a confrontation with the West, the West was now explicitly excluded from the realm of democracy. The strong emphasis on the indigenous system, however, kept this anti-Western position from being purely negative. Through it, Sukarno hoped to achieve what in his opinion was not possible with the system of the West: social justice.

All this recalls the Ratu Adil movements—the uprising of the Javanese in order, by driving out the Dutch, to found their own kingdom, one that conformed to their hopes and wishes, to their image of social justice. They were animated by expectations much like those expressed here by Sukarno. And of this no one was more conscious than Sukarno himself when he asked the delegates, directly following the rejection of Western democracy: "What is meant by Ratu Adil? Ratu Adil—that *is* social justice. People want happiness. . . . They wish, under the leadership of a Ratu Adil, to create for themselves a world in which there is justice. Let us, therefore, if we really understand and love the Indonesian people, adopt this principle of social justice." [16]

But although the old wishes had been translated into modern terms, there was no great difference between the Ratu Adils at the close of the nineteenth century, who called upon their adherents to ignore Dutch rule and follow them if they wished to win paradise, and the modern Ratu Adil who promised them the kingdom of social justice if they would keep away from Western democracy. Nor was Sukarno's fifth and final principle,

[15] *Lahirnja Pantjasila*, p. 27.   [16] *Ibid.*

"belief in Almighty God" (Ketuhanan jang Maha Esa) in any way alien to the Ratu Adil movements. For as the state of euphoria wore off, they had become aware of their own impotence; and so it was for Sukarno. There had been a place for God in his philosophical system from the beginning, ever since 1926. But it was a belief subject to fluctuation: when the need was greatest, God was closest—in prison, in exile, during the Japanese occupation, when every hope appeared illusory.

Sukarno worshiped not the God of Islam, who demanded total submission to his commandments, but rather the God of Fate, who could be justified on the basis of developments in the world's history, and from whom inspiration was received and interpreted according to one's own discretion. God was for him the all-powerful being who animated the world, the essence of all being and of every religion. He once described God as the "great unity," and all that came from him as "parts of this great unity." [17]

This definition is still the best expression of Sukarno's belief. Likewise in his Pantja Sila speech, he identified the varieties of belief as part of the "great unity." Every religion, he told the delegates, ought to serve God in its own way: that of the Christian according to the teaching of Jesus, of the Moslems according to the teaching of Mohammed, of the Buddhists according to their own sacred scriptures. Each of these religions had given a magnificent witness to tolerance, and it was this tolerance that must be guaranteed, through mutual respect in the state that was to be.[18]

Such was the original formulation of the Pantja Sila, the five pillars of the future state. It was an attempt to give Indonesia's heterogeneous political tendencies a common foundation in the new state, just as Sukarno upon his first appearance in the movement, nearly two decades earlier, had attempted to establish a common denominator for all political movements in the fight for independence.

As he declared at the beginning of his speech, it was a matter of finding a world view for Indonesia to which all classes of the population *could* consent—and in this he had obviously suc-

[17] AR, December 9, 2604, p. 3.   [18] *Lahirnja Pantjasila,* pp. 28f.

ceeded, as the hearty applause at the end of his speech bore witness, with the concept of the Pantja Sila.

Every attempt to regard the Pantja Sila apart from this intended goal—to criticize it, for example, on the basis of specific cultural traditions in the islands—must fail. For the state in the process of being established, the Pantja Sila amounted to a program rather than a philosophy, the program for a movement that had as its first task to form an "Indonesia" out of the archipelago—and this has been overlooked in the only detailed review of the Pantja Sila undertaken thus far.[19]

Sukarno declared in 1946: "The Pantja Sila are no product of recent years. Decades before Japan pushed southward, these ideals were already alive in the Indonesian movement. Now we want to put them into practice so that they can become the foundation of the state." [20]

Sukarno, the Javanese

Certainly the five principles had been alive for decades in the Indonesian movement: the nationalist idea in the various nationalist parties, in Budi Utomo, in the Indonesian Study Club of Dr. Sutomo, and the regional associations; the idea of a humanitarian internationalism among the Moslems and the communists; the democratic idea in the sense of Mufakat, repre-

[19] J. M. van der Kroef, *Indonesia in the Modern World* (1956), Vol. 2, pp. 198ff., deals with the Pantja Sila in themselves, without discussing Sukarno's argument. He contends that the Pantja Sila are a "bowl without content." And it is true that so little content had been poured into the "bowl," despite Sukarno's repeated demands, that in 1954, when van der Kroef wrote his essay, the Pantja Sila as the basis of the Indonesian state had indeed become questionable. This development, however, could not have been anticipated in 1945, when the Pantja Sila were generally agreed upon. The third principle, for instance, was a plea for a Mufakat-democracy that would have prevented the parties from becoming the decisive factor in Indonesian politics. It was only after the implementation of liberal democracy that the Pantja Sila became the "symbolism of disorder."

[20] "Enam bulan merdeka [Six Months Independent]," foreword to *Merdeka, Nomor peringatan 6 bulan Republik Indonesia* [Commemorative issue on the occasion of six months' existence of the Republic of Indonesia] (1946).

senting people of all classes, especially among the minorities; the hope for social justice among the masses, and more explicitly in the Marxist factions; the belief in God, finally, in the religious communities and among all those who "needed" God.

There was, however, only one channel through which these various currents passed, in which they were separated as by a prism and then harmoniously recombined to form a new pattern; and that was Sukarno himself.

Since making his independent appearance in the movement, and having been strongly impressed by the split in the Sarekat Islam at the beginning of the 1920's, he had seen as his chief task the re-creation of the "great unity." As a fanatic believer in the laws of progress, he had sought from the beginning to hasten the evolution of various groups by forcing all schools of thought into a system that could only strangle progress: for unity meant submission.

For Sukarno, proof that all movements were basically one, as though made to form a united front, was not difficult. With his magic weapon Nanggala, the discovery of "misconceptions," he always had at hand an instrument for lending force to his summons to the great unity. "We must be able to receive, but we must also be able to give. That is the secret of unity"—this was his motto, and he himself stood by it through all the years of his activity in the Indonesian movement. Again and again he regarded as his chief task the discovery of a common denominator for the various political currents. In 1926 it had been a nationalism as broad as the air, providing room for all creatures to live. In 1932 it had been Marhaenism, the attempt to draw as many groups as possible into the revolutionary struggle along with the proletariat. In 1936, in his preoccupation with Islam, he had found a no less simple formula: "Islam is a religion that is broad and strives for the unity of mankind." [21] And in 1945, finally, it was the Pantja Sila, which was to provide a common basis for all schools of thought.

That again and again Sukarno was able to find a common denominator had a simple explanation: he had not seriously come

[21] DBR, p. 346.

to grips with any of the three tendencies he studied intensively one after another—with nationalism, Marxism, or Islam. He examined all of them primarily for their strategic value.

Where nationalism was concerned, he went beyond the boundaries implicit in the concept, so as to draw all Asian peoples into it in their struggle against the West.

In Marxism, what interested Sukarno above all was the promise offered by its dialectic of victory for the oppressed in the struggle against capitalism. That the conditions of production had also to be taken into account as an unalterable hypothesis did not disturb him. He reinterpreted Marxist theories so as not to forfeit his desire for the participation of all classes.

With Islam it was the same. Islam was not submission to the will of Allah, it was "progress." The high authority Ameer Ali was made to proclaim his own opinion, and was then declared correct in his view that the laws of Islam were "flexible as rubber."

Under these conditions the synthesis of nationalism, Marxism, and Islam was no problem for Sukarno, and it becomes understandable that he could describe himself as a "mixture of all these isms." His way of thinking avoided troublesome details and concentrated instead on broad outlines. As he once expressed it in a radio address to the peoples of Asia, "We, the Indonesian people, have learned to think not in centimeters or meters, not in hours or days. We have learned to think in continents and decades." [22]

His self-assurance in identifying his own way of thinking with that of the "Indonesian people" is characteristic. Among his comrades in the struggle for Indonesian independence were a great number who thought in centimeters, who concerned themselves with details rather than ignoring them, and who attempted to act politically rather than to inflame the spirit—Sjahrir, Hatta, Natsir, to name only the most prominent of Sukarno's rivals. Throughout the present study they have been depicted wherever they were in conflict with him, so that by means of the contrast further light could be shed on the pecu-

[22] AR, September 4, 2604, p. 1.

liar role played by Sukarno. And fundamental to that role was the self-assurance he displayed and with which he developed his theories, all the while denying real problems and handing out praise and blame as though he bore the absolute measure within himself. This self-confidence was contagious, and gave him in the eyes of the masses the aura of a chosen one, a Ratu Adil. It was the true secret of his unique ability to address the masses and to carry them with him, whether he promised them paradise or proclaimed a life-or-death struggle.

For the masses Sukarno was no mystery. Never did the opponent change, and neither did the ideal. He had little genuine grasp of the political tendencies he embraced, and rarely did he come to grips with the adversary. Not once during the period covered here did Sukarno seriously examine or alter his prejudice against the West. Whatever name he gave the adversary—whether it was individualism or liberalism, capitalism or colonialism, Holland, England, or the United States—it was always the West. Toward it he was as uncompromising as he was ready for compromise within his own ranks.

Sjahrir, on the other hand, had written in exile: "We can never engage in an essential struggle between East and West—never; for we are intellectually dependent on the West, not only in scientific but also in cultural matters. Culturally we are closer to Europe or America than we are to the Borobudur [temple] or the *Mahabhrata*." [23] This was true for him and for a number of young intellectuals who had studied in Europe and who, like him, "felt at home" there.[24] But it was not true for Sukarno. His emphasis on the native Indonesian process of Permusjawaratan and Mufakat, from the Indonesian federation of 1927 down to the Gotong-Rojong Parliament of the early 'sixties, makes this fact clear, as does the no less long-standing "holy war" against the West and all its political and philosophical systems, which Sukarno failed to understand because he had no wish to understand them.

The same fact is clear from Sukarno's striving for unity at any price within his own ranks. Was this only a tactical device? In 1926, tactical considerations may have played a role, since a

[23] Sjahrir, *Overpeinzingen*, p. 61.   [24] *Ibid.*, p. 161.

united front would clearly have been more effective than a group of parties fighting each other. But in 1932 at the latest, when Sjahrir made it clear that the united front—described by Sukarno at the time as "part of my life"—must weaken the movement because a multitude of considerations would cripple its ability to act, the tactical point of view lost its value. Yet Sukarno held fast unflinchingly to his striving for unity, down to Nasakom. He revised Marxism and Islam—for the sake of unity. Why? Sukarno must have known that among Moslems as well as Marxists he would have more enemies than friends if he distorted their teachings. Why, then, this emphasis on unity at any price?

In the conflict with Sjahrir, who in the spring of 1932 so resolutely opposed Sukarno's efforts for unification, it became clear that for Sukarno unity was more then a tactic, it was a basic principle of order. Hence his uncompromising attitude toward an opponent who did not adapt himself to but rather set himself above the Tåtå, the cosmological order of the ancient Javanese. Hence his readiness to compromise with any political group that would agree to this Tåtå—groups such as the Christians or the Marxists. Java, which in past centuries had fused Hinduism, Buddhism, and Islam with its own culture, producing a unique syncretism, could also absorb modernism so long as it permitted itself to be "adapted." Of all this Sukarno's synthesis is a classic example.

But from the beginning the whites had put forward claims to dominance, and had threatened the order. From the command of the Javanese prince who in the early seventeenth century called on his subjects "to drive the Dutch out of Djakarta," all through the revolts of princes and the Ratu Adil movements among the people down to the Sarekat Islam and Sukarno himself, they had been perceived as aliens and disturbers of the Tåtå, the well-ordered harmony of the Javanese world view.

It would seem to be no coincidence that those who were most critical in opposing Sukarno's efforts at unification—Sjahrir, Hatta, Natsir, and Salim (who had previously opposed Sukarno's teacher Tjokroaminoto)—were natives not of Java but of Sumatra. There was less of this strongly pronounced syncretism among the Sumatrans; for them there was no such Tåtå to be protected, and thus they had neither the rigidly uncompromising attitude toward the outside nor the eagerness to compromise within. Moreover, the conceit that Raden A. Kartini calls one of the "vices of the Javanese," [25] and which is so pronounced in Sukarno, was quite foreign to all these opponents.

In Java, indeed, conceit was a quality of the one who inherited the Wahju Tjakraningrat, the mission of preserving the order, the mission of rule. And that one, in the eyes of the Javanese people, had long been Sukarno. The people had always understood him. There was a grain of truth in his vaunting statement: "Why is it that people ask me to make speeches to them? . . . The answer is that what Bung Karno says is in fact already written in the hearts of the Indonesian people. The people wish to hear their own thoughts spoken, which they cannot voice themselves." [26]

These thoughts of the people led Sukarno to conceive of the Pantja Sila, which were to become the cornerstone of a new order, no longer limited to Java, but including all of Indonesia.

Once again, the magic ingredient of this new order was—unity. "Bhinneka tunggal ika" (unity in diversity) was the secret of the greatness of nations, Sukarno explained as he displayed for the first time the motto of the wise Tantular [27] that appears today on the Indonesian coat of arms. "All things are one" was the deepest insight of Javanese philosophy. Thus Sukarno in his Pantja Sila address lost no time before expatiating on the unity subsumed within his five principles. After devoting a moment to the symbolism of the number five, so full of meaning in Javanese culture,[28] Sukarno turned to the delegates and

25 R. A. Kartini, *Door duisternis tot licht* (1912), p. 40.

26 W. A. Hanna, *Bung Karno's Indonesia* (1960), Report 13, p. 3.

27 AR, November 8, 2604, p. 3.

28 The reference was to the four winds and the center where they are forged into a unity. See Th. Pigeaud, *Javaanse beschavingsgeschiedenis*, Vol. III, *Geloof en Godsdienst*, which has been consulted in manuscript by the kind permission of the author, and from which important suggestions for this chapter have been derived. See also J. M. van der Kroef, "Javanese Messianic Expectations: Their Origin and Cultural Context," *Comparative Studies in Society and History*, 1958/59, pp. 301, 320f.

asked whether perhaps some were not in accord with the number five, but desired only three principles? This could be achieved without difficulty. Nationalism and humanitarianism could be easily combined in one term, and the principle of Socio-nationalism would be the result. And out of the combination of principles three and four (democracy and social justice) would come Socio-democracy.[29]

Sukarno had arrived at the two concepts of the 1930's as the natural result of the four first principles. Nationalism and humanitarianism were simply the "Eastern nationalism" of the 1920's—or, following his study of Marxist literature, the Socio-nationalism of the 1930's. Socio-democracy was the "political and economic democracy" that he had always held up as an ideal in contrast to parliamentary democracy—an ideal which, according to Sukarno's conception, could best be achieved by the Indonesian practice of mutual support among all groups (Gotong-Rojong) according to Mufakat, the all-inclusive consensus. In addition to these two concepts there remained as a third principle the belief in God, just as it had always been a component in Sukarno's synthesis of nationalism, Marxism, and Islam.

In Western eyes these three movements represent fundamental positions, incapable of further adjustment. Not so for Sukarno, the engineer to whom analytical thought had remained foreign, the revolutionary who avoided the principle of contest that drives the revolution forward, the Javanese who looked to synthesis—in which already Aristotle saw the basis of all error—for salvation and the solution of all problems. As one who thought in other categories, he regarded further compromise in the search for unity as perfectly possible:

Perhaps you are not at all in accord with these three principles, but would ask for the Eka Sila, the one single principle? Very well, I shall make them one. . . . If I compress the five into three and then these three into one, I have a genuine Indonesian expression for the result—the concept of Gotong-Rojong. . . . The principle of Gotong-Rojong between rich and poor, between Moslems and Christians, between those who come from elsewhere and their chil-

[29] *Lahirnja Pantjasila,* p. 29.

dren who are born in Indonesia—this, gentlemen, is what I recommend to you! [30]

Sukarno had found his unity, one that could no longer be expressed in Western terms. He had found it in his own culture, which seemingly had more understanding for this kind of striving.

[30] *Ibid.,* pp. 29f.

Glossary

Adat	Indonesian customary law
Barisan Pelopor	Pioneer Corps of Indonesian nationalists under the command of Sukarno within the Djawa Hokokai
Bharata Judha	Mythical decisive battle from the *Mahabhrata* between Pendawas and Kaurawas
Bima	The second of the five Pendawas, warlike by nature, portrayed as a holy man in Javanese literature
Budi Utomo	Pure Endeavor; aristocratic Javanese party founded in 1908
Dalang	A puppeteer, performer of the Wajang
Desa	Javanese village
Dewa	A god
Djago	Warrior, champion
Djajabaja	Supposed prophet of the Ratu Adil. Historically, he was King Jaya Bhaya of Kediri in the twelfth century
Djawa Dipa	Javanese language reform movement against the submissiveness inherent in Kromo (the language used in addressing Javanese of higher social status)
Djawa Hokokai (Japanese)	People's Service Association in Java (March 1944–August 1945)
Djihad	Holy war
Djimat	Charm supposed to confer invulnerability
Erutjakra	(also Heru Tjokro) Synonym for Ratu Adil; originally Vairocana, the supreme Buddha
Gotong-Rojong	Mutual help
Hakko Ichiu	Brotherhood of Nations (a Japanese expression)
Karno	Mythical hero of the *Mahabhrata,* leader of the Kaurawas reawakened after the Bharata Judha

Kaurawas   Opponents of the Pendawas, whose hereditary
                    kingdom they have usurped, and who are
                    defeated in the Bharata Judha

Kijais   Teachers of religion in Java

Kromo   "Little man"; frequently used of proletarians

Ksatrija   Noble knight of Javanese mythology

Mahabhrata   Indian epic, which underwent certain changes
                    in Java and was incorporated in the themes
                    of the Wajang

Marhaens   All the poor of Indonesia, not just the prole-
                    tariat

Merdeka   Independence, freedom; free (originally, "rich")

Mufakat   Unanimous consensus

Musjawarah   General discussion of a consultative character,
                    with Mufakat as its goal.

Nanggala   Magic weapon of the mythical hero Kokrosono,
                    who received it from a god for the purpose
                    of freeing his land

Pantja Dharma   "Five duties" of Indonesians during the Pacific
                    war, announced in November 1944

Pantja Sila   "Five basic pillars" (of the Indonesian state),
                    set forth by Sukarno on June 1, 1945

Pemudas   Adult youth and youth associations

Pendawas   Heroes of the *Mahabhrata,* victorious in the
                    Bharata Judha after fighting against the
                    Kaurawas for their hereditary kingdom
                    (Ngastina)

Permufakatan   Consensus (see Mufakat)

Permusjawaratan   General discussion (see Musjawarah)

Prijajis   Javanese bureaucratic nobility

Putera   Son; see also Abbreviations

Ramayana   Indian epic which, like the *Mahabhrata,* was
                    incorporated into the Wajang

Ratu Adil   "Just Prince"; the Javanese Messiah prophesied
                    by Djajabaja

Sanas and Sinis   "Those who stand *there*" and "those who stand
                    here": terms for the enemies and friends of
                    the independence movement; synonyms for
                    Kaurawas and Pendawas

Sarekat Islam   Islamic Association which in 1912 replaced the
                    Sarekat Dagang Islam (Islamic Trading As-
                    sociation)

Sita	Goddess abducted by Rahwana in the *Ramayana*
Tjondobirowo, Pantjasana	Magic sayings from the Wajang, which protected the heroes in their battle
Tåtå	Javanese concept of order as a reflection of the cosmos in their own realm
Ulamas	Islamic legal scholars
Wahju	(Divine) inspiration; Wahju Tjakraningrat: mission to rule for the protection of the Tåtå
Wajang	Javanese shadow play on themes from a mythical history, projected on a lighted screen by a Dalang using leather puppets

Bibliography

Unpublished Sources

Gobee Collection, Koninklijk Instituut voor Taal-, Land- en Volkenkunde, The Hague.

Indische Collectie (RVO-IC), Rijksinstituut voor Oorlogsdocumentatie, Amsterdam.

Beppan (Sixteenth Army staff concerned with opinion research). RVO-IC 005798f, 008223f, 006524-35.

Gunseikanbu (Military Government), Record of the process of the Independence movement (1945). RVO-IC 005869-78.

Ichibangase, Y. (Vice-President, BPKI). RVO-IC 005850-55.

Imamura, H. (Saiko Sikikan, Sixteenth Army, until November 1942). A Tapir in Prison. RVO-IC 002460.

Maeda, T. (Head of Bukanfu). RVO-IC 005802-06, 006825-28, 006894-6902.

Myoshi (Employee of Gunseikanbu). RVO-IC 005846-47, 005857, 05397 (pp. 17f.)

Nakamura, H. (Officer of Somubu). RVO-IC 011155-57.

Nishijima, S. (Employee of Bukanfu). RVO-IC 006076-89.

Nishimura (Somubucho, December 1944–August 1945). RVO-IC 059330 (pp. 1–8), 0593331.

Saito, G. (Employee of Somubu). RVO-IC 005838-42.

Shimizu, H. (Head of Sendenbu). RVO-IC 005842, 006585-91, 059397 (p. 16).

Shimura (Somubucho in Sumatra). RVO-IC 009405.

Yamamoto, N. (Somubucho, March 1943–November 1944; Gunseikan, November 1944–August 1945). RVO-IC 016898-016904.

Kern Collection, Koninklijk Instituut voor Taal-, Land- en Volkenkunde, The Hague.

Amir, M. De Japanese tijd. Unpublished manuscript. Rijksinstituut voor Oorlogsdocumentatie.

Brunsveld van Hulten, E. Rapport over de Japansche invloede op de Merdeka-beweging en de gebeurtenissen in de Augustdagen

(1945). Unpublished manuscript. Rijksinstituut voor Oorlogs-documentatie.

Surio Santoso, R. S. De Japaansche propaganda en de Islam. Un-published manuscript. Rijksinstituut voor Oorlogsdocumentatie.

Weerd, K. de. The Japanese Occupation of the Netherlands East Indies (Tokyo, 1946). Unpublished manuscript. Rijksinstituut voor Oorlogsdocumentatie.

Published Sources

Writings and Speeches of Sukarno up to 1945

Sukarno. *Dibawah Bendera Revolusi. Djilid pertama* [Under the Banner of the Revolution. Vol. I]. K. Goenadi and H. M. Nasu-tion, eds. Djakarta: Panitia Penerbit Dibawah Bendera Revolusi, 1959. Essays, articles, and letters of Sukarno, 1926–41, chronologi-cally arranged.

——. *Indonesia Menggugat: Pidato pembelaan Bung Karno dimuka hakim kolonial* [Indonesia Accuses: Bung Karno's Address to the Colonial Court, December 1930]. Djakarta: Departemen Penera-ngan, 1961.

——. *Indonesië klaagt aan.* Amsterdam: N. V. de Arbeiderspers, 1931. A translation into Dutch of Sukarno's address to the colonial court, shortened and not always accurate.

——. *Mentjapai Indonesia Merdeka* [Toward Indonesian Indepen-dence]. Djakarta: Indonesian Department of Information, 1959. Also reprinted (with some discrepancies) in DBR.

——. *Tindjauan Islam* [Views on Islam] Ir. Soekarno, Hamka dan A. M. Pamuntjak. Ar. Muchlis [M. Natsir], ed. Tebingtinggi: Pustaka al Hambra, 1947.

——. "Lahirnja Pantjasila [The Birth of the Pantjasila]," in *Civics: Manusia dan Masjakarat Baru di Indonesia* [Civics: The New Man and the New Society in Indonesia]. Djakarta: Indonesian Ministry of Information, 1960. Stenographic transcript of an address given June 1, 1945.

——. *Lahirnja Pantajasila—The Birth of Pantjasila* [in English]. Djakarta: Indonesian Ministry of Information, 1952. The best existing translation of the address of June 1, 1945.

——. *Het ontstaan van de Pantjasila.* The Hague: Indonesian Em-bassy, 1952. The same address in Dutch, greatly shortened.

——. *Menudju Indonesia Merdeka* [Toward an Independent Indonesia]. N.p., n.d. A pamphlet issued in the spring of 1945. Parts were reprinted in *Pradjurit,* May 30, 2605.

Official Publications

Bantam-Rapport. Rapport van de commissie voor het onderzoek naar de oorzaken van de zich in de maand November 1926 in verscheidene gedeelten van de residentie Bantam voorgedaan hebbende ongeregeldheden, ingesteld bij Gouvernemensbesluit van Januari 1927, No. 1. Weltevreden: Landsdrukkerij, 1928.

Handelingen Volksraad [Minutes of Volksraad Sessions], Vol. I, Batavia 1918–19.

Jaarboek der Technische Hoogeschool te Bandoeng. Bandung, 1935.

Kaigunsireikan et al., eds. *Untuk apa sekarang Nippon berdjuang?* [What Is Japan Now Fighting For?] Kepada anggota Seinendan [To the members of the Seinendan]. Djakarta, July 1944.

Kan Po—Berita Pemerintah [Announcements of the Military Government]. Djakarta: Gunseikanbu, Bag. Kikakuka [Military Government, Information Section], 2602–05 [1942–45].

Mededeelingen der Regeering omtrent enkele onderwerpen van algemeen belang. Weltevreden, 1917–30.

Oendang-Oendang dari Pembesar Balatentara Dai Nippon, Nomor 1–20 [Laws of the Commander in Chief of the Japanese Army, Nos. 1–20]. Batavia: Gunseikanbu [Military Government], June 1942.

Orang Indonesia jang terkemuka di Djawa [Prominent Indonesians in Java]. Djakarta: Gunseikanbu [Military Government], 1944. A kind of *Who's Who* of the military government.

Overzicht van de inlandsche en maleisch-chineesche pers [IPO]. Weltevreden: Bureau voor de Volkslectuur, 1918–41.

Programma der Technische Hoogeschool te Bandoeng. Bandung, 1921–26.

Publicaties Hollandsch-Inlandsch onderwijs-commissie. No. 2: Het leerlingenverloop en de bestemming der Abiturienten bij de instellingen van Westersch onderwijs in Nederlandsch-Indië. 2 vols. Buitenzorg, 1929.

Sarekat Islam Congres. 1e, 2e en 3e nationaal-congres. Behoort bij de geheime missive van den Wd. Advizeur voor inlandsche zaken. 3 vols. in 5 parts. Batavia, 1916–18.

Statuten der Sarekat Islam. Weltevreden: Visser, 1919.

Verslag van de commissie tot herziening van de staatsinrichting van

Nederlandsch-Indië. Ingesteld bij Gouvernementsbesluit van den 17. December 1918. Weltevreden, 1920.

Westkust-Rapport. De gang der communistische beweging ter Sumatras Westkust. Deel I (politiek gedeelte). Rapport van de commissie van onderzoek ingesteld bij het gouvernements-besluit van 13. Februari 1927, No. 1a. Weltevreden, 1928.

Newspapers and Periodicals

Asia Raya [Greater Asia]. Daily; Indonesian text. Djakarta, April 29, 1942–September 8, 1945.

Bijdragen tot de Taal-, Land- en Volkenkunde van Nederlandsch-Indië. The Hague, 1853–1968.

Djawa: Driemaandelijksch Tijdschrift, uitgegeven door het Java-Instituut. Weltevreden, 1921–41.

Djawa Baroe [New Java]. Fortnightly; Japanese and Indonesian text. Djakarta, January 1943–August 1, 1945.

Hindia Poetra [Son of Ind(ones)ia] Monthly; Dutch text. The Hague, 1916–17, 1923. (See *Indonesia Merdeka.*)

Indische Gids, De. Tevens nieuwe serie van het Tijdschrift voor Nederlandsch-Indië. Amsterdam, 1879–1940.

Indisch Tijdschrift voor het Recht: Orgaan der Nederlandsch-Indische Juristenvereeniging. Weltevreden, 1931.

Indonesia Merdeka [Independent Indonesia]. Bimonthly. The Hague, 1923–33. (The first volume was issued under the title *Hindia Poetra.*)

——. Fortnightly. Djakarta, April–July 1945.

Koloniaal Tijdschrift: Pub. Vereeniging van ambtenaren bij het Binnenlandsche Bestuur in Nederlandsch-Indië. Batavia, 1912–41.

Koloniale Studien. Tijdschrift van vereeniging voor studie van koloniaal-maatschappelijke vraagstukken. Batavia, 1917–41.

Locomotief, De. Daily. Semarang, 1851–1941. Issued beginning 1923 under the title *De Locomotief-Overzee-editie,* for distribution within the Indonesian archipelago. Beginning March 1934, issued also as *Overzee-editie voor Nederland.*

Oranje: Tijdschrift voor de Nederlandsche en Nederlandsch gemeenschap in de Zuid Pacific. Melbourne, 1943–44.

Pandji Poestaka [Banner of the People]. Indonesian text. Weltevreden, 1923–45. Originally issued twice weekly, later weekly, and fortnightly from late 1943 to March 1945.

Pradjoerit [Hero]. Fortnightly. Djakarta, September 1944–July 1945.

Soeara Miai [Voice of the Islamic federation, MIAI]. Fortnightly. January–November 1943. Succeeded by *Soeara Muslimin Indonesia.*

Soeara Muslimin Indonesia [Voice of the Indonesian Moslems]. Fortnightly. December 1943–December 1945.

Stuw, De. Orgaan der vereeniging tot bevordering van de maatschappelijke en staatkundige ontwikkeling van Nederlandsch-Indië. Batavia, 1930–33.

Suara afd[eeling] Djocja. Monthly (irregular). Jogjakarta, 1923–25.

Suluh Indonesia Muda [Torch of Young Indonesia]. Text partly in Indonesian, partly in Dutch; twelve issues published. Bandung, 1927–29.

Suluh Rakjat Indonesia [Torch of the Indonesian People]. Weekly; Indonesian text. Surabaja, 1927–30.

Taak, De. Algemeen Indisch Tijdschrift. Weekly. Weltevreden, 1917–25.

Wederopbouw. Tijdschrift aan de Jong-Javanen-Beweging en het Javaansch geestesleven gewijd. Monthly. Weltevreden, Jogjakarta, 1918–23.

Special Issues and Commemorative Volumes

Asia Raya. Special issues: September 1942 (six months after end of colonial rule); April 1943 (one year of appearance).

Gedenkboek Indonesische Vereeniging, 1908–1923. The Hague: Commissie van Redactie, 1924.

Kongres Ra'jat Indonesia ke-1 [First Indonesian People's Congress]. Indonesian text. Batavia, 1939.

Merdeka. Special issue, six months after founding of the Indonesian Republic. February 1946.

Parlement Indonesia. Indonesian text. Batavia, 1939.

Tien jaar Volksraad-Arbeid, 1918–1928. Weltevreden, 1928.

Tien jaar Volksraad-Arbeid, 1928–1938. Weltevreden, 1938.

30 jaar Perhimpunan Indonesia 1908–1938. Jubileumsnummer van het Vereenigingsorgaan, Indonesia. Leiden, 1938.

Dictionaries and Encyclopedias

Coolsma, S. *Soendaneesch-Hollandsch Woordenboek.* Leiden: A. W. Slijthoff, 1913.

Dowson, J. *Hindu Classical Dictionary*. London: Trübner's Oriental Series, 1913, 1914.

Echols, J. M., and H. Shadily. *Indonesian-English Dictionary*. Ithaca, N.Y.: Cornell University Press, 1961.

Encyklopaedie van Nederlandsch-Indië. 8 vols. The Hague: M. Nijhoff; Leiden: E. J. Brill, 1917–38.

Ensiklopedia Indonesia. 3 vols. Bandung and The Hague: W. van Hoeve, 1954.

Enzyklopaedie des Islam: Geographisches, ethnographisches und biographisches Wörterbuch der muhammedanischen Völker. 4 vols. Leiden: E. J. Brill; Leipzig: Harrassowitz, 1908–34.

Gonggrijp, G. F. E. *Geillustreerde Encyclopaedie van Nederlandsch-Indië*. Leiden: Leidische Uitgeversmaatschappij, 1934.

Kähler, Hans. *Grammatik der Bahasa Indonesia*. Wiesbaden: O Harrassowitz, 1956. (Porta Linguarum Orientalium, Neue Serie II.)

Karow, Otto, and Irene Hilgers-Hesse. *Indonesisch-Deutsches Wörterbuch*. Wiesbaden: O. Harrassowitz, 1962.

Oplt, M. *Bahasa Indonesia: Ucebnice indonestiny* [Indonesian Language]. Prague: Statni Pedagogicke Nakladatelstvi, 1960.

Pigeaud, Th. *Javaans-Nederlands Handwoordenboek*. Groningen and Batavia: J. B. Wolters, 1938.

Poerwadarminta, W. J. S., and A. Teeuw. *Indonesisch-Nederlands Woordenboek*. Groningen and Djakarta: J. B. Wolters, 1952.

Survey of Literature

Aichele, W. "Oudjavaansche bijdragen tot de geschiedenis van den wenschboom," *Djawa*, VIII (1928), 28–40.

Alers, H. J. H. *Om een roode of groene Mendeka*. Eindhoven: Vulkaan, 1956.

Ali, Ameer. *The Spirit of Islam*. Rev. ed. London: Christophers, 1922.

Alisjahbana, S. T. "The Indonesian Language—By-product of Nationalism," *Pacific Affairs*, XXII (1949), 388ff.

——. *Indonesia: Social and Cultural Revolution*. Kuala Lumpur, London and Melbourne: Oxford University Press, 1966.

Alkema, B. *De Sarikat Islam*. Utrecht: G. J. A. Ruys, 1919.

Amelz, ed. *H. O. S. Tjokroaminoto: Hidup dan perjuangannja* [H. O. S. Tjokroaminoto: His Life and Struggle]. Djakarta: Bulan Bintang, 1952.

Anderson, B. R. O'G. *Some Aspects of Indonesian Politics under*

the Japanese Occupation, 1944–45. Ithaca, N.Y.: Cornell University, Modern Indonesia Project, Interim Reports Series, 1961.
——. "Japan: 'The Light of Asia,'" in J. Silverstein (ed.), *Southeast Asia in World War II: Four Essays.* New Haven: Yale University, Southeast Asia Studies, Monograph Series No. 7, 1966. Pp. 13–50.

Arx, A. von. *L'évolution politique en Indonésie de 1900 à 1942.* Dissertation, Fribourg, 1949.

Aziz, M. A. *Japan's Colonialism and Indonesia.* The Hague: M. Nijhoff, 1955.

Babad Tanah Djawi [Chronicle of Java up to 1647]. Translated into Dutch by W. L. Olthof. The Hague: M. Nijhoff, 1941.

Bauer, Otto. *Die Nationalitätenfrage und die Sozialdemokratie.* Vienna: Wiener Volksbuchhandlung, 1924.

Bekki, ——. *Geopolitiek Asia Timur Raja* [Geopolitics of Greater East Asia]. Djakarta: Djawa Shimbun Sha, 1944.

Benda, H. J. "The Beginnings of the Japanese Occupation of Java," *Far Eastern Quarterly,* XV (1956), 541–60.
——. *The Crescent and the Rising Sun.* The Hague and Bandung: V. Hoeve, 1958.
——. "Tradition und Wandel in Indonesien," *Geschichte in Wissenschaft und Unterricht* (1963), pp. 46–53.
—— and Lance Castles. "The Samin Movement," a paper presented to the Congress of Asian Studies, Kuala Lumpur, 1968.
—— and R. T. McVey. *The Communist Uprisings of 1926–27 in Indonesia: Key Documents.* Ithaca, N.Y.: Cornell University, Modern Indonesia Project, 1960. Translated from the Bantam and Westkust reports (see Official Publications, above).
——, J. K. Irikura, and Koichi Kishi. *Japanese Military Administration in Indonesia: Selected Documents.* New Haven: Yale University, Southeast Asia Studies, Translation Series No. 6, 1965.

Berg, C. C. "Indonesia," in H. A. R. Gibb, ed., *Whither Islam? A Survey of Modern Movements in the Moslem World.* London: V. Gollancz, 1932. Pp. 273–311.
——. "Ratoe Adil," in *Katholieke Encyklopedie,* Vol. 20, p. 419.
——. "Sarekat Islam," in *Enzyklopaedie des Islam,* Vol. 4 (1934), pp. 174–81.

Bijleveld, J. "De Saminbeweging," *Koloniaal Tijdschrift,* XII (1923), 10–24.

Blumberger, J. Th. Petrus. *De communistische beweging in Nederlandsch-Indië.* Haarlem: Tjeenk Willink und Zoon, 1928.

——. *De nationalistische beweging in Nederlandsch-Indië.* Haarlem: Tjeenk Willink und Zoon, 1931.

——. *Politieke partijen en stroomingen in Nederlandsch-Indië.* Leiden: Leidsche Uitgeversmaatschappij, 1934.

Boas, J. H. *Het Indonesische vraagstuk en de Britische pers.* Leiden: Nederl. Genootsch. v. Internation. Zaken, 1946.

Bodenstedt, A. A. *Sprache und Politik in Indonesien: Entwicklung und Funktionen eiener neuen Nationalsprache.* Dissertationsreihe des Südasien-Instituts der Universität Heidelberg. Heidelberg, 1967.

Boer, D. W. N. de. *Wat iedereen weten moet.* . . . The Hague: Indië in Nood, 1946.

Bouman, H. *Enige beschouwingen over de ontwikkeling van het Indonesisch nationalisme op Sumatras Westkust.* Groningen and Batavia: J. B. Wolters, 1949.

Bousquet, G. H. *La politique musulmane et coloniale des Pays-Bas.* Paris: Paul Hartmann, 1938.

Brandes, J. "Iets over den ouderen Dipanegara in verband met een prototype van de voorspellingen van Jayabaya," *Tijdschrift voor Indische Taal-, Land- en Volkenkunde,* XXXII (1889), 368ff.

Brooshooft, J. P. M. *De ethische Koers in de koloniale politik.* Amsterdam, 1901.

Brouwer, B. J. *De Houding van Idenburg en Colijn tegenover de Indonesische beweging.* Dissertation, Amsterdam, 1958.

Brugmans, I. J. *Geschiedenis van het onderwijs in Nederlandsch-Indië.* Groningen: J. B. Wolters, 1938.

——, H. J. de Graaf, A. H. Joustra, and A. G. Vromans. *Nederlandsch-Indië onder Japaansche bezetting: Gegevens en documenten over de jaren 1942–45.* Franeker: Uitgave T. Wever, 1960.

Cohen-Stuart, A. B. "Eroe Tjakra," *Bijdragen tot de Taal-, Land- en Volkenkunde van Nederlandsch-Indië,* Third series, VII (1872), 285ff.

Cohen Stuart-Franken, M. *Van Indië tot Indonesië. Voor, in en na het kamp.* Amsterdam: W. ten Have, 1947.

Colijn, A. W. *Japan et het extremisme.* The Hague: Van Stockum en Zoon, 1946.

Colijn, H. *Koloniale vraagstukken van heden en morgen.* Amsterdam: De Standaard, 1928.

Deventer, C. Th. van. "Een eereschuld," *De Gids* (1899), reprinted in H. T. Colenbrander and J. E. Stokvis, *Leven en werk van*

Mr. C. Th. van Deventer, Vol. 2. Amsterdam, 1916. Pp. 1–47.

Dimyati, M. *Sedjarah perduangan Indonesia* [History of the Indonesian Struggle]. Djakarta: Widjaja, 1951.

Djojopoespito, S. *Buiten het gareel.* Utrecht: W. de Haan, 1940.

Douwes Dekker, E. F. E. *De Indische partij. Haar wezen en haar doel.* Bandung: Fortuna, 1913.

——, Tjipto Mangunkusumo, and Suardi Surjaningrat. *Onze verbanning.* Schiedam: De Toekomst, 1913.

Drewes, G. W. J. *Drie javaansche goeroes. Hun leven, onderricht en messias prediking.* Leiden: A. Vros, 1925.

——. "The Influence of Western Civilization on the Language of the East Indian Archipelago," in B. Schrieke, *The Effect of Western Influence on Native Civilizations in the Malay Archipelago.* Batavia: G. Kolff, 1929. Pp. 126–57.

Duynstee, J. F. M. *Nieuw Guinea als schakel tussen Nederland en Indonesië.* Amsterdam: De Bezige Bij, 1961.

Elsbree, W. H. *Japan's Role in Southeast Asian Nationalist Movements 1940–45.* Cambridge, Mass.: Harvard University Press, 1953.

Ende, E. C. v. d. *Hoe verder met Indië?* The Hague: Blommendaal, 1946.

Engers, J. F. *Het Indonesische vraagstuk in de Amerikaansche pers.* Leiden: Nederl. Genootsch. v. Intern. Zaken, 1946.

Febre, W. le. "Taman Siswa en de nationalisatie van het onderwijs in Indonesië," *Orientatie,* No. 43 (1951), 378–80.

Feith, H. *The Decline of Constitutional Democracy in Indonesia.* Ithaca, N.Y.: Cornell University Press, 1962.

——. "Dynamics of Guided Democracy," in Ruth McVey, ed., *Indonesia.* New Haven: HRAF, 1963.

Fischer, L. *The Story of Indonesia.* New York: Harper & Brothers, 1959.

François, J. A. *37 jaar Indonesische Vrijheidsbeweging.* Amsterdam: De Driehoek, 1946.

Furnivall, J. S. *Netherlands India: A Study in Plural Economy.* Cambridge: Cambridge University Press, 1939.

Geertz, Clifford. "The Javanese Kijai: The Changing Role of a Cultural Broker," *Comparative Studies in Society and History,* II (1959–60), 228–49.

——. *The Religion of Java.* Glencoe, Ill.: The Free Press, 1960.

Goedhart, J. F. *Een revolutie op drift.* Amsterdam: G. A. van Oorschot, 1953.

Goris, R. "Stormkind en geestes zoon," *Djawa,* VII (1927), 110–13.

Graaf, H. H. de. *Geschiedenis van Indonesië.* The Hague and Bandung: V. Hoeve, 1949.

——. "The Indonesian Declaration of Independence," *Bijdragen tot de Taal-, Land- en Volkenkunde,* CXVIII (1959), 305–27.

Grunebaum, G. E. von, ed. *Unity and Variety in Muslim Civilization.* Chicago: University of Chicago Press, 1955.

Haastert, W. K. S. van. *De Sarekat Islam.* Batavia: Albrecht en Co., 1916.

Hanna, W. A. *Bung Karno's Indonesia: A Collection of 25 Reports Written for the American Universities Field Staff.* New York, 1960.

Harjaka Hardjamardjaja, O. Carm. *Javanese Popular Belief in the Coming of Ratu Adil, a Righteous Prince. Excerpta ex dissertatione ad lauream in Facultate Theologica.* Rome: Pontifica Universitatis Gregoriana, 1962.

Hatta, M. *Indonesia vrij.* The Hague: Perhimpunan Indonesia, 1928. (Hatta's speech in his own defense, March 1928.)

——. *Verspreide geschriften.* Djakarta, Amsterdam and Surabaja: V. d. Peet, 1952.

Hazeu, G. A. J. *Bijdrage tot de kennis van het Javaanse tooneel.* Leiden, 1897.

Herrfahrdt, H. *Sun Yat-sen: Der Vater des neuen China.* Hamburg: Drei Türme Verlag, 1948.

"Indonesien: Politik und Weltanschauung des Präsidenten Dr. Achmed Sukarno," *Aus Politik und Zeitgeschichte* (Supplement to the weekly *Das Parlement,* No. 18 [1958]), 209–27.

Juynboll, Th. W. *Handbuch des islamitischen Gesetzes.* Leiden: E. J. Brill; Leipzig: Harrassowitz, 1910.

Kadt, J. de *De Indonesische tragedie. Het Treurspel der gemiste kansen.* Amsterdam: V. Oorschot, 1949.

Kahin, George McT. *Nationalism and Revolution in Indonesia.* Ithaca, N.Y.: Cornell University Press, 1952.

Kartini, R. A. *Door duisternis tot licht. Gedachten over en voor het Javaansche Volk.* (Ed. J. H. Abendanon.) The Hague, 1912.

Kasman Singodimedjo, ed. *Negara Republik Indonesia* [The Republic of Indonesia]. Djakarta, 1945.

Kat Angelino, A. D. A. de. *Staatkundig beleid en bestuursbezorg in Nederlandsch-Indië.* 3 vols. The Hague: M. Nijhoff, 1930.

Kautsky, K. *Ethik und materialistische Geschichtsauffassung.* Stuttgart: J. H. W. Dietz, Nachf., 1906.

——. *Parlamentarismus und Demokratie.* Stuttgart: J. H. W. Dietz, Nachf., 1893, 1911.

——. *Sozialismus und Kolonialpolitik.* Berlin: Vorwärts, 1907.

Kern, H. *Verspreide Geschriften.* 15 vols. The Hague: M. Nijhoff, 1913–28.

Kertapati, Sidik. *Sekitar proklamasi 17 Agustus 1945* [On the Proclamation of 17 August 1945]. Djakarta: Jajasan Pembaruan, 1964.

Koch, D. M. G. *Batig Slot. Figuren uit het oude Indië.* Amsterdam: Djambatan, 1960.

——. *Koloniale vraagstukken. Verzamelde opstellen.* Weltevreden: Javasche Boekhandel en Drukkerij, 1919.

——. *Om de Vrijheid.* Djakarta: Jajasan Pembangunan, 1950.

——. *Verantwoording. Een halve eeuw in Indonesië.* The Hague and Bandung: V. Hoeve, 1956.

Kraemer, H. "Beschouwingen met betrekking tot de inlandsche beweging," *Koloniale Studien,* XI (1927), 1–15.

——. *Een javaansche primbon uit de zestiende eeuw. Inleiding, vertaling en aantekeningen.* Leiden: Trap, 1921.

Kroef, J. M. van der. *Indonesia in the Modern World.* 2 vols. Bandung: Masa Baru, 1954 and 1956.

——. *Indonesian Social Evolution.* Amsterdam: V. d. Peet, 1958.

——. "Javanese Messianic Expectations: Their Origin and Cultural Context," *Comparative Studies in Society and History,* 1958–59, 299–323.

——. "Sukarno and Hatta: The Great Debate in Indonesia," *The Political Quarterly,* XXIX (1958), 238–50.

——. "Sukarno, the Ideologue," *Pacific Affairs,* XLI (1968), 245–61.

Lev, D. S. *The Transition to Guided Democracy: Indonesian Politics, 1957–59.* Ithaca: Modern Indonesia Project, Cornell University, 1965.

Löben-Sels, T. M. A. van. *Het ontstaan van de Repoeblik Indonesia.* Arnhem: Browen en Zoon, 1946.

Logemann, J. A. H. "Nieuwe gegevens over het ontstaan van de Indonesische grondwet van 1945," *Mededeelingen der Koninklijke Nederlandse Academie van Wetenschappen,* New Series, XXV (1962), 691–712.

McVey, Ruth. *The Rise of Indonesian Communism.* Ithaca: Cornell University Press, 1965.

——. "Taman Siswa and the Indonesian National Awakening," *Indonesia* (Cornell University) No. 4 (October 1967), 128–49.

Malik, A. *Riwajat dan perdjuangan sekitar proklamasi Kemerdekaan Indonesia 17 Agustus 1945* [History and Struggle over the

Proclamation of Indonesian Independence, August 17, 1945].
Djakarta: Widjaja, 1956.

Mangkupradja, Gatot. "The Peta and My Relations with the
Japanese," *Indonesia,* No. 5 (1968), 105ff.

Mangunkusumo, Tjipto. See Tjipto Mangunkusumo.

Meyer, D. H. *Japan wint den oorlog! Documenten over Java.*
Maastricht: Leiter-Nijpels, 1946.

Moens-Zorab, M. V. "De intocht der Pendawas in Ngastina," *Djawa,*
IV (1924), 145f.

——. "De Pendawas van Java," *Djawa,* V (1929), 258–62.

Mook, H. J. van. *Indonesia, Nederland en de wereld.* Amsterdam:
De Bezige Bij, 1949.

Mossman, J. *Rebels in Paradise: Indonesian Civil War.* London:
J. Cape, 1961.

Multatuli [Douwes Dekker]. *Max Havelaar.* Amsterdam: Gebr.
Binger, 1909.

Nagazumi, Akira. "The Origin and the Earlier Years of the Budi
Utomo, 1908–1918." Doctoral dissertation, Cornell University,
1967.

Nasution, M. Y. *Riwajat ringkas penghidupan dan perdjuangan
Ir. Sukarno* [Sketch of the Life and Struggle of Ir. Sukarno].
Djakarta: Pustaka Aida, 1951.

Natsir, M. *Capita Selecta.* 2 vols. Bandung and The Hague: V.
Hoeve, 1955.

Niel, R. Van. See Van Niel, R.

Nishijima, Shigetada, and Kishi Koichi. *Japanese Military Administration in Indonesia.* Washington: U.S. Department of Com-
merce, Joint Publications Research Service, 1963.

Notosutarso, R. M. *Het drama van Indië.* The Hague: Indië in
Nood, 1946.

Overdijkink, G. W. *Het Indonesische problem, de feiten.* The
Hague: M. Nijhoff, 1946.

Pakpahan, G. *1261 hari dibawah sinar Matahari Terbit* [1261 Days
Under the Rays of the Rising Sun]. Djakarta: n.p., 1947.

Palmier, L. *Indonesia and the Dutch.* London: Oxford University
Press, 1962.

Pauker, G. J. "The Role of the Military in Indonesia," in J. J.
Johnson (ed.), *The Role of the Military in Underdeveloped
Countries.* Princeton: Princeton University Press, 1962, 185ff.

Picard, H. W. J. *De waarheid over Java.* The Hague: V. Hoeve.
1946.

Pigeaud, Th. "Eruçakra Vairoçana," in *India Antiqua: A Volume of Oriental Studies, Presented by His Friends and Pupils to Jean Philippe Vogel* (Leiden: E. J. Brill, 1947), 270–73.

——. "Javaanse Beschavingsgeschiedenis." Unpublished manuscript, Koninklijk Instituut voor Taal-, Land- en Volkenkunde, Leiden.

——. *Javaanse Volksvertooningen*. Batavia, 1938.

Pijper, G. F. "De Ahmadijah in Indonesia," in *Bingkisan Budi: Een bundel opstellen aan Dr. Ph. S. van Ronkel*. Leiden: A. W. Slijthoff, 1950, 247–54.

——. *Fragmenta Islamica*. Leiden: E. J. Brill, 1934.

Pluvier, J. N. *Overzicht van de ontwikkeling der nationalistische beweging in Indonesië in de jaren 1930 tot 1942*. The Hague: V. Hoeve, 1953.

Prijohoetomo. *Nawaruçi. Een middel-javaansch prozatekst, vergeleken met de Bhimasoetji*. Groningen, The Hague, and Batavia: J. B. Wolters, 1934.

Pringgodigdo, A. G. *Perubahan kabinet presidensiil mendjadi kabinet parlementer* [The Change from a Presidential to a Parliamentary Cabinet]. Jogjakarta: Jajasan, 1955.

Pringgodigdo, A. K. *Sedjarah pergerakan rakjat Indonesia* [History of the Indonesian People's Movement]. Djakarta: Pustaka Rakjat, 1950.

——. *The Office of President in Indonesia as Defined in the Three Constitutions in Theory and Practice*. Translated by A. Brotherton. Ithaca, N.Y.: Cornell University, Modern Indonesia Project, Translation Series, 1957.

Raffles, T. S. *The History of Java*. 2 vols. London: Black, Parbury and Allen; J. Murray, 1817.

Raliby, O. *Documenta Historica I. Sedjarah documenter dari pertumbuhan dan perdjuangan Negara Republik Indonesia* [Documentary History of the Development and Struggle of the Republic of Indonesia]. Djakarta: Bulan-Bintang, 1953.

Rassers, W. H. "Over de zin van het Javaanse drama," *Bijdragen tot de Taal-, Land- en Volkenkunde van Nederlandsch-Indië*, LXXXI (1925), 311–81.

——. "Over den oorsprong van het Javaansche tooneel," *loc. cit.*, LXXXVIII (1931), 317–450.

Rauch, G. von. *Geschichte des bolschewistischen Russland*. Hamburg: Fischer-Bücherei, 1963.

Salim, H. Agus. *Djedjak Langkah Hadji A. Salim. Pilihan karangan utjapan dan pendapat beliau dari dulu sampai sekarang*. [The

Path of Hadji A. Salim. Selections from his Writings, Speeches and Opinions from Early Times until the Present.] Djakarta: Tintamas, 1954.

Samkalden, I. *Het college van gedelegeerden uit den Volksraad.* Doctoral dissertation, Leiden, 1938.

Sarkisyanz, E. *Russland und der Messianismus des vorderen Orients.* Tübingen: J. C. B. Mohr, 1955.

Sartono, Kartodirdjo. *The Peasants' Revolt of Banten in 1888.* The Hague: H. L. Smits, 1966.

——. *Tjatatan tentang segi-segi messianistis dalam sedjarah Indonesia* [Notes on Messianic Aspects of Indonesian History]. Penerbitan Lustrum ke-2. Jogjakarta: Universitas Gadjah Mada, 1959.

Schepper, J. M. J. *Het vonnis in de PNI-Zaak.* Batavia: De Unie, 1931.

Schomerus, H. W. *Indische und christliche Enderwartungen und Erlösungshoffnung.* Gütersloh: C. Bertelsmann, 1941.

Schrieke, B., ed. *The Effect of Western Influence on Native Civilizations in the Malay Archipelago.* Batavia: G. Kolff and Co., 1929.

Schrieke, B. J. O. "De Javaansche messias voor en tijdens den Islam": Résumé in *Jaarboek Oostersch Instituut 1941* (Leiden, 1942), 77–79.

Selosoemardjan, *Social Changes in Jogjakarta.* Ithaca, N.Y.: Cornell University Press, 1962.

Serruier, L. *De Wajang poerwa.* Leiden: E. J. Brill, 1896.

Silverstein, J., ed. *Southeast Asia in World War II: Four Essays.* New Haven: Yale University, Southeast Asia Studies, Monograph Series No. 7, 1966.

Singh, V. "The Rise of Indonesian Political Parties," *Journal of Southeast Asian History,* II (1961), 43–65.

Sitorus, L. M. *Sedjarah pergerakan kebangsaan Indonesia* [History of the Indonesian Nationalist Movement]. Djakarta: Pustaka Rakjat, 1951.

Sjahrazad [S. Sjahrir]. *Indonesische overpeinzingen.* Amsterdam: De Bezige Bij, 1945.

Sjahrir, S. *Out of Exile.* New York: John Day, 1949.

——. *Perdjuangan kita* [Our Struggle.] Djakarta: Pertjetakan Republik Indonesia, 1945.

——. *Pikiran dan perjuangan* [Thought and Struggle]. Djakarta: Pustaka Rakjat, 1947.

Slamet, M. *Japanese Machinations*. 4 parts. Batavia, 1946.
Snouck Hurgronje, C. *Colijn over Indië*. Amsterdam: Brecht, 1928.
——. *Verspreide geschriften*. 6 vols. Bonn, Leipzig: K. Schroeder; Leiden: E. J. Brill, 1924–26.
Soekarno—President of Indonesia. Djakarta: Ministry of Information, 1956.
Sprang, A. v. *En Soekarno lacht*. The Hague: V. Hoeve, 1946.
Staargaard, W. F. *Oost en West in Nederlandsch-Indië*. Haarlem: Tjeenk Willink en Zoon, 1928.
Stern, A. H., ed. *Lenins 21 Punkte. Der 2. Kongress der 3. Internationale in Moskau*. Berlin, 1920.
Stoddard, L. *The New World of Islam*. London: Chapman and Hall, 1921.
Stutterheim, W. F. "Een oud-javaansch Bhima Kultus," *Djawa*, XV (1935), 37–64.
Sukarno. *Marhaen and Proletarian*. Translated by Claire Holt. Ithaca, N.Y.: Cornell University, Modern Indonesia Project, Translation Series, 1960.
——. See further listings under "Writings and Speeches of Sukarno up to 1945," above.
Sukarno: An Autobiography as Told to Cindy Adams. Indianapolis: Bobbs-Merrill, 1965.
Supardi, I. *Bung Karno sebagai Kokrosono* [Bung Karno as Kokrosono]. Surabaja: Pustaka Nasional, 1950.
Suriokusumo, R. M. S. "De Wajang als leidraad tot karaktervorming," *Wederopbouw*, IV (1921), 174ff.
——. "De Wajang of het schaduwenspel," *Wederopbouw*, IV (1921), 121ff.
——. "*Het Heilige Schrift in Beeld, de Wajang*," *Wederopbouw*, VI (1923), Nos. 1–3.
Sutjipto Wirjosuparto, R. M. *Sedjarah Indonesia, Djilid II: Abad Ke-16 sampai sekarang* [Indonesian History, Vol. II: From the 16th Century to the Present]. Jogjakarta: Indira, 1960.
Swellengrebel, J. L. *Korawaçrama. Een oudjavaansch prozageschrift, uitgegeven, vertaald en toegelicht*. Dissertation, Leiden, 1936.
Tan Malaka. *Massa-Actie* [1926]. Djakarta: Pustaka Murba, reprinted 1947.
Tjan Tjoe Siem. *Hoe Koerapati zich zijn vrouw verwerft. Jav. Lakon in het Nederl. vertaald*. Dissertation, Leiden, 1938.
Tjantrik Mataram, ed. *Peranan ramalan Djojobojo dalam revolusi kita* [The Role of Djajabaja's Prophecy in Our Revolution]. Bandung: Masa Baru, 1950.

Tjipto Mangunkusumo. *De beweging in India* [Foreword by Sukarno]. Bandung: Suluh Indonesia Muda, 1928.

——. *Het communisme in Indonesië: Naar aanleiding van de relletjes.* Bandung: Fadjar Hindia, 1926.

——. *Het Saminisme. Rapport uitgebracht aan de Vereeniging Insulinde.* Semarang: Benjamins, 1918.

——. "De Wajang," *De Indische Gids,* 1914, pp. 530–39.

Tjokroaminoto, H. O. S. *Islam dan Socialisme* [1924]. Newly published by A. and H. Tjokroaminoto. Djakarta: Bulan Bintang, 1950.

Treub, W. F. M. *Het gist in Indië.* Haarlem: Tjeenk Willink en Zoon, 1927.

——. *Nederland in de Oost.* Haarlem: Tjeenk Willink en Zoon, 1923.

Vandenbosch, A. "Nationalism and Religion in Indonesia," *Far Eastern Survey,* XXI (1952), 181–85.

Van Haastert, W. K. S. See Haastert, W. K. S. van.

Van Niel, R. *The Emergence of the Modern Indonesian Elite.* The Hague and Bandung: V. Hoeve, 1960.

Veer, P. v. 't. "Soekarno," in *Kopstukken uit de twintigste eeuw,* Vol. XV. The Hague: Kurseman, 1964.

Vlekke, B. H. M. *Nusantara: A History of the East Indian Archipelago.* Cambridge, Mass.: Harvard University Press, 1943.

——. *Nusantara: A History of Indonesia.* Rev. ed. The Hague and Bandung: V. Hoeve, 1959.

Vries, D. de. *Culturele aspecten in de verhouding Indonesië-Nederland.* Amsterdam: Vrij Nederland, 1947.

Wal, S. L. van der. *De Volksraad en de Staatkundige ontwikkeling van Nederlandsch-Indië.* 2 vols. Groningen: J. B. Wolters, 1964, 1965.

Weatherbee, D. E. *Ideology in Indonesia: Sukarno's Indonesian Revolution.* New Haven: Yale University, Southeast Asia Studies, Monograph Series No. 8, 1966.

Wehl, D. *The Birth of Indonesia.* London: Allen and Unwin, 1948.

Weise, W. *Die Entstehung der nationalistischen Bewegung in Indonesien und ihre Entwicklung bis zum Jahre 1927.* Dissertation, Hamburg, 1953.

Weiss, C. *Sukarnos tausend Inseln.* Hamburg: Christian Wegner, 1963.

Wertheim, W. F. *Indonesian Society in Transition.* The Hague and Bandung: V. Hoeve, 1956.

——. *Nederland op den tweesprong: Tragedië van een aan traditie gebonden mensch.* Arnhem: V. Loghum-Slaterus, 1946.

Wiselius, J. A. B. "Djajabaja: Zijn leven en profetieën," *Bijdragen tot de Taal-, Land- en Volkenkunde van Nederlandsch-Indië,* Third Series, VII (1872), 172–207.

Woodman, D. *The Republic of Indonesia.* London: The Cresset Press, 1955.

Yamin, Muhammad. *Naskah persiapan Undang-Undang Dasar 1945* [Documents on the Preparation of the Constitution of 1945]. Djakarta: Jajasan Prapantja, 1959.

——. *Proklamasi dan konstitusi Republik Indonesia.* Djakarta and Amsterdam: Djambatan, 1951.

Index